D1758854

University of
Hertfordshire

## Learning and Information Services

College Lane, Hatfield, Hertfordshire, AL10 9AB

For renewal of Standard and One Week Loans,
please visit the website: http://www.voyager.herts.ac.uk

This item must be returned or the loan renewed by the due date.
The University reserves the right to recall items from loan at any time.
A fine will be charged for the late return of items.

4827/KM/DS

# ROMANTIC VAGRANCY

CAMBRIDGE STUDIES IN ROMANTICISM

*General editors*
Professor Marilyn Butler      Professor James Chandler
*University of Oxford*            *University of Chicago*
Editorial Board
John Barrell, *University of York*   Paul Hamilton, *University of Southampton*
Mary Jacobus, *Cornell University*   Kenneth Johnston, *Indiana University*
Alan Liu, *University of California, Santa Barbara*   Jerome McGann,
*University of Virginia*   David Simpson, *University of Colorado*

This series aims to foster the best new work in one of the most challenging fields within English literary studies. From the early 1780s to the early 1830s a formidable array of talented men and women took to literary composition, not just in poetry, which some of them famously transformed, but in many modes of writing. The expansion of publishing created new opportunities for writers, and the political stakes of what they wrote were raised again and again by what Wordsworth called those "great national events" that were "almost daily taking place": the French Revolution, the Napoleonic and American wars, urbanization, industrialization, religious revival, an expanded empire abroad and the reform movement at home. This was an enormous ambition, even when it pretended otherwise. The relations between science, philosophy, religion and literature were reworked in texts such as *Frankenstein* and *Biographia Literaria*; gender relations in *A Vindication of the Rights of Woman* and *Don Juan*; journalism by Cobbett and Hazlitt: poetic form, content and style by the Lake School and the Cockney School. Outside Shakespeare studies, probably no body of writing has produced such a wealth of response or done so much to shape the responses of modern criticism. This indeed is the period that saw the emergence of those notions of "literature" and of literary history, especially national literary history, on which modern scholarship in English has been founded.

The categories produced by Romanticism have also been challenged by recent historicist arguments. The task of the series is to engage both with a challenging corpus of Romantic writings and with the changing field of criticism they have helped to shape. As with other literary series published by Cambridge, this one will represent the work of both younger and more established scholars, on either side of the Atlantic and elsewhere.

*For a complete list of titles published see end of book*

# ROMANTIC VAGRANCY

*Wordsworth and the simulation of freedom*

CELESTE LANGAN

*University of California, Berkeley*

CAMBRIDGE
UNIVERSITY PRESS

CAMBRIDGE UNIVERSITY PRESS
Cambridge, New York, Melbourne, Madrid, Cape Town, Singapore, São Paulo

Cambridge University Press
The Edinburgh Building, Cambridge CB2 2RU, UK

Published in the United States of America by Cambridge University Press, New York

www.cambridge.org
Information on this title: www.cambridge.org/9780521475075

© Cambridge University Press 1995

First published 1995
This digitally printed first paperback version 2006

A catalogue record for this publication is available from the British Library

Library of Congress Cataloguing in Publication data

Langan, Celeste.
Romantic vagrancy / Celeste Langan
p.   cm. – (Cambridge Studies in Romanticism)
Includes index.
ISBN 0 521 47507 4
1. Wordsworth, William, 1770-1850 – Political and social views.   2. Literature and society
– England – History – 19th century.   3. Homelessness in literature.   4. Liberalism in
literature.   5. Vagrancy in literature.   6. Walking in literature.   7. Romanticism –
England.   8. Poets in literature. I. Title.   II. Series.
PR5892,S58L35   1995
821'.7 – dc20   94-49735   CIP

ISBN-13  978-0-521-47507-5 hardback
ISBN-10  0-521-47507-4 hardback

ISBN-13  978-0-521-03510-1 paperback
ISBN-10  0-521-03510-4 paperback

# Contents

# Acknowledgments

Someone once suggested to me that, given the way in which my digressive imagination seemed to prohibit my ever finishing this project, I should dedicate the book "To My Surprise." The people I acknowledge here are the agents of that surprise, who helped me to articulate rather than passively to imitate the spectacle of vagrancy. My most immediate debts are to James Chandler and Alan Liu, who enthusiastically supported the book even as they offered crucial advice for revision; my longest-standing debts are to my teachers, Stuart Curran (who introduced me to Romanticism so many years ago), Marjorie Levinson, and Elaine Scarry. I thank as well Berkeley colleagues who offered incisive but generous comments on various drafts: Paul Alpers, Cathy Gallagher, David Lloyd, and my reading group, Catherine Bergeron, Timothy Hampton, Leslie Kurke, Lydia Liu, and Michael Lucey. Irene Tucker was far more than a research assistant; she was a skillful editor and a generous friend. Long-distance though they have become, the "friends from Philadelphia" – Michael Awkward, Chris Flint, Pidge Molyneaux, Joe Valente, and Athena Vrettos – continue to provide a model of community. Wherever this project has taken me in the last several years, Steve and Cathy Goldsmith have been there too, always providing food for body and spirit, a home away from home. I am honored by their friendship. Finally, I dedicate this book to my family, especially my parents, because the home that they have created for me can never be lost, even if 114 Undercliff Road one day has new owners.

# Abbreviations

B&G    William Wordsworth, *Lyrical Ballads and Other Poems, 1797–1800*, ed. James Butler and Karen Green. Ithaca: Cornell University Press, 1992.

BL    Samuel Taylor Coleridge, *Biographia Literaria*. London: Dent, 1977.

C    Karl Marx, *Capital*, ed. Frederick Engels, New York: International, 1984.

CF    Immanuel Kant, *The Conflict of the Faculties*, trans. Mary J. Gregor. Lincoln: University of Nebraska Press, 1979.

CJ    Immanuel Kant, *Critique of Judgment*, trans. J. H. Bernard. New York: Hafner Press, 1951.

CL    Samuel Taylor Coleridge, *Collected Letters*, ed. Earl Leslie Griggs. Oxford: Clarendon, 1956–71.

CW    Thomas DeQuincey, *Collected Writings*, ed. David Masson. London, (1890).

D    Jean-Jacques Rousseau, *Rousseau, Judge of Jean-Jacques: Dialogues. Collected Writings of Rousseau*, vol. 1. ed. and trans. Roger D. Masters and Christopher Kelly. Hanover: University Press of New England, 1990.

DWJ    Dorothy Wordsworth, *Journals of Dorothy Wordsworth*, ed. Mary Moorman. New York: Oxford University Press, 1981.

E    Jean-Jacques Rousseau, *Emile*, trans. Barbara Foxley. London: Dent, 1982.

EB    Karl Marx, *The Eighteenth Brumaire of Louis Bonaparte*. New York: International, 1987.

EY    Ernest de Selincourt (ed.), *The Letters of William and Dorothy Wordsworth: the Early Years*. Oxford: Clarendon, 1939.

GI    Karl Marx and Frederick Engels. *The German Ideology*, ed. C. J. Arthur. New York: International, 1986.

*KN*   Slavoj Zizek, *For They Know Not What They Do*. London: Verso, 1991.

*LB*   William Wordsworth and Samuel Taylor Coleridge, *Lyrical Ballads, 1798*, ed. W. J. B. Owen. Oxford University Press, 1987.

*OC*   Jean-Jacques Rousseau, *Œuvres Completes*, ed. Bernard Gagnembin and Marcel Raymond. 4 vols. Bruges: Bibliothèque de la Pléiade, 1959.

*OR*   Jean-Jacques Rousseau, *The First and Second Discourses together with the Replies to Critics and Essay on the Origin of Languages*, ed. and trans. Victor Gourevitch. New York: Harper, 1990.

*PrW*   William Wordsworth, *The Prose Works of William Wordsworth*, ed. W. J. B. Owen and Jane Worthington Smyser. 3 vols. Oxford: Oxford University Press, 1959.

*PW*   William Wordsworth, *The Poetical Works of William Wordsworth*, eds. Ernest de Selincourt and Helen Darbishire. 5 vols. Oxford University Press, 1940–49.

*R*   Jean-Jacques Rousseau, *Reveries of the Solitary Walker*, trans. Peter France. New York: Penguin, 1979.

*SC*   Jean-Jacques Rousseau, *The Social Contract and Discourses*, trans. G. D. H. Cole. London: Everyman's Library, 1986.

*SO*   Slavoj Zizek, *The Sublime Object of Ideology*. London: Verso, 1989.

# A methodological preamble

The development of each human fate can be represented as an uninterrupted alternation between bondage and release, obligation and freedom ... What we regard as freedom is often in fact only a change of obligations; as a new obligation replaces one that we have borne hitherto, we sense above all that the old burden has been removed. Because we are free from it, we seem at first to be completely free – until the new duty, which initially we bear, as it were, with hitherto untaxed and therefore particularly strong sets of muscles, makes its weight felt as these muscles, too, gradually tire. The process of liberation starts again with this new duty, just as it had ended at this very point.
>               Georg Simmel, *The Philosophy of Money* (1907)

Walking, then, is a perpetual falling with a perpetual self-recovery.
>               Oliver Wendell Holmes, "The Physiology of Walking" (1883)

I begin by adjoining two passages – one about freedom, the other about walking. By what odd logic does their mere proximity suggest an equation or an identity between the central terms? Perhaps the transformation of contiguity into sequence that reading produces offers one clue; reading the passages in succession, we are inclined to complete the implicit syllogism, and conclude that "freedom is walking." We are accustomed to expect from narrative a progressive expansion of knowledge, and Holmes's description of walking, since it follows Simmel's description of the freedom made possible by money, may seem to consolidate the abstract language of the first. But this *narrative* logic cannot explain the full force of the equation between descriptions of walking and freedom that occurs as a consequence of their symmetrical arrangement. For by means of a recursive logic, Holmes's description of walking as a perpetual activity takes on a certain pathos in relation to Simmel's allusion to "human fate": walking becomes a Sisyphian task. A neighboring

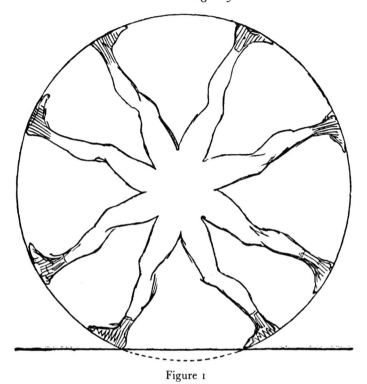

Figure 1

passage *inflects* the other, donating a tone, or an absent trajectory: the abstract is given figural form, the fact a moral significance.

But these passages are only "neighbors" by virtue of an ex-propriation. They are placed in an *absolute* relation, which is why, finally, the logic of their equivalence cannot be fully determined: the logic of *analogy*, I contend, is neither progressive nor retrospective, but rather the logic of infinite circulation. Analogy, we might say, is a perpetual alternation rather than a progress. Notice, for example, that analogy works by an ahistorical or anachronistic logic whereby Holmes can seem to "explain" the concept of freedom years before it is articulated by Simmel.

The absolute relation or logic of equivalence which joins the terms of an analogy differentiates it from metaphor, in which tenor and vehicle can still be identified. Analogy subverts all such relations of subordination by subordinating both tenor ("freedom") and vehicle ("walking") to the logic of equivalence. Its structural mirroring of the mathematical equation means that analogy cannot be regarded as the merely rhetorical decoration of a given proposition, its "literary" aspect, for analogy is itself propositional. What analogy proposes is the mediation of discourses, the different "terms" of the equation. Again, however, that mediation is achieved not by the introduction of a third term, outside or beyond the proposed equivalence, but rather by a perpetual negotiation.

The analogy between walking and freedom I have proposed is designed to suggest that liberalism is an idea of human community partly modeled on the logic of analogy: determined wholly neither by its economic name of *laissez-faire* capitalism nor its political name of representative democracy, liberalism is itself their negotiation. But the performance of this negotiation by the liberal subject may entail the subtraction from identity of all elements unassimilable by the logic of equivalence.

Holmes's essay, "The Physiology of Walking," contains two illustrations. In an extension of the symmetrical logic of analogy, it will seem that the first (Figure 1) represents Simmel's philosophical, and the second (Figures 2–5) Holmes's more physiological interests. I would also like tentatively to suggest that they represent two alternate ways of imagining the logic of equivalence – and of human community. First we have a purported "illustration" which, like Simmel's philosophy of freedom, makes no room for the contingencies of locomotion: terrain, leg-length discrepancies, speed. But without such historical and spatial coordinates, walking here (Holmes describes it as representing the "idea" that "man is a wheel" [129]) is purely circular; it represents the reduction and abstraction of the body in terms of its locomotive power.

The second illustration is actually a series of four drawings (Figures 2–5). Holmes prefers their explanatory value to the "mathematical formulae" of French anatomists, contending that new techniques – specifically photography – enable greater descriptive accuracy:

We have selected a number of instantaneous stereoscopic views of the streets and public places of Paris and New York, each of them showing numerous walking figures, among which some may be found in every stage of the complex act we are studying. Mr. Darley [the illustrator] has had the kindness to leave his higher tasks to transfer several of these to our pages, so that the reader may be sure that he looks on an exact copy of real human individuals in the act of walking. (124–5)

Those details lending us assurance that the "walking figures" are "real human individuals," however, are precisely what we need to

Figure 2            Figure 3

Figure 4            Figure 5

erase in order to conceive this series as the equivalent of the earlier walking circle. Yet clearly this motive of reproducing the circle operates as the principle of selection: the outstretched leg of figure 2 maps onto the right leg of figure 3 and so on, until what emerges into focus is not four "real human individuals," but once again two (eight) "legs" – the organs containing, as it were, the abstract "labor-power" of movement.

Yet the "complexity of the act we are studying" fully appears in the residual effect of these figures. For who does not attend to their costumes, which give them a social (and historical) identity, and suggest the distinctive social inflections of the gait they so variously enact? Holmes himself suggests surprise at the evident length of stride in figure 2 (it "arrests our attention") and the sharp-angle tilt of the heel-strike in figure 5, claiming that "no artist would have dared to draw a walking figure in attitudes like some of these" (127). He does not call the extended stride "masterful," nor relate the jaunty angle of figure 5's hat to the sharp angle of his step, but we can hardly help but do so. The more measured knee-bends of figures 3 and 4 – may we call them the peasant and the soldier? – likewise seem in keeping with the downward cast of their gaze, and, possibly, their lower expectations. Placing the series in an analogical relation, a certain democratic effect is achieved, whereby sundry persons with distinct interests are united in a nonetheless common activity: walking. Walking then is what remains when the contingent details are removed, as a kind of transcendental surplus.

That same analogical relation, however, allows us to see the pathos of imagining the "transcendental" community as one which merely walks. Take, for example, Dorothy Wordsworth's *Journals*. A similar logic of community might seem to be at work in her frequent preamble to the observations registered: "We walked." Like the streets of Paris and New York, Grasmere and its environs are populated by numerous walking figures:

Poor Fellow, he straddled and pushed on with all his might but we soon outstripped him. (86)

I saw Jane Ashburner driving the cow along the high road ... she had a stick in her hand and came tripping along in the Jig step, as if she were dancing. (100)

On the Rays we met a woman with 2 little girls one in her arms the other about four years old walking by her side, a pretty little thing, but half starved. She had on a pair of slippers that had belonged to some gentleman's child, down at the heels – it was not easy to keep them on, poor thing! young as she was, she walked carefully with them. (121)

All these figures are walking, but the collateral details give to that activity a social inflection. Only by erasing the social dimension – replacing it perhaps with an entirely physiological focus and analysis – can we achieve the *pure* analogy, whereby all walkers are made the same.

Figure 6

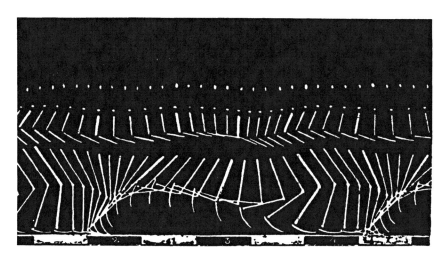

Figure 7

Perhaps the model of pure analogy, achieved by an increase of focus that erases contingent details, culminates in Marey's cinematographic studies of human locomotion. Figures 6 and 7 are from one such study.[1] We may take the cinematographer's reliance on the black costume inscribed with a white line, which followed the imaginary center of body and limbs, as emblematic of the erasures, also a visual impoverishment, effected by the purely analogical relation, and the logic of progress which emerges in the event of these erasures. If the analogy between and among different walking figures produces a figure of abstract (discursive) community, here the analogy, operating between different moments in the serial deportment of an individual, may be said to produce a figure of the abstract subject (Kant: the "subject without properties"). Let us suppose this figure is the purest *exposition* of a concept – but let us rename that concept: not walking, nor even, in the sense that walking represents "the human being's capacity to move out beyond the boundaries of his or her own body," Simmel's freedom; but instead, vagrancy – the condition of having nothing to do and nowhere to go.[2]

In that case, then, the work of art represented in figure 8, Van Gogh's *Old Boots with Laces*, can represent the material remainder of the Kantian subject, his property. Like each of the other "illustrations" I have considered, Van Gogh's painting belongs neither to the historical period nor to the culture of Romanticism "proper"; yet I would argue that the painting nonetheless helps to conjure an image of something that might be called "Romantic vagrancy." If its subject matter and tone were not sufficient to afford Van Gogh's shoes this place, the series of theoretical representations that now frame the painting would make the case.

In his famous essay, "The Origins of the Work of Art" (1935), Heidegger refers to "a well-known painting by Van Gogh" to exemplify the status of "equipment," a category equidistant between "thing" and "work." What has commanded attention, however, is less the philosophical context than the sheer *pathos* of Heidegger's description, evoking the image of a solitary reaper:

From the dark opening of the worn insides of the shoes the toilsome tread of the worker stares forth. In the stiffly rugged heaviness of the shoes there is the accumulated tenacity of her slow trudge through the far-spreading and ever-uniform furrows of the field swept by a raw wind. On the leather lie the

Figure 8　Vincent van Gogh, *Old Boots with Laces*

dampness and richness of the soil. Under the soles slides the loneliness of the field-path as evening falls. In the shoes vibrates the silent call of the earth, its quiet gift of the ripening grain. (34)

Notice how the allusive fullness attributed to the painting, what Heidegger calls its disclosure of "truth," depends on the vacancy of the shoes, not only their emptiness but also their dislocation; as Heidegger remarks, "there is nothing surrounding this pair of peasant shoes in or to which they might belong – only an undefined space" (33).

Heidegger's reference to Van Gogh is determined by two elements that are equally "Romantic." First, he chooses as his example of utility "a common sort of equipment – a pair of peasant shoes"; second, he fails to name the particular Van Gogh painting he has in mind, although acknowledging that the artist "painted such shoes several times" (33). In each case, the elevation of one object to the status of representative example depends on an idea of the "common" that is patently Romantic. What, after all, makes a "pair of peasant shoes" a *common* piece of equipment in 1935? A nostalgic pastoralism seems clearly at work in this representation of the "common" that may be read as parallel to Wordsworth's analogy between "rustic" and "common" language in the 1800 Preface. Similarly, the iconic status of the painting depends on its *textualization*: Heidegger alludes less to a single *authoritative* representation than to a *series* of representations, since the sheer number of Van Gogh paintings of such shoes (and, of course, their frequent reproduction and exhibition) is what makes them "common" (well known, familiar) enough to serve as a general example. Two competing ideas of the common are thus collapsed, one historical, the other formal. The peasantry and its shoes, representing the "historical" common, have almost disappeared, threaten to fall into disuse. The common where those shoes formerly stood, walking and working, is now the artificial terrain of representation; representation seems to restore, produce, or simulate our sense of the "common."

Even more interesting than this refraction of the (rural–nostalgic) content and (serial-discursive) form of Romanticism in Heidegger's reading of the painting is the subsequent critical discussion it generates, which repeats this Romantic double-exposure of the "common," and through which we can trace recent trends in Romanticist criticism. In 1968, Meyer Shapiro disputed Heidegger's attribution of the shoes to an imaginary peasant woman, claiming that "they are clearly the artist's own shoes, not the shoes of a peasant," and moreover that the artist was "by that time a man of the town and city" (quoted from Derrida, *Truth in Painting*, 365). Finally, Shapiro argues that even if we were to imagine such a painting, the shoes would still revert to Van Gogh: "Let us imagine a painting of a peasant woman's shoes by Van Gogh… [Still] Heidegger would have missed an important aspect of the painting: the artist's presence in the work" (*ibid.*, 369). Titling his essay "The Still Life as Personal Object," Shapiro reads Van Gogh's representations of objects as displaced self-portraits. Both the time-frame and the ideological impetus of Shapiro's account seem consonant with the critical spirit that rescued Romanticism from its association with the rural–nostalgic and the commonplace, rendering it instead "a drama of consciousness," a *binding* of nature to imagination (the allusion is to Hartman).

In 1984, Fredric Jameson makes a somewhat more casual reference to Van Gogh's shoes in his seminal essay, "The Cultural Logic of Late Capitalism" (in *Postmodernism*). He also disputes Heidegger's rural–nostalgic evocation of the peasant-woman, but primarily by rereading the hallucinated landscape as one "of agricultural *misery*, of stark rural *poverty*, and the whole rudimentary world of back-breaking peasant toil" (7; emphases mine). Jameson represents the painting as an historical allegory, a "Utopian gesture" whereby a "drab peasant object" is transformed into "the most glorious materialization of pure color in oil paint"(7).[3] Jameson's reading, then, corresponds with those more recent accounts of the Romantic project, often called "new historicist," which read the text as it variously idealizes, erases, allegorizes, or otherwise transforms the "raw materials" of historical, economic, and biological existence. The new historicist allegory is an allegory of *production*, moreover; the "work" of art is to reconfigure the "work" of "backbreaking peasant toil," as the work of narrative is to reconfigure historical agency.

Although Jameson uncritically accepts Heidegger's description of the shoes as those of a peasant, he still shares with Shapiro an understanding of the painting as a self-representation; in effect, his reading reflects Van Gogh's own claim that "I am a painter of peasants ... and it is there that I feel in my element."[4] The nostalgia Heidegger apparently projects onto the painting is relocated in Van Gogh himself, although it is a less idealizing nostalgia. Implicitly, then, Van Gogh is once again "by this time a man of the town and the city," who identifies the peasant world as "there" – elsewhere. Thus situating the artist as socially and historically separable from the object of representation enables Jameson to posit another historical difference, perhaps nostalgic as well, between Van Gogh's painting and "postmodern" representation. For Jameson, the difference between a peasant's shoes and an artist's shoes, between now and then, is decidable; it is the difference between the rural object and painterly form. The postmodern, by contrast, is defined as a "fundamental mutation in the object-world itself – now become a set of texts or simulacra" (9).

But what happens when we consider the question of "whose shoes" in relation to the *seriality* of Van Gogh's representations? In *The Truth in Painting*, Derrida undertakes precisely this task. He traces the error of "restitutions" of the shoes both to the peasant and to the artist, noting the crucial *detachment* of the shoes, not only from a given subject, whether peasant woman or artist, but also from each other: they may not even constitute a "pair." Their represented condition reinforces this detachment: worn and unlaced, the shoes attract Heidegger's attention in the first place because they are in a state of disuse, or *désoeuvrement*. Neither working nor walking, the shoes are out of order. As such, they "belong" neither to the peasant nor to the artist in the sense of that term bestowed by the discourse of property.

Or at least not to the discourse of property traditionally associated with the "peasantry."[5] As Derrida remarks, Shapiro's reattribution of the shoes to Van Gogh "contest[s] the rights of agricultural property," asserting instead a kind of *absolute* property right, for by the logic of Shapiro's account, Van Gogh can paint nothing that is not his own. All collateral objects devolve into "the presence of the artist," and we might retitle the painting, as Derrida suggests, *Hoc est corpus meum* (369). Or rather, given the seriality of Van Gogh's self-representation, perhaps *Van Gogh fuit hic.*[6]

It is Marx who most famously claimed that the difference between a "peasant" world and modernity turned on a conflict between "the rights of agricultural property" and *absolute* property rights. Thus the appropriateness with which Shapiro's description of the shoes, as absolutely the property of the artist, entails the "expropriation" of the agricultural producer from the terrain of the painting.

When Van Gogh "renders himself" in the shoes, it is true that he mirrors the activity of a subject no longer tied to the land. But that subject is less the bourgeois (that man of the town and city) than the vagrant, dispossessed of a stable identity. (Marx: "the laborer could only dispose of his own person after he had ceased to be attached to the soil" [*C* 668–9]). For both – both the "subject" of Van Gogh's shoes and the expropriated laborer – "rendering oneself" will therefore be a serial event, a continual "disposition" of his or her own person. The point here is not just that an apparently aesthetic issue depends upon an economic mutation; as I have tried to indicate, that mutation is inseparable from a symbolic mutation, a logic of equivalence. Perhaps that mutation is represented in the indeterminate background of Van Gogh's painting, which helps to establish the shoes in a purely analogical relation to each other: not a pair, but a shoe and its double. This background is itself the aesthetic equivalent of the public space, that space in which the *absolute* subject of modernity appears. As an abstraction of the "common," the public space has as much a political as an economic resonance; Lefort, for example, identifies it as "the heart of democracy" (43). It is for this reason that I seek to identify the public space with liberalism, and the vagrant who occupies it with the liberal subject.

Rather than merely supporting Marx's critique of "progressive" liberalism as the ideological instrument of capitalism, the vagrant also confounds or undoes Marx's own dialectic of progress. Identifying capitalist accumulation as "a negation of individual private property as founded on the labour of the proprietor," Marx writes that "capitalist production begets its own negation. It is the negation of the negation" (*C*, 715), but mistakenly identifies that negation as the proletarian rather than the vagrant. For the capitalist and the proletarian are a pair; together, they work, they "walk" and function as the motor of historical progress. But the vagrant is the *real* "negation of the negation," the hallucinatory double of capital, his endless mobility and identity shorn of all contingent properties simulating the endless circulation of capital.

In *The Poetics of Primitive Accumulation*, a study of Renaissance culture, Richard Halpern has also suggested that the vagrant is both the hallucinatory double of capital and "a precocious and night-marishly exaggerated image of modernity" (74). I believe this "anticipatory" aspect of the vagrant, a figure of what "will have been" the condition of the postmodern subject, is a consequence of the vagrant's formal imitation of an abstract concept: negative liberty. In the same way, I will argue, the Romantic poem's formal reduction of freedom of expression to a "common" meter, the equalized lines of iambic pentameter, or the ventriloquized epitaph disables our tendency to regard even the most rambling story as a narrative of progress. In this sense, it is peculiarly "postmodern," for Romanticism denies us a belief that modernity "occurs," except as a retrospective illusion.

# Introduction

In the 1805 *Prelude* Wordsworth offers a retrospective account of how he decided on the form and content of the kinds of rambling stories that make up *Lyrical Ballads*. Rejecting books of moral philosophy, Wordsworth takes to the "public road" on which he hopes to gather an estimate of

> The dignity of individual man –
> Of man, no composition of the thought,
> Abstraction, shadow, image, but the man
> Of whom we read, the man whom we behold
> With our own eyes.              *(Prelude* XII.83–7)

Why should an encounter with a stranger on the public road become the empirical paradigm of social knowledge, and the social contract? Not only is the project itself – essentially, the rendering of freedom as sheer mobilization – an historically contingent response to philosophical, political, and economic abstractions of "man", but the poem presents this project in characteristically Wordsworthian terms. Repeating the word "man," Wordsworth allows repetition itself to substantialize the abstraction. Indeed, the passage might fairly be paraphrased by the tautology "Man is...man." For even as he then proceeds to list the attributes of this positive "man," Wordsworth can offer at best a negative litany: man is *not* an abstraction, *not* a shadow, etc. Moreover, the finally positive definition – "the man of whom we read" (87) – has an entirely recursive logic, especially in the context of Wordsworth's previous renunciation of books of moral philosophy: the man of whom we read is the word "man" of whom we read in the subsequent lines of the poem. It is for this reason that Wordsworth can equate this "man" – *which* (not *whom*: the word, not the "reality") we as readers behold with our own eyes – with the "Strolling bedlamites" and "uncouth vagrants" *(Prelude* XII.157,

158) over whom his own eyes travel as they are passed and repassed on the public thoroughfare.

Walking and reading, it seems, are related practices of mobilization. Reading, of course, implies "time to spare and money to spend" (Plumb, 267). But walking may *seem* to imply a similar leisure; the bedlamite "strolling" and the uncouth vagrant seem unconstrained by dearth of time, at least. This figuration whereby reading and vagrancy are made analogous is a crucial part of the rejoinder Wordsworth makes to books of moral philosophy, where propositional content dominates rhetorical form. In Wordsworth's text, the propositional content – a negative litany – is itself a product of the passing of lines that constitutes verse's turnings and returnings. The recursive effect of Wordsworth's tautological structures suggests that "the dignity of individual man" – the *ethos* of liberalism – far from being self-evident, is instead manufactured by a logic of infinite circulation – capitalism and the money-form.

This book, then, is an examination of the *pathos* of liberalism. It situates that *pathos* in Romanticism – specifically, in what I contend is the framing issue of Romantic form and content: vagrancy. When we read Wordsworth's initially enthusiastic plans for the abandoned epic *The Recluse* – "I have written 1,300 lines of a poem in which I contrive to convey most of the knowledge of which I am possessed. My object is to give pictures of Man, Nature, and Society. Indeed I know not anything which will not come within the scope of my plan" – we recognize in the vaunted encyclopedism and fragmentary nature of its expression the distinguishing marks of the Romantic project. Those 1,300 lines, of course, were largely made up by what we now know as "The Ruined Cottage." Why did Wordsworth feel that he had, in narrating the encounter of the passerby and the former inhabitant/now vagrant, enabled an infinite project? In extracting the encounter between vagrant and passerby as the crux of social, political, and economic life from among various alternative configurations, Wordsworth will give pathological expression to the shaping ideology of that infinite project he seeks to represent: liberalism.

Romanticism is a discourse coincident with the emergence of liberalism and, according to the argument advanced by Lacoue-Labarthe and Nancy in *The Literary Absolute*, coincident with the emergence of "literature" as a privileged form of knowledge. Literature claims this privilege not despite but rather in the name of its disability, its pathology: "an inability to produce the concept that it promises" (*Literary Absolute*, 92). We may regard the familiar difficulty that attends critical attempts to define Romanticism as the contagious effect of the Romantic paradigm of literature: *the juxtaposition of surplus and distress, or excess of representation as a symptom of failed presentation.* Rousseau's lament in the *Rêveries* – "Amidst so many riches, how may I keep a faithful register?" (36) – will be the annunciation of this equation of literature with the disabling surplus. His solution to that surplus which, by its very hyperpresence, tends to disable the *project* is the invention of the solitary walker, the reduction to "moi-même."

But where the *Rêveries* demonstrates how the epistemological subject of Enlightenment thought is an *asocial* subject, the Romantic project, by contrast, restores that subject to a social setting – the encounter with another subject. Moreover, this restoration of the paradigmatic subject to a social context effectively returns this subject to a condition of duality. The identity of the epistemological subject – an identity always dialectically achieved by the relation between the subject and the object of perception – is no longer inherent or sovereign but stretched out, infinitely attenuated, by the fact that the object of knowledge itself is the condition of vagrancy. For insofar as we read the modern subject as coincident with the emergence of liberalism, we must notice that the *transcendental* subject is the product of so many juxtapositions, and so itself a shadow, abstraction, image. Liberalism places the three subjects of modernity – the political subject, the economic subject, the private epistemo-logical or psychoanalytic subject – into an *analogical* relation, and, in locating itself at the intersecting sameness of these disparate identities, transforms a series of relations of content into a purely formal identity. Argument by analogy thus stands as the logic – and the methodology – of the liberal subject.

But if the *idea* of analogy ought theoretically to reveal an equally ideal liberal subject, the particular poetic practice of analogy produces instead a series of paradoxes. Let us take as the ethical ideal of liberal democracy Benjamin Constant's imagination of freedom: the right of individuals "to come and go without permission, and without having to account for their motives or undertakings" (311). Most striking is the evident contradiction, in practice, of this theoretical expression of right: within the structure of the poem, both the poet and the vagrant render an account of their comings and goings. This rendering of accounts is the chief method by which the poem produces a figurative identity – an analogy – between the poet and the vagrant; hence, within the regime of the text, such a rendering of accounts appears necessary. Even where origin and destination are included in these accounts, however, what matters is the fact of traveling; it is on the basis of *actual* mobility rather than *intentional* mobility (desire) that figurative identity – and political equality – is achieved. Similarly, the poem pays greater attention to the *style* of speech – its "measured" or methodical quality – than to its referential content.

The fact that *talking* rather than *walking* – or talking *as well as* walking – is the ground upon which identity or equality between the poet and the vagrant rests suggests a further paradox. Contextualized by the passing encounter with the vagrant which is its characteristic narrative elaboration, Wordsworth's representation of the Romantic formal revolution as the adoption of a *common* language as its medium of written expression must strike us as ironic. The poet and the vagrant speak the same language only insofar as a common practice – the logic of infinite circulation represented as "coming and going" – has detached their speech from the regional affiliations that might identify it as a dialect. The common language of the Romantic poem – a language validated by the logic of democracy – has become also the *pathological* expression, the *pathos*, of that logic: its *patois*.

Lacoue-Labarthe and Nancy offer a salutary reminder that the Romantic is the language of the vernacular, but it is a dialect "freed" from its regional associations; local expressions will take on, in the written text, a "wildish destiny." Although the *Oxford English Dictionary* (*OED*) claims that the etymological origin of *patois* is unknown, we may use its definition of the term to elucidate the relation of *patois* to dialect, and (by analogy) of Romantic vagrancy to (liberal) freedom:

French scholars distinguish *dialects* as the particular forms presented by a language in different regions, so long as there does not exist a common written language. When a common language has become established as the medium of general literature, the dialects lose their literary standing and become *patois*.

The identification of regional accents as *patois* depends on the increased mobility represented here by the circulating text of the "common written language," but represented in the Romantic text by the writer carrying, perhaps, his pocket-copy of Thomson or Dante. With the increased circulation of print-language, dialects "lose their standing" or autonomy, and enter into linguistic circulation as so many pathological expressions. Oddly, however, *patois* is also the mirror of that print-language, or the "common" language attached not to the soil but to technology: *patois* also comes to name languages that emerge from linguistic exchanges brought about by trade, or business. "Patter," that English cognate of *patois* (and *pathos*, perhaps), derives from "pedlar's French," or language disfigured by another logic of infinite circulation. The linguistic analogy between *patois* and patter makes tangible (audible, perceptible, and hence pathetic) how the process of negotiation between discourses, here reduced to a verbal unit, requires an abstraction *that is also a destitution*: "patter" is language reduced to its material component, sound; it is articulation disarticulated ("then all at once the air was still / And showers of hailstones patter'd round" ("A Whirl-blast"). It is now common because it affords no sense of belonging.

This, then is the first of the semantic trajectories by which "Romantic vagrancy" may be construed: Romantic vagrancy is the Romantic representation of vagrancy, a representational practice particularly concerned with those aspects of vagrancy susceptible to analogy and subsequent idealization: first, the mobility that appears to guarantee to the vagrant a residual economic freedom, despite his or her entire impoverishment; second, the speech-acts that appear to consolidate a residual political identity. The poet and the vagrant together constitute a society based on the twin principles of freedom of speech and freedom of movement.

"Romantic vagrancy," then, describes a certain idealization of the vagrant: a reduction and an abstraction. The vagrant's mobility and expressivity are abstracted from their determining social conditions – the fiscal–military state that effectively produces the vagrant's mobility and the specific purpose of the vagrant's speech: entreaty, or begging. This reduction and abstraction crucially elevate the vagrant to the status of the poet's double. But in reducing and abstracting the condition of vagrancy to walking and talking, "Romantic vagrancy" as a representational practice threatens to dissolve into a self-identification, a self-representation: Romantic vagrancy describes not an external object but an internal condition. This threat is obliquely acknowledged by Wordsworth when, in the 1800 Preface

to *Lyrical Ballads*, he reacts so vituperatively to Johnson's parody of
the Romantic vernacular:

> I put my hat upon my head
> And walked into the Strand,
> And there I met another man
> Whose hat was in his hand.

The parody is "superlatively contemptible" not because of its style or
language, but because of "the *matter* expressed," Wordsworth claims.
But what, really, is the "matter" with this poem? In four lines,
Johnson effectively parodies not only Romantic form, but also
content (its matter): the encounter on a public road between the
bourgeois and the beggar.[1]

The logic of analogy that identifies poet and vagrant enables a
certain conflation of otherwise contradictory qualities of liberalism,
contradictions that become apparent at the moment the purely
analogical relations of likeness are replaced by the actual meetings of
beggars and "citizens." Consider a recent representation of the
competing claims of the beggar and the passerby in Berkeley,
California as "the free speech of solicitors and the well-being of the
solicited."[2] The competing claims represent what political theorists
describe as the difference between *civil* and *substantive* rights, negative
and positive liberty – the *état du droit* and the welfare state, those two
configurations of liberalism.[3] Our (perhaps liberal) tendency is to
regard the beggar's interests as consistent with substantive, the
(bourgeois) passerby's with civil rights. Thus it may strike us as
peculiar that the City Council desires to protect the *civil* rights of the
beggar and the *substantive* rights of the passerby (whose "well-being"
is guaranteed in the preamble to the US Constitution as the right to
"general welfare"). This peculiarity is revealing, however. First, it
suggests the logical inconsistency of our (liberal) tendency to regard
the beggar (the solicitor) not as a political entity but as a social being
and socioeconomic product – a body. After all, the two activities
symbolically constitutive of her or his identity – mobility and speech
(the entreaty as a *cahier des doléances*) – describe the political subject.
Moreover, unlike the passerby, who resides elsewhere, the vagrant
has being *only* in the public sphere (except when private charitable
institutions afford a temporary residence). Insofar as citizenship
describes a purely public persona, therefore, the beggar or vagrant
appears to be the essential unit of the state, rather than evidence of its

malfunction. Second, it suggests our (liberal) tendency to *disregard* the social being – the body – of what was called, in the initial newspaper account, the "citizenry" – a category identified with the passerby. When, in the name of the citizen, the City Council proposes "relief" in the form of "hassle-free streets," we discover that the apparently political being of the passerby (the solicited) is only a social being in disguise. Free speech will be accorded to those with substantive needs (or desires); well-being will be guaranteed to those whose chief value is self-expression. The juxtaposition of the vagrant and the passerby thus exhibits important evidence of the essentially *serial* concept of liberalism: the relation between public and private freedom is an *analogical* one. Political theories of liberalism can construe freedom as belonging to either private being or public being, but the split into public and private means that one cannot possess these freedoms *at the same time*.

The second semantic trajectory I wish to assign to Romantic vagrancy, then, has to do with the implicit contention of my subtitle: that in the literary (paradigmatically Romantic) text, the formalization of freedom – the reduction and abstraction of walking to produce the concept of "freedom" – is a simulation in Baudrillard's sense: "to feign to have what one hasn't" (Baudrillard, *Simulations*, 5). Perfectly expressive of the negative liberty enshrined in liberalism as "freedom from," the alienated condition of vagrancy is the *pathos* of this negative liberty: the "freedom to come and go" become the obligation to mobility.[4] Also, however, the reverse: freedom, that description of the condition of transcendental surplus, may be no more than a refracted image of an exigency.

I therefore wish "Romantic vagrancy" to be read as a juxtaposition of the aesthetic and the political, the aesthetic and the social: my project attends to the way in which Romanticism inflects and is pathologized by a certain historical experience. I read that experience – the peculiar conjunction of a rationalized political and a rationalized economic agenda – phenomenologically; the body politic and the invisible hand are noumena which the poet encounters in their phenomenal form: the impolitic body of the abandoned woman and the slackened hand of the discharged soldier. The poet as private epistemological subject, released from his political identity, encounters the vagrant, released from *economic* affiliations. In the attempt to thematize their dual displacements as a singular liberation, Wordsworth activates the constitutive logic of liberalism: the subject is a series of successive discursive representations – political, economic, psychological.

Indeed, this encounter, which I will call, after Adorno, a meeting of *the transcendental surplus and the empirical deficit*, is exactly what mandates walking as both the formal protocol and the thematic content of the Romantic text. In a series of strategic misreadings, the Romantic project uses the reduction to the body to exhibit the transcendental principle. First, the Romantic poet misunderstands the nature of negative liberty (the unimpeded pursuit of "happiness"), giving the freedom to come and go a purely physiological *patois*: freedom is walking. Next, the Romantic text extends this misunderstanding by juxtaposing the two walking-consciousnesses most peripheral to the coming and going imagined in negative liberty: the vagrant and the liberally educated subject – the passer-by.[5] Through an interrogation discovering a residual consciousness not fully determined by walking (the Old Man traveling "moves with thought"), the Romantic text completes the essential tautology: walking is freedom. Hence the passion with which Wordsworth, in "The Old Cumberland Beggar," will defend the "right" to outdoor relief: in walking, the Beggar alters his horizon with each step and so demonstrates his freedom from determination.

But because walking takes place, not only in a network of transportational signs, but also in real space, a far more immediate obstacle to exercising the right "to come and go" emerges: private property threatens to diminish the subject's ability to "exercise" his freedom. Hence the impossibly formal geography of liberalism, the negated referentiality of origin and destination. This impossible formal geography is well represented in the old Cumberland Beggar's "one little span of earth" (line 50) – itself a corollary, perhaps, of the smooth gravel path that was Wordsworth's preferred landscape of composition.[6] Both imply that the geographical boundary of liberalism is the *aesthetic* space.

Thus it is not only the activity, but also the domain, of freedom that the Romantic text pathologically misunderstands and misrepresents. For most of us, the freedom to go and to return would seem to suggest an intention relative to origin and destination: I am here, I wish to go there as a consequence of some interest or antipathy; if I am allowed to pursue my project, I am free. In the Romantic *patois*, coming and going becomes, *in itself*, the pure form of freedom, an absolute unmarked by origin and destination, by interest or antipathy. Wordsworth's apostrophic turn to public roads in book XII of *The Prelude* ("Therefore did I turn / To you, ye pathways, and ye lonely roads" [123–24]) is emblematic of the pathological conversion of means into ends that characterizes the logic enabling the identification of freedom with vagrancy. This apostrophe is an ironic fulfillment of the poem's destination and destiny, reinflecting an initial indecision – "Whither shall I turn, / By road or pathway" (1.29–30) – as the space of freedom.

We may summarize these reductions of the metaphysic of liberalism (social mobility, freedom of speech) to walking and conversation simply: the Romantic text turns the Kantian "subject without properties" into the "subject without property."[7] The poet's "disposition to be affected more than other men by absent things as if they were present" (1800 Preface) takes on a different aspect in proximity to the beggar who may be even more profoundly affected by "absent things" – that is, by the condition of privation, indigence. Ironically, the transcendental surplus becomes available to the poet *only* in proximity to the figure of empirical deficit.

Let us now read outward, from the pathological expression toward the determining condition. Wordsworth inaugurates the Romantic project with his first published poem, *An Evening Walk*. Walking seems an appropriate activity for a subject who, in his authorizing signature, can claim only a metaphorical social space, or estate: "Fellow of St. John's College, Cambridge." (An ironic sidenote: the "plot of ground" upon which St. John's College stands was given to Cambridge by a burgess named Henry Frost "to build an hospital, for the use of the poor and infirm." [Dyer, 1.228]) Alan Liu has described the poem's formal balancing of picturesque and loco-descriptive elements as an entirely transitory achievement, soon to be disrupted by the intrusion of "history" (*Wordsworth: the Sense of History*). Thus he names *An Evening Walk* "The End of Repose." But in Rousseau, this picturesque priority of repose (or "station") has already become entirely nostalgic, sentimental; notice the formal compulsion that structures the *Rêveries*: the daily walk. Roger Gilbert calls attention to a similar compulsion in the Romantic project when he notes the signifying importance of the indefinite article in Wordsworth's title; in contrast, for example, to Cowper's *The Task*, which consists of representative walks, "now the poem claims to represent only a single evening walk" (43). On the other hand, in order to have any representative function, the poet must continue to walk, since only insofar as he walks is he free, and free to represent. Hence the end of repose and the beginning of vagrancy.

In signaling "The End of Repose," Liu remarks in passing that what emerges in the aftermath of the evening walk is "something very like a beggar's story" (*Wordsworth*, 130). The literal aftermath of evening – night – effects an erasure of the positive contents of the descriptive scene: "Last evening sight, the cottage smoke no more"; "Nought else of man or life remains behind" (lines 369, 375). In this sense, we must regard the title of *An Evening Walk* as a *double entendre*: walking is a leveling – an "evening" – of difference.[8] Specifically, this evening will affect the status of "is" and "is not"; this opposition is mediated by a new contention: "is, as it were." This *evening* of difference, whose method is not the sequential logic of the loco-descriptive genre, but, rather, that of *free* association, makes possible the poem's comparison of a swan the walker sees to a female beggar he imagines. The *evening* walk is thus the literary equivalent of what Constant identifies as the operative distinction between liberalism and classical democracy: the former offers a "guarantee of obscurity" to the individual. Like the scene that is projected as his epistemological reflection, the *evening* walker is similarly evacuated of his positive contents.

The notion of an "evening" walk carries yet another connotation: the walk in which attention is paid to the even spacing of one's stride. To maintain composure while unemployed: this is the free enterprise – a "freedom from" enterprise – of the Romantic text. Antony Easthope has already pointed out that "pentameter has what might be called a *constitutionalist* significance" (67; emphasis mine), but restricts his analogy to freedom of *speech* exercised against the abstract metrical pattern. Since a metrical pattern is derived, at least metaphorically, from walking, we may allege that the walking which gives to Wordsworthian pentameter its distinctively physiological inflection has a similarly constitutional significance. By disregarding the idea of progress toward some end that attaches itself to walking, the Romantic poet enables escape from the recursive threat of deprivation; each step is ideally equal in value, neither closer to nor further from a destination or an origin. Even where the Romantic text will posit a *telos*, it takes an ironic form: the right to come and go is the funeral march, its constitutional form Simonides' epitaph: "We are all debts owed to death."

The fact that we may regard an "evening" walk according to (at least) three semantic trajectories suggests the third way in which the concept of "Romantic vagrancy" will be played out in subsequent chapters: as a synonym for the aesthetic. In the Romantic paradigm imagination itself takes on the double aspect of the poet/vagrant, the formalism that is also an objectlessness. In the "Essay, Supplementary," Wordsworth correlates the mental operation with the word itself, claiming that "imagination" is "a word which has been forced to extend its services far beyond the point to which philosophy would have confined [it]" (*PrW III*, 81). This forcible expropriation of "imagination" from its etymological link to the object-world (imagination as a mental imaging of sense impressions) is a consequence, he alleges, of the "*poverty* of language"; because we have no "proper" word for the formal reflection of the mind on its own operations, we must resort to the word "imagination" as to a metaphor. The word "imagination" here functions as the Romantic image does, as the vagrant does: expropriated from a determinative context, it holds the place of the unimaginable, the abstract.

Thus the "poverty" of imagination is the aspect that most suits it for Romantic representation. We may read Wordsworth's description of the *forcible* expropriation of the word from its etymological roots as the aesthetic equivalent of Rousseau's famous paradox: the citizen "will be forced to be free" (*SC* 195). Etymology – the historicist law of the word – represents for Wordsworth an incomplete liberation:

Here, as in other instances throughout the volume [William Taylor's *English Synonyms Discriminated*], the judicious Author's mind is enthralled by Etymology; he takes up the original word as his guide and escort, and too often does not perceive how soon he becomes its prisoner, without liberty to tread in any path but that to which it confines him (*PrW III*, 30).

An Enlightenment science, etymology liberates understanding from subjection to a superstitious belief in the relation between word and thing only to subject it in turn to new enthrallments: history and sensation. The Romantic poem, by contrast, depends on an equivocation – a multiplication but also an evening – of the word's referential field. It seeks to preserve for the reader a "liberty to tread in any path," but eliminates the right of residence.

The expropriation of imagination from reference, I suggest, is what determines the Romantic privileging of *form*. In the Romantic paradigm, a poem's form and its content are no longer alienable; this inalienability is what defines the *literary absolute*. I use Wordsworth's formal experiments as emblematic of the literary absolute because the random encounter that structures his poems draws attention to the *exigency* of this formal constraint. It suggests the subjection of literary composition to precisely those forces – historical, economic, social (those *public* forces, in other words) – that it wishes to subordinate to absolute freedom of expression.

This formal exigency provides a crucial link to the explicitly political discourse of liberalism. Here too, we discover a strange, even self-reflexive symmetry between form and content. The political writings of Constant, whose essay distinguishing "Ancient and Modern Liberty" is held to inaugurate the discourse of classical liberalism, were undertaken amid "otherwise disorderly habits and incessant travelling," his editors report. Incessant mobility is the historical context, in other words, of Constant's proposition that political liberty is "the liberty to come and go without permission."

To compensate for these situational exigencies, Constant developed an index-card system of notation: "legend claims that he began this practice by writing on the back of a pack of tarot cards" (32). This "legend" excavates a certain obscure philosophical *legacy*. In writing his political theory on the obverse of tarot cards, Constant merely embellishes upon the example of Rousseau, that fellow Genevan whose political writings Constant would challenge, but whose notes for *Rêveries du promeneur solitaire* were written on the backs of playing cards. By modeling his *political* theory on the form of Rousseau's *literary* method, Constant may unwittingly suggest how the transitory reflections of the private subject, the solitary walker, will replace the political declarations of *citizen* subject (Rousseau's explicitly political corpus). With Constant, one might say, the marginal method and fragmentary form of Romantic composition are elevated to the status of political principle; indeed, Constant's "Fragments d'un ouvrage abandonné" (1800–3, in *Political Writings*) was revised and published in 1815 as *Political Principles*.

Constant's possession of tarot cards may serve as an emblem of liberalism's (and Romanticism's) partial rejection of Enlightenment and the Revolutionary law of transparency. We know also that Rousseau's playing cards, carried by someone in 1793, might be construed under the Law of Suspects as evidence of private interest – as property not cleansed of historical and ideological content; images of kings and queens had been replaced by a revolutionary icongraphy by that time. It is precisely because iconic representation is so charged with historical reference that playing cards inscribed on the back are most truly the "walking papers" of the liberal subject, and may serve as the emblem of Romantic representation. By inscribing the back, so to speak, the subject *textualizes* the card, demoting the pictorial, referential aspect of the representation to the status of enabling background; his own "plebeian" self-representations take the place of "departed potentates" (I draw here on Wordsworth's representation of card games in *The Prelude* [1.540–62]). Thus despite the apparent redolence of autobiographical detail and fact in the Romantic text, its *pictorial* aspect – what used to be regarded as its elevation of Nature – represents not a positive content, but the effacing or obscuring of positive content. What is left in the empty space is the subject's self-inscription.

We should also recall that what makes the tarot or the playing card (or the *carte de civisme*, for that matter) so susceptible a material surface for this inscription is its *portability*. The pathological remainders in the *ethos* of liberalism – the freedom to come and go and the right to private property – constitute the liberal subject as one who, in Rousseau's resonant image, "carries all of himself." The regime of liberalism is enabled by and enables a crucial *mobilization of property*; as enacted by the Romantic text, this mobilization of property takes the form of the "moving spectacle" – where the transcendental surplus, the "all," is reduced to that possession which most indicates an absolute destitution; for example, the "last" of a flock or the disfigured playing card. This destitution, in turn, displays the absolute transcendence of imagination.

I call the figure of Romantic vagrancy *analogical* rather than metaphorical, metonymic, or allegorical in order to suggest how the prolixity we associate with Romantic representation is a pathological symptom – the substitution of the implicit relations of metaphor by analogy's explications. Merleau-Ponty explains this pathology: a patient

does not even understand such simple analogies as: "fur is to cat as plumage is to bird"... or "eye is to light and colour as ear is to sounds." In the same way he cannot understand, in their metaphorical sense, such common expressions as "the chair leg" or "the head of a nail," although he knows what part of the object is indicated by these words. (128)

The disabled patient's difficulty with metaphor – the clinical term is *apraxia* – is not a *rational* incapacity; in fact, the dysfunction requires him to resort to reason, to articulate (rather than intuit) the posited identity *as an analogy*:

If we described analogy as the apperception of two given terms under a co-ordinating concept, we should be giving as normal a procedure which is exclusively pathological, and which represents the roundabout way in which the patient makes good the normal understanding of analogy. This freedom in choosing a *tertium comparationis* on the patient's part is the opposite of the intuitive formation of the image in the normal subject. (128)

A similar disability, I suggest, obtains in the Romantic text. In describing freedom as the "moving spectacle" of walking, the Romantic poet freely chooses a *tertium comparationis* by which to draw the poet and the vagrant into an analogical relation. But walking becomes the third term precisely because the relation between the poet and the vagrant – their identity as liberal subjects, which should go without saying – is something that the poet "does not understand." The "roundabout way" of analogy – a fine description of Romantic method – is a pathological expression of *freedom of association*. (We may recall that liberalism's early translation of this freedom into law delegitimated all but purely random associations: the workers' corporation, that grouping for economic and political empowerment, was outlawed by the Le Chapellier law of 1791.[9])

The critic who would explain the analogical relation between the subject of liberalism and the vagrant of capitalism by reference to the third term, *literature*, will find herself in the position of the apraxic who obsessively *represents* or subjects to articulation processes (walking and talking) that make up our social being and ought *to go without saying*. Like grasping the logic of a metaphor, walking and talking become pathological when fully articulated into serial components. The underrecognized contribution of phenomenology is to remind us that the body does not walk as the consequence of (ideological) representations that are then relayed to the material nervous system of the body. (Merleau-Ponty: "It is true, as Marx says, that history does not walk on its head, but it is also true that it does not think with its feet" [xix].) But this is precisely why we should be interested in the Romantic representation of freedom – a representation that depends upon the (dis)articulation of thinking and walking, and therefore equates freedom with *apraxia*, that condition Rousseau called *désœuvrement*, or the body "out of order," out of *the* order of production.

If the structural vagrancy of the liberal subject is indeed a consequence of the attempt to negotiate a series of differential determinations of freedom – political, economic, aesthetic – it will not be surprising that I have found it impossible to say, in the chapters that follow, "Here walking has a political, there an economic dimension; here it is a product of thought, there a physiological habit." By proposing that *vagrancy*, rather than the errand, the stroll, or the march, is the paradigm of Romantic walking and talking, I claim that the transcendental surplus – freedom – depends on the negation of any single discursive trajectory. Perhaps Wordsworth offers the best representation of Romantic vagrancy when he imagines the drunkard: "In some parts of England it is quaintly said, when a drunken man is seen reeling towards his home, that he has business on both sides of the road."[10] This "quaint" saying suggests the diverse and pathological elements of Romantic representation as I have outlined them: the saying is "quaint" because it is confined to "parts" of England, indicating a regional origin or affiliation – the language of dialect. Expropriated into the "common" language of print culture, it takes on the aspect of the thing it seeks to describe: the "quaint" saying is a kind of slurred speech, a corrupted *patois* produced by trading in too many discourses. The critic confronting the itineraries and speech patterns of the Romantic poem is similarly susceptible to the fallacy of imitative form. But it should be clear that any critical method claiming the privilege of an historical or objective distance – a "freedom from" its object of analysis – itself falls subject to the thing it would avoid: Romantic ideology or liberal idealism. I therefore consciously adopt a method that is dialectical but not synthetic, producing two pathologies instead of one.

Chapter 1, "Rousseau Plays the Beggar: the Last Words of Citizen Subject," lays out evidence for my fundamental contention that the liberal subject is constituted by a regime of texts. While Rousseau's political philosophy can hardly be characterized as "liberal," what interests me is the way in which his negotiation between his political and his literary selves brings about a "fall" into print whose "disfigurement" prefigures liberalism's incapacity to embody the universal. From this process of negotiation the most consistent self-representation emerges: "ma personne fut affichée par mes écrits" ("my person was advertised by my writings"). This "negotiation" of an identity produces a literary form that replicates its content:

Rousseau's invention of the pedestrian *excursion* has the status of an *excursus*, a supplement to or digression from the "proper" text. This status subverts any possibility of literary autonomy; like Rousseau himself, these texts are said to "go begging." Rousseau's representation of the text's failure to find its "public" – the "all" that is the abstraction of liberalism's body politic – configures the "literary" as the self-expression of citizen vagrant. The affective disorder of literature – talking to itself – is the formal equivalent of the self-referential but hardly autonomous subject of liberalism.

Each of the remaining chapters considers Wordsworth's representation of Romantic vagrancy. Focusing on three different formal experiments – the 1800 edition of *Lyrical Ballads*, *The Prelude* and *The Excursion* – I read the Wordsworthian subject as the (negated) historical incarnation of Rousseau's imaginary citizen. If democratic revolutions appear to make the universal "man" an historical reality, the chief interest of Wordsworth's poetry lies in its display of that historical existence as a kind of vagrancy. Historical experience registers the identity of the subject freed from determination as one that "will have been," a registering that requires the rhetorical form of the negative litany (he will have been what I *am* not) and the structural form of the literary excursion. Such a form depends for its material subsistence on the random encounter.

Because I read Romantic vagrancy as a version of the "literary absolute" that would subsume all competing discourses according to the logic of liberalism, each of the chapters on Wordsworth reads the figuring of vagrancy against extraliterary discourses upon which the construction of the liberal subject depends. In chapter 2, "Money Walks: Wordsworth and the Right to Wander," for example, I discuss the relation between the thematic of impoverishment in *Lyrical Ballads* and the idea of literary "property" evident in Wordsworth's two-volume revisionary expansion of the 1800 edition. To illuminate the relation between form and content, I read the poems in reference to what might be called the "form" and the formal critique of capitalism – double-entry bookkeeping and Marx's *Capital*. I propose that Wordsworth employs two discourses – story and number, or the literary and the economic – to represent vagrancy. But in *Lyrical Ballads*, that notoriously hybrid literary form, these two discourses are employed to negate each other, and so themselves correspond to the "double-entry" form of accounting that makes purely formal the categories of credit and debit, and enables the long-term and large-scale business enterprise. Romantic vagrancy is the representation of the expropriated peasant, but it is also the representation of the difference between neighbor and passerby as another purely formal distinction that makes possible the poet's address to a transhistorical "public."

In chapter 3, "Walking and Talking at the Same Time: the 'Two Histories' of *The Prelude*," I set out to describe the formal features of the transhistorical liberal text, and to suggest why that text will fail fully to repress its pathological content: vagrancy. The "two histories" identified in my title refer to the form and the content of Wordsworth's poem, heuristically reduced, in my account, to the "glad preamble" and the encounter with the discharged soldier. They also refer, implicitly, to two competing ways of reading the historical "references" to the French Revolution in the poem: Alan Liu's recent persuasive argument (in *Wordsworth*) that "Napoleon" is the referent for the expropriated and expropriating word "Imagination" in the famous apostrophic interruption of *The Prelude*'s narrative (vi, 525ff. [1805]), and Marx's proleptic – even postmodern – reading of the historical referentiality of the French Revolution in *The Eighteenth Brumaire of Louis Bonaparte*. The double history of *The Prelude* – the autobiographical account and the history of the composition of that account (content and form) – has long been of interest to critics, who have either implicitly or explicitly suggested the centrality of the poem's formal self-reflexiveness to the emergence of the modern subject. I propose a radical rereading of *The Prelude* by demonstrating how the formal history negates the anecdotal autobiography. By figuring the "man" of whom we read, *The Prelude* only conjures the vagrant; the poem's form of address – the physiologically inflected apostrophic "oh" of the glad preamble – is finally indistinguishable from the vagrant's "groans scarcely audible."

I use chapter 4, "The Walking Cure," as an opportunity to bring together the diverse elements of my argument that Romantic vagrancy is the pathos of liberalism. Its subject is the longest poem Wordsworth published in his lifetime, *The Excursion*. I take issue with the prevailing account of the poem as a failure, arguing instead that the poem is entirely consistent with the representation of Romantic vagrancy elsewhere in Wordsworth's corpus. To this end, I foreground two aspects of *The Excursion*: its structuration as a series of interlocutions and its representation of the *dead* body politic. First, I demonstrate the deep ambiguity of the poem's central figure, the Pedlar-turned-Wanderer; initially unrecognized as he stands stationary in a public thoroughfare, later established "in residence" at the site of the ruined cottage, the Wanderer is at once vagrant and (liberal) host. Wordsworth's representation of the transcendental/ transient, the Wanderer, as one who "could afford to suffer" is another collapsing of discourses, and I read the "psychic economy" that emerges as the subject of *The Excursion* as evidence of the last (or latest) incarnation of citizen subject: the therapeutic subject, or hypochondriac. Using Freud's essay, "Mourning and Melancholia," to explain the relation between "The Ruined Cottage" – that emblematic narrative of Romantic vagrancy – and the graveyard books of *The Excursion*, I explain why the Solitary's affective disorder, melancholia, is a *political, economic*, and *historical* disorder: a disorder of liberalism. Prophetic of the gradual transformation in the nineteenth century of the cemetery into the park, the graveyard books of *The Excursion* reconfigure the public sphere literally as the space of the subject who "will have been." The dead afford to the philosophical concept of "society" a positive (and negative) content, and the elegiac march of the funeral procession becomes the forerunner of our own versions of society, the "democracy to come" of Derrida and the "inoperative community" of Nancy.

# CHAPTER I

# Rousseau plays the beggar: the last words of citizen subject

Of the features of Rousseau's corpus that compel a resurgent recognition of his critical and philosophical importance, none is as crucial nor as problematic as the imaginary fault line that separates his "political" or "public" writing from the autobiographical or ostensibly "private" documents. On the one hand, Rousseau's "literary" reputation appears to rest on the *Confessions*, regarded by many as marking the emergence of the modern (liberal) subject. On the other, the *Social Contract* is a crucial text for political theorists now engaged in rethinking the relation between the political subject of democracy and the private subject of liberalism. But the very nature of Rousseau's texts complicates any attempt so to "discipline" or separate into private and public spheres the question of the subject and the question of the citizen, the confession and the contract. *Both* the subject *and* the citizen owe their preeminence as essential units of thought in the regime of liberalism to a metaphorical logic by which one derives its justification from the other. If we are now at a point where we wish to ask, with Jean-Luc Nancy, *Who Comes After the Subject?*, we may wish, with Etienne Balibar, to use Rousseau to ground our response: "*After the subject comes the citizen*" (38).[1]

What does it mean to "return" to Rousseau, and the citizen, in this manner? How does such a return promise to escape or at least to criticize the metaphorical interchangeability of citizen and subject? At first, such a return to Rousseau might seem to identify a postmodern critical agenda with the logic of infinite circulation. If we recognize certain ideological limitations in the category of the (epistemological) subject, nonetheless the subject of liberalism has been regarded as an improvement upon the citizen. Disillusioned with the discourse of rights, the negative freedom of the citizen, liberalism (after Constant) invents the "obscure" subject, replete

31

with desires, as the citizen's afterlife, and democracy's afterword. After the citizen comes the subject: this is the historical narrative of progress. As the chronology of his corpus suggests, even Rousseau *begins* with the citizen and *ends* with the subject. But note how, in Rousseau's *œuvre*, the two figures, citizen and subject, seem to require for their resolution a supplementary narrative: the citizen writes the "history" of the subject (the autonomous individual who chooses with each step and exchanges his independence for rights via the contract), as Rousseau does in the *Discourse on the Origins of Inequality* and the *Social Contract*; the subject writes the history of the citizen (the public Rousseau) in the autobiographical texts.

Even those critics most responsive to Rousseau's work have tended to emphasize *one* supplementary history over the other, deeming that the irony so characteristic of Rousseau's rhetoric renders the political writings literary rather than the reverse. Paul de Man, representing those whose interest in Rousseau is primarily "literary," characterizes strictly political interpretation as "the literal reading that fails to take into account the figural dimensions of the language" (136); yet his exemplar of political interpretation, Louis Althusser, had already located an essential displacement operating between the political and literary dimensions of Rousseau's work. In his essay on the *Social Contract*, Althusser argues that a serial "play on words" constitutes and determines the logic of the contract and the nature of Rousseau's ideology. But if de Man argues that such literary play with words means that "the political writings can then become a reliable way of access to the problematics of self in Rousseau" (138) – we might argue with equal validity the reverse: the autobiographical writings, or what Althusser calls his "unprecedented *literary* work," may serve to illuminate the problematic of the citizen in Rousseau.[2]

Althusser argues that the conceptual discrepancies in Rousseau's idea of the citizen are furtively "resolved" by the emergence of the autobiographical – and literary – subject. I wish to argue here instead that those discrepancies are purposely *exposed* by the *disfiguration* of the subject at work in the autobiographical project as a whole, particularly in the history of that project that emerges in the texts titled or structured as "afterwords" to the *Confessions*: the *Dialogues*, its curious appendage, the "Histoire du précédent écrit," and the *Rêveries*. For if the differential construction of subject and citizen (the one writes the "history" of the other and so produces itself) emerges in the relation between the *Social Contract* and the *Confessions*, these later texts threaten or promise to unravel that differential construction and produce its critique.

The metaphorical interchangeability of citizen and subject depends in large part on what is perhaps Rousseau's major contribution to the ideology of liberalism: the equation of freedom with mobility, the formulation of citizenship *as* mobility. In the *Social Contract*, Rousseau complains that the French have misunderstood the nature of citizenship, a misunderstanding visible through an irresponsible "play on words" which takes "un bourgeois pour un Citoyen." In other words, the French imagine, represent, or *figure* citizenship in terms of fixed and immobile property. To be a citizen of Geneva, on the other hand, one needed only to be a man; one's body was sufficient property, according to Rousseau.[3] If Althusser is right to suggest that Rousseau idealizes the citizen as artisan, that artisan is nonetheless a journeyman, the one able to carry "all" of himself as he travels. The valorization of mobility is everywhere at work in Rousseau's "political" writings: in the *Discourse on the Origins of Inequality*, the independent savage "chooses with each step"; in the *Social Contract*, the citizen "runs to assemblies"; in *Emile*, the student is trained by a pedestrian pedagogy to resist the stationary contemplation Rousseau suggests is the epistemological form of tyranny and to prepare for the "retraining" so frequently necessary in an increasingly mobile society. The effect of this equation between freedom and mobility is to deinstitutionalize citizenship, which helps to explain the peculiarly paradoxical fact that even as Rousseau will consistently praise as model citizens the citizens immobilized within Geneva's walls, his own identity as "citoyen singulier" requires his exit from those walls on foot. Thus even if we were to see that exit as producing the "citizen subject," a hybrid whose political freedom consists paradoxically in the distance he can log from the public sphere, we must acknowledge that the freedom of Rousseau's "subject," like that of the citizen he may be said to replace, resides in *mobility*.

As we try to assess Rousseau's relation to the liberal tradition which, as Andrzej Rapaczynski has recently argued, explains the liberty guaranteed by the social contract as "a completely innocuous 'absence of external impediments to motion'" (226) (and so identifies democracy with *laissez-faire*), we may at first be drawn to conclude with Rapaczynski, as with Althusser before him, that Rousseau's prescient critique of liberalism is limited by his failure "to realize the fundamental role that economic production would play" or to "attune his political proposals to the coming age of capitalism" (273). In this light, we may regard the equation of citizenship with the artisan's mobility as evidence of Rousseau's nostalgia for an economy of handicrafts and a society of corporations; or we may regard his embrace of mobility as a capitulation to the displacements inaugurated by the consolidation of capital. In so doing, however, we overlook the *critique* of mobility offered in the autobiographical project, specifically in its "afterwords" as we watch the pedestrian traveler subjected to repeated *disfigurement*. The suggestion as we watch these quite literal disfigurements occur is that mobility is only a *metaphorical* freedom, and that before Althusser, Rousseau recognized that the discourse of rights in a liberal regime amounts to a "play on words." Although Rousseau begins his political theory by positing a difference between the bourgeois and the citizen, he may be said to conclude by positing an identity between the citizen and the vagrant. Far from substantiating an equation between mobility and freedom, these narratives subvert the claim to autonomy of self at the same time as they undermine or compromise any claim to "literary" autonomy that might be made in the name of the text.[4] Like Rousseau himself, the last manuscripts are said to "go begging."

One contention at work here is that the regime of liberalism, in part constituted by the division between public and private made in the political writings and apparently reinforced by the structure of Rousseau's corpus, entails a new valorization of mobility – certainly mobility of property but also individual mobility. Therefore the *critique* of liberalism may be partly accomplished by the disfiguration of mobility. This is true primarily because individual mobility, as it defines a "liberal" society, is already conceived of differentially, as Baudrillard reminds us: as "each individual and each group searches out his–her place in an order, all the while trying to jostle according to a personal trajectory," that place is established by "the disparity between intentional mobility (aspirations) and real mobility (objective chances of social promotion)" (38). The *valorization* of mobility, as opposed to the real increase in mobility of populations characteristic or perhaps constitutive of the liberal regime, is thus primarily *metaphorical*, as the expression "upward mobility" suggests. But if Rousseau's figuration of freedom in the wandering subject finally ironizes an ideology of mobility by equating the "autonomous" pedestrian with the vagrant, we need not conclude, *à la* de Man, that the equation of freedom with "absolute randomness" signals "the moment of dispossession in favor of the arbitrary power play of the signifier" and that therefore Rousseau's political theory itself amounts to a "play on words." Rather we ought to see Althusser's concession of this fact as an indication of the profoundly political implications of Rousseau's final representation of the citizen as vagabond. We may reach, in the process, an understanding of Deleuze and Guattari's claim, in *Anti-Oedipus: Capitalism and Schizophrenia*, that "the schizo, continually wandering about, migrating here, there, and everywhere as best he can... deliberately seeks out the very limit of capitalism; he is its inherent tendency brought to fulfillment, its surplus product, its proletariat, its exterminating angel" (35).

If the *Social Contract* and the *Confessions* stand as testaments to their respective authors – the citizen and the subject – the writing that follows these "unprecedented" forays into the discourse of individuality is the *Dialogues*, which, in its self-conscious splitting of man from citizen (Jean-Jacques from the "author" of certain texts) refigures individuality as duality or schizophrenia. In the odd "Dedication" to that text, which therefore serves as the most immediate "afterword" to the *Confessions*, Rousseau's prayer is that the reader might "read *all* of it before making use of it" ("le lire tout entier avant que d'en disposer") (659). To read the *Dialogues* "tout entier" means to finish by reading the "Histoire du précédent écrit," which narrates the debilitating failure of Rousseau's pedestrian attempts to find an audience for his address "A tout Français." As he wanders the streets and promenades of Paris, depending on the kindness (or justice) of passersby and thus miming the activities of that city's increasing horde of the dispossessed, we witness a transformation: walking becomes not only the cure offered by liberalism, but also the disease produced by it; the privacy newly discovered by the solitary walker is interrupted by the recognition that privacy may be experienced as privation. My argument is that the autobiographical writings might profitably be read as histories "des précédents écrits" which ironize the positivist or liberal tendencies of Rousseau's sociopolitical thought by refiguring freedom as "un désœuvrement du corps." In the *Rêveries du promeneur solitaire*, which functions in the corpus as Rousseau's *last* such afterword, mobility and freedom of thought, or walking and reverie, are radically transformed in a way that should recall his account of the dispossession undergone by the subject (of the prince) in favor of his subsequent incarnation, the citizen: "even the wise saw that they had to make up their mind to sacrifice one part of their freedom to preserve the other, as a wounded man has his arm cut off to save the rest of his body." By the fact that his pedestrian excursions subject him to a variety of bodily accidents, and either physical or textual disfigurement, Rousseau seems to discover that mobility and *agency* are on a collision course, constitute a contradiction rather than an identity. Language participates in the "mouvement machinal" which outspeeds the subject's intentions, but only insofar as it has been monopolized by the "corporations" that would control public opinion as the guilds had, in an earlier age, impeded the free movements of the journeyman.

The *Dialogues* and its appended "history" suggest that this transformation is a consequence of the transformation of the social contract (a transformation partly effected, one must grant, by Rousseau himself). As writing supplants the feudal form of covenant, the "aveu," which constituted identity as a fixed place in a determinate social order – the subject as "subject to" the prince or lord – we discover the "discrepancy" noted in a different context by Althusser: the new "contract" has only one party; there is neither a recipient nor a guarantor. Such a discrepancy reduces the subject citizen, who "declares" his identity and his rights, to the status of *un sans-aveu*: beggar, vagabond, stranger. Not only does this transformation expose the false synonymy between mobility and its valorization as freedom, but it allows Rousseau to render the failure of the social contract as a failure of *liberality* (or rather, compassion: liberality is compassion based upon a falsely assumed superiority). The abstract political relation replaces the *social* relation which is ostensibly its aim. Because a liberal regime utilizes the ideology of the welfare state (the consolidation of power and wealth justified as necessary to ensure the welfare of all – Rousseau's "general interest") to support dispossession and displacement, it conforms to the model of usurpation that Rousseau lays out: the contract is the work of *homo fabulator* who would, by sleight of word, construct "this is mine" as "right" (the first conflation of bourgeois and citizen). Without an absolute "faith" in the word that "aveu" implies, the "sans-aveu" is in the position of disillusionment; this disillusionment is what the gradual disfigurement of "pedestrian Rousseau" into the vagrant accomplishes.

When Rousseau represents himself as leaving Geneva on foot, walking originates as an image of entrepreneurship, self-education, and even liberation – to a condition of pure social mobility: "sans avoir aucun état moi-même, j'ai connu tous les états... Admis chez tous comme un homme sans prétensions et sans conséquence, je les examinais à mon aise" ("without having an estate myself, I have known them all... Admitted to everyone's house as a man without pretensions and without consequence, I have studied them at my leisure") (*OC* 1.1150). As soon as the *Confessions* and other autobiographical texts begin to narrate the history of his writing career, however, the representation of mobility becomes far more problematic. Such are the vagaries of civil society – or, with more historical precision, such is the emerging contradiction of liberalism – that the very behavior symbolic of political freedom simultaneously connotes social disenfranchisement. The story of the "illumination" on the road to Vincennes which begins Rousseau's public career is the first of a series of "accidents imprévus" whose effect on Rousseau is described as a "bouleversement" that throws him to the side of the road. Because of the hot summer and the long journey,

In order to ease my journey [pour modérer mon pas] I decided to take something to read. One day I took the *Mercure de France*, and glancing through it while walking I fell [et tout en marchant et le parcourant je tombai] on this question proposed by the Academy of Dijon... Whether the progress of the arts and sciences had contributed to corrupt or improve morals? (*OC* 1.351)

Rousseau's "fall" into print is then literalized: "no longer able to breathe while walking, I let myself fall under one of the trees lining the avenue" ("ne pouvant plus respirer en marchant, je me laisse tomber sous un des arbres de l'avenue") (*OC* 1.351). A second "history" of this event (du précédent écrit) in the *Rêveries* focuses even more sharply the problematic of mobility; Rousseau writes that his walking reveries, where freedom is represented as a meandering, autotelic movement, are *displaced* at the moment he encounters the text of the *Mercure*: "once thrown by outside forces into a literary career, I felt the weariness of mental labor and the exigency of an unhappy fame" ("une fois, jetté dans la carrière littéraire par des impulsions étrangères, je sentis la fatigue du travail d'ésprit et l'importunité d'une célébrité malheureuse") (*R* 107; *OC* iv.1062). We witness here what Paul Virilio, in *Speed and Politics*, calls "the obligation to mobility" ("No one yet suspected that the 'conquest of the freedom to come and go' so dear to Montaigne could, by a sleight of hand, become an *obligation to mobility*") [30]. Rousseau first adopts a pedestrian mode of travel in order to participate in the increase of speed and social circulation represented by the world beyond Geneva's walls, a world where newspapers advertise competitions for social advancement. But when he most fully becomes the mobile subject ("je devins [*sic*] un autre homme," he writes in the *Confessions*), he is least an agent; the man that he becomes, as the *Dialogues* will demonstrate, is "un gueux" – a beggar.

Rousseau died before seeing the French Revolution articulate this division in a declaration of the rights of "man *and* citizen." But the rationalization and reorganization of many aspects of eighteenth-century French society suggest how that declaration had many precedents. One aspect of the increase of social legislation has particular relevance to this discussion: the policing of the poor. The historian Olwen Hufton summarizes the problem:

> To Montesquieu, to Rousseau, to the innumerable pamphlet-writers of the eighteenth century, to government officials (though most recognized they had no substitute to offer for voluntary charity) and, very importantly, to the *Comité de mendicité*, concerned in 1790 to endow France with a new poor law, indiscriminate Catholic charity, rather than soundly based, objective state assistance to the truly poor in the form of work, was alone responsible for the gross inflation in France of the number of paupers who were for the most part idlers parasitic on the rest of society. (3)

Hufton offers no references to help us identify passages in texts where Rousseau justifies the welfare state or criticizes random acts of charity;[5] indeed, insofar as the political theory supports such an interpretation, the autobiographical texts establish another major "discrepancy," given the number of such random acts performed and narrated by Rousseau in the *Rêveries* and his querulous opposition to their rationalization. Actually, Hufton's assumption that Rousseau supported the rationalization of charity, derived no doubt from his argument for the subordination of the particular to the general interest in the *Social Contract*, was a contemporary understanding as well – a contemporary *mis*understanding, according to Rousseau, as we will see by complaints he makes in the second *promenade*. What is *not* a misunderstanding, however, is the implicit mapping of a political model onto apparently "social" issues. Once the "history" of the individual citizen is narrated by the autobiographical project, we discover that the abstracted unit of citizenship most closely resembles – the vagabond. As a postscript to the politics, Rousseau's representation of the subject of history may be read as Rousseau's attempt to historicize, and thereby critique, the concept of the welfare state.

Let me explain why Rousseau's implicit concern with the problem of vagrancy and poor laws is particularly relevant to the link established between the political and the literary, and how the figure of the beggar traverses the distance between these two discourses, thereby becoming the locus of Rousseau's critique of his own theory of the social contract. We know that Rousseau was among the first political theorists to refuse to posit as the basis for society a "natural sociability." Instead, society is an effect of the institution of property and the consequent historical development of desires into *needs*. One enters society, in other words, in a condition of dependency. If the contingencies of climate allow a certain latitude of first speech – in Rousseau's imagination, the scarcity of the north produces one kind of address ("aidez moi") whereas in southern climates, the more direct address is "aimez moi" – nonetheless language is *a priori* political, since the act of address itself reveals a social – and *unnatural* – dependency. For this reason, I contend, Rousseau sees his own entry into social discourse as analogous to that of the beggar/ vagabond.

This self-representation is everywhere at work in Rousseau's rhetoric: his repeated apologies for the inability to follow a consistent plan, his acknowledged antipathy to "travail," his *manie ambulante*, these plainly identify him with the vagabond. Jean Starobinski has called attention to the series of negating litanies – for example, "sans biens, sans emploi, sans fauteurs" – that constitute not only Rousseau's distinctive rhetorical style, but also his typical self-representation; this rhetoric – a figure of destitution – *is* Rousseau's critique of the newly mobilized citizen subject.

Evidence that Rousseau regards vagabondage ultimately as a kind of destitution rather than as a positive freedom becomes visible as we examine his modes of address. Rousseau demonstrates that the prevailing ideology of social contract is modeled on the beggar's address, and thereby delegitimates any declarations of right based on such a model as capitulating to a regime of duty and inequality rather than freedom and equality. When in the later texts Rousseau replaces the formula of (self-authorized) declaration with a *simulation* of that address (a figurative or *literary* address), Rousseau exposes the fictive nature of the ostensibly *political* claim to authority.

In the *Dialogues* which preface the "histoire," Jean-Jacques is attacked for a self-disfigurement central to my argument: "he *plays the beggar* even though he is rich" ("[il] *fait le gueux* quoiqu'il soit riche") (*OC* 1.720), claims the prosecutorial Frenchman. "Rousseau," the other interlocutor and empirically minded advocate, operates almost in the manner of one of eighteenth-century France's many Comités de Mendicité in attempting to judge the worthiness of his favorite author, asking: "if he plays the beggar, does he then receive or request alms? Because that is all that distinguishes the beggar from the poor man, who is no richer than he but who contents himself with what he has and demands nothing from anyone" (*s'il fait le gueux*, il reçoit donc ou demande l'aumone? Car voilà tout ce qui distingue le gueux du pauvre, qui n'est pas plus riche que lui mais qui se contente de ce qu'il a et ne demande rien à personne") (*OC* 1.720). The logic of this defense – that simulation without a motive of self-interest is no crime – is the same offered by Rousseau about dissimulation in the *Rêveries*, where he argues in the fourth promenade that to lie "sans necessité, sans profit" is to enter the realm of the literary, where for example Montesquieu's preface to *le temple de gnide* is "a positive lie" ("un mensonge bien positif") yet its author not an impostor. It is significant also to recall in this context Rousseau's allusion to Boudin, in the *Discourse on Political Economy*, as an authority for regarding "those who impose or contrive the taxes [les *impôts*]" as *imposteurs*, because they disguise their class interest behind the mask of general welfare; an impostor is one who demands payment unjustly (*SC*, 128). Thus were Rousseau to adopt the guise of a beggar, such a self-refashioning would only be ethically suspect were he to demand, against justice and according to self-interest, alms or charity not due to him. On the other hand, adopting the address or *formal* posture of the beggar Rousseau offers to criticize all *im*postures of the state, precisely by suggesting that when the state appears in the guise of benefactor, all of its subjects are thereby reduced to beggars.

In the case he lays before us in the *Dialogues*, Rousseau goes further: those who adopt the guise of "friends" and benefactors to

Rousseau demand his gratitude, even as they seek to do his reputation irreparable harm. Their strategies – the misappropriation and misrepresentation of Rousseau's corpus through the careful control of collected editions – are similarly reminiscent of strategies employed by "those that the world calls honest" ("ces gens qu'on appelle vrais dans le monde"), and criticized by Rousseau in the fourth promenade. Just as the latter take care accurately to cite place, time, and person and to narrate with no exaggeration, embellishment, or fiction in even the most casual conversation, thereby building credit for the fables they tell when their interest is at stake, so the "benevolent" friends of the *Dialogues* conceive of producing "fine editions which, because of their typographical perfection, would be preferred to preceding ones and remain in libraries" ("des belles éditions qui par leur perfection typographique fissent tomber les *précédents* [écrits] et restassent dans les bibliothèques") (*OC* 1.959; *D* 232). This representation of textual "history" in the *Dialogues* reveals that Rousseau regards the conspiracy against him as utilizing protocapitalist techniques of accumulation and expansion, even as its agents are aligned with tax collectors attempting to centralize and to control wealth not their own. He writes,

Among the peculiarities that distinguish our century from all others is the methodical and consistent spirit that has guided public opinion for twenty years. Until now, these opinions meandered [*erraient*] without order and without regulation at the whim of men's passions, and these passions continually colliding made the public go back and forth from one to the other with no steady direction. It is no longer the same today. Prejudices themselves have their progression and rules.

(Parmi les singularités qui distinguent le siècle où nous vivons de tous les autres est l'esprit méthodique et conséquent qui depuis vingt ans dirige les opinions publiques. Jusqu'ici ces opinions *erraient* sans suite et sans règle au gré des passions des hommes, et ces passions s'entrechoquant sans cesse faisaient flotter le public de l'une à l'autre sans aucune direction constante. Il n'en est plus de même aujourd'hui. Les préjugés eux-mêmes ont leur marche et leurs règles.) (*OC* 1.964–5; *D* 236–7)

He points out how the academies and the Encyclopedists have become a corporate body, and how by blatant misrepresentations of Rousseau they attempt to determine "just how far their credit extends" ("jusqu'où leur credit pouvait s'étendre") (*OC* 1.965). Not only does this analysis suggest that, contrary to Rapaczynski's claim, Rousseau is very much aware of how altered modes of production threaten the free operation of consensus, it also suggests that Rousseau did indeed take "the last step in the direction of the 'denaturalization' of man, which would make it entirely impossible to analyze even a single aspect of human life in terms of a theory of nature" (264). Although we may find in the early, public discourses a theory of justice, for example, that appeals to a distinction between "natural" and "unnatural" needs, again we find that the auto-biographical "afterwords" problematize such a distinction, by recognizing discursive manipulations of the category of need on a par with editorial manipulations of Rousseau's manuscripts. Any original "truth" may be overwhelmed by history's new *consolidation of opinion*. In a way, this is a far more dangerous effect than the consolidation of material wealth (as capital), for it disallows the political liberty – freedom of opinion – liberalism offers as social inequality's chief compensation.[6]

However, such a consolidation of opinion *does* have a dangerous economic effect, rendered in the *Dialogues* as the unsuccess with which Rousseau attempts to resist the "charity" of his benefactors. The form of the general conspiracy, as it is identified by the Frenchman, is to give him alms on the sly, and thereby transform his "honest" poverty into an apparently unjust demand upon the resources of the public: "this charity, which they zealously publicize, has perhaps contributed more than anything else to debasing him as much as his friends desired" ("cette charité, qu'on s'attache à rendre bruyante, a peut-être contribué plus que tout autre chose à le déprimer autant que le désiraient ses amis") (*D* 46; *OC* 1.718). The conspiracy which attacks individual autonomy and splits Jean-Jacques from Rousseau, public author from private subject, is thus both the consolidation of opinion and the consolidation of money it makes possible; theories of the "welfare" state allow – even en-courage – the monopolization of a properly democratic power to take place behind the mask of solicitousness for the general welfare.

By undertaking his critique of the welfare state on the rhetorical level of self-disfigurement – playing the beggar – Rousseau manages not only to demonstrate the effects of this imposture on the agency of the "citoyen singulier," but also to suggest its logical inadequacy, or why such reasoning creates a social impasse. In the *Discourse on Political Economy*, Rousseau pointed out the rhetorical contradiction of a social compact rendered as a one-sided *demand* ("You have need of me, because I am rich and you are poor. We will therefore come to an agreement. I will permit you to have the honor of serving me, on condition that you bestow on me the little you have left, in return for the pains I shall take to command you" [162]), and the effect on liberty of this "compact" is rendered by an example of unequal mobility later allegorized in the *Rêveries*: "Fifty honest pedestrians quietly going about their business had better be crushed to death than an idle [rich] man be delayed in his coach" (*SC* 161). In the public document Rousseau attempts to illuminate the rhetoric of contract by narrative; in the autobiographical texts, I would suggest, the reverse is the case: the narrative of paranoia is set in motion by the "imposture" (or imposition) of contract.

Let us therefore turn to the obvious corollary of the coach's collision with a pedestrian: Rousseau's apparently *a*political second promenade. Careful attention to this promenade is warranted because the question focusing critical discussion of the *Rêveries* concerns the event which precedes its composition, which Rousseau describes in the first walk as "un événement aussi triste qu'imprévu." The second promenade narrates just such an event.

Speculation concerning the nature of the event that finally led Rousseau to abandon his desire to find an appropriate audience and instead to write "for myself alone" has often turned to the "Histoire du précédent écrit" for evidence, despite chronological contradictions (as Raymond points out, the events narrated in the "Histoire" take place at least six months before October 1776, whereas Rousseau speaks of only two months' calm). But reference to the "Histoire," the narrative of Rousseau's unsuccessful attempts to "publish," does establish one crucial fact: that the "events" narrated in the *Rêveries* concern the disfigurement of Rousseau's figurative corpus – his books – at least as much as his body.

By regarding the *Rêveries* as an extended "afterword" – a textual apparatus – we may escape the biographical impulse which dominates Rousseau studies and lend our attention to the text's verbal echoes – especially the rhetorical resonance Rousseau establishes between the unrecorded "événement imprévu" of the first promenade and "l'accident imprévu" of 4 October 1776 narrated in the second walk. As I have tried to suggest, Rousseau's self-representation as *promeneur* offers numerous narrative examples of "accidents" which literally marginalize him; the incident that I am about to recount is thus as much a redaction of those narratives as it is a history of the "event" itself.

Walking alone on a road deserted because the wine harvest is finished and workers have quit the country, Rousseau is startled by the onrush of a Great Dane leading a speeding coach.

I judged that my only hope of avoiding being knocked down was to leap into the air at precisely the right moment to allow the dog to pass underneath me. This lightning plan of action, which I had no time either to examine or to put into practice, was my last thought before I went down.

(Je jugeai que le seul moyen que j'avais d'éviter d'être jeté par terre était de faire un grand saut si juste que le chien passât sous moi tandis que je serais en l'air. Cette idée plus prompte que l'éclair et que je n'eus le temps ni de raisonner ni d'éxécuter fut la dernière avant mon accident.) (*R* 38; *OC* 1.1005)

Not only do we find here an indication of Rousseau's acknowledgment that the agency of the pedestrian citizen is an inadequate defense against the consolidation of speed; we also discover that theoretical speculation, specifically the valorization of pure mobility (mobility as the "flight" into ideology) emerges from an exigency – a real difference in social power. The fact that his accident cannot be blamed on the coach, which swerves to avoid running him over, allows Rousseau later, in the eighth walk, to differentiate himself from "les infortunes" who mistakenly personify (rather than "classify") oppression. For Rousseau, the speed that is the efficient cause of his "bouleversement" is linked with the consolidation of opinion and wealth that are the political and economic faces of the emergence of liberalism. Therefore, the critique is lodged not in the narrative of the accident itself but in the history of *texts* which directly follows upon the accident, although we should note that Rousseau indicates the nature of his concern when, awaking as if unfamiliar with the language and remembering neither place names nor those Christian and family names that operate as social reminders, he emerges from this "state of nature" when he is addressed by those who wish to help him: "A man whom I did not know had the *charity* to accompany me" ("Un monsieur que je ne connaissais pas ... eut *la charité* de m'accompagner") (*OC* 1.662). Significantly, Rousseau refuses to surrender his agency when advised by this benefactor to take a cab: "I thought that, since I could walk without pain, it would be better thus to continue my journey on foot than to expose myself to perish of cold in a cab" ("je pensai que, puisque je marchais sans peine, il valait mieux continuer ainsi ma route à pied que de m'exposer à périr de froid dans un fiacre") (*OC* 1.662).

The history of two "texts" follows upon this refusal, suggesting how the consolidation of opinion threatens to overwhelm the solitary walker's attempts to preserve agency. As his mobility had been rendered nought by the speed of the Great Dane, his face and identity disfigured by the collision, so Rousseau finds that published accounts of his accident – "this account... changed and disfigured" ("cette histoire... changée et défigurée") – render him even more completely immobile. News of his death carried by the *Avignon Courier* easily outdistances the slow pace of the solitary walker, whose presence in the world makes itself felt in only a few isolated encounters.

The economic injustice of such a consolidation of power – Rousseau's critique of "liberality" (the newspaper announces a subscription to be taken up for the publication of his *œuvre*) – accounts for the seemingly disproportionate weight given in the second promenade to the person and novel of Mme. d'Ormoy, who visits him during his convalescence. Rousseau becomes suspicious again as a consequence of unwelcome charity: "little affected presents, frequent visits, without purpose and without pleasure, marked well enough for me a secret object" ("de petit cadeaux affectés, de fréquentes visites, sans objet et sans plaisir, me marquaient assez un but secret") (*OC* i.1007). But it is the form of her novel – its rhetorical texture and mode of address – which reveals the secret. At first Rousseau is only annoyed by the novel's preface, whose apparent solicitousness toward Rousseau betrays its author's self-interest: "coarse flattery is never attached to [true] benevolence" ("la rude flagornerie ...ne s'allia jamais avec la bienveillance]") (*OC* i.1008). But as the history of the novel's reception is told by Mme. D'Ormoy herself – "She told me that her book was causing a sensation because of one of the footnotes" ("Elle m'apprit que son livre faisait le plus grand bruit à cause d'une note") (*OC* i.1008), he discovers once again that his writing has subjected him to a *disfigurement*: the wording – "la tournure" – of the note, imitating Rousseau's style, allows it to be attributed to him. It is crucial that this note, which Rousseau himself finds "blameable," concerns the nature of the welfare state:

This man who cannot support himself requires his rights from his King; how is he repaid? He is stashed without compassion on a straw mat; the Tax Collectors ignore the cries of his wife and children which surround him... If Sovereigns were made aware of all the evil that is done in their name, they would wish no longer to be Kings. Royalty desires nothing but the welfare of its people... It is in misfortune that one knows the man.

(Cet homme qui ne peut se nourrir, doit un droit a son Roi; comment le payera-t-il? On le mettra sans pitié sur la paille: les pleurs d'une mère et des enfants dont il est entouré, n'attendrissent pas les Collecteurs... Si les Souverains pouvaient connaître tout le mal qu'on fait sous leur nom, ils gémiraient d'être Rois. La royauté n'est à désirer que pour la félicité des Peuples... C'est dans l'infortune qu'on connaît l'homme; les revers n'abattent point son courage, le vice seul lui fait horreur.) (*OC* iv.1776–7)[7]

The second part of this note seems to offer the best evidence of the imitative "tournure" which allows the note to be misattributed, particularly in light of my contention that Rousseau's self-representation takes the form of a negative litany; it would seem that "dans l'infortune," as Rousseau "plays the beggar," one finds "l'homme" (by identifying the sources and techniques of his disfigurement). Moreover, it coincides with the contention in the *Dialogues* that there is virtue in the poverty content with what it has. But the note conflates this idealization of poverty with an attack on the monarch who neglects his people's welfare, implicitly limiting the "rights of man" (since "l'homme" is identified with "l'infortune" in the latter part of the note) to this demand for charity.

In the sixth promenade, Rousseau describes how the desire for society articulated by the initial address (aidez moi/aimez moi) is blocked when that desire is disfigured as demand or right. The crippled boy, a beggar, with whom Rousseau establishes a social relation – "I struck up a kind of acquaintance with this little gentleman" ("J'avais fait une espèce de connaissance avec le petit bonhomme") (*OC* i.1050) – changes his mode of address; where at first in "requesting alms from passersby" ("demandant l'aumone aux passans") (*OC* i.1050) the boy elicits a kind of natural compassion, the repetition of address turns the spontaneous act of charity into an obligation – une espèce de devoir" – particularly because to preface his request, "he never failed to address me as M. Rousseau so as to show that he knew me well ("il ne manquait jamais de m'appeller souvent M. Rousseau pour montrer qu'il me connoissait bien") (*OC* i.1050–1). The effect?

My first favors were in the eyes of those who received them no more than an *earnest* of those that were still to come... the first freely chosen act of charity was transformed into an indefinite right to anything else he might subsequently need, nor was my inability to provide it enough to excuse me.

(Mes premiers services n'étaient aux yeux de ceux qui les recevaient que *les erres* de ceux qui les devaient suivre...et ce premier bienfait libre et volontaire devenait un droit indéfini à tous ceux dont il pouvait avoir besoin dans la suite, sans que l'impuissance même suffit pour m'en affranchir.) (*R* 95; *OC* I.1052)

Perhaps Rousseau uses "les erres," the archaic form of "*les arrhes*" ("down-payments"), in order to indicate the nature or structure of the disfiguration. Compassion is refigured as generosity through a logic by which the social contract joins parties in infinite debt (infinite false credit); like the King in Mme. d'Ormoy's note, Rousseau now "owes." Similarly, the disfigurement of language (or discourse in general) endemic to history turns an image of freedom – les *erres* (wandering, vagabondage) – into an economic "assujetissement" – *les arrhes*.

When Rousseau laments that the crippled boy has learned the proper form of address, he appears to indict discourse itself for the disfigurement that, in the narrative of the sixth promenade, is rendered as "un *détour*." Here de Man's representation of language as a machine seems apropos; it is after all the "mouvement machinal" of the boy's address that has turned Rousseau from his intended road: another bouleversement, as it were, analogous to those set in motion by the *Mercure de France* and the *Avignon Courier*. On the other hand, it is important to recall Rousseau's claim, at the commencement of the sixth walk, that we can discover the operations of the machine, and recognize the obstacles to social understanding they set in place – if we reflect on or historicize them.

Rousseau's compulsion to write histories of writing, not only by structuring his autobiographical corpus as a series of afterwords but also by choosing archaic turns of phrase, calls attention to the ways in which the social imbrication of the language machine may be held accountable for the apparent conspiracy to misrepresent Rousseau as "un gueux." If Rousseau's fictive poverty is disfigured as mendicancy through an unforeseen and unwelcome charity that constitutes the "plot" of the *Dialogues*, just as his philosophical position on the state and welfare is misrepresented in a novel with an apparently charitable preface, so we also find, in keeping with Rousseau's claim that it is a mistake to personify the conspiracy, that the very language with which Rousseau seeks to defend himself threatens a similar disfigurement. I have already drawn attention to the series of negating litanies by which Rousseau identifies himself; they represent a certain "tournure" of phrase that might secure for him a recognizable identity. However, such litanies do not *belong* to Rousseau; they have a history – for example, the *Déclaration du Roi, concernant les vagabonds et les Gens sans aveu*, August 1764. If the negating litany is a technique by which Rousseau rhetorically simulates poverty, a similar language practice helped to "identify" – and thereby disfigure – the poor in eighteenth-century France. Note how the language of the de L'Averdy Commission on Mendicancy of 1764 *dispossesses* the poor of distinguishing features through the negative litany:

Those will be called vagabonds... who, for six consecutive months, have exercised neither profession nor trade, and who, having neither estate nor means of subsistence, cannot be sworn or certified as to their good life and morals by people of dignified reputation.

(Seronts réputés vagabonds... ceux qui depuis six mois révolus n'auront exercé ni profession ni métier, et qui n'ayant aucun état ni aucun bien pour subsister, ne pourront être avoués ou faire certifier de leurs bonne vie et moeurs par personnes de digne foi.) (Hufton, 162)

In addition to newly defining categories of mendicity and regulating the amount and nature of state relief, such commissions retained the long-standing identification of mendicants as "les sans-aveux" – a reference to the feudal "aveu" between vassal and lord. Even if Rousseau's self-representation as a man "sans biens, sans emploi, sans fauteurs" does not *intentionally* echo such language, therefore, nonetheless his attempt at self-representation (soi-disant) is undermined by the corporate legal definition, which conspires to identify him as a *sans-aveu*, even as an extraordinary mobility leaves him without neighbors or "friends" to corroborate his self-representations.

Lynn Hunt argues in *Politics, Culture and Class in the French Revolution* that the deluge predicted by Louis XIV was "a deluge of words, in print, in conversations, and in political meetings." In his study of mendicancy in eighteenth-century France, Robert Schwartz notes a similarly large discursive increase:

After 1750 mendicity became a virtual *cause célèbre*. An outpouring of books and pamphlets addressing the critical problems of employment and mendicity marked the intensified concern of the propertied classes... At the same time, provincial academies also took up the issues of poverty and mendicity. Academies solicited and received hundreds of essays and tracts that circulated in manuscript and remained unpublished. (154)

Without suggesting that the rise of print culture was peculiarly focused on the problem of mendicity, I do wish to claim a discursive relation between theories of the state and the regulation of welfare. In both cases we see print contributing to what Rousseau had described as the "consolidation of opinion" made necessary by the attenuation of social relations, itself a consequence of increased mobility. Rousseau's criticism of this development – analogous to his resistance to definitive collected editions of his own work – calls into question our assumption that print culture is a democratizing force; at the same time, it suggests the importance of the regime of texts in the triumph of liberalism. Rousseau's adoption of the rhetoric of mendicity implicitly criticizes the way language – that instrument of sociability – increasingly poses obstacles to its exercise, most notably by restricting and regulating the motivating principle: compassion.

Rousseau complains that charity was never oppressive until he became a writer. Once he makes himself a public spectacle by his writings ("ma personne fut affichée par mes écrits"), Rousseau claims, he becomes a General Delivery post office ("je devins le bureau général d'adresse de tous les souffreteux ou *soi-disant* tels..." [*OC*.1052]). This self-representation as "bureau général" seems to conflict with the more pervasive self-identification in the *Rêveries* and elsewhere as one of the "soi-disant" sufferers. Yet in fact even here Rousseau's *disfigurement* by print culture (he is *marked* by his writing) allies him to the vagabond class. A 1724 edict had provided for the branding of those applying for relief or arrested on related charges (*M* for *mendicant*, *V* for *vagabond*) so that repeat offenders might be identified. Like the crippled boy's attempt to identify his patron as "M. Rousseau," however, the letter both always and never reaches its destination; real identity is abstracted by the social marker.

Although it is difficult to see the effects of this abstraction on the autonomy and agency of the poor except perhaps through Rousseau's self-representations, there is some anecdotal evidence to support the "history" we will see offered in the "Histoire du précédent écrit." Hufton reprints the following note, found attached to an abandoned child near the end of the seventeenth century:

Messieurs et dames qui avez inspection sur les pauvres enfants je vous supplie très humblement d'avoir la charité de recevoir mes deux enfants que j'ai mis à votre porte...deux filles dont l'aînée s'appelle Louise âgée troize ans et la cadette Jeanne âgée de douze mois, mais elle tette encore...Je les laisseray le moins que je pourray et aussi vous aurez la charité de conserver le billet afin que lorsque je pourray les reprendre je puisse vous les redemander. (333)

(Ladies and gentlemen who have inspection of poor children, I humbly entreat you to have the heart to take in my two children I have left at your door ... two girls, the older one named Louise, thirteen years old and the younger, Jeanne, twelve months old. I leave them what I can, and hope you will take care to save the note so that, when I am able, I can ask you and take them back.)

Hufton claims that such notes became less frequent even as vagrancy and the numbers of abandoned children skyrocketed in the latter half of the eighteenth century. Whereas in periods of economic crisis poor families had frequently abandoned children temporarily, the onset of deteriorating economic conditions was marked by an increase in the abandonment of babies without "a distinguishing mark, a ribbon or coloured rag pinned to ... clothing, or a letter revealing ... origins and making future identification easy" (333). Although Hufton reads this shift only as an indication of a more generalized economic trauma, it is also the case that the attempted regulation of charity tended to generate this silence. As the monarchy attempted to limit payments to *hôpitals*, they justified the curtailment by claiming the mendicity was mendacious, that foundlings were "exposé par leurs propres parents que pour se débarrasser de leur nourriture jusqu'à ce qu'ils aient atteint l'âge de 7 ans" (341). Any name, any mark of legitimacy – including the speck of salt denoting baptism – might end in the refusal of charity and the return of the child to its parents via parish records.

This historical retreat into silence bears a remarkable similarity to Rousseau's literary project as it shifted between the *Dialogues* and the *Rêveries*. The self-represented Rousseau, likewise a parent accused of having "played the beggar" in abandoning five children at the Foundling Hospital, discovers no one who will have the charity to conserve "le billet"; that, in a nutshell, is the story of the "Histoire du précédent écrit."

On the face page of the *Dialogues* to which that "Histoire" refers, where a dedication, advertisement, or address would normally find its place, we find the following negation of such rhetorical gestures:

If I dared address a prayer to those into whose hands this writing will fall, it would be to read all of it before making use of it and even before talking about it with anyone. But very certain beforehand that this favor will not be granted to me, I keep silent and give everything over to providence.

(Si j'osais faire quelque priére à ceux entre les mains de qui tombera cet écrit, ce serait de vouloir bien le lire tout entier avant que d'en disposer et même avant que d'en parler à personne; mais très sûr d'avance que cette grace ne me sera pas accordée, je me tais, et remets tout à la providence.) (*OC* 1.659)

To address a prayer is, of course, to make a solicitation, to ask, *demander*. If we refer back to Rousseau's self-defense against charges "qu'il fait le gueux," the erasure Rousseau effects here is more readily understood. Already the importunity of the gesture is mitigated by the fact that it is addressed, as it were, to no one ("je me tais"). Like the blind beggar of Wordsworth's *Prelude*, who wears his story pinned to his chest, or the discharged soldier whose trust "is in the God of Heaven / And in the eye of him who passes me," Rousseau's representation of literary authority initially suggests a social transcendence: like them, he does not *ask* for charity. However, the suggestion that the practice of literature in general might escape "incorporation" or identification with a particular social position or class interest is undone when Rousseau later identifies the conditions of a literary culture (reading as the sign and practice of a leisure class defined by its valorization of privacy – and private interest). Like the speculative transcendence that promises a momentary escape from the real in the second promenade, the "history" of literature (defined here as the self-sufficient or self-referential address) contained in the appended "Histoire du précédent écrit" promises a rude fall.

Providence, to which Rousseau addresses himself in default, refers as much to the "histoire subséquente" of the *Dialogues*, or history itself, as to a transcendent condition. We might regard this alternative to the personal address as the social contract remanded to the future anterior. The "contract" thus imagined to obtain between writer and future reader appears to have much in common with Derrida's exploration of apostrophe in "The Politics of Friendship." There, Derrida contends that to address another, *even* in the apostrophic and therefore self-canceling mode of the philosopher who begins, "O my friends, there is no friend" (it should be easy to read Rousseau's prayer as this apostrophe in paraphrase), is to enter into a social relation via the common language. It is possible, however, also to find Rousseau challenging this presumption, since the immediately preceding writing – an epigraph from Ovid – both by its foreignness (it is quoted in Latin) and by its translated content ("Here I am the barbarian because no one understands me"), challenges the possibility of a truly *common* language. In any case, the ends imagined for the text – its fall into the hands of various strangers, Rousseau's rejection of that avenue and his decision to "remit" the manuscript to providence – must call to mind the "Histoire du précédent écrit" which, in narrating the story of the text's attempted distribution, suggests the immediate failure of literature to produce a just social relation.

The story may be familiar, since it is often recounted as an indication of Rousseau's growing paranoia. On Saturday, 24 February 1776, at two o'clock, Rousseau walks to Notre Dame, as he has many times before, this time preparing to deposit his manuscript on the Great Altar. Upon entering the cathedral, he meets with "un obstacle imprévu": a grill separating the nave from the choir and preventing Rousseau from reaching his goal. His reaction to this unforeseen obstacle repeats a well-established narrative pattern: Rousseau is "seized with vertigo like a man who falls into an apopleptic fit, and this vertigo was followed by an upheaval of my whole being" ("saisi d'un vertige comme un homme qui tombe en apoplexie, et ce vertige fut suivi d'un bouleversement dans tout mon être") (980).

Reflecting on his attempt to "conserve" his text in the aftermath of its failure, Rousseau implicitly associates the "address" to Notre Dame with an old regime, for he had imagined that eventually his manuscript would appear "sous les yeux du Roi" (978). The desire that his text might fall under sympathetic eyes not only identifies Rousseau with beggars who carried "les piques," or cards signed by parish priests recounting their misfortunes and legitimating their vagabondage, it also suggests a regime within which the address can only be conceived as a prayer for charity. Failing to leave the manuscript at Notre Dame, moreover, is the acting out or narrative of the withheld "prayer" inscribed on the dedicatory page; this accounts for the choice of Notre Dame as "dépôt." The dedicatory inscription has already rejected such an avenue, or suggested the impasse which prevents it; insofar as literary authority represents Rousseau's model of the social contract, which has no guarantor, the "old regime" of charity offers no succor. The church and state had been reasonably well equipped to respond to the problems of a temporary exigency, but Rousseau's text, as its form of address indicates, represents a structural exigency. To that, the gates of Notre Dame are closed.

The rhetorical subtext of the second episode recounted in the "Histoire du précédent écrit" therefore relates Rousseau's revised plan for textual distribution to the address redirected to "providence" in the dedicatory inscription. Refusing an address to the King or his mediator the priest, Rousseau refigures the audience of his address as a totality. This address recalls (or prefigures) the logic by which Thomas Paine's dedication of the second part of *The Rights of Man* to Lafayette was excised by his French editors: "The French can no longer endure dedicatory epistles. A man should write privately to those he esteems: when he publishes a book his thoughts should be offered to the public alone" (386). For it is indeed an address to the "public" Rousseau attempts.

This episode too is perhaps well known: Rousseau decides to write "A kind of advertising circular addressed to the French nation" ("un espèce du billet circulaire adressé à la nation française") and to distribute copies "along the walks and in the streets to strangers whose physiognomy pleased me most" ("aux promenades et dans les rues aux inconnus dont la physionomie me plairait le plus") (*OC* 1.984). In one sense, of course, Rousseau may be exonerated from playing the beggar here; the producer of a manuscript for distribution, he rather occupies the position of an artisan, a figuration supported when he mentions in the *Dialogues* that the autobiographical project of self-justification has proceeded in spite of the conspiracy because Rousseau has used India ink – that is, has written by hand, rather than printed or "published" (made public) the documents. This is Rousseau as the music copyist, that "honest profession." But the fact that he can induce neither interest nor exchange tends to undermine such an identification, or at least to suggest its inadequacy for representing the "social condition" of the citizen subject. Instead, this figure who stands on street corners with advertising circulars no one wants to take suggests the image of Benjamin's sandwichman, proleptically described in the sixth promenade ("ma personne fut affichée par mes écrits"). The text itself – literature reduced to the status of "advertising circular" – may further remind us of Benjamin's description of the commodity as that which "takes on the character of a demand." In attempting to escape social parameters by which the address, ideally the sign of the subject's sociability, is transformed into the expression of private interest and need – the transformation of "aimez moi" into "aidez moi," of autonomy into dependency – Rousseau's abstracted address dooms the social contract to identification with that exchange of goods and services from which he had so carefully distinguished it.

Having written in the form of a letter, Rousseau addresses himself "To all Frenchmen who still love justice and truth" ("A tout Français aimant encore la justice et la vérité") (*OC* 1.984). Although such an address is truly to a "bureau général," Rousseau admits that "I never imagined that any one would dare refuse such an address" ("je n'imaginais pas que sur cet adresse aucun l'osât refuser") (984). The adjectives here – "tout" and "aucun" – presage the failure of Rousseau's attempt to mitigate the "discrepancy" of the social contract, for they presuppose what is, according to Althusser, the organizing logic of that discrepancy: the binary logic of totality and the individual. His initial surprise that "hardly anyone accepted it" ("presque aucun ne l'accepta") forces a reassessment that may bring to mind the Abbé de Sieyès's revolutionary ontology: "What is the third estate? All. What has it been? Nothing. What does it wish to be? Something." For despite the apparently universal appeal, he can generate no audience. The mode of address itself seems to generate his failure, for without reading even the first page of the *Dialogues*, let alone the entirety as Rousseau had hoped, they read only the "title" of the letter and return it to him saying, "It is not addressed to me" ("Il ne s'adressait pas à [moi]") (984).

What logic enables this refusal? It is the division of public from private that generates the categories of particular and general. When they read that the circular is addressed to a public entity (all "Frenchmen"), they are excused: these are particular individuals ("aucun") whose pedestrian excursions along the streets and parks of Paris resemble neither Rousseau's own disinterested practice of "botanizing along the sidewalks" nor the exertions of those citizens of old who "ran to assemblies," but are rather motivated by getting and spending, the pursuit of self-interest. The written form of Rousseau's address is even less successful than a more traditional verbal appeal for help – even on Berkeley's Telegraph Avenue, the beggar expects a better response ratio than "presque aucun" – because writing encourages the practice of privacy. Rousseau's own person is lost to the gaze of passersby as they behold his reinscription on the circular put before their eyes. Hence the ambiguity of the pronominal reference: does "il" refer to the circular itself (it), or Rousseau himself as its author (he)?

Does the "Histoire du précédent écrit" then narrate the failure of literature to institute the sociability that ought to replace the relations of domination and subordination that disfigure the social contract as it is currently enforced, and therefore suggest that literature inevitably functions as a retreat from politics? On the contrary: by the "play on words" which characterizes literary discourse Rousseau achieves the exposure of historical "reality" as a simulation. In the circular, subsequent to the initial address, Rousseau demands that his readers "abandon the old name of *Franks*; it ought to make you blush" ("ce vieux nom de *Francs*; il doit trop vous faire rougir") (*OC* 1.990). When they identify themselves as lovers neither of truth nor of justice by their refusal of the circular, Rousseau declares, "That was the only *frank* speech I had had from a *French* mouth in fifteen years" ("Voilà la seule parole *franche* que depuis quinze ans j'aye obtenue d'aucune bouche française") (984). The "archaic," that is "natural" or proper, name of the Frenchman is revealed (connotations of "frank" as open, transparent, "honest," are relevant here) at the moment when each interlocutor is reduced to "presque aucun" – almost nobody. Rousseau as the social cipher that is the vagrant and the Frenchman as the increasingly privatized subject (since the address is to "all," the passerby's failure to respond indicates that he is also "almost nobody") are established in a new metaphorical identity. Although the "frankness" of the pedestrian is ironized here, is Rousseau's own honesty any less so? Reflecting on a life dedicated to the truth, *Vitam impendere vero*, Rousseau in the fourth promenade admits the "bizarre inconséquence" of being able to lie frequently and without remorse. Thus the "Histoire du précédent écrit" ends in the moment Rousseau spoke of as both preceding the moment of the original contract and following its corruption:

the last stage of inequality and the extreme point that closes the circle and touches again upon our point of departure. Here all private individuals again become equal because they are nothing. (*OC* III.191)

"Here" – ostensibly the state of nature – is represented in the text by the advertising circular, which reduces its producer, its distributor, and its potential consumer each to the status of extreme privacy (or privation) – a privation which their continuing mobility figures as vagrancy.

The misdirection of the circular – its failure to reach an intended addressee – is made possible by the ambiguity, or metaphoricity, of

its identifications. The public document, *sans* signatory, appears to
"refer" to its distributor, the person of Rousseau; but a possible
discrepancy between the document and the person – the corpus and
the corps – is simultaneously hidden and revealed in the pronoun
"il." This gap opened between public and private is also at work, as
I have suggested, in the totalization and abstraction of the audience
he seeks. In a sense, the passerby is quite justified in his refusal of the
circular. The very "grammar" of his singularity precludes appropriate response to the plural address. In whose name can he
respond? To reply, he would need to take the title of "tout," "the
people" – and that would be a usurpation indeed.

Rousseau's employment of the advertising circular to indicate the
end point of the valorization of mobility accomplishes two things.
First, it indicates how that valorization completes itself in a reification
by which the commodity – here that ideological commodity *par
excellence*, the advertisement – usurps the mobility and freedom which
was to have been lodged in citizen subject. Second, in its loss of
specific direction, the commodity mimes the movements of that most
singular representative of *laissez-faire* political and economic culture:
the vagrant. Thinking through the "history" of the advertising
circular that might be written, one imagines the rejected circular
eventually falling to the ground, drifting in the wind along sidewalks
and gutters, those habitations of the homeless.

The representation of writing in the *Rêveries* echoes such a
speculation, as notes for the *Rêveries* are written on the backs of
playing cards during one walk and conserved only that they might
nourish his imagination on another. The revolutionary contention of
the *Rêveries* – "I write for myself alone" ("Je n'ecris...que pour
moi") (*OC* 1.1001) – may seem like an attempt to move beyond the
public/private dichotomy ("I neither hide them nor display them"),
but it also completes the inherent circularity of the ostensibly
"democratic" address of the advertising circular; now, so to speak, *il
ne s'adressait qu'à moi* (it is addressed *only* to me).

Thus Rousseau himself demonstrates how the logic of the social
contract, essentially an act of address, proceeds by a supremely
*literary* logic, a "play on words," self-referential and therefore self-
sufficient. Do we then agree with the implications of de Man's claim
that far from being a "repression of politics" (Althusser, "Social
Contract"), literature is "the truly political discourse" (157)?
Rather, the tendency to regard the metaphorical logic that under-

girds the logic of the commodity and the logic of democracy within the regime of texts (liberalism) as having no reference to the real is exactly what Rousseau resists by continuing to put the literary *parole* in the mouth of the vagrant, that figure whose impassive body takes precedence over his "proper name." Like Deleuze and Guattari's schizophrenic, Rousseau's vagrant "mistake[s] words for things" (23), but not in the de Manian manner. When Rousseau, whether on the streets and street corners or on the page, publicly solicits compassion, he denies the political or the literary address any claim to social neutrality. Moreover, the figure joins the body and the address, the corps and the corpus. As such the figure of the vagrant represents the structure of *Rousseau*'s corpus, where increasingly importunate explanations and histories attempt to resist the commodification and abstraction that occur with his entry into the public sphere.

In this light, my attempt to link the literary and the political through, on the one hand, the problem of literary form and, on the other, the problem of destitution, may seem less arbitrary. For some time, we have recognized a lack of agency in the literary text; one of the most powerful recent formulations of this problem is Lacoue-Labarthe and Nancy's emphasis, in their attempt to identify the emergence of the literary with and as Romanticism, on *exigency*. This exigency has a formal dimension – the importance of the fragment and the dialogue, for example – and is actually described, following Blanchot, as *un désœuvrement* that "insinuates itself throughout the interstices of the romantic work" (57). This emphasis seems to me a muted tribute to Rousseau, whose *Rêveries* narrate "ce désœuvrement du corps."

This understanding of the literary as a text which unravels like the worn uniform of a discharged soldier sits well with our current theoretically informed understanding of the subjugation of individual texts to history and to the sociocultural machine, but becomes more problematic when we consider another, equally pervasive, understanding of the literary as *absolute*, in a sense that Lacoue-Labarthe and Nancy also acknowledge: standing alone, unconnected to other discursive formations, political, social, or economic; but rather, like the soldier, discharged, or like Rousseau, feeding off his own substance.

The question raised by the emergence of the literary – is the text in a state of exigency or autonomy? – also addresses the status of citizen vagrant. And finally, as I have suggested, the problems of autonomy and exigency haunt the foundations of liberalism, that regime of texts in which the practice of liberality suggestively provides not only a name but also a justification and a social structuration.

Although I share with Rapaczynski the opinion that Rousseau was "in no sense a liberal," my reading of these texts demands disagreement with his contention that Rousseau's critique of its political face is limited by his antecedence to capitalism. Rapaczynski does not consider how the consolidation of the welfare system prefigures capitalist formations, nor how Rousseau's obsessive concern with the production, distribution, and consumption of his writing in the autobiographical texts belies any alleged ignorance of the importance of new modes of production to social formations and relations. As is so often the case, Rousseau's best readers fail him by not reading "tout entier."

CHAPTER 2

# *Money walks: Wordsworth and the right to wander*

Wordsworth was once journeying to Lowther Castle to attend a
dinner in his honour, at which the Lord Chief Justice and Mr.
Justice Coleridge were to be present. They passed down
Patterdale by Ullswater, then, leaving the chaise, they struck
across some fields toward the castle. Suddenly the path ended in
a blind wall. The poet muttered something and attacked the
wall as if it were a living entity, crying out, "This is the way, an
ancient right of way too," and passed on. That evening after the
ladies had left the room, Mr. Justice Coleridge said to Sir John
Wallace who was a near resident: "Sir John, I fear we have
committed trespass today; we came over a broken-down wall on
your Estate." Sir John seemed irate and said that could he have
caught the man who broke it down, he would have horse-
whipped him. The grave old bard at the end of the table heard
the words, the fire flashed into his face and rising to his feet he
answered: "I broke your wall down, Sir John, it was obstructing
an ancient right of way, and I will do it again. I am a Tory, but
scratch me on the back deep enough and you will find the Whig
in me yet.'

(Howard Hill, 40)

In fact, ce n'est que le premier pas qui coûte.

(Marx, *Capital* 1.127)

## I: COUNTING (AND ACCOUNTING FOR) STEPS

My account of Wordsworth's manifesto of the Romantic project of
literature, the second, two-volume edition of *Lyrical Ballads* (1800),
is constructed as a meditation on Marx's insistence, in the first
volume of *Capital*, that "in fact, ce n'est que le premier pas qui
coûte" ("it is only the first step that costs"). Marx's recourse
to a proverbial expression to establish an essential homology

between the commodity- and the money-form would appear to underscore the potential relation between his analytical procedures and Wordsworth's interrogation of the ballad-form. Both the proverb and the ballad achieve their value, their truth-status, by dint of repetition and circulation; as with the money-form, they exhibit a collusion between form and substance. For example, Marx reads the "so-called primitive accumulation" that serves as capitalism's justifying myth, its "original sin," as itself the product of repetition, its being "so-called" (*sogenannt*). According to Marx, "its origin is supposed to be explained when it is told as an anecdote of the past" (*C* 667). In a sense, then, the justifying myth of "primitive accumulation" is a tautology, an *apparently* logical concept or propositional truth devoid of substance, or whose substance consists of pure repetition.

But it is also crucial that Marx resorts to a proverbial expression in a "foreign" language, expropriated from its original territory or "natural" context into the general economy of *Capital*. The section begins with Marx's description of coin as so many "different national uniforms worn at home by gold and silver as coins, and doffed again in the market of the world" (*C* 125). Dressing his argument in the uniform of the French expression offers Marx two distinct advantages, both emanating from the single word "pas" and thereby suggesting the "two-fold character" of the commodity-form. "Pas" means both "step" and "not" (in the vernacular, "pas" alone can perform the negation of the negative adverb *ne...pas*); thus, the proverbial expression might be translated *either* as "it is only the first step that costs" *or* "it is only the first *not* – negation – that costs."[1]

The double allusion to "step" and negation subtly furthers a formal equivalence left unrealized in the explicit argument of *Capital*: that between the commodity-form and the expropriated peasant. In addition to foreshadowing his historical account of this latter expropriation, Marx's recourse to the proverbial expression recalls his famous description of commodity-fetishism:

A commodity appears, at first sight, a very trivial thing, and easily understood. Its analysis shows that it is, in reality, a very queer thing, abounding in metaphysical subtleties and theological niceties. So far as it is a value in use, there is nothing mysterious about it, whether we consider it from the point of view that by its properties it is capable of satisfying human wants, or from the point that those properties are the product of human labor. It is as clear as noon-day, that man, by his industry, changes the forms of the materials furnished by Nature, in such a way as to make them useful to him. The form of wood, for instance, is altered, by making a table out of it. Yet, for all that, the table continues to be that common, every-day thing, wood. But, so soon as it *steps forth* [*auftritt*] as a commodity, it is changed into something transcendent. It not only stands with its feet on the ground, but, in relation to all other commodities, it stands on its head, and evolves out of its wooden brain grotesque ideas, far more wonderful than "table-turning" ever was. (*C* 76; emphasis mine)

Marx's idea of the "transcendent" here (literally, *ein sinnlich übersinnliches Ding* – a sensuous non-sensuous thing) is thus immediately connected both to walking and to walking as *désœuvrement*. When the commodity is not "in use," when its usefulness is not in view, it walks. This is perhaps why, in Marx's estimation, "ce n'est que le premier pas qui coûte." The step which costs, so to speak, is the step Derrida (after Blanchot) describes as *le pas au-delà* – the step (not) beyond.[2] What characterizes this step – which is precisely not a step, but rather a *pas* – is the movement from matter into the immaterial. As one recent translator expressed the problem, "Because of the double meaning of *pas* ('step' and 'not'), every step becomes a false step" (Blanchot, *Step Not Beyond* xvi).

By translating his image of the commodity-form "stepping" into circulation into a French proverb, Marx with his "play on words" implicitly contends that, with the advent of capitalism if not before, the economy is structured like a language whose logic is that of tautology. What Marx uses the proverb to explain – how the circulation of coin and the consequent disparity between nominal and real weight, nominal and real value, creates the "purely symbolic value" (*C* 127) of paper money that itself merely *repeats* the "transcendental" surplus exhibited in the commodity-form – is in this sense the mere material instantiation of a more general and operative "truth": repetition produces a total (a totalization) greater (and less) than the sum of its elements.

Recall in this context how tautology and repetition will be crucial to Wordsworth's poetic "experiment" of *Lyrical Ballads*: not only does he adopt the ballad-form (which Antony Easthope usefully characterizes by its structure of "incremental repetition" [86]); he also explicitly defends apparent tautology in his account of "The Thorn." But his interest in what we may call the "bilateral" effects of repetition – positive and negative – is also displayed in his representation of the value of meter: the power of poetic "numbers" to confer iterability works to diminish pain and increase pleasure.[3]

By placing the Marxian proverb and the lyrical ballad in an analogical relation, I wish to illustrate how the Romantic project of literature entails turning the commonplace into the common tale – the common *place*, that is, into a discursive effect. Although the content of the *Lyrical Ballads* will often concern an actual displacement of a person from a location, the *form* of the lyrical ballad will entail the negation of that displacement. The historical "first step" of agricultural expropriation is itself expropriated into a deterritorialized landscape of poetic iterability. Repetition, or the "steps" of poetic meter, in other words, will have the effect of blinding us to the "first step," or the event narrated by the poem; it will negate the historical cause. As in Marx, the effect of this negation-repetition will indeed cause certain tables to turn.

The kind of table-turning explored in *Lyrical Ballads*, I will argue, has less to do with mesmerism than with accounting. Figuratively, "turning the tables" implies a bringing into balance, a balancing act. The second volume of *Lyrical Ballads* is an experiment with numbers, with (ac)counting. Its means of balancing accounts, moreover, corresponds with what Max Weber long ago identified as the rhetorical form of capitalism, double-entry bookkeeping. But the final "balancing" implicit in both *Capital* and *Lyrical Ballads* will be the establishment of a formal equivalence between capital and vagrancy. Insofar as circulation of capital entails infinite expansion, its movements correspond with the vagrant's, whose comings and goings are similarly without end. Money "walks," so to speak, like the vagrant. Its steps are, finally, *beyond* counting.

## Double-entry bookkeeping

Given the two available ways of "counting" the proverbial "pas," we may wish to consider more closely the method of accounting that developed partly to rationalize the costs and profits of any given enterprise: double-entry bookkeeping. Introduced into the "vernacular" in Italy in the fifteenth century, double-entry bookkeeping was standard in England by the eighteenth century. Its central feature is a formal repetition: "What was characteristic of double-entry methods was the fact that all transactions were entered twice, once as a debit and once as a credit... The terms debit and credit are purely conventional and do not denote a decrease or an increase" (Carruthers and Espelande, 37). This lack of reference to an exterior decrease or increase suggestively marks the relation between book-keeping and *literature*; Weber, for example, speaks of the "fictions" enabled by double-entry – such as the idea that one could buy and sell to oneself.

"Double-entry" bookkeeping was the first fully rationalized system of accounting, and provided the basis for subsequent developments in accounting that made use of its "bilateral," non-chronological form:

Bilateral accounts, including double entry, involved the extraction of records of transactions from a continuous narrative and their placement in a tabular arrangement... The extraction of items from a chronological flow inevitably involves abstraction and simplification. Extraneous detail can be identified and eliminated. Qualitative differences can be reduced to quantitative differences. The amount of information is reduced as items are decontextualized. (*ibid.* 56–7)

According to Weber, the double-entry form of accounting was motivated by the desire "to check in the technically most perfect manner on the profitability of *each step or measure*" (*Economy and Society*, 93; emphasis mine). This segmenting of a series of "steps" may itself be tied to another cognitive effect of double-entry bookkeeping. If the bilateral, tabular form of accounting reformulated and streamlined the original "manuscript" (called a "waste-book" in accounting textbooks of the eighteenth century and earlier) into a non-chronological organization, this reformulation had an initially problematic effect: there was now no "natural" end to the transaction, as there had been in the typical account-book prior to the advent and standardization of double-entry. The "running" account, or tab, is the emergent form of mercantile conceptualization.

The elimination of the "natural" end of the business cycle – whether we imagine that end as the completed individual trans-action, the agricultural season or the three-month "future" of the merchant ship – contributed to the reconceptualization of the busi-ness venture. No longer was business to be understood as a local transaction, nor even, perhaps, segregated into separate fields of operation (agriculture, pasturage, textile manufacture); instead, it came to be perceived as "a continuous, abstract enterprise" (Carruthers and Espelande, 54). The periodization of business was entirely arbitrary, and recognized as such. With the external referents for the periodization of accounting diminished, the self-reflexive measurement of each "step" alluded to by Weber appears to have emerged in their place. This formalization also has explanatory value, I would suggest, for a different kind of – poetic – accounting. Think, for example, of the way in which the "steps" of common meter in a poem like "Goody Blake and Harry Gill" will replace an apparently "natural" chronology of agricultural seasons by a logic of incremental equivalence:

> In March, December, and in July,
> 'Tis all the same with Harry Gill;
> The neighbors tell, and tell you truly,
> His teeth they chatter, chatter still.                    $(9-12)$[4]

### *Deterritorialization and* le pas au-delà

This replacement of history by entirely arbitrary periods, represented as so many "steps" entered in the account-book, also entails the erasure of location, a deterritorialization of economic activity and the economic agent. Here we may add to the picture Marx's *historical* explanation of the emergence of capital: the expropriation of the agricultural laborer. The historical "first step" or "so-called primitive accumulation" again acquires a telling literalness in Marx's account: the expropriation of the agricultural laborer sets capitalist production "on its own legs [*Füßen* – feet]" (*C* 668). Like the commodity-form of the table, land itself is transformed into an alienable – and therefore mobile – property. With capital, *mortmain* is lifted, as it were, and the land enters, on a larger scale than heretofore, the circuit of exchange. Land itself becomes a "unit of account." This is the economic aspect of Enlightenment and the revolutionary principle of *freedom*: its epitome may be the French *assignat*, which converted seized church property (the classical locus of *mortmain*) into public credit. The social effect of this discursive displacement, the translation of land into a money-form, is the expropriation of those whose subsistence depended upon access to underutilized parts of a landed estate – for example, the unenclosed common – and the consequently enormous increase, chronicled not only in Wordsworth's poems but also by contemporary historians and political economists, and referred to by judges negotiating customary and property rights, of an unemployed surplus-population, newly mobilized and inhabiting the roads. If the old proverb held that it was the first step that "counted," thenceforward that will only be the case because the subsequent steps do not bear counting, are beyond measure.

Just as Marx captures the relation of capital to the "rhetorical" form of double-entry bookkeeping with his punning proverb about steps, so he also reduces the historical tranformation of land into a discursive "unit of account" to a telling phrase: "Transformation of arable land into sheepwalks was its cry" (*C* 672). This "cry" (*Losungswort*), identified with the first phase of large-scale enclosure in the sixteenth century, continued to resonate through the eighteenth and early nineteenth centuries, as political economists justified measures undertaken to increase the production of wool as the achievement of geographical proportion. Sir Frederick Eden, author in 1797 of *The State of the Poor*, contended that

The due proportion between arable land and pasture had to be established. During the whole of the 14th and the greater part of the 15th century, there was one acre of pasture to 2, 3, or even 4 of arable land. About the middle of the 16th century, the proportion was changed of 2 acres of pasture to 2, later on, of 2 acres of pasture to one of arable, until at last the just proportion of 3 acres of pasture to one of arable land was attained. (quoted in *C* 681)

Eden's concern with the due proportion or the just balance is congruent with the aesthetic logic of double-entry bookkeeping, whose inventor, Pacioli, had argued that only the *evening* of debit and credit could justify commerce and distinguish it from usury. Eden's emphasis on a *numerical* equivalence almost suggests an unconscious echoing of this logic, even if the achievement of "justness" is not a balance but a proportion, not 2:2 but 3:1. In any case, Eden's account certainly indicates a geographical rationalization, or deterritorialization; his idea of proportion obeys a logic extrinsic to the "nature" of England, a logic of production. It was, after all, the increasing importance of trade and the rise of textile manufactures that led to a transformation of the landscape into "sheepwalks" (*Schafweide*); where land was not susceptible to cultivation (and even where it was), it was turned into "pasturage."

The Marxian cry of "sheepwalks" is particularly telling not because it accurately describes the landscape of *Lyrical Ballads* – by the late eighteenth century, improvements in agricultural production made it equally likely that waste land or commons would be enclosed as "tillage," transforming the landscape into what Wordsworth will call "*wastes* of corn." Rather, the cry of "sheepwalks" generally works to suggest how the most profitable landscape had become, by the eighteenth century, a depopulated landscape, not only because of the increased productivity of enclosed land, but also because owners were not responsible for providing relief for itinerant laborers. Marx quotes Arthur Young's analysis, which seems to oppose profit and population, to indicate the entirely *erudite* meaning which comes to be attached to the idea of land "use": "of what use, in a modern kingdom, would be a whole province thus divided [in the old Roman manner, by small independent peasants], however well cultivated, except for the mere purpose of breeding men, which taken singly is a most useless purpose?" (221).[5]

Wordsworth calls into question Young's entirely erudite notion of "use," as I have suggested, with the image of "wastes of corn"; like the cry of "sheepwalks," this image too, oxymoronic and "literary" as it might appear, can be culled from the discourse of political economy. What Wordsworth will call "wastes of corn" are acres of tillage that are transformed by economic speculation into an abstraction from need. Roy Porter reports that "Corn output grew from 17,353,000 quarters in 1770 to 21,102, 000 in 1800" (334), yet these were also years of an enormous increase of both the price of corn and the level of vagrancy. Out of this paradox, modern economic discourse arose, according to Keith Tribe; debates over the various Corn Laws occasioned by this paradoxical (because "unnatural") rise both of price and production led to the invention of two concepts crucial to economic discourse, both of them relevant to the *literary* discourse of *Lyrical Ballads*. First, Ricardo's rational explanation of this paradox is a "ground rent" theory that explains the economic significance of the equalization or deterritorialization of land implicit in Eden's description of the "just proportion." According to Ricardo, the costs of production rise as "waste" land is cultivated; and the cost of corn does not reflect a *local* cost of production but rather the *general* cost of production for the annual (and national) crop. Not only is there a literal "evening" as waste land is transformed into pasture or tillage (notice how this "evening" operates by a logic opposite to the traditional "common"), but there is also a purely formal "evening" as local costs and profits are balanced by reference to a *general* economy. Second, Tribe points out that explanation, justification, or criticism of the Corn Laws and the apparently artificial high price of provisions depends upon a posited antagonism between the landlord and capitalist farmer. In this perceived antagonism, according to Tribe, we find registered one of the crucial indices of an economic discourse: instead of the untheorized conception of populations among whom a national product circulates, Classical Political Economy constructs distribution as occurring between theoretically defined economic agents. For the first time it is possible to construct economic, rather than political, legal or even human agencies. (127)

Tribe's formulation of this "economic agent" in contradistinction to other discursive constructions of agency is crucial, of course, for it discloses this agency, like the others, as a negation. "Occupying" what Tribe calls "the terrain of an economy" rather than a polity, this economic agent, a subject split by a structural antagonism, is also the subject of *Lyrical Ballads*. The chief terms of the antagonism that structures Wordsworth's subject will be credit and debt, terms that replace the old ontology of the subject – being and having.

Finally, the cry of "sheepwalks" is a rural–nostalgic representation of the "steps" of money. For the sheepwalk, a product of enclosure, requires that the shepherd or laborer follow a more "roundabout" route. The *Public Health Report* of 1865, summarizing the effects of enclosure on people who walked for a living, establishes the connection between deterritorialization and vagrancy:

Large proprietors…have but to resolve that there shall be no labourers' dwellings on their estates, and they shall henceforth be virtually free from half their responsibility for the poor. How far it has been intended, in the English constitution and law, that this kind of unconditional property in land should be acquirable, and that a landlord "doing what he wills with his own," should be able to treat the cultivators of the soil as aliens, whom he may expel from his territory, is a question which I do not pretend to discuss…To [the laborer's] daily toil there will then have to be added, *as though it were nothing*, the daily need of walking six or eight miles for power of earning his daily bread. (quoted in *C* 639–40; emphasis mine)

Unlike the sheepwalk, the laborer's walk signifies not potential surplus but "nothing," an *ontological* lack. When they no longer occupy the land but instead occupy a purely discursive territory as wage-laborers, the necessity of walking can occasion a literal deficit, whereby the wages of a shepherd's wandering are diminished by his travel to and from work:

To reduce the long trudges over these wide plains, the beautiful pastures of Leicester and Northampton, the shepherd used to get a cottage on the farm. Now they give him a thirteenth shilling a week for lodging, that he must find far away in an open village. (639 n. 1)

Although the thirteenth shilling appears to be an increase, the manifest difficulty of obtaining appropriate lodging for one shilling a week, plus the expenditure of time and energy on travel, renders this apparent credit a deficit. This transformation of land, of status and property into credit and deficit is for Marx the "real" effect of the cry of "sheepwalks."

Noticing how this transformation crucially involves the coin – the thirteenth shilling is, as it were, "lodged" in the hand or pocket of the shepherd to replace his lodging – we are in a better position to understand Marx's elaboration of the relation between mobility and negation (*pas*) in reference not to the sheepwalk but to what he calls the "track of money," *le cours de la monnaie*. The course of money is distinguished from the circulation of commodities; where the commodity "first steps into circulation" only "to fall out of circulation again" when it is purchased, according to Marx "the currency of money is the constant and monotonous repetition of the same process" (*C* 116). This currency is "restless" (*rastlosen*) and a kind of "*perpetuum mobile*" (*C* 130). Thus, although the commodity-form is the "first step," its *cost*, so to speak, and what prevents a final accounting from ever being taken, is this *pas au-delà* of money: "hence the movement directly imparted to money takes the form of a constant motion away from its starting-point" (*C* 116).

Marx represents the circulation of commodities by the *apparently* tautological symbol C–M–C (Commodity–Money–Commodity). Such "circulation" is not in fact tautological because the symbolic equivalency of commodities represented in the abstraction "M" is not true of their use-values; the weaver who sells his cloth for a Bible and the Bible-seller who buys brandy, that "eau de vie," after having received the purchase price of "the water of everlasting life" (*C* 114), receive different use-values out of their equivalent exchange-values. In fact, C–M–C registers the logic of analogy, which establishes a temporary equivalence. According to Marx, "it is otherwise in the circulation M–C–M" (*C* 148). The *difference* which explains the money trail in commodity-exchange – which we may imagine as money's departure from lodging in one commodity to residence in another – then becomes a mathematical formula: the original *qualitative* difference between commodities' use-values now is represented in the *quantitative* difference between the original capital and the profit (represented as M–C–M'). But now it is the *difference*, rather than the similitude, that is momentary, since the exchange returns to the pockets of the financier the same substance he had previously owned. Summarizing the difference between the two forms of movement, Marx writes,

The simple circulation of commodities – selling in order to buy – is a means of carrying out a purpose unconnected with circulation, namely, the appropriation of use-values, the satisfaction of wants. The circulation of money as capital is, on the contrary, an end in itself, for the expansion of value takes place only within this constantly renewed movement. The circulation of capital therefore has no limits. (*C* 150)

Marx helps us to envision this second kind of circulation by the invention of its persona, Mr. Moneybags. Mr. Moneybags is the "economic agent" invented by economic discourse, devoid of other contingent sources of identity. "As a conscious representative of this movement, the possessor of money becomes a capitalist. His person, or rather his pocket, is the point from which the money starts and to which it returns" (*C* 151). This reduction of the person to the pocket, made explicit in the capitalist's "proper name," will be the equivalent to Marx's representation, in *The Eighteenth Brumaire*, of the "political agent" of liberalism, the small property-owner (the peasant) transformed by an analogous logic of equivalence into the "tatterdemalion" [*zerlumpten Individuum*] whose identity resides in his rags. Although the implication is that property and identity (self) perfectly coincide in these agents, Mr. Moneybags and the tatterdemalion, that coincidence functions as a negation of substantial identity. Expropriated peasants, for example, are those who "have nothing to sell but their own skins" (*C* 667); rather than representing the conjunction of property and propriety, their example only testifies to an exquisite alienation of the body. These two *dramatis personae*, to use Marx's description of his economic agents, figure importantly, I believe, in the metamorphosis of commodity-exchange into capital-exchange. They represent the social effect of this metamorphosis, a congealing into surplus and dearth of an "identity" whose political equivalent is described by Rousseau in the split between "Jean-Jacques" and "M. Rousseau" (the one regarded as a "Mr. Moneybags" by the crippled boy, the other accused of "playing the beggar").

We may imagine the circulation of commodities as taking place in one of two ways: either these economic agents converge at a marketplace, or they "meet," so to speak, through their intermediaries – the itinerant peddler or the stationary retailer. In C–M–C, this convergence or meeting is represented by the connective tissue of the formulation: the dashes represent spatial and temporal distance. Since the goal is the achievement of the commodity-exchange, Marx can render not only those lines but indeed the middle term itself, money, as "a transient existence": "its functional existence absorbs, so to say, its material existence" (*C* 129). In the second model, the "transient existence" of money becomes permanent, at the same time as it is incarnated in a mobilized Mr. Moneybags. We speak of a life, that species of transient existence, as having been "spent"; so Marx speaks of money in commodity-exchange. But for the circulation of capital, a different metaphor is required: "the money, therefore, is not spent, is it merely *advanced*" (*C* 147; emphasis mine).

This mere *advancement* of money, distinguished by Marx from the exchange of commodities, describes a tautological movement: the formerly "transient" life of money, representing the distance between commodities, is abstracted into a permanent value; Mr. Moneybags's advancement, or walking, is an end in itself. Marx claims that Mr. Moneybags's dark double is the miser. By emphasizing the nature of the capitalist "venture," I wish rather to suggest that it is the vagrant. For the miser inversely represents only the subjective, psychological interior of Mr. Moneybags, whereas the vagrant is the product of his advancement. The historically specific vagrant I mean here to indicate is one produced by a money economy; as Simmel notes,

Poverty, like avarice and greed, appears in its purest and specific form only at a certain stage of the money economy. In natural conditions which are not yet regulated by a money economy, and as long as agricultural products do not circulate merely as commodities, that is, as money values, the total destitution of the individual is less common. (252)

The vagrant who will be the subject of interest to Romantic speculation, is precisely this all-too-familiar figure: the vagrant *says* that he "will work [or walk] for food," but that "translation" of labor-power into use-value is rarely possible, given the structural "detour" of provisions such as corn into the money-form. The vagrant begs for food rather than money only because the rhetoric of social relations and of the welfare state lags behind that of economic relations. Simmel again explains:

humane and sympathetic feelings towards poverty are more easily aroused in these circumstances [begging for food] than when what the poor lack and what one can help them with is not what is most immediately necessary to them. In purely monetary relationships, sympathetic feelings have to make a detour before they reach the point of their genuine interest. They often flag during this detour. For this reason, practically helpful and charitable people prefer to come to the aid of the poor with food and clothing rather than money. (252)

Thus, for example, such figures as "The Old Cumberland Beggar," whose reduction to mere existence by age or infirmity as well as poverty, and whose location in a rural and semi-agricultural region allows a bypass of the prevailing money economy, can more easily become figures of sentimental attachment than the more ambivalent figures of law and the letter: those branded with the "V" in Elizabethan times because of the conjunction of an able body and the specter of unemployment.[6]

Yet even in "The Old Cumberland Beggar," Wordsworth suggests that *location* no longer distinguishes the (local) beggar and the (deterritorialized) vagrant. Already, as Wordsworth notes, beggars of provisions – a class that "will probably soon be extinct" – received alms "*sometimes in money*, but generally in provisions" (B&G, 228; emphasis added). Indeed, I would argue that Wordsworth's representation of the Old Beggar is significant – and significantly Romantic – precisely because the Beggar's own represented epistemology is more sophisticated than that of the villagers to whom he offers moral comfort. The beggar scans his food "with a fixed and serious look / Of idle computation" (11–12) as if the number of food scraps were valued more highly than their ostensible use-value: nourishment. If his poverty is miserable, it is also that of a miser, who laments any occasion that requires him to exchange his own "unit of account" (the coin) for some object which represents accumulation less purely than money, which represents the abstract *power* of accumulation.[7] The Beggar's hands, those instruments of acquisition, are "palsied," and scatter the food even as he tries to eat it, as if in parodic imitation of the "invisible hand" in Smith's *Wealth of Nations* that encourages circulation and distribution. Certainly the fact that a coin is "lodged" (line 28) with him must be read ironically; far from representing the secure depositing in a bank, the "lodging" of a coin in a (vagrant) beggar's hand suggests how the Beggar, with his "stated round," merely redoubles the entirely abstract "industry"

– of circulation – elsewhere represented in the poem; Wordsworth cites the toll-gate keeper and the post-boy, both of whom derive their sustenance, like the Beggar, from circulation and mobility.

The "first step" described in *Capital* marks a number of decisive shifts to modernity as above all involving a *formal* mutation in what Marx calls "the language of real life." That this mutation is formal requires that we pay at least as much attention to the *forms* of representation as to their contents. On the one hand, this means noting the "literary" and "figurative" dimension of economic discourse. On the other hand, it means we need to come to terms with the relation between this "language of real life" and literature itself, particularly the Romantic idea of literature as a *lingua communis* that balances competing histories or economies by producing a third term, the pure form of the poem itself. For poetry itself is a kind of bookkeeping, fully caught up in the deterritorialization and dehistoricization it implies. In this context, it is significant that the question of *copyright* becomes a privileged locus for the adjudication of property rights during the Romantic period. The concept of "property" itself has becomes entirely discursive, because the traditional sources of property – imagined as emanating (a) from "the labor of his body and the work of his hands" or (b) from natural largesse, the "richness" and fruitfulness of the earth – are no longer available. Similarly, the value of land is no longer natural, but depends on the social relations between the landlord and the capitalist farmer; land is ground rent, or pure exchange-value. It is this symbolic mutation of property – from land and person to the discursive unit of account – that explains why, in both *Capital* and *Lyrical Ballads*, legal and economic measurements of property will be reduced to a formalized accounting of "steps," and associated with vagrancy. The discourse Wordsworth invents as literature, also exhibited in the consciously rhetorical dimensions of *Capital*, is a conflation of story and number, historical and economic discourse, into a *literary* discourse that also entails their collapse.

II: *LYRICAL BALLADS*: THE DOUBLE NEGATIVE OF TAUTOLOGY

In *Wordsworth: Language as Counter-Spirit*, Frances Ferguson emphasizes the way in which *tautology* structures not only many of Wordsworth's poetical experiments, but his theoretical accounts of those experiments as well; tautology is, according to Ferguson, "a characteristic Wordsworthian tactic which prompted both his contemporaries and subsequent critics to accuse him of loose and unsystematic thought" (8). Here is Wordsworth's own defense of repetition and tautology, appearing in the note to "The Thorn" included in the 1800 edition of *Lyrical Ballads*:

There is a numerous class of readers who imagine that the same words cannot be repeated without tautology: this is a great error: virtual tautology is much oftener produced by using different words when the meaning is exactly the same. Words, a Poet's words, more particularly, ought to be weighed in the balance of feeling, and not measured by the space which they occupy upon paper. For the Reader cannot be too often reminded that Poetry is passion: it is the history or science of feelings; now every man must know that an attempt is rarely made to communicate impassioned feelings without something of an accompanying consciousness of the *deficiencies* of language. During such efforts there will be a *craving* in the mind, and as long as it is unsatisfied the Speaker will cling to the same words, or words of the same character. There are also various other reasons why repetition and apparent tautology are frequently beauties of the highest kind. Among the chief of these reasons is the interest which the mind attaches to words, not only as symbols of the passion, but as *things*, active and efficient, which are of themselves part of the passion. And further, a mind *luxuriates* in the repetition of words which appear successfully to communicate its feelings. (Ow, 140; emphases mine)

As I have indicated by the italicized words, this passage represents tautology in terms not only of passion but also of need; Ferguson has usefully characterized the relation between these two economies: "Passion never knows what is not a need" (64). But Wordsworth's economics of tautology is even more complex. Not only does an impassioned need (a "craving") produce a tautology which serves not to fulfill the need but to display the word's representational *deficiencies*, so too does surplus: effective communication results in the speaker's *luxuriating* in the word's richness – the *thingness*, what de Man would call the *materiality* of the letter, or its residual being in the aftermath of its communicative function. In the first case, the case most apropos of the poem to which the note is attached ("The Thorn") tautology is a kind of hoarding associable with the *miser*, who likewise appreciates the *thingness*, rather than the communicative or symbolic function, of the representative object. For our purposes, we can say that the former speaker, exemplified in Martha Ray, produces out of linguistic impoverishment a "beggar's cant" that substitutes repetition for an extensive vocabulary or a narrative rationale. All words come equally to express the pervasive condition of misery or destitution, and the poem itself is reducible to the single self-definition "Woe is me." In the latter instance, words are only spoken that their author might appreciate their sonorities, the phonetic aspect of words that offers to reorder their relation not in terms of semantic "sense," but in terms of an aesthetic *sensation* or style.

In his double-edged criticism and defense of Wordsworth's imitation of the "apparent tautologies" of demotic speech, Coleridge only defends the second type of tautology. He first describes tautology in a manner suggestive of Cobbett's analysis of paper-money,[8] arguing that "the property of passion is not to *create*, but to set in increased activity," and that the adoption of "unmeaning repetitions, habitual phrases and other blank counters" is analogous to a stage production in which "the same player pops backwards and forwards, in order to prevent the appearance of empty spaces" (*BL* 200). However, Coleridge goes on to defend "*apparent* tautologies" as accurate renderings where the passion described cannot be "exhausted or satisfied by a single representation" (*ibid.*). "The best part of human language," so Coleridge contends, "is derived from reflections on the acts of the mind itself" (197). The familiar divergence of "manners" that prevented Wordsworth and Coleridge from proceeding with their joint poetic project as planned might then appear to be this difference between Coleridge's idea of a self-reflexive language and Wordsworth's alleged "matter-of-factness."

We can think of few discourses more matter-of-fact than accounting, perhaps. It is "repetitious, detail oriented, and methodical" (Carruthers and Espelande, 31); the preference of the bookkeeper for numbers over anecdotes is a consequence of the fact that statistical evidence tends to be regarded as more objective and "factual" than observation and verbal recounting. Jerome Christensen, however, describes how even verbal recounting became subject to a rationalization similar to that which differentiates the "waste-book" from the ledger in double-entry bookkeeping: he describes the development, in the early nineteenth century, of stenography. The development of stenography, like the development of double-entry bookkeeping, offers a useful example of an historical or material "dialectic" in which language becomes *self-reflexive*:

The dialectic of stenography actively contributed to the regulation of public discourse. The stenographer recorded a pulpit utterance in shorthand, which was later decoded and written in longhand in order that it could be printed and sold … in handbooks of model sermons available for the plunder of preachers eager to economize on sermon preparation. Pulpit oratory rapidly adapted itself to the technology available to reproduce it. The history of change … eventually leads to Stones's radical system, which abbreviates to a distinctive character a conventional phrase that the stenographer was largely responsible for turning into formula in the first place. (Christensen, 203)

Coleridge's idealization of language that is the product of the mind's colloquy with itself is here translated into a technology of "formula." Perhaps it should surprise us, therefore, that, as Christensen points out in a note, Coleridge's own language was peculiarly resistant to the stenographer's reduction:

a very experienced short-hand writer was employed to take down Mr. Coleridge's lectures on Shakespeare, but the manuscript was almost entirely unintelligible. Yet the lecturer was, as he always is, slow and measured. The writer … gave this account of the difficulty: that with regard to every other speaker whom he had ever heard, however rapid or involved, he could almost always, by long experience in his art, guess the form of the latter part, or apodosis of the sentence, by the form of the beginning; but that the conclusion to every one of Coleridge's sentences was a *surprize* upon him. He was obliged to listen to the last word. (quoted in Christensen, 400)[9]

It may seem that the characteristically Coleridgean mode of expression – irreducible to stenography because the end bears no predictable relation to the beginning – could not be farther removed from the circular repetitions of tautology. But we can see how the double-entry form of a tautology might confuse the would-be stenographer. For in fact, tautology is precisely what one *doesn't* expect from a propositional statement; one expects predication to fill out the abstraction. How might the stenographer positively represent the aching gap that lurks between the subject and predicate of such tautologies as "God is … God" or "Law is … law" or Wordworth's "Man is … the man of whom we read"[10]? The absence of this content is what defines Romantic vagrancy, whether that absence takes the form of "matter-of-factness" or the more avowedly abstract "reflection of the acts of the mind itself."

This unacknowledged common interest in the structure of tautology may in fact have enabled the joint project of *Lyrical Ballads*. It is certainly true that it was prompted by the experience of debt, a debt made correlative in accounts of the project with walking. In the Fenwick notes, Wordsworth claims that the literary collaboration between himself and Coleridge was undertaken with a view toward the periodical publication of a single poem ("The Rime of the Ancient Mariner") for which they hoped to receive, perhaps, five pounds. Wordsworth's explanation of their financial situation is important; according to his account, the collaborative venture begins *in medias res*:

> In the Spring of the year 1798, he [Coleridge], my Sister, and myself started from Alfoxden, pretty late in the afternoon, with a view to visit Linton and the Valley of Stones near it, and as our united funds were very small we agreed to defray the expence of the tour by writing a Poem to be sent to the New Monthly Magazine. (B&G, 4)

Since the walking tour is well underway, the defraying of expenses must of necessity be imagined as occurring after the fact, as the paying off of a debt incurred. Reinforcing the imputation of improvidence this context lends to the experiment is Wordsworth's allusion to the late-afternoon time of their departure, inappropriate to the length of the journey and indicative of an absence of forethought. This same absence of forethought appears to affect the composition of the "Ancient Mariner"; "as we endeavoured to proceed conjointly, our respective manners proved...widely different"; finally, the poem *exceeds* the original conception (it "grew & grew until it became too important for our first object"). Wordsworth's organic metaphor here, like the implicit differentiation, to be confirmed by Hazlitt's observations, between the collaborating authors' manners of walking, obscures the economic identity of the poem they wish to produce; designed without reference to use-value, the original ballad is a commodity of which Christensen has recently said, "The commodity is not a ruin; it is neither natural nor subject to natural processes, although it is always being naturalized" (192).

### The female vagrant

Absence of forethought also characterizes "The Female Vagrant," a fragment excerpted from an earlier project for inclusion in *Lyrical Ballads*. Thus the very *form* of the poem reinforces the expropriation that will be its moral, political, and economic themes. "The Female Vagrant" is cut off, by Wordsworth's decision to publish, from its "proper" context, the neighborhood of "Salisbury Plain." But if, by the end of the historical narrative offered in the poem, we come to identify vagrancy with a historical moment (war and its aftermath) and an economic condition (unemployment and destitution), the poem also nonetheless attributes to the female narrator a certain vagrant *attitude*, preexisting the series of catastrophes which mark her historical existence. One cost of the mobility represented in both the form (expropriation) and content (vagrancy) of the poem is, apparently, the inability to identify a "first step," or to tell a story with a "proper" beginning and ending.

First, even before she becomes a vagrant, the companion of gypsies and a beggar of bread, the female vagrant is occupied by tasks which are themselves conducive to a passive mental attitude: they are versions of gleaning, of an extractive industry dependent upon an original or natural largesse: "With thoughtless joy I stretch'd along the shore / My father's nets, or watch'd, when from the fold / High o'er the cliffs I led my fleecy store" (5–7). Shepherding is "watching," or the mind's eye wandering in imitation of the object-world.

Taught to read by a father similarly dependent on "what the *neighbouring* flood / Supplied" (3–4), the female vagrant extends her gleaning to *books*:

> I read, and loved the books in which I read;
> For books in every neighbouring house I sought,
> And nothing to my mind a sweeter pleasure brought. (16–18)

I emphasize Wordsworth's repetition of "neighbouring" here in order to demonstrate the way in which such a species of courtesy might inform one's attitude both to intellectual and "real" property. "Neighbourage," legally defined as "the collective surroundings and outside conveniences of a plot of land" (*OED*), represents an extension of property rights beyond "pre-established codes of decision," as it were; neighborage was the principle upon which usufruct was founded.[11] Given Wordsworth's representation of "neighbouring" in the poem, it is difficult – indeed, I would argue, impossible – to determine whether the female vagrant's "wandering" into neighbors' houses is a consequence of the wandering eye she develops through reading, or of familiarity with the principle of "neighbourage" that enables her father to procure a living. In a note to the poem, Wordsworth appends information about usufruct which reinforces the connection between reading and neighborage: "Several of the Lakes in the north of England are let out to different

Fishermen, in parcels *marked out by imaginary lines drawn from rock to rock*" (*LB*, 43). Neighborage is marked by *imaginary* lines which traverse the space already marked out by the *deed*, or original title, of property. Perhaps a familiarity with the imaginary character of such lines suggests to the female vagrant that the property line too is strictly imaginary.

The female vagrant describes the landlord who eventually forces her expropriation as one unfamiliar with the concept of neighborage: "No joy to see a neighbouring house, or stray / Through pastures not his own, the master took" (41–2). Because of the ways in which "neighbouring" has already been deployed in the poem, the description offers us a wealth of information about the new landlord; since the implicit joy (pleasure) with which the female vagrant might view a neighboring house is associated with the books she might find there, we can say that, in her description, she means to suggest that the landlord does not like to *read* either. Certainly he is oblivious to the "imaginary lines" that mark out her father's range of water; his rights are "denied" (51). The landlord's entirely negative concentration of pleasure in things that are "his own" is thus an attitude associated with "pre-established codes of decision" (absolute property rights and poetic "propriety") according to which poetry has a "propriety" that the reader may appropriate and effectively consume by purchasing a volume.

With the female vagrant as its exemplar, we see how poetry can be conceived as a subversion of absolute property rights, however. The poem itself has only *imaginary* boundaries, and is in fact attached to "neighbouring" discourses (politics, economics, law, those languages of real life) in the way that Wordsworth's note on usufruct is attached to the poem: as a neighborage, not impertinent to the question of the property's (and the poem's) value. A taste only for poetry, then, is an exquisite refinement parallel to the female vagrant's discovery of the "pure form" of being: "Oh! dreadful price of being to resign / All that is dear *in* being" (118–19). The assertion of absolute property rights is also the reduction of land, text, or person to "itself" – and as such an impoverishment.

Alerted by the asterisk that supplementary information is in the vicinity, our eyes stray to the page's margins in order to appreciate the "whole." Thus the concept of neighborage, by contrast to the assertion of absolute property rights, whether emanating from "title" or labor, suggests a reading practice that might reinvest the *forms* of thought with wider significance. The correspondence between reading and wandering can be established only by reference to those "extrinsic" issues to which Wordsworth alludes in the footnote: the legal "reading" of rights of property and rights of common, the latter described by law as *easements* of absolute property right by the principle of neighborage.

### The displacement of the neighbor and the right to wander

But "neighbourage" itself is a problematic concept in a volume which so chronicles the historical moment as one of *displacement*.[12] We cannot forget, in other words, that the former "neighbour" of Derwent is now a vagrant, whose narrative is reported by a likewise nameless interlocutor. Even the textual history of the poem to which I have already alluded reinforces this sense of a *loss* of neighborhood: because "The Female Vagrant" is excerpted or expropriated from the "Salisbury Plain" manuscript, we cannot even locate her in *that* "neighbourhood."

The displacement of the neighbor by the stranger, of neighborhood by mobility (and vagrancy), is also a problem for those "readers" of the imaginary lines of usufruct, the law courts. Most cases which attempted to clarify the nature of easements were doomed in their efforts to decide the cases before them, because "easements" were common-law mitigations of absolute property rights based on a principle of neighborage largely superseded by a newly mobilized population. Holdsworth's *History of English Law* summarizes the problem to be presented by the concept of *jus spatiandi*, an allegation of the (inalienable) right to wander:

it was settled that the extent of an easement was limited by the needs of the tenement to which it was attached. But if an easement in gross was allowed to be created, no such limitation of its extent was possible. It would therefore in effect be a new incident attached to the enjoyment of property, which could not be limited, as customary right was limited. (236)

The "democratic" right to wander was alleged by or on behalf of plaintiffs who no longer occupied the "station" or position of the traditional peasant, whose "tenement" had frequently been eliminated by enclosure; these displaced inhabitants alleged the right to wander as a kind of supplement to the lost traditional rights of common. But the presiding judge in one such case, *Fitch* v. *Rawling* (1795), did not hesitate to declare the impossibility of reconciling the stranger's right with the neighbor's custom (or, one might say, Godwinian with Burkean discourse): "what is common to all mankind can never be claimed as a custom" (*English Law Review* v. 126, 616–17). The context of his decision suggests how the meaning of "rights of common" is disrupted by the background noise of the assertion of democratic rights, common to all. The plaintiffs in the case argued their customary right to play on a green owned by the local landlord; the judge denied their petition claiming that

a custom for all the inhabitants of a parish to have the liberty of exercising and playing at all kinds of lawful games at seasonable times, at their free will and pleasure, is bad. *There is great uncertainty in the description of inhabitants*; it includes all servants, visitors, women, and children; it depends neither on time nor estate: their interest is transitory, and not in general noticed by law. (614–15; emphasis mine)

The language of the decision suggests that the enjoyment of property was no longer thought to consist merely in use or profit, but now extended to the exercise of privilege, of *exclusive* use, and consequently *exclusion*: the depopulated landscape is the *sublime* of property.[13]

For some, this was a dangerous refinement of property, another kind of *imaginary* line. A dissenting judge in the later case of *Blundell* v. *Catterall* (1821) regarded the protection of privilege in cases where utility and profit were not in question as an egregious assertion of privilege:

the principle of exclusive appropriation must not be carried beyond things capable of improvement by the industry of man. If it be extended so far as to touch the right of walking over these barren sands, it will take from people what is essential to their welfare, whilst it will give to individuals only the hateful privilege of vexing their neighbours. (1197)[14]

Thus there appear to be two ways of reading the "imaginary line" of property. In most cases, the law equated wandering, except when confined to one's own property, with trespass; that is, the courts held that the representation of property as an *imaginary* and therefore permeable line was a species of courtesy. Such is the language of Farwell, the presiding judge in a case at the turn of the nineteenth century which would deny the right to wander across Salisbury Plain:

the liberality with which landowners in this country have for years past allowed visitors free access to objects of interest on their property is amply sufficient to explain the access which has undoubtedly been allowed for many years to visitors to Stonehenge from all over the world. It would indeed be unfortunate if the Courts were to presume novel and unheard of trusts and statutes from *acts of friendly courtesy*, and thus drive landowners to close their gates in order to preserve their property. (*Attorney General* v. *Antrobus*, 200; emphasis mine)

In essence, nineteenth-century property law courts and property owners would argue forcefully (and successfully) for the elimination of easements; the razing of tenements and the depopulation of the countryside by Acts of Enclosure meant that the *customary* claims, based on neighborage, were voided. When petitioners sought to invent in their stead a general, positive right, *jus spatiandi*, the courts held that the right to wander could not be described as an *easement* because easements were granted for *use*, usufruct. But the petitioners in the Farwell decision, themselves habitual wanderers across Salisbury Plain, cited a different precedent: "these public rights have been enjoyed long before the site was private property" (192). Wandering, they would claim, precedes and supersedes the law; that is why property is an imaginary line. This is the history written in "The Female Vagrant."

### *Balancing accounts: reading the second volume of* Lyrical Ballads

Recognizing the analogy between the "imaginary line" of property and the poetic line – also a "species of courtesy" according to the 1800 Preface – may enable us to "balance" the competing claims of *Lyrical Ballads*, represented in its hybridized title. "The Female Vagrant," "The Brothers," and "Goody Blake and Harry Gill" are emblematic of the interest of *Lyrical Ballads* in legal disputes about property that end in the victory of absolute property rights and a consequent expropriation. In these poems, vagrancy appears to be a represented *content*. But "Expostulation and Reply" and "The Tables Turned," the two companion or "neighbor" poems Wordsworth chose to begin the second volume of the 1800 edition of *Lyrical Ballads*, suggest how Wordsworth implicates reading and writing – the practice of literature – in the legal and economic disputes which otherwise might strike us as the mere alienable *content* of the poems, rather than, as I contend, their enabling ground. The two companion poems, I will argue, represent the economic and legal aspects of the poet's own wandering eye/I.

Wordsworth represents himself (as "Poet") in the 1800 Preface as a descendant "cut off" from an inheritance (the "private stock" of language that constitutes poetic diction), a claim which reinforces the anonymous authorship of the original volume; Wordsworth has no title to authority.[15] And, if the Poet is thereby "liberated" – unlike the Historian or the Biographer, he is not beholden to "facts" – his audience has been subjected to a similar liberation. No longer is any specialized knowledge, knowledge that might be acquired by the practice of a craft or profession ("a lawyer, a physician, a mariner, an astronomer, a natural philosopher"), required. Wordsworth's is an audience unemployed in more than one sense. *Gleaning* – a traditional right of common – becomes the paradigm of reading in *Lyrical Ballads*. But it is a gleaning deprived of use-value, a purely recreative walk through a landscape. Such non-appropriative use mirrors the language of the law as it tried to mediate the absolute rights of property and threatened rights of common. But in English property law, this mediation – *jus spatiandi*, the right to wander – is consistently denied. Wordsworth can therefore find no adequate paradigm for the mediation of property rights so long as property is imagined as land. His project, instead, is to make the poem represent the book as the paradigmatic form of property.

Let us take William Hazlitt, the reputed interlocutor ("Matthew") of "Expostulation and Reply" and "The Tables Turned," as representative of one version of reading, modeled not only upon absolute property rights but also upon the practice of consumption which, according to the historical arguments of McKendrick, Brewer, and others, developed in the eighteenth century, and which Wordsworth attacked more explicitly in the 1800 Preface.[16] De Certeau offers to explain how central a practice reading was to this model of consumption:

In the eighteenth century, the ideology of the Enlightenment claimed that the book was capable of reforming society, that educational popularization could transform manners and customs, that an elite's products could, if they were sufficiently widespread, transform a nation... the idea of producing a society by a "scriptural" system has continued to have as its corollary the conviction that although the public is more or less resistant, it is moulded by (verbal or iconic) writing, that it becomes similar to what it receives, and that it is *imprinted* by and like the text which is imposed on it. (166–7)

To be what one consumes, to take on the aspect of the proximate object – this is the imitative fallacy writ backwards as the goal of reading. It will certainly underlie Wordsworth's defense of his poetical experiment with the language of "low and rustic life" whose practitioners "hourly communicate with the best objects from which the best part of language is originally derived" (B&G, 744). Later, a similar proximity will account for the superior "domestic attachments" of yeomen farmers; moreover, Michael notoriously *reads* the landscape he inhabits. But unlike the classic Enlightenment ideology de Certeau describes and criticizes, Wordsworth imagines an *exchange* taking place in the act of reading; the landscape is humanized or textualized as much as reading is naturalized. "Proper" reading may appear to engrave ("imprint") the subject, but for Wordsworth this "oppressive" model of reading (as the writing or informing of the subject) may be countered by a model of the "impression" – here used to signify both a casually affective reading and a reading that itself affects the text, leaving, as it were, the impression of a footprint across its surface.[17] This is the point of the chiasmatic metaphors which structure the companion poems. In "Expostulation & Reply," the Hazlitt figure imagines books in nature's terms; they are "light" and "spirit" (air), and although these elements are etherealized by the overly metaphysical speaker, who imagines an *inner* light and a musty air ("breath'd / From dead men to their kind" [6–7]), they are eminently literalizable, as we see in "The Tables Turned." There, "inner light," upon which the "preacher" might be said to have a premium, now belongs to the throstle, and the source of inspirational light, or grace, is not books and their doctrines but "things," including the setting sun.

What do we imagine – what are our *impressions* – when we read the first stanza of "Expostulation & Reply"? Take the first four lines:

> "Why, William, on that old grey stone,
> "Thus for the length of half a day,
> "Why, William, sit you thus alone,
> "And dream your time away?

Only the next line, "Where are your books?" forces an opposition between this representation and reading; in fact, I would suggest, without that line we are quite likely to imagine the seated William as engaged in the activity of reading. Normatively, reading is both a sedentary and a private activity; one might sit thus alone to read. Moreover, the half-day's duration of the "dreaming" activity – as opposed to the companion poem's subtitle, "An *Evening* scene" – suggests that light is necessary for its operation. "Books" truly become "a dull and endless strife" when night advances to "even" the difference between the word and the page. Thus when the speaker of "The Tables Turned" instructs or advises the book-reader to abandon his activity, to "quit your books," the reasonableness of his advice appears to be reinforced by the waning light; we notice, of the discursive experiences he proposes as potential alternatives, that their auditory form requires no light; one might hear the woodland linnet and the throstle when reading (at least out of doors) is no longer possible. The instruction to "come forth into the light of things," in other words, occurs at the moment when quotidian light is vanishing. As such, it is an invitation to *imagine*, in the way that Wordsworth will define that activity in contradistinction to the visual image, or reproduction of the object; it is an activity that depends upon absence, and dearth. (I refer here to Wordsworth's "definition" of imagination in the "Essay, Supplementary"; imagination "has no reference to images.")

In the absence of its representation on the page, let us "imagine" William reading upon the old grey stone, apparently flat, that may serve as an emblem of the (written) tablet of law or of literature; recall that, in *The Prelude*, the youthful Wordsworth discovers that his "little yellow canvas-covered book" (v.483), an abstract of the *Arabian Nights*, is "but a block / Hewn from a mighty quarry" (487–8). William's "reading" cannot be construed as particularly attentive; as with his reading of *Don Quixote* in *The Prelude*, however, we may regard reading as the impetus for the dreaming so reprehended by the expostulating Matthew. In the latter poem (*The Prelude*), even the geometry text becomes an occasion for the solitary, sedentary dreaming which is Wordsworth's representation of the *poet's* reading habits; John Newton parts company with his fellow castaways and takes his book "to spots remote and corners of the isle" (vi.170–1). Crucially, in light of the ethos of "purpose" to be adumbrated in the first poem, we should recall that Wordsworth's defense of indolence is written in a "pocket-copy" of Thomson's poem on the subject (see "Stanzas Written in a Pocket-Copy of Thomson's 'Castle of Indolence'"). James Chandler, who suggests that the "argument" of the poems is to resist argument, to offer "pleasure" and representation as alternatives to argument, also refuses to take the poems as a simple repudiation of books: "If William is not rejecting conversation as such, neither is he … rejecting books, only a mistaken view of them" (286).

This "mistaken view" appears to be the connection made by Matthew between books and purpose – more generally, between books and the law (the moral law, of doctrine, particularly – but also the law of "propriety" more generally). That this law specifically concerns property is made amply clear by the fact that the dreaming poet is criticized for appearing to regard earth as (to use a later Wordsworthian phrase) an "inheritance new-fallen":

> "You look round on your mother earth,
> "As if she for no purpose bore you;
> "As if you were her first-born birth,
> "And none had lived before you!" (9–12)

I would like to contend here that the poet's wandering eye (wandering as that movement opposed to the "unit of account," the measured step) originates in his reading experience, and, as it were, teaches him to disregard the laws of inheritance and primogeniture by which light may be "bequeath'd" (5) and air communicated "From dead men to their *kind*" (7; emphasis mine). In this way "William" becomes a type of the female vagrant, similarly "educated" by books, neighborage, and their imaginary lines to wander and finally to disregard property rights altogether.

Chandler's reading of "Expostulation and Reply," a reading which marks an advance over the critical tendency to paraphrase the poem and its companion as straightforward endorsements of a philosophy of "wise passiveness," usefully constructs the problematic in light of a vague literary allusion.

> "Think you, mid all this mighty sum
> "Of things for ever speaking,
> "That nothing of itself will come,
> "But we must still be seeking? (25–8)

is read as a redeployment of *King Lear*'s "nothing will come of nothing." Chandler remarks that the play is "obsessed with the problems of causality" (152), but it is even more centrally concerned with problems of inheritance, and it is to this problem that the language of the poem explicitly directs our attention.[18]

Frances Ferguson's reading (in *Solitude and the Sublime*) of another of the *Lyrical Ballads*, "We Are Seven," may serve to illuminate the connection between a rhetoric of mathematics (the subtraction / addition / multiplication / division of "nothing") in "Expostulation and Reply" and its thematics of property and inheritance for,

like the central line about "nothing" and its products in "Expostulation and Reply," "We Are Seven" concerns numerical concepts.
According to Ferguson, we may read the latter poem as a staging of
the contemporary contest between the concept of meaning (that
"property" of the text) as an authoritarian imposition or as a formal
accident. The conflict represented in the poem between two ways of
counting the dead (positively and negatively) suggests the way in
which what comes of nothing is a "sum" very much open to dispute.
Only according to one concept of number, Ferguson argues, are number and numbering – enumeration or *counting* – equivalent. According to another, more modern, conception, which she argues is allied
with Kantian formalism, number represents the equivalent of the
*name*, which may continue to exist independent of the referent it may
originally have named. (Number stands here in relation to its referent
as coinage and paper-money may to gold, it should also be noted.)
If William in "Expostulation & Reply" behaves as if none had
lived before him, the girl of "We Are Seven" behaves as if none could
die. Their use of number, particularly their refusal to regard "nothing" (as "not being," death may serve as its phenomenal equivalent)
as altering the "all" of existence, is not only an indication of the
pantheism that critics used to find in the early Wordsworth, in poems
like "A Slumber Did My Spirit Seal." The crucial number, as it turns
out, in questions of literature as well as of property, is the zero – the
non-use-value exposed by wandering (and the sheepwalk, and wastes
of corn).[19]

### *The companion poems: credit and debit*

Let us sketch out the ideology of property in the poems. First, we need
to consider whether William and Matthew count property in the
same way. Matthew's interest in "seeking" seems a product of the
economic anxieties accruing to auxiliary family members in a system
of primogeniture, where to live "as if life's business were a summer
mood" is behavior appropriate to a certain class of men (those "first-
born"), but not to the poem's two interlocutors. For them,
apparently, acquisition is everything, since they are else "forlorn."
Hence Matthew is apparently confounded by the seated William's
evident complacency in a condition – aloneness – which approximates forlornness.[20] An expostulation – the demand of a reason –
may be said to be the rhetorical form of the content of Matthew's next
question: "Where are your books?" (5), since the proper reply to the

initial demand for an explanation would involve, no doubt, an enumeration (of reasons), in the same way that Matthew appears to regard property as necessarily plural. Here, "books" have become units of account; one "keeps" books in the way one keeps track of one's acquisitions in a ledger.

Idleness and aloneness – which combine to produce the specter of vagrancy, as Matthew's remonstrance makes clear – are analogous conditions, made so by the absence of external reference which helps to constitute them as such. To break down the absoluteness of these conditions, Matthew seeks reasons (discursive "purposes") and books, the latter affording to mere being a certain content, an identifiable property. In the first case ("Why?") Matthew wishes to substitute *doing* for being; in the second case ("Where?"), *having* for being. In both cases, the substitution is regarded as a necessary compensation for a primary deprivation; the subject is not "first-born" – by analogy, noble – so that being can confer no status or identity. This deprivation is responsible for Matthew's preference for metaphors of inheritance – the bequest and the ancestral relation. Like Burke's veil of illusion, the *metaphor* of blood relation and family bonds helps to naturalize the exclusion.

The poet's actual response to Matthew's expostulation is rendered silently in the text, as an *imaginary* line, a kind of erased neighborage, and parallels the answer offered in "Anecdote for Fathers" to a similar expostulation: "I knew not why" (14). The similarity between the two poems suggests that we regard William's subsequent speech as on the order of the child's explanation of his preference by a *lack*: "At Kilve there was no weathercock, / And that's the reason why" (55–6). Yet at least initially, his "response" appears instead to emphasize a certain repleteness, a natural *plenum*, which culminates in his description of the world as "this mighty sum / Of things" (25–6). On one level, this description itself offers an adequate riposte to the contention that merely to be is to be forlorn; it draws upon the classical principle that one has property in the earth. On another level, however, the poetical argument is more complex, invoking not only the context of "moral philosophy" (the 1798 Advertisement's allusion to Hazlitt, author of the *Essay on the Principles of Human Action*) but also the political philosophy of the social contract. Unlike Rousseau's political subject, Wordsworth's physiological subject does not appear to be born free; embodiment is registered as a loss of will. Attached to eyes, ears, and other organs of sensation, which represent a kind of inalienable "neighborage," mental activity becomes no choice at all; the subject can *only* perceive. In this context, the stillness that sedentariness approximates might be seen (cannot but be seen?) as precisely the exercise of will that Matthew mistakenly (according to William) ascribes to activity and intentionality. Since the eyes and ears function involuntarily, an anorexia of sensation is perhaps the best way to "Feed this *mind* of ours" (23).

On the other hand, can it be said that the poet, in idly dreaming, is feeding his mind with fewer images and sensations than the "seeking" reader of texts? Once we admit that "nothing" is an experiential or phenomenal impossibility, how does that affect the various mathematical formulae of the poem? The importance of this question emerges as we attempt to understand Wordsworth's motives in producing "The Tables Turned" as a companion poem. Chandler has pointed out two senses in which this poem does not appear to answer the claims made by the title. First, "Expostulation & Reply" itself contains, at least ostensibly, both sides of the staged debate; insofar as "William" in the poem in fact refuses to respond to the expostulation, except to say (implicitly) "Ask not wherefore," the first poem already turns the tables on the initial stanza. Second, as Chandler puts it, "'The Tables Turned' offers not even the slightest gesture toward realizing the promise of symmetry implied in the title phrase" (153).

On the other hand, the second poem's subtitle affords a premise for establishing the poem's relational identity with the first; it is "An evening scene, on the same subject." As I have already suggested, "evening" may often be taken in a Wordsworthian context as a *double entendre*, implying not only a specific quotidian event but also a "balancing" perspective. Only if we have misidentified the subject of the first poem do the second's apparent interests appear not to correspond to the "argument" of this first. When we read "Expostulation & Reply" as essentially concerned with mathematical formulae as "units of account" – the relations between one (the subject alone), many ("books"), all (the "mighty sum"), and "nothing" – then the latter poem's interest in "evening," sameness, and doubling comes into focus. Whereas Matthew's questions reveal an anxiety whereby solitude represents an impoverishment, for the speaker of "The Tables Turned" (presumably William), a different anxiety manifests itself. Here, the acquired plenitude represented by the plural "books" is a threat to integrity: "Up! Up! my friend, and quit your books, / Or surely you'll grow double" (3–4). Note the tautological "balancing" of this line: the repetitive formula "Up! Up!" suggests that, with or without books, the subject will grow (or has already grown) double. The poem's "argument," however, is that the one is precisely "enough," whereas surplus (the plural) is connected with "toil and trouble" and "endless strife." Thus, the singular instance provides the structuring unity of the poem: to "books" are opposed, one at a time, the sun, the woodland linnet, the throstle. The description of each is isolated by successive stanza breaks, for the point here is not to employ the obscure evening light in service of a vaguely synaesthetic effect of light and sound, but rather to uphold the efficacy of "*one* impulse from a vernal wood" (21; emphasis mine).

In contrast to the ethos of bequest, property, and inheritance propounded in "Expostulation & Reply," "The Tables Turned" celebrates a vernal impulse, an organic principle of "seeking" whose chief representative, perhaps, is the (ironically) setting (or sitting) sun. Whereas the light of knowledge is subject to laws of property, inhering in books and transmitted by legacy, the sun's light is dispersed in an entirely "evening" manner:

> The sun, above the mountain's head,
> A freshening lustre mellow
> Through *all* the long green fields has spread,
> His first sweet *evening* yellow.  (5–8; emphases mine)

This stanza departs from the present indicative of the rest of the poem; it is the only emphatic durative in either of the two companion poems. As such, it may be taken as an example of the way in which a certain model of time (the past of inheritance, the future of legacy) may be dreamed away – and as an answer to "how" if not "why" the poet's own work of "evening" (in this context explicitly a gerund) is performed. Certainly the parallels between the sun's "wise passiveness" and the poet's are pronounced; both are explicitly associated with the modifier "sweet," for example, if the more important positional identification – between the poet who sits upon an old grey stone and the sun whose ascendancy over the mountain's "head" is purely temporary – is left implicit. Similarly, both poet and sun may be said to "look round [their] mother earth" – or rather, insofar as the sun is mythically and symbolically judged to *precede* the earth, Wordsworth has found an iconographic way of suggesting that, far from being its second-order birth, the poet gives life – luster – to the earth.

The implication is that rather than "nothing," "all" emerges from the subject ("itself"), as does the repetition of "Up!". Such an implication is reinforced by the fact of the poems themselves: both arise, discursively, from the spectacle of the poet doing nothing. Yet, insofar as the poems are upon "the same subject," the multiplication of discourses made possible by this indolence does not seem to achieve fully independent existence; rather, like the threat posed by multiple texts to its reader, they seem to "grow double" – and we cannot tell, entirely, whether this doubling is a multiplication or a division – two models of organic reproduction. As the organic "impulse" of the verb *grow* suggests, Wordsworth implies that the effects of reading are entirely different from those of accumulation propounded by Matthew.

De Certeau differentiates between writing and reading in a way helpful to unraveling the difference between Matthew's and William's attitudes toward books:

Far from being writers – founders of their own place, heirs of the peasants of earlier ages now working on the soil of language, diggers of wells and builders of houses – readers are travellers; they move across lands belonging to someone else, like nomads poaching their way across fields they did not write, despoiling the wealth of Egypt to enjoy it themselves. Writing accumulates, stocks up, resists time by the establishment of a place and multiplies its production through the expansionism of reproduction. Reading takes no measures against the erosion of time (one forgets oneself *and* also forgets), it does not keep what it acquires, or it does so poorly. (174)

We may recall in this context Wordsworth's own representation of a pseudo-Egyptian nomad, the Arab Bedouin of book v ("Books") of *The Prelude*, who attempts to conserve the "enough" of science and of art by burying them in forms (a stone and a shell) that would make their excavation a fruitless enterprise, since their difference from other objects upon which "natural" history is written – that is, other stones and shells – is negligible. In contrast to de Certeau's nomad, Wordsworth's Bedouin is driven by motives of economy, the desire to save the book from consumption. His solution – to "prevent death by prevenient burial," as Susan Eilenberg has put it (209) – will be parallel to that of other nomadic types in Wordsworth's corpus. His task, in other words, is a similarly "evening" one.

We may thus more or less establish two economies of reading at issue in the poems. The first regards books as a bequest, the "voice" of dead men that would organize the wandering eye and reading practices for a given purpose, according to an Enlightenment ideology: to *inform* the subject. The second appears to generalize that economy, and to make indistinguishable the voice of the book and those "things for ever speaking" or objects in the world regarded as so many texts by the dreaming poet. Thus, although the speaker of "The Tables Turned" privileges the singular, his ability to regard each object as a potential "preacher" or "teacher" may be attributed to his exposure to books in the plural: a liberal education, rather than the largely biblical education of "high livers" in Scotland, for example. Sacred authority is displaced by a regime of texts, none of which can claim priority; each discourse is equally valid. The dreaming poet is a type of the modern scholar, who resists orthodoxy by opposing to "intensive" (close) reading "extensive" reading: "consuming many texts, passing without constraint from one to another, granting little consecration to the object read" (Chartier, 57). Although he may be said to be "fed" by this kind of activity, Wordsworth appears to have in mind a consumption that is at least as "wise" as it is passive. De Certeau describes the difference: "This misunderstanding [of consumption] assumes that 'assimilating' necessarily means 'becoming similar to' what one absorbs, and not 'making something similar' to what one is, making it one's own, appropriating or reappropriating it" (166). This second economy of consumption helps to explain the characteristically tortured syntax by which Wordsworth figures the subject–object relation: "Nor less I deem that there are powers, / Which of themselves our minds impress" ("Expostulation," 21–2); we may read the latter clause taking as its subject either (external) "powers" or "our minds." Read in the latter sense, as in "our minds themselves produce powers which then appear as their effect," Wordsworth's imagining of the subject–object relation duplicates his subsequent question: "Think you... / That nothing of itself will come[?]" (25–7). By the logic of apposition, the mind is registered at once as "nothing" and, of course, as the power of thought capable of such a registering – grammatical proof, as it were, of the implicit contention that the mind, *in addition* to being subject to impressions (through the sensations that occur "against, or with our will" [20]), is also the producer of those impressions. A "mighty sum" indeed.

Unlike de Certeau's formulation, Wordsworth's mathematical

formula moves us away from the discourse of economy into epistemology. What might in economic discourse be taken as a description of the accumulation of capital – growing double as doubling one's investment, for example – appears in the context of "The Tables Turned" almost as a visual impairment, the effect of eyes crossed by too-intensive study. Similarly, "seeing double" may describe the particular effect of the literary text, the poem itself, in contradistinction to the "books of moral philosophy" to which Wordsworth, in a note to the poem, suggests that his "friend" is overly attached. In the crucial clause which we have just examined, for example, "seeing double" is the effect of consuming the text in two different ways, reading both for sound and sense; that is, attempting to account for the effect that the rhyming impulse (a product of the fact that "we cannot bid the ear be still" [19] despite the modern practice of silent reading) has on sense, or what happens when "impress" moves to the end of the line. But seeing double may only serve as the equivalent of the wandering eye – looking "round" – when both senses are put in play (both semantic trajectories, but also both hearing and sight). In other words, what lends the poet so much assurance in his prognostication ("*surely* you'll grow double") is his own familiarity with a world constructed as so many texts. For the image of the "double" is itself ambiguous; if, on the one hand, it suggests self-reproduction, on the other it is represented later as "barren leaves" ("Tables," 30).

In the characteristic rhetoric of the period, political economists regarded the mathematics of doubling or reproduction with similar ambivalence. Godwin, for example, writes that "vast *numbers* of their inhabitants are deprived of almost every accommodation that can render life tolerable or secure" (89). Poverty is always a matter of adding and subtracting:

In England there is less wretchedness and distress... In England the poors' rates amount to the sum of two pounds sterling per annum. It is calculated that one person in seven of the inhabitants of this country derives at some period of his life assistance from this fund. If to this we add persons who, from pride, a spirit of independence, or want of a legal settlement, though in equal distress, receive no such assistance, the proportion will be considerably increased. (90)

As in other poems in *Lyrical Ballads* – many critics, for example, have noticed the way in which "The Last of the Flock" reconsiders the Godwinian attack on private property – in "Simon Lee," allusions to Godwin seem quite conscious. Wordsworth's characterization of Simon Lee, that *ne plus ultra* of poverty ("So vain was his endeavour / That at the root of the old tree / He might have worked for ever" [86–8]), seems clearly to revisit the place in Godwin's *Enquiry* where the social relations between the poor and the bourgeois are described, the former "perpetually and vainly endeavouring to secure for themselves and their families the poorest conveniences" (91). The conflation of aesthetic image or symbolic object with figures of economic destitution in so many of the *Lyrical Ballads* allows us to contend that Wordsworth's apparent dismissal of those discursive contexts through which the poetic articulation of "nature's lore" might "grow double" (political economy or law, for example) is in fact a demonstration of the way in which, despite that dismissal, the "powers" of language are such that these contexts will resonate. Wordsworth will demonstrate that even (especially) statistical language – that epitome of information – is capable of doubling, is subject to rhetorical indeterminacy. When the speaker of "The Tables Turned" contends that the man who does not quit books will become double, he does not promise, as might seem, that their rejection will assure singularity – propriety. For the speaker seated alone in the first poem himself has apparently grown double: though "alone," he is found nonetheless "Conversing as I may" (30).

Equally important, Wordsworth's interest in growing double may have derived from "conversing" with a friend other than Hazlitt, also present during the period of the poems' composition: Coleridge. Although the latter will expand upon his understanding of synonymy and desynonymy fully only in the *Biographia Literaria* of 1817, we know that a distinction between imagination and fancy central to its logic helped to construct the dual plan of *Lyrical Ballads*. It is thus perhaps important to recall that Coleridge attributes *desynonymy* – the progressive distinction of meanings and proliferation of new words – to "an instinct of growth" (*BL* 50), and also that one of his examples is the historical desynonymization of "property" and "propriety" (50 n.; see Hamilton, *Coleridge's Poetics*). Coleridge also provides a metaphor for this linguistic "growing double" derived not from the technology of the printing press, that technology for doubling books, but instead from "nature's lore":

There is a sort of minim immortal among the *animalcula infusoria* which has not naturally either birth, or death, absolute beginning or absolute end: for a certain period a small point appears on its back, which deepens and lengthens till the creature divides in two and the same process recommences in each of the halves now become integral. This may be a fanciful but it is by no means a bad emblem of the formation of words, and may facilitate the conception of how immense a nomenclature may be organized from a few simple sounds by rational beings in a social state. (*BL* 50)

Here we have an organic form that demonstrates, as it were, the necessity of distinguishing between property and propriety. The body itself, since Locke the locus of property rights, is subject to the vicissitudes of growing double; its "integral" or "proper" aspect is subject to displacement. This organic "growing double" explains the desynonymization of property and propriety that takes place, according to my argument, in relation to their antonyms, neighborage and vagrancy. For Coleridge declares that desynonymy is often effected "by giving to the one word a general, and to the other an exclusive use" (*BL* 50 n.); and, despite his attribution of the difference between property and propriety to "mere difference or corruption in the pronunciation of the same word," we recognize in the implicit reference to vernacular *circulation* (and consequent corruption) an analogy to the coin's vagabond life, and the related emergence of the paper *ideal*. The transcendental surplus of "property" depends on the loss of *propriety*: the unit can appear in both columns of the double-entry account. Surely "Expostulation & Reply" and "The Tables Turned" represent just such a process of growing double, each poem "integral" and yet organized by a single conversation.

To return to Matthew's economic anxiety: we can see, now, how this model of "growth" in the social state may serve as a riposte to Matthew's belief in the determinative law of primogeniture. Because he connects books with land, property is a mere sum; according to such an economy, doubling (of offspring) can only mean division and diminution (clearly, this will be the logic the parish demands of the shepherd in "The Last of the Flock"). But according to a different economy, doubling yields a mighty sum; what began in the walking tour of 1798 as a *division of labor* produced a poem "too important for our first object, which was limited to our expectation of five pounds" (*LB*, 4).

In the second edition of *Lyrical Ballads*, as Susan Eilenberg has pointed out, the even greater disproportion between the number of Wordsworth's poems and those of Coleridge problematizes the notion of the "joint" project, as does the appearance of Wordsworth's name as author of the poems and the Preface. As *Lyrical Ballads* "grows" from one to two volumes, there is some question as to whether the 1800 edition constitutes the same "book" at all. But this appears to be precisely the question Wordsworth wishes us to address. As if to indicate the way in which the poems provide us with a methodological key to the poetic experiment, Wordsworth displaced Coleridge's "Rime" as the first poem of *Lyrical Ballads* and chose instead to elevate "Expostulation & Reply" and "The Tables Turned" to its position of priority. We may also note that the poems added to the second volume – particularly the two most ambitious, "The Brothers" (a poem that Coleridge thought should *open* the volume) and "Michael" (which closes the volume) continue to thematize issues of doubling and inheritance.[21] In that "The Brothers" indicates by its title that it will thematize and narrativize the concept of doubling, and because it reinscribes the relation between reading and impropriety (neighborage) represented in "The Female Vagrant," I believe we can read the poem in a way that will suggest how issues of reading are a "shorthand" for issues of property and identity in *Lyrical Ballads*.[22]

### *Growing Double: "The Brothers"*

"The Brothers" has a more than passing interest for readers wishing to extrapolate from the companion poems under discussion Wordsworth's attitude toward reading and – more important – the relation posited between modes of reading and modes of symbolic exchange. The poem narrativizes several of the epistemological contentions of the earlier poems; for example Leonard, who "in those hours / Of tiresome indolence would often hang / Over the vessel's side, and gaze and gaze" (50–2) appears as a type of the dreaming poet. As the doubling of "gaze" in line 52 suggests, the effect of his indolent or passive "reading" is to produce his double. As a sailor he suffers the "calenture," seeing in the green waves the image of green fields, and even his own mirror image: "Shepherds clad in the same country grey / Which he himself had worn" (61–2). Like the companion poems and "The Female Vagrant," moreover, "The Brothers" opens abruptly (for which Wordsworth apologizes in a footnote); and the Priest of Ennerdale criticizes "Tourists" on the same grounds upon which Matthew's expostulation is based: they lead lives far from "profitable" (2) and "sit perch'd" (7) when they

might walk twelve miles or reap an acre of their *neighbour's* corn (10).
(Of course, the point is that the tourist, the passerby, *has* no
neighbors: he is deterritorialized.)

If we imagine the recreational enterprises criticized in the figure of
the tourist as reading and writing (as we imagined the dreaming
William reading), that imagining will be both counteracted and
reinforced. The Priest is particularly confounded, as Matthew had
been, by a dreaming (growing double) without benefit of books:
Leonard gazes at neither sketchpads nor travel guides – nor even
epitaphs.

> In our churchyard
> Is neither epitaph nor monument,
> Tomb-stone nor name, only the turf we tread,
> And a few natural graves.                    (12–15)

Leonard's extended gaze upon the churchyard barren of monuments
will be the means by which Wordsworth achieves a poetic "calenture" in reverse, an "evening" of seascape and landscape.[23]
Earlier Leonard had gazed upon "the broad green wave" (53); now,
as if in imitation of the *trance* by which his shepherd brother James has
apparently fallen to his death, Leonard gazes upon a similarly broad
green expanse:

> He had found
> Another grave, near which a full half-hour
> He had remain'd, but, as he gaz'd, there *grew*
> Such a confusion in his memory,
> That he began to doubt, and he had hopes
> That he had seen this heap of turf before,
> That it was not another grave, but one
> He had forgotten.              (81–8; emphasis mine)

Again, Wordsworth figures a visual doubling as an organic
"growth"; and again, perhaps, two economies contend. At issue is
the "value" to be accorded an accretion – "Another grave was
added" (81) – that clearly represents a *loss*, at least to Leonard.
"Another grave," that is, figures as the "nothing" (death as not-
being, hence nothing) of "Expostulation & Reply" and "We Are
Seven."

Coleridge poses the problem of the calenture in more familiarly
economic terms in the *Biographia* when, attempting to distinguish
between an opposition and a contradiction, he cites the following
example: "if a man's capital be ten and his debts eight, the
subtraction will be the same, whether we call the capital negative

debt or the debt negative capital" (*BL* 163). In Wordsworth's formulation, however, the difference between capital and debt, positive and negative, is literally a matter of life and death. By subtracting the apparently "new" grave (whose topographical form – the hollowed ground and the raised mound – is a materialization of the mathematical paradox by which "nothing" is doubled) from the churchyard, Leonard can restore James to (an imagined) life; whereas if he allows the addition to take place, he suffers a deep loss. To Leonard, "another grave" signifies in its simplest sense negative capital – loss, or debt. But in destabilizing the "fact" before him by an intensity of focus (the cross-eyed "growing double" of "The Tables Turned") that produces a sense of *déjà vu*, a sense that the grave was always already there, Leonard performs that act we had earlier associated with the Arab Bedouin: a prevenient burial to prevent death. Leonard's imaginary addition is in fact a kind of subtraction; this subtraction, in its turn, functions as "negative" debt – the *negation* of debt, and a psychic gain.

In *Lyrical Ballads* the mariner is opposed to the shepherd repeatedly in a personification of competing economies. The economy of the land-owning (not yet displaced) shepherd, who derives his subsistence and profit from the land, and who consequently venerates real estate value, privileges addition. Perhaps the shepherd of "The Last of the Flock" is the preeminent example of this first economy; he takes an almost miserly pleasure in the pure form of acquisition – counting:

> Of sheep I number'd a full score,
> And every year encreas'd my store.
>
> Year after year my stock it grew.
> And from this one, this single ewe,
> Full fifty comely sheep I raised.                    (29–33)

The mariner, by contrast, has typically acquired whatever "stock" he possesses through *trade*; hence the speaker of "The Thorn" is imagined as the retired "Captain of a small *trading* vessel" (B&G, 350), and Leonard has achieved the small surplus enabling his return to Ennerdale by trade ("Some small wealth / Acquir'd by traffic in the Indian Isles" [63–4]).[24] Trade, which corresponds to the mathematical formula of equation rather than addition, also requires a certain aptitude for *subtraction*. As Marx spells it out, this subtraction – in fact an abstraction – is an essential moment in the constitution of the commodity:

If we make abstraction from its use-value, we make abstraction at the same time from the material elements and shapes that make the product a use-value; we see in it no longer a table, a house, yarn, or any other useful thing. Its existence as a material thing is put out of sight. (*C* 45)

It is by virtue of this negation that the commodity "steps" into circulation; in order for exchange to take place, an equivalency must be established which negates the positive content (use-value) of the objects for exchange, at least temporarily: "The two things must therefore be equal to a third, which in itself is *neither the one nor the other*" (*ibid.*; emphasis mine). This third term is also *money*, the (negating) profit or transcendental surplus that emerges from the transaction.

Thus Leonard, as a mariner whose "wandering through the world" (Marx's description of monetary circulation) has included training in the principles and profits of exchange, can by a simple act of speculation (gazing) reduce a positive content – another grave – to its opposite: "it was not another grave" (87). However, we should note that this subtraction is accomplished by a dehistoricization. An intensity of focus – close reading – produces Leonard's experience of *déjà vu*; he is able to make James's grave disappear because he begins to believe his memory plays him false, that he has seen that grave before. This intensity of focus Coleridge will later describe as essential to the operation of what he calls the "negative faith" employed in reading the literary text:

This illusion, contradistinguished from delusion, that *negative* faith which simply permits the images presented to work by their own force, without either denial or affirmation of their real existence by the judgment, is rendered impossible by their *immediate neighbourhood* to words and facts of known and absolute truth. (*BL* 256; emphasis mine)

We should recall that Coleridge's definition of "negative faith" (equivalent to the more well-known "willing suspension of disbelief") appears in the context of his criticism of that other "wanderer through the world" (see below) who achieves a small surplus by trade, the Pedlar of *The Excursion*. Coleridge wishes to deny the relevance of occupational history to mental operations, patterns of imagination. But Coleridge's own "geography" of negative faith suggests why Wordsworth might insist upon the relevance of the Pedlar's occupation, and why Leonard's own occupation of mariner – and the "occupational hazard" of the calenture – is important to the thematic of "The Brothers." The increased range of these occupations, their extraordinary mobility, renders void the concept of "immediate neighbourhood" – and so renders facts less known or absolute, and more available to speculation, or negative faith. We will find in "The Brothers" that the "immediate neighbourhood" of the dramatic conversation – Leonard and the Priest are bounded by the churchyard and a neighboring pasture – will be subject to such speculation, and that each (the churchyard and the pasture) will lose its "propriety" or identity by reference to a third term, the (double-entry) book or ledger.

And yet, if there is an opposition between the shepherd and the mariner, there is also a similarity (hence the implicit logic of the poem: despite their different occupations, Leonard and James continue as "brothers").[25] Although his relation to the land may be seen as one of dependence, the shepherd in *wandering* appears as a type of the mariner; both the mariner and the shepherd thus might be described, at least symbolically, as *nomadic*, in the sense that Marx gives to that term:

Nomad races are the first to develop the money-form, because all their worldly goods consist of moveable objects and are therefore directly alienable; and because their mode of life, by continually bringing them into contact with foreign communities, solicits the exchange of products. (*C* 92)

Here "nomad races" perform the task or the operation also performed, according to Marx, by circulating coin:

In the course of its friction against all kinds of hands, pouches, pockets, purses, money-belts, bags, chests, and strongboxes, the coin rubs off, loses one gold atom there and another one there and thus, as it wears off in its wandering over the world, it loses more and more of its intrinsic substance. By being used it gets used up...The longer a coin remains in circulation...the greater the discrepancy between its form as coin and its actual gold or silver substance. What remains is *magni nominis umbra*. The body of the coin becomes but a shadow...While other beings lose their idealism in contact with the outer world, the coin is idealized by practice, becoming gradually transformed into a mere phantom of its golden or silver body. (*Political Economy*, quoted in Eilenberg, 261)[26]

It may be that Wordsworth's contribution to the critique of political economy in *Lyrical Ballads* and elsewhere lies in his representation of certain "circulating" occupations as involved in a similar process of "idealization by practice": as the Pedlar modulates into the

Wanderer, so the "grey-headed Mariner" modulates into a com-
pulsive tale-teller, a type of the Poet – *and the shepherd, that classical
representative of circulating occupations, becomes the beggar.*

This latter transformation occurs because the shepherd's "wandering over the world," to use Marx's phrase, not only contributes to his
own etherealization, but to the etherealization (commodification) of
mobile property – and eventually the land itself as well. We may
recall in this context the operation of the Speenhamland system,
which demanded that the poor "alienate" all surplus in order to
receive relief; this is the story of "The Last of the Flock." A wagoner
in a similar condition (with "two cows and a few pounds") is quoted
by one historian in explanation: "Whilst I have these things I shall
get no work; I must part with them all; I must be reduced to a state
of beggary before anyone will employ me." The irony here is that the
very surplus by which we may identify the shepherd or the wagoner
(whose "trade" is similarly nomadic) as a "man of property"
becomes the means of his reduction, in the last decade of the
eighteenth century, to a condition of beggary and destitution. Marx
notes that "The *first step* made by an object of utility towards
acquiring exchange-value is when it forms a non-use-value for its
owner, and that happens when it forms a superfluous portion of some
article required for his immediate wants" (*C* 91; emphasis mine). If
surplus – the identification of alienable property, grammatically
represented in the distinction Coleridge had noted between property
and *propriety* – is one side of the coin, destitution is the other (in that
destitution is the remainder, the new mathematical formula of the
"self" – alone).

Initially, of course, Wordsworth's shepherd regards the multiplication of his flock as an *aesthetic* value (a related form of
etherealization); the sheep are "comely" and "pretty." But the
Speenhamland system, in regarding the excess sheep as so much
*exchange*-value, uses the same process of abstraction, whose *first step*, as
Elaine Scarry has suggested, may be counting (see Scarry, *Literature
and the Body*). As if to indicate that alienability which is the essence of
exchange-value, Wordsworth reserves the most pathetic instantiation
of the shepherd's counting to represent the form of *subtraction*:

> Another still! and still another!
> A little lamb, and then its mother!
> It was a vein that never stopp'd,
> Like blood-drops from my heart they dropp'd.                    (61–4)

Again we see repetition or doubling as both an addition and a loss.

What makes the case of "The Brothers" even more intriguing a poem in terms of Wordsworth's representation of competing economies (the propertied shepherd's primitive counting versus the mariner's double-entry *accounting*, which turns the former's surplus into dearth) than "The Last of the Flock" is the fact that what Leonard counts and subtracts is *land*. Leonard's observation that "the dead man's home / Is but a fellow to that pasture field" (170–1) is perhaps the crucial line of the poem, for this equivalence brings into play the thematic of kinship (the field and churchyard are "fellows") as well as the thematic of vagrancy and destitution, since the churchyard is the *only* home of the dead man (James), once the Ewbanks have lost their property. Wordsworth writes in the *Essay on Epitaphs* that a churchyard placed by the side of a footpath, as the Ennerdale churchyard is, will often evoke "lively and affecting analogies of life as a journey – death as a sleep overcoming the tired wayfarer – of misfortune as a storm that falls suddenly upon him" (*PW* v.448). In "The Brothers," these are not analogies: the shepherd James is a dromomaniac (sleepwalker) whose penchant for wandering leads finally to his sudden "fall" and death. The activation or realization of these analogies, I would suggest, is a consequence of the transformation of property into circulating capital. There is no place left.

The wandering of both brothers contributes to an indifferentiation of the land – indeed, of the entire world, since the "calenture" induced by mobility makes land and sea indistinguishable as well. But that wandering is itself the product of the money-form, or, more precisely, the transformation of land into a unit of account. Prior to the series of bonds and mortgages which burden the Ewbank land, it seems that what the Priest now points to as "those few green fields" (205) had been under cultivation; the Priest refers to the family debt as "other burdens [on the land] than the crop it bore" (210). Of course, it is impossible to determine from the poem the relative proportion obtaining between tillage and pasture on the Ewbank estate, but our inability to differentiate between the two, captured in the vague designation "fields," may be precisely the point. For there is a third kind of calenture represented in the poem. Wordsworth emphasizes the distinctive feature of the Ennerdale churchyard: the absence of monuments. The fact that the churchyard is indistinguishable, *except symbolically*, from any "pasture field" (171), as

Leonard puts it, helps us to situate the poem within the context of the money-form of land, its deterritorialization.

Land, frequently defined as "immobile property" and classified as a part of "fixed" capital, seems the most unlikely of commodities (indeed, as Marx points out, land appears generally as a commodity-form only in the seventeenth century [*C* 92]); thus it should not surprise us if the same land changes its character (i.e., its topography or geography) in this new arrangement. We have earlier cited both Eden and Marx on the nature of this change; a classic modern history ratifies Marx's representation of the transformation of arable land into "sheepwalks": "During the first two-thirds of the eighteenth century the reduction in the number of small holdings was followed, as in the days of the Tudors, by the extension of pasture land" (Mantoux, 173).[27] In a way, the perception of land as an exchange-value entails not only a change of character but indeed a *loss* of character, that characteristic *anonymity* of money, according to Simmel.

In his historical account of this transformation, Marx refers specifically to the French *assignat*, that paper security drawn on church lands nationalized (and desacralized) by the Revolutionary government. To indicate how the *economic* revolution enacted by the Constituent Assembly might have been as much of concern to Wordsworth as the *political* revolution more generally acknowledged as a crucial influence on his literary project, we need only recall Burke's representation of the *assignat* as a kind of "negative faith":

These gentlemen perhaps do not believe a great deal in the miracles of piety; but it cannot be questioned, they have an undoubting faith in the prodigies of sacrilege. Is there a debt which presses them – issue *assignats* ... Are the old *assignats* depreciated at the market? What is the remedy? Issue new *assignats*. (251–2)

The *assignat* is the third term, "neither the one nor the other," that effects an equivalence between land (negative debt) and the national debt (negative capital). But it is also, according to Burke, a means of beggaring the nation.

Although it is a "churchyard" only in a metaphoric sense that the French Revolutionaries turn to "pasture" when they confiscate church property as the basis for the *assignat*, Burke's attitude toward their depredations may not unreasonably be compared to the disdain that the Priest of Ennerdale reserves for the tourist, who represents the loss of neighborhood. And indeed, the dramatic conversation of "The Brothers" is staged as a debate between Leonard (the mariner/speculator) and the Priest (e.g., pastor, shepherd) of Ennerdale over the stability of land value, its trustworthiness as a sylvan historian.

Our judgment of their debate is affected by the apparent obtuseness of the Priest. Since Leonard, the apparent "stranger" (so called, and so misrecognized, by the Priest) must point out the changes wrought in the surrounding landscape, the Priest's unreliable memory undercuts his preference for "these vallies" (164) over the inscriptions of historians or stonecutters. Leonard's repressed capacity to perceive change has been finely honed by his experience of "trade": he not only registers changes in the landscape but also tends to perceive those changes as loss.

> I remember,
> For many years ago I pass'd this road,
> There was a foot-way all along the fields
> By the brook-side – 'tis gone – and that dark cleft!
> To me it does not wear the face
> Which then it had.                               (128–33)[28]

The Priest's response to the latter observation – "for aught I know, / That chasm is much the same" (133–4) – reinforces the poetic pattern, observed elsewhere in *Lyrical Ballads*, that places subtraction and equation in apposition. Imagining a change wrought on the face of a chasm, we are placed in the position of Leonard regarding another grave: alteration means hollowing, loss. But the cleft remains a cleft, or chasm – hence, "the same."

Even as the past and present of the chasm are rendered "much the same" by equivalent negation, so it is the *absence* of a tombstone (that "house" of the dead) or shepherd's cottage that produces the most important equivalence in the poem, between the churchyard and the pasture, those "fellow" fields. When Leonard suggests that the unmarked churchyard implies Ennerdale is "heedless of the past" (166), the Priest responds for the inhabitants of Ennerdale, raised in the shadow of mountains, that "*we* want / No symbols" (179). The priest contends that no engraving is necessary to ensure the legibility of what is a "plain tale" to those in the immediate neighborhood, but ironically, it is the very plainness of the churchyard's tale that renders it the equivalent of the pasture field. Hence its plainness is no protection against the "speculations" of tourists or economic agents.

The economic problem under implicit consideration – how to *count* "another grave", whether it represents negative capital or negative debt – is made to correspond, in the poem, with this disputation concerning change in the landscape. Leonard's observation that " the dead man's home / Is but a fellow to that pasture field " (170–1) is the central image of brotherhood in the poem, I contend, because unlike the "brother fountains" usually taken as marking the place of James and Leonard in the landscape, the correspondence between churchyard and pasture registers James' death not as a permanent loss but as a kind of deferred balancing. The difference between the two economies of memory is effectively marked by a classic Italian textbook describing the advantages of double-entry bookkeeping as a memorial. The double-entry form

not only preserve[s] and keep[s] in memory all transactions, but they are also a means to avoid many litigations, quarrels, and scandals. And they also cause literate men to live thousands upon thousands of years...And undoubtedly, a merchant must not rely upon memory, for such reliance has caused many persons to err. (Carruthers and Espelande, 44)

Now, both the Priest and Leonard seem subject to errors of recollection: to the Priest, the chasm at first appears "the same" (that is, he fails to register a loss); to Leonard, the graveyard at first appears different ("another grave" is added). The advantage of the double-entry mode of accounting adopted by "The Brothers" will be a balancing of loss and gain, the transformation of loss into negative capital and of gain into negative debt. In both cases, a psychic pain will be deferred by the speculative gaze.

In addition, as I have indicated, the correlation Leonard posits between pasture and churchyard places the family narrative in the larger context of economic and political revolution represented by the *assignat.* It is this context, perhaps, that Wordsworth means to invoke when the Priest responds to Leonard's observation about the identity between pasture and churchyard: "Why, there, Sir, is a thought that's new to me" (172). We might ask ourselves: why should the metaphoric equivalence between a churchyard and a pasture be "new" to the Priest? After all, the Christian church has traditionally represented itself by means of a pastoral rhetoric. Here again the Priest appears vaguely obtuse, misrecognizing his own (symbolic) identity as shepherd/pastor.

This misrecognition appears to occur because of the very proximity of the *actual* pasture, deictically indicated by Leonard: "that pasture field." In the "immediate neighbourhood" of the real (recall Coleridge's criticism of Wordsworth's "matter-of-factness"), the "illusion" of metaphor ceases to operate, and the prevailing difference between the field devoted to profit and the churchyard consecrated to community reemerges. Hence, perhaps, the Priest's specifically economic observation on the "truth" of Leonard's comparison: "The stone-cutters, 'tis true, might beg their bread / If every English church-yard were like ours" (173–4). It is as if the Priest has intuitively registered the relation between enclosure or engrossment and the increase of vagrancy; when the land is not inscribed, either by furrows or tombstones, its former inhabitants are rendered homeless. Or, in Leonard's more exact rendering, they find a home only in the grave – "the dead man's home."

James Turner writes of an earlier era, where – according to Coleridge – the gradual desynonymization of property and propriety occurred:

"Land" and "place" are equivalent to "propriety" – meaning in seventeenth-century English both *property* and *knowing one's place*... Place is identity. Things out of place are not properly themselves, and move as living forces toward their natural home. (5–6)

In Wordsworth's poem, property and propriety "grow double" – in this case, become distinct – because the self is "left alone" (334) without a place. "Knowing one's place" is an achievement of which neither the mariner nor the shepherd, neither the passerby nor the resident, appears capable any longer. As Leonard has difficulty locating his brother, so the Priest cannot identify Leonard, despite numerous clues afforded by Leonard's anxious interjections. Finally, the knowledge offered by "The Brothers" is that one *has* no place.

### Vagrancy: the "brother" of capital

Although the Priest imagines stonecutters beggared by the "doubling" of pasture, it is James – the brother "left alone" – who most notably feels the impact of the interest and mortgages that overwrite and override the Ewbank claim to a place. Forced to sell the estate, Leonard leaves; but his transient existence is largely invisible, as is suggested by the fact that Priest and villagers believe he has died, or is languishing in slavery. It is James's homelessness that becomes most immediately visible – this despite the characteristically

Wordsworthian arithmetic by which the Priest reckons James's
estate: "If he had one, the Lad had twenty homes" (383). As he had
claimed that the Ennerdale inhabitants "want no symbols," the
Priest claims that James "wanted neither food, nor clothes, nor love"
(341), and there is no reason to dispute his claim. The *speculative*
moment, the subjunctive construction, arises only in relation to the
question of shelter – of home, or place. For even by the Priest's own
logic, James is rendered homeless: since he has *not* one home, but *none*,
then he has not twenty either. Double nothing is not twenty, but
nothing.

James's condition, then, appears to be precisely that of having no
place, but being instead a placeholder – a naught, a mark of absence.
Only with the onset of his homelessness does he become a dromomaniac:

> And, when he liv'd beneath our roof, we found
> (A practice till that time unknown to him)
> That often, rising from his bed at night,
> He in his sleep would walk about.                    (345–8)

Wordsworth suggests that sleepwalking is an etherealization of the
shepherd's activity (and thus a type of Marx's "wandering through
the world") by representing James's accidental death. Accompanying other shepherds, James lingers behind as they proceed on
"further business" (356). The local "conjecture" is that he fell asleep
and walked in his sleep off a precipice. Identifying for Leonard the
place of his death, the Priest describes a spot "that looks like one vast
building made of many crags" (359–60), as if to suggest the way in
which the "illusion" or negative faith of metaphor and the
consciousness of the sleepwalker are to be related, for certainly we
imagine James, in the "calenture" of dreaming, transforming the
abyss into more pasture, as the Priest has transformed the rocks into
a building. In addition, James's sleepwalking appears to reinforce the
identification of the brothers as "kindred": sleepwalking occurs
when one is "asea" in acres of the English countryside, and James's
death is the consequence of a kind of calenture on solid ground.

The aftermath of James's death appears to return us to a strictly
pastoral economy; as if in imitation of the parable of the good
shepherd, the Ennerdale inhabitants go and search for James once he
is discovered to be missing. This discovery is itself an accident,
however; his companions had assumed his return, and only a chance

visit to "the house / Which at this time was James's home" (370–1) reveals the fact that he is missing. Few missing-persons reports are filed for the homeless, after all – both because their displacement is regarded as more or less permanent and therefore hardly "news," and because few if any know where they are supposed to be.

Another factor also contributes to a sense that Ennerdale is no longer a "place" entirely distinguishable from an England opened to the two hemispheres, in Burke's phrase, by trade. Let us say that the Priest is well aware of the social conditions everywhere contributing to the increasing displacement of his "flock," the rural population, as his reflection on the condition of stonecutters and his opinion that Leonard will not return, despite his promise to that effect, would seem to indicate. His act of "prevenient burial" to the latter loss is to give Leonard a Bible, as if, now that the land can no longer provide a stable place, the book must take up its former function of identification. At least that is the implication when the Priest reports that

> The very night before he went away,
> In my own house I put into his hand
> A Bible, and I'd wager twenty pounds,
> That, if he is alive, he has it yet.           (281–4)

This donation of Bibles is, apparently, the "new" way in which the pastor tends his flock; therefore, we expect that by the end of the poem a recognition will have been effected by Leonard's possession of this book, since there seems to be little other reason for the inclusion of this narrative detail. Contrary to such expectations, however, Leonard goes away unrecognized, and identifies himself only subsequently, by correspondence. This contravening of expectations suggests that we should focus more critically on the nature of the Priest's speculation concerning Leonard's property. Is it not similar in kind to his "speculation" on the number of James's homes?

The Priest's willingness to "wager" twenty pounds (the amount exactly duplicates the number of homes which, according to the Priest's multiplication of nothing, accrue to James in his destitute condition) seems vaguely sacrilegious, a "trading" on the value of the good book not unlike Marx's example in *Capital* of the exchange of a Bible for brandy. In addition, it is an act reminiscent of the Revolutionary "speculation" on the value of church property. Though the Priest expresses his conviction that family property and local attachment are of paramount (sacred) value to Leonard (as he has good reason to believe; even as a youth, Leonard has taken unusual care of his books [see 259–67]), the means he chooses to express that conviction suggests that he himself values the book as a commodity. Perhaps more important, the Priest evidently regards money – that abstraction of the commodity-form – not as a means by which to acquire commodities with a particular use-value (C–M–C) but as a means by which to reproduce or to multiply money (M–C–M). At best, the twenty pounds is an arbitrary sign of his conviction, as, implicitly, the possession of a Bible would be of Leonard's "faith." In this context, the fact that no Bible makes its appearance suggests the extent to which Wordsworth writes "The Brothers" as a parable of "negative faith."

In a section of *The Philosophy of Money* entitled "Money's congruence with those who are marginal," Simmel writes that "the contrast that existed between the native and the stranger has been eliminated, because the money form of transactions has now been taken up by the whole economic community" (227). It is in the context of this observation, which Simmel supports by a report of "advice I once overheard" (227) – not to have financial dealings with friends or enemies – that I believe we must place the double representation Wordsworth offers us in "The Brothers."[29] Once James is dead and gone, Leonard becomes, as it were, his own double – he is *both* native and stranger, made equivalent by the precedence of a money economy. The Priest, who within an old order might have represented the point of greatest resistance to that precedence through his association with church property, has already symbolically converted church property into "twenty pounds," a fraction of the universal equivalent. Simmel explains the peculiar value and often *religious* significance attached until the modern era to land:

One might say that landed property had no equivalent; the sequence of values in which it stood terminated with landed property. Whereas movable objects might be exchanged against one another, immobile property was – *cum grano salis* – something incomparable: it was value as such, the immovable ground above and beyond which real economic value was carried on…The inalienability of the Church's landed property was only the conscious and legal character of this inner character. It demonstrated that the movement of values terminated here and that the ultimate limit and finality of the economic sphere had been attained. (241)

Simmel's description of the "inner character" of land value suggests why Wordsworth, confronted with historical evidence that the apparent foundation of value, the churchyard, could indeed be alienated by economic and political revolutions, would seek to relocate that "inner character" in poetic value. "The Brothers" renders sea and land, pasture and churchyard, equivalent, and so establishes a metaphorical or literary "ground" capable of representing once again "a certain dignity which distinguishes it from all other kinds of possession." This transformation of the stable "ground" of value into the relative "ground rent" of the poem – the shift in focus, in other words, from its content to its form, the latter assuring at least a *methodological* consistency – comes at a cost, however. Poetic value is conditioned by loss; the Bible is no longer read literally, as it were (for *we* have great need of symbols).

### *"Goody Blake and Harry Gill": property and tautology*

Coleridge too will make a case that the value accruing to church property is no longer sacred and permanent but metaphorical and essentially *mobile*. Indeed, Coleridge quotes *Job* to suggest that symbolic value is now embodied in the parish clergyman:

That to every parish throughout the kingdom there is transplanted a germ of civilization... this it is which the patriot and the philanthropist cannot estimate at too high a price. "It cannot be valued with the gold of Ophir, with the precious onyx, or the sapphire. No mention shall be made of coral, or of pearls: for the price of wisdom is above rubies." (*BL* 129–30)

Coleridge's effusion is complicated by the fact that he has apparently a strictly economic issue in mind: what can the literary man (he does not consider the case of the woman writer) do to earn a living? Having taken as his motto the advice "*never pursue literature as a trade*" (*BL* 127), Coleridge considers the role of clergyman as the appropriate occupation of the poet: "Still the church presents to every man of learning and genius a profession in which he may... unite the widest schemes of literary utility with the strictest performance of professional duties" (*BL* 129). He imagines, for example, the clergyman writing a history of the Bible: "to give the history of the Bible as a book would be little less than to relate the origin and first excitement of all the literature and science that we now possess" (*BL* 131).

   If we consider more carefully the source of the clergyman's living, of his independence, we must acknowledge a peculiar effect of the fact that in England, the church was strictly a state institution, and tithing a form of taxation with a different name. Coleridge explicitly imagines church property as a kind of *national* wealth, a negative debt produced by the aggregation of so much "negative capital" or taxation of profits:

revenues of the church are in some sort the reversionary property of every family that may have a member educated for the church or a daughter that may marry a clergyman. Instead of being foreclosed and immovable, it is in fact the only *species* of landed property that is essentially moving and circulative. (*BL* 130)

Thus church property, which affords the clergyman an independence necessary for the production of literature, is imagined as a kind of national trust. Coleridge particularly criticizes the objections made by farmers to tithing:

among the instances of the blindness, or at best the shortsightedness which it is the nature of cupidity to inflict, I know few more striking than the clamours of farmers against church property. Whatever was not paid to the clergyman would inevitably be paid at the next lease to the landholder. (*ibid.*)

Indeed, it is often the case that Coleridge will criticize farmers as those particularly myopic in relation to large-scale capital enterprise, and the ideas implicit in negative capital and negative debt. For Coleridge, in other words, the farmer represents the economy of mere *addition* that Wordsworth associates with the primitive (not yet dispossessed) shepherd. When criticizing Wordsworth's matter-of-factness in *Lyrical Ballads* and the contention in Wordsworth's 1800 Preface that the sentiments and expressions of the poems are derived from – according to Coleridge – "occupations and abode," or "low and rustic life" (*BL* 190), he will use farmers as an example of "rustics" singularly unenlightened by their occupation and abode. Where such enlightenment occurs in rural communities, Coleridge argues, it is less the proximity to mountains than to a few books (particularly the Bible) that affords the inhabitants of such regions the "vantage-ground" (*BL* 191) necessary for an elevated appreciation of rural life. His negative proof is the case of the *farmer* without such an education:

Let the management of the Poor Laws in Liverpool, Manchester, or Bristol be compared with the ordinary dispensation of the poor rates in agricultural villages, where the farmers are the overseers and guardians of the poor. If my own experience has not been particularly unfortunate...the result would engender more than scepticism concerning the desirable influences of low and rustic life in and for itself. (*ibid.*)

Here again farmers are deplored, primarily for an apparent unwillingness to tax themselves, or to recognize the concept of a communal wealth, whether in the "negative debt" sense of "church" land held in a kind of national trust or in the "negative capital" sense from which poor laws largely derive: a recognition that poverty is often a local effect of measures taken to increase the gross national product.

Coleridge imagines the mobile and classically or liberally educated subject as the antithesis of the "narrow" view connected with the largely sedentary condition of the landed farmer; as I have suggested, this is to imply that liberal education consists of acquaintance with *many* rather than few books. Indeed, *acquaintance* seems to characterize the kind of knowledge of which the liberally educated subject – paradigmatically the transplanted "vicar" – seems possessed: "a neighbour and a family man whose education and rank admit him to the mansion of the rich landholder, while his duties make him the frequent visitor of the farm-house and the cottage" (*BL* 130). In a similar vein, the narrators of many of Wordsworth's *Lyrical Ballads* will seem to have easy access to the different classes of society, but Wordsworth usually suggests that the observer is at most a visitor, and a "neighbour" only in a loosely metaphorical (also democratic) sense.

This is paradigmatically the case with "Goody Blake and Harry Gill." One of my purposes here is to explain the relevance and resonance of the moralizing lines with which the poem concludes: Now think, ye farmers all, I pray, / Of Goody Blake and Harry Gill" (126–7). But as we attempt to identify the "class-characteristics" (Coleridge's phrase; *BL* 192 n.) of the speaking subject, "I," and the designated audience – all farmers – the first relevant information is provided for us in the poem's italicized subtitle, "A True Story." This subtitle appears brilliantly to illuminate the project of *Lyrical Ballads*, and seems especially appropriate as the subtitle for a poem which works to unite in a single lyric the supernatural naturalism and natural supernaturalism according to which Wordsworth and Coleridge claimed to have divided their labors. As distinguished from the immediate neighborhood of fact, the story may be true according to two logics: first, that it indisputably occurred (i.e., is *literally* true);

second, that it has a poetic *power* – that it operates, in Coleridge's phrase, as a "poetic analogon of faith" (*BL* 257), or in Wordsworth's, that it possesses a "general and operative" truth, and is "its own testimony." As if to engage both logics, Wordsworth calls special attention to the poem and its subtitle in the 1798 Advertisement and the 1800 Preface, writing that "The tale of Goody Blake and Harry Gill is founded on a well-authenticated fact which happened in Warwickshire" (*LB*, 4). Different from the plain fact, the *authenticated* fact is certified by writing. As Marjorie Levinson comments, "Almost every edition of Macpherson's and Chatterton's work was prefaced with essays intended to validate or discredit the historical authenticity of the poems" (*Romantic Fragment Poem* 37). Though the assurance that "Goody Blake and Harry Gill" is based on an authentic fact seems to distinguish the poem from fiction, the apparent necessity of authentication suggests an increased distance from the fact, since a number of mediations have been required for its authentication.

What exactly *is* the source of authentication? As many editors and critics have pointed out, Wordsworth appears to derive his material for the poem from Erasmus Darwin's *Zoonomia*. Owen usefully reprints the relevant passage:

I received good information of the truth of the following case, which was published a few years ago in the newspapers. A young *farmer* in Warwickshire, finding his hedges broke, and the sticks carried away during a frosty season, determined to watch for the thief. He lay many cold hours under a hay-stack, and at length an old woman, like a witch in a play, approached, and began to pull up the hedge; he waited till she had tied up her bottle of sticks, and was carrying them off, that he might convict her of the theft, and then springing from his concealment, he seized his prey with violent threats. After some altercation, in which her load was left upon the ground, she kneeled upon her bottle of sticks, and raising her arms to Heaven beneath the bright moon then at the full, spoke to the farmer already shivering with cold, "Heaven grant, that thou never mayest know again the blessing to be warm." He complained of cold all the next day, and wore an upper coat, and in a few days another, and in a fortnight took to his bed, always saying nothing made him warm, he covered himself with very many blankets, and had a sieve over his face, as he lay; and from this one insane idea he kept his bed above twenty years for fear of the cold air, till at length he died. (*LB*, 132; emphasis mine)

Thus Wordsworth's "well-authenticated fact" appears as a species of what Paine in the *Age of Reason* described as "second-hand rev-elation": for Wordsworth, the story is "authenticated" by its appearance in a published text (with some scientific authority, although the author of *Zoonomia* also authored poems like "The Botanic Garden" and therefore occupied an unstable place between literature and science, "negative faith" and fact). But Darwin has not witnessed the event himself; the story is authenticated for him by an unidentified, and therefore unimpeachable, authority. Notice how the *economy* of authentication assumes a loss of neighborhood, or immediate proximity, to the event or to the original report; but also how access to *books* (Wordsworth borrowed Darwin's book from the eventual publisher of *Lyrical Ballads*, Joseph Cottle) increases the range of one's knowledge (and also one's authority, the property which enables one to authenticate). The speaking "I" of the poem is purposefully distinguished by Wordsworth from the "neighbours" ("The neighbours tell, and tell you truly" [11]). And if he need not be imagined as the retired captain of a small trading vessel, he nonetheless is associated with mobility, having known, presumably elsewhere, of "*Two* poor old dames" (34) in a situation similar to Goody Blake's, and testifying to only perhaps a stranger's familiarity with his subject and her condition: "*Any* man who passed her door, / Might see how poor a hut she had" (23–4; emphasis mine).

As to the question of audience, the problem may be posed as follows: why does Wordsworth address himself to *farmers*? Few critics in their discussion of the poem reproduce Darwin's account, because they appear to suppose that the account offered by the poem is largely identical. And so it is; with one notable exception.[30] In Darwin's account, "Harry Gill" is a Warwickshire *farmer*; in Wordsworth's he is a *drover*. Why, in addressing farmers, does Wordsworth seek to give Harry Gill a different occupation? In one sense, I suppose we may conclude that the shift is explained as a retreat from attacking farmers outright, from representing them – through Harry Gill – as unneighborly and miserly. But this still does not entirely account for Wordsworth's decision to cast him as a *drover*, which the *OED* defines as "a dealer, trafficker"; "one who drives droves of cattle, sheep, etc., esp. to distant markets." In light of the conflict already outlined between tillage and pasture, Wordsworth's identification of Harry Gill as a *drover* is more than a deflection of criticism away from the farmer; insofar as the drover is the economic antagonist of the farmer, to criticize the drover as closefisted will hardly encourage self-criticism in farmers. In fact, allusion to the economic antagonism between farmers and drovers is important to

the logic of *being* that the poem expresses: even as "farmer" and
"drover" become purely differential identities (A = A'), so *being* will
be the sum of what one *has not*.

The identification of Harry Gill as a drover is important for other
reasons as well. First, it establishes a coherent general economy:
Harry Gill is a dealer in sheep, and Goody Blake is a spinner
(presumably, of wool). Since spinning is a part of the textile industry
in closer proximity to the final product of woollen cloth, one might be
surprised that it is Goody Blake who is "ill clad" and Harry Gill who
has various kinds of woollen clothing, including "good duffel grey
and flannel fine" (6). That we are *not* surprised that the spinner has
less clothing than the trader only indicates the extent to which we
have *abstracted* the value of human labor. The distinction implicitly
posited between the two "rural" occupations of spinner and drover
is evacuated by that general economy: all labor, and all products of
labor, are subject to exchange; as money disables the distinction
between native and stranger, so it makes possible the event that a
spinner might have no wool, or wear woollen cloth manufactured in
another region. The address to the farmer cannot stand apart from
this context, for precisely in question in enclosure movements was the
fate of rights of common such as that exercised by Goody Blake when,
after a storm, she gathers "lusty splinter[s]" and "rotten bough[s]":
it was a kind of *gleaning* related to the "common of *estovers*," or the
right of local inhabitants to cut wood if trees grew on a common
(Mantoux, 148–9). As a "liberty of taking *necessary* wood" (Blackstone ii,iii, 27), the common of estovers appears to be based upon a
superseded economy, which determined property in relation to use-
value.[31]

The identification of Harry Gill as a drover, despite evidence that
his property includes tillage (he stands behind a "rick of barley" [73]
and the moon shines on a harvested "stubble-land" [76]), also helps
to explain the central paradox explored in the poem – that Harry has
no negative capital: "Of waistcoats Harry has no lack" (5). "No
lack" here is a version of that mathematical conundrum we have
been examining, the "cost" and profit of the commodity-form. To
have a certain number of clothes is to have "wealth" in one respect;
but Wordsworth's inverted formula, which identifies Harry Gill's
property as consisting of a double-negative, produces an equivalence
between surplus and nothing. Of course "no lack" is not exactly the
same as "no *thing*," but it does correspond to Coleridge's description

of capital as negative debt. Thus we can see at work in Wordsworth's curious way of representing Harry Gill's property the rhetoric of the double-entry. On the one hand, the reduction of Harry's property to the formula of the double-negative – the representation, in other words, of capital as "negative debt" – answers the purpose of legitimating commerce, hiding evidence of possible usury; Carruthers and Espelande comment that according to the moral law of the church, "a just transaction was one characterized by equality of exchange" (38). On the other, it has the effect of dematerializing, or etherealizing, property, transforming Harry's surplus from a series of items into a version of Coleridge's (and Wordsworth's) representation of the literary as a value *beyond* measure.

Moreover, the double-negative corresponds with the double-interrogative with which the poem opens: "Oh! what's the matter? what's the matter?" (1), where repetition, this time apparently of a positive content (matter), has the effect of transforming that content, making it mean metaphorically. One might inflect these two identical questions each in a different way. First, in a paraphrase offered in the second line, what is *wrong* with Harry Gill? What "ails" him? Second, in light of the fact that his ailment is psychosomatic: what is the nature of matter? The effect of this "double-entry" is to ambiguate "matter," to define it as loosely, perhaps, as is possible: matter is "no lack."

The insistent rhyming of matter with "chatter" suggests that a particular kind of matter is at stake in the poem. The joining of matter and chatter redirects our attention back to the subtitle: a true story. In what way does chatter – story, or discourse – alter "matter," the stuff of fact and truth? Is chatter – discourse reduced to its "material" form – the zero-sum of "no lack"? If so, does it perform a similar "balancing" of the transcendental surplus and the empirical deficit? Property is, of course, only matter with a hedge surrounding it; in this light, the "trespass" of Goody Blake calls attention to the discursive construction of property.

Justification for describing Harry Gill's property by a double-negative comes near the conclusion of the story, where Wordsworth's narrator reports that Harry's acquisition of coats and blankets "was all in vain, a useless matter" (113). The fact that the coats do not keep Harry warm suggests that his property has been abstracted (by poetic fiat, the "truth" that is the discursive equivalent of the psychosomatic symptom) to pure exchange-value – *useless* matter.

Goody Blake's "curse" is also an economic mirroring; in the same
way that the products of her spinning cannot keep her warm, because
she must exchange them for wages – wages apparently so meager
that they do not even "pay" (a crucial verb, exposing the economy
in operation) for candlelight – so Harry's surplus affords him no
comfort, and does him no good. This surplus is represented not only
by the *numbering* of waistcoats (always essential, as we have seen, to
Wordsworth's representation of abstraction), but also by Harry's
attitude toward the hedge. Although the waistcoat has a certain use-
value, it is primarily an item of fashion, a sign worn by the man of
property.[32] So too the hedge; it has a certain value in protecting fields
from natural and human depredations, but only the poor tended to
regard the hedge, like clothing, as a source of warmth. For property-
owners like Harry Gill, it tends to represent the exclusionary *principle*
of property; clearly the exercise of a right of common in this case does
not damage Harry's estate *materially*, but rather symbolically. Those
prosecuting similar acts of alleged trespass often invoked the danger
of creating a precedent (a "first step"; also a trespass – *le pas au-delà*)
that appeared to dilute the absolute right of property. For them, good
hedges made good neighbors. In Wordsworth's poem, by contrast,
two acts of trespass are represented: Goody Blake's against the
material property of Harry Gill, and Harry Gill's against what Alan
Bewell calls the "law of charity" (156).

When Wordsworth uses the word "trespass" to describe the crime
– "Now Harry he had long suspected / This trespass of old Goody
Blake" (65–6) – he invokes a specifically legal discourse. Trespass
describes every violation of a law, although in the development of the
English legal tradition, it tended to be confined in application to the
*private* sphere; crimes against the state, like treason, were rarely if ever
called trespasses. But "trespass" also figures in religious discourse,
where the idea of Christian *neighborhood* negates the criminality of
trespass: "Forgive us our trespasses, as we forgive those who trespass
against us." *Both* of these trajectories of trespass – legal and religious,
positive and negative – are at work in "Goody Blake and Harry
Gill," in yet another balancing act.

These days, the word "trespass" will conjure an image immediately relevant to the poem: the "No Trespassing" sign. By a
process of what we may call desynonymy, trespass in legal and
religious discourse has a general meaning – transgression – that
appears only metaphorically related to "trespass" as it circulates in

the vernacular. There, it tends to evoke a specific *kind* of transgression, just such an incident as that narrated in the poem: the pedestrian violation of a property boundary.

The fact that trespass describes a far more extensive range of legal violations suggests that this image – and the corresponding incident narrated in the poem – has a peculiarly symbolic value. Even in legal definitions of trespass, the pedestrian violation is accorded an exemplary status. Consider Blackstone's classic definition in the *Commentaries*:

> In the limited and confined sense...it signifies no more than an entry on another man's ground without a lawful authority, and doing some damage, *however inconsiderable*, to his real property. Every unwarrantable entry on another's soil the law entitles a trespass by breaking his close. (III.xii, 209; emphasis mine)

"Breaking his close," in this context, need not entail the *literal* breaking (of the hedge) that we see Goody Blake perform. By 1817, at least, the law would regard enclosure as an intrinsic feature of landed property:

> The land of every owner or occupier is enclosed and set apart from that of his neighbour, whether by a visible and tangible fence...or by an ideal invisible boundary...Hence every unwarrantable entry upon the land of another is termed a trespass by breaking his close. (Selwyn, II.1216).

This latter registering of a property maintained by an "invisible" boundary is only a playing-out of Blackstone's inclusion (which I have italicized) of damage "however inconsiderable"; by 1765, a judicial decision destined to become an important precedent held that

> The great end, for which men entered into society, was to secure their property. That right is preserved sacred and incommunicable in all instances, where it has not been taken away or abridged by some public law for the good of the whole. By the laws of England, every invasion of private property, *be it ever so minute*, is a trespass. No man can set his foot upon my ground without my license, but he is liable to an action, *though the damage be nothing*; which is proved by every declaration in trespass, where the defendant is called upon to answer for bruising the grass and even treading upon the soil. (*Entick* v. *Carrington*, 137; emphases mine)

In this frequently cited decision, we notice two peculiar features: first, the political theory with which the legal decision is now imbued, suggesting the emergence of a specifically liberal ideology; second, the detail with which the trespass over a possibly imaginary boundary is represented – the bent blade of grass, the merest footprint being, potentially, evidence of an actionable offense. It is as if the increasingly abstract principles upon which property is defined necessitate a recursion to the sensuous, tangible, *literary* sign of its existence.

There is a third feature of the language of the decision worth noticing, however, because it is a feature consistently present in the legal discourse of rights. Despite the obvious aim of the judge to uphold property as an absolute right, he nonetheless acknowledges certain conditions limiting its sway: "where it has not been taken away or abridged by some public law for the good of the whole." As soon as we enlarge our concept of private property, directing our attention away from the captivating image of the "real" estate (its reality, we should note, is partly a consequence of the fact that one can *measure* it) toward the full complement of goods and chattel by which private property is generally defined (for example: nine waistcoats, three riding-coats, and sundry blankets; also, perhaps, fifty sheep, or the profits accruing from their sale) then we can read in the *Entick* v. *Carrington* decision a justification of taxation – a subtraction or abridgement of exclusively private property rights for the good of the whole.

Let us return, with this legal context established, to "Goody Blake and Harry Gill." The poem appears to represent the social polarization of having and being described in "The Female Vagrant" ("Oh! dreadful *price* of being to resign / All that is dear in being" [118–19; emphasis mine]). Like other "borderers" interrogated by the passerby in *Lyrical Ballads*, Goody Blake has a distinguishing characteristic: she is alone. Emphatic solitude increases the effectiveness with which Wordsworth is able to convey impoverishment, as in "Simon Lee," where repeating the same initial phrase, "no man," implicitly reinforces a sense that Simon is "the poorest of the poor" (60), for Wordsworth has eliminated all possible objects of comparison. If such figures achieve a slightly supernatural or symbolic agency, at the same time their otherworldliness tends to derive from the fact that they have no "place" – or the poorest of places, in Goody Blake's case.

The rich "being" such figures achieve thus comes at the expense of all capacities of possession, sometimes even of the body: Simon Lee has only one eye and Goody Blake a withered arm. By contrast, conventional wealth confers no such richness: the poem wonders aloud whether there is any "matter" (or substantial value) to Harry Gill, as it will later total up the exchange-value of Goody Blake's spinning: "Alas! 'twas hardly worth the telling" (27). To have no lack, therefore, is to have so exercised the power of possession that being appears to fall away; in fact, the falling away of being, or embodiment, is made quite literal by Wordsworth: "Harry's flesh it fell away" (117). The ruddiness and bodily warmth that at first distinguishes Harry from Goody Blake – he is "lusty" and "stout," suggesting a certain *surplus* of energy and flesh – has been alienated by a certain kind of telling, or (ac)*counting*. Now Harry's substance is an alienable clothing, his surplus of riding-coats and blankets working like the "poisoned vestments" Wordsworth describes in the *Essay on Epitaphs*. I quote the relevant passage in full because the context – that of language – is significant:

> If words be not... an incarnation of the thought, but only a clothing for it, then surely they will prove an ill gift; such a one as those poisoned vestments, read of in the stories of superstitious times, which had power to consume and alienate from his right mind the victim who put them on. (*PrW* II.85)

It is hard to believe that Wordsworth was not thinking of "Goody Blake and Harry Gill" when he wrote this sentence, since one of the pivotal lines of the poem – "and icy-cold he turned away" (104) – is in part a resurrection of a dead metaphor, that "clothing" of thought. Bewell has demonstrated the way in which Goody Blake is invested with qualities associated with witchcraft; Wordsworth's invocation of "superstitious times" in this manner converts one construal of "icy-cold" – a (dead) metaphor of unkindness – into another, literal or material construal: having waited so long to capture Goody Blake, Harry has caught his death of cold.[33]

The *sum* of the poem (notice the title has the form of a sum, an addition) is not merely the marriage of the natural and the supernatural, however. Rather, in Wordsworth's lyrical ballads the supernatural tends to be defined as a cultural form, but one that is economic rather than religious or spiritual in nature. If Wordsworth is among the first, he will not be the last, to represent the effects of that most "supernatural" of economic forms, capital, upon the "primitive encounter" (Bewell's phrase). After more than 600 pages of economic analysis, Marx in *Capital* returns to the scene of "so-called primitive accumulation":

In themselves money and commodities are no more capital than are the means of production and of subsistence. They want transforming into capital. But this transformation can only take place under certain circumstances...two very different kinds of commodity-possessors must come face to face and into contact; on the one hand, the owners of money, means of production, means of subsistence, who are eager to increase the sum of the values they possess...on the other hand, free labourers, the sellers of their own labor-power. (668)

Marx's point is that this face-to-face encounter is by no means "natural," between persons, but rather the result of an expropriation that negates all but economic agency:

The process, therefore, that clears the way for the capitalist system, can be none other than the process which takes away from the labourer the possession of his means of production; a process that transforms, on the one hand, the social means of subsistence and of production into capital, on the other, the immediate producers into wage-labourers. (*ibid.*)

Marx's already-cited description of these wage-laborers as those with "nothing to sell except their own skins" (667) is a description peculiarly relevant to a poem in which one character – the wage-laborer – has been reduced to skin and bones, but manages, via a "withered" arm, to render the man who wishes to seize this last of her means of production her mirror-image.

Of course, Goody Blake does not effect this transformation by means of her arm alone, nor is Wordsworth's poem merely an allegory of the forcible expropriation of the poor from neighborhoods to permit larger-scale agricultural enterprise and livestock accumulation. As I have tried to indicate, the poem is an exploration of the "sum" of this event, which the poem classifies as "useless matter." In an important way, this phrase identifies the poem itself as the sum of the encounter; "useless matter" is, after all, an apt description of the aesthetic. Moreover, the poem will associate uselessness with *repetition*, which, as we have seen, Wordsworth associates both with his characteristic poetic figure, tautology, and with verse. In the 1800 Preface, for example, he expands the commentary offered by the Advertisement on "Goody Blake and Harry Gill":

I might perhaps include all which it is *necessary* to say upon this subject by affirming what few persons will deny, that of two descriptions either of passions, manners, or characters, each of them equally well executed, the one in prose and the other in verse, the verse will be read a hundred times where the prose is read once... In consequence of these convictions I related in metre the Tale of GOODY BLAKE and HARRY GILL, which is one of the rudest of this collection. I wished to draw attention to the truth that the power of the human imagination is sufficient to produce such changes even in our physical nature as might almost appear miraculous. The truth is an important one; the fact (for it is a *fact*) is a valuable illustration of it. And I have the satisfaction of knowing that it has been communicated to many hundreds of people who would never have heard of it, had it not been narrated as a ballad, and in a more impressive metre than is usual in Ballads. (*LB*, 174)

Consider Wordsworth's contention about the poem, usually regarded primarily as a restatement of Darwin's argument that the incident illustrates *mania mutabilis*, or mistaking "imaginations for realities" (*LB*, 132), in light of the larger contention about the effect and value of meter. Having posed an equivalence between prose and verse – that is, equal skill – Wordsworth "proves" the greater value of the poem by reference to its greater use, its wider distribution. When he argues that the poem "has been communicated" to hundreds of people, he does not specify the means of its distribution, but subsequent reference to an audience that has "heard" of the ballad suggests that he means verse, particularly the "common meter" of the ballad-form, is susceptible of oral transmission or communication and therefore accessible to, for example, the illiterate or those without the means to buy *Lyrical Ballads*. Wordsworth's notorious early aversion to publishing – Susan Eilenberg has documented it well – might even be related to this valorization of the *oral* communication of poems.

Moreover, oral communication has everything to do with the poem's representation of the "useless matter" of the event narrated. The poem foregrounds a peculiar *kind* of oral communication – in fact *not* communication as we might normally describe it. After hearing Goody Blake's prayer/curse, Harry no longer talks to anyone but he is not silent either: "No word to any man he utters, / ... / But ever to himself he mutters" (121–3). The difference between uttering and muttering thus consists of another mathematic opposition: "no word," like "no lack," functions as a kind of double-negative (recall that Wordsworth in the "Essay, Supplementary" claims that the "poverty of language" gives meaning to the word "imagination"); in its wake emerges an endless flow, represented in the oxymoronic "chatter still." The rhyming of "chatter" with "matter" confirms one's sense that, in the poem, Wordsworth seeks to explore the physiological dimension of verse; indeed, in one line, the poem, like Harry's "speech," is reduced to what we might call the pure form of sound and rhythm: "Chatter, chatter, chatter still" (4). The question – is such repetition a "useless matter"? – is perhaps answered when we reflect that the "progressive" logic or incremental knowledge afforded by the feet of the ballad-refrain (its steps) mirrors what we learn of Harry Gill's perceptual faculties: "'Tis all the same with Harry Gill" (10, 14). Oddly, then, the sound- and rhythm-dominated quality of verse becomes the linguistic symptom of Harry Gill's economic proclivity for "trade," and his denigrated tendency to convert all use-value, including the hedge, into pure exchange-value, and finally, capital. Moreover, Wordsworth accomplishes a successful traversing of the distance between mental and physical by exhibiting that perceptual tendency in Harry's chattering, an effect at once of bodily temperature and "cold-heartedness."

### Chatter: literature as tautology

Somewhat ironically, perhaps, the Harry Gill who has "no lack" of clothes stands in close relation to the similarly literary fiction of the emperor with "no clothes." Even more ironically, he himself is the "chatterbox" who, like the child in Andersen's fairy tale, effectively reveals the central "lack" in symbolic power. Slavoj Zizek reminds us of the crucial role of the "chatterbox" (his term) in such an exposure; he argues that the boy who declares the lack, or the negation, "who with disarming innocence states the obvious," is "usually taken as an exemplar of the word which delivers us from stuffy hypocrisy and forces us to confront the actual state of things" (*KN*, 11). This exposure (and consequent "coldness"), as in Andersen's story, signals the breakdown of community, for community is based on illusion. In this light, Zizek suggests that

the time has come to abandon the usual praise of the child's gesture and rather conceive it as the prototype of the innocent chatterbox who – by blurting out what should remain unspoken if the existing intersubjective network is to retain its consistency – unknowingly and involuntarily sets off the catastrophe. (*KN*, 12)

But Zizek also makes us realize that the exposure performed by the chatterbox (or by "chatter") can only occur because the *form* of illusion upon which community rests is tautology. Goody Blake's prevenient mirroring of Harry Gill's eventual coldness ("her old bones were cold and chill") reverses the chronological relation between cause and effect *narrated* in the poem, even as it collapses the difference between them. The *logic* of the poem is that of tautology.

This understanding is crucial to reading the concluding moral that has been the object of our attention ("Now think, ye farmers all, I pray, / Of Goody Blake and Harry Gill"). My repeated contention that vagrancy determines not only the narrative content of *Lyrical Ballads* but also its form means that the implicit injunction to neighborliness will have been contaminated by the money-form that disables a spatial configuration of neighbors, or their differentiation from strangers. In fact, the last line of the poem, representing a "double-entry" of the title, suggests that Wordsworth redirects our attention to the poem itself; that is, we are directed to think of "Goody Blake and Harry Gill." This redirection (also a repetition) is yet another version of the poem's questioning of the nature of discursive "matter"; neighborhood has become entirely the product of an imaginary line. Only by so redirecting our attention do we manage to discover the intentional tautology as the central "matter" of the poem; the intentional tautology is the figure that, according to Zizek, lurks at the center of liberalism.

As I have argued, "Goody Blake and Harry Gill" is a poem about breaking the law, but *which* law (the law of property or the law of charity) has been broken, or which broken law represents a severer violation, remains in question. Also in question, we should recall, is the poem's initial interrogative: "What's the matter?" We learn, via the written representation of Harry's muttering, that "Poor Harry Gill is very cold" (124); this diagnosis, offered in the last stanza, must strike us as an anticlimax, or even a tautology. The implicit question – what has *made* him so cold that his teeth chatter? – is also answered only implicitly – first by the narrative, then by the oblique moral. But more importantly, it is answered within the formal dimension of the poem, for the repetition of chatter is what suggests that Harry's symptoms are not those of a *common* cold (or rather, are precisely those of the "coldness" induced by an entirely abstract notion of the "common"). Harry's disease is tautology, one might say.

In his chapter "On the One," Zizek implies that tautology is the best way to understand the model of analysis obtaining both in Hegel and in Marx – in other words, dialectic.[34] He takes as his example –

again an example relevant to "Goody Blake and Harry Gill" and its theme of transgression ("trespass" or *le pas au-delà*) – the statement "law is law," and suggests that the very tautological structure necessitates two readings:

The first law ("law is...") is the universal law insofar as it is abstractly opposed to crime, whereas the second law ("... law") reveals the concealed truth of the first: the obscene violence, the absolute, universalized crime as its hidden reverse. (We can sense this concealed dimension of violence already apropos of the everyday, "spontaneous" reading of "law is law" – is not this phrase usually evoked precisely when we are confronted with the "unfair," "incomprehensible" constraint that pertains to law?) (*KN*, 35)

To say "law is law" is at once to be a positivist and to perform a nominalist critique; to complain of the seemingly incontrovertible (because grammatical, logical) power that can confer legitimacy on whatever it names. Repetition gives to identity a problematic status; rather than reinforcing the self-evidence of identity, tautology evacuates the apparently positive term of its content. Hegel, Zizek's source for this analysis, gives another example which, even more than "Law is...law," displays the crucial role that the temporal structure of tautology – which represents, we might say, the "pure form" of the proposition, or truth-statement – plays in the subversion of identity:

If anyone open his mouth and promises to state what God is, namely God is – God, expectation is cheated for what was expected was a *different determination*... Looking more closely at this tedious effect produced by such truth, we see that the beginning, "The plant is – ", sets out to say *something*, to bring forward a further determination. But since only the same thing is repeated, the opposite has happened, *nothing* has emerged. Such *identical* talk therefore *contradicts itself*. Identity, instead of being in its own self truth and absolute truth, is consequently the very opposite; instead of being the unmoved simple, it is the passage beyond itself into the dissolution of itself. (Hegel, quoted from Zizek, *KN*, 35)

Recall that, in the 1798 Advertisement, Wordsworth contends that the major purpose of his experiment was to encourage readers to resist "pre-established codes of decision" (*LB*, 3); Hegel's analysis suggests why tautology might have become for Wordsworth a preeminent technique of that experiment. Hegel's foregrounding of expectation implicitly posits what Wordsworth's Advertisement makes explicit: the audience. As Zizek comments,

The effect of contradiction can take place only within the framework of a dialogical economy. The first part ("God is...") provokes in the interlocutor the *expectation* determined by the very form of the proposition (one *awaits* a predicate *different* from the subject, a specific determination of the divine universality: God is... omnipotent, infinitely good and wise, and so on.) The expectation thus provoked is then *disappointed* by the second part ("...God") in which the *same* term recurs. This dialogical economy therefore implies a purely logical *temporality*: a temporal scansion between the moment of expectation and the moment of its disappointment, a minimal *delay* of the second part of the tautology. Without this minimal temporality, the proposition A = A remains a simple affirmation of identity and cannot produce the effect of pure contradiction. (*KN*, 36)

In a way, the dialogical encounter between Goody Blake and Harry Gill places the two tautologies we have examined in apposition/ opposition; Harry's power or authority derives from the law (one discursive function of "trespass"), whereas Goody Blake cites God as her authority (Harry too has trespassed, against the moral law of the Christian neighbor; trespass is here implicitly invoked as a unit of religious discourse).

Perhaps the tautological character of these citations is most visible in their gesticulated expression. Although Harry speaks in the language of the pure form of the law, he must nonetheless seize hold of Goody Blake in a banal literalization of *habeas corpus*; in this he imitates the gesture of Goody Blake, who in "pointing" to her God signifies a faith in supernatural power associated with the "rude" ballad-form and a precapitalist idea of neighborhood as constituted by proximity (God is "never out of hearing" [99]). The grasping and pointing together represent the logical impasse of tautological predication.

We are now in a position to reconsider the form of the poem itself, in relation to Wordsworth's emphatic claim for "Goody Blake and Harry Gill": that it is a *true story*, a "fact." He thus lends to the poem the aura of proposition, an aura placed in direct competition with (and apparent contradiction to) what he describes as the "rude" elements of the ballad – especially its *orality*. In traditional accounts of the ballad-form, its formulaic quality – "the simple rhymes, the incremental repetitions, the obligatory epithets, the magical numbers" (Easthope, 79) – derives from the fact that it depends for its transmission on oral communication; the formulaic features as well as the "simple" rhymes make it easier to remember.[35] But those who read or hear a *lyrical* ballad are positioned rather like Coleridge's would-be stenographer, unable to predict what will follow because of the disruption of temporality and the expectation of progress that pure analogy – tautology – generates.

On an even more formal level consistent with its apposition/ opposition of form and content, the poem renders its most philo- sophical proposition as a double-rhyme: "matter" is "chatter." The normative medium of the proposition is a prose which eschews the sensuous and material aspects of language in order to distance propositional "truth" from rhetorical effect – to deny that truth is a discursive phenomenon. By contrast, Wordsworth's decision to cast the poem's "matter" in the form of a double-rhyme is an act that foregrounds the coincidence, or phonetic "accident," by which that proposition comes into being. We may say, in the spirit of argument, that the proposition aspires to a state of pure being, seeks to divest itself of alien "properties," of sound or rhythm, for example. Insofar as "Goody Blake and Harry Gill" represents the only truth-claim explicitly made by *Lyrical Ballads*, the rudeness indicated by the "feminine" or double-rhyme suggests the way in which the universal (truth) is caught up in a larger opposition between being and having that is more (and less) than propositional or grammatical. The *form* of being (and truth) is at once its excess and its impoverishment.

In sum: to have no lack is, in "Goody Blake and Harry Gill," potentially worse than the condition of absolute poverty. It is also, so to speak, the poverty of philosophy. Thus we are back to the propositional dispute with which the second volume of *Lyrical Ballads* began: what is the worth of *books*? Moreover, what is the relevance of this question to *farmers*?

These two questions require that we consider more closely the law case that would serve as a *topos* and precedent for law regarding trespass, particularly cases involving disputed rights of common: *Entick* v. *Carrington*. What I left out of an earlier discussion of this case, with its veneration of every blade of grass as matter sanctified by property, was a singular fact: *Entick* v. *Carrington* had nothing to do with the trespass of *land*. Rather, the case concerned the state appropriation of private papers; in finding against the state, the court used the rhetorical figure of land in order, apparently, to evoke the image of a substantial right, a material connection between the citizen and his mental (verbal) projections.

## Conclusion: Wordsworth and copyright

In *Lyrical Ballads*, I have contended, Wordsworth addresses the effect of the money-form on "the language of real life." The discursive shift that takes place when money becomes a value primarily as a "unit of account" represents a material revolution similar to those brought about by the men of science in whose footsteps the poet, according to the 1800 Preface, is to follow. Primarily, Wordsworth follows the effect of the money-form on *reading* – reading lines of poetry, reading also "imaginary lines" of easements and of property. He appears to argue that the abstraction to which these lines have become increasingly subject requires a counteractive reading: we must stray, turn aside from the public way, if we are to discover "what's the matter." That is, he directs attention to the effect *reading* might have on the money-form. Books, if "The Female Vagrant" and "Expostulation & Reply" may serve as any indication, are according to Wordsworth a valuable tool for mediating customary ("common") rights and statutory ("democratic") ones: if the law allows for no general right of *pleasure* ("such rights constitute mere rights of recreation, possessing no quality of utility or benefit, and as such cannot qualify as easements" – *In re Ellenborough Park* [1956]),[36] Wordsworth creates a new contract between author and reader whose only condition is pleasure.

Therefore we must be tempted, in considering Wordsworth's ardent support for the extension of copyright in the 1830s, to regard his assertion of property rights in the context of his own work as evidence of the political and moral tergiversation with which he is so often charged. What follows is an attempt to problematize that evidence, and to suggest that for Wordsworth, copyright is a legal invention necessary to his own understanding of the text as taking the place of a "common" which had proved to be an illusion – unlike the "tautology" of private property.

Legal historian Bryan Harris explains this latter tautology:

The expression "privately owned" land is in a sense tautological: all land in England and Wales, even the subsoil of highways and other public places, has an individual owner. Categorizing owners according to whether they are "private" or "public" would be meaningless, since there is no such thing as "publicly owned" land. Perhaps the nearest concept in English law to "publicly owned" land is land held in trust for the public, and such land itself may be subject to restrictions on public access. Even land forming a highway is not normally subject to the right to wander at large, though conversely areas of land used by the public for this purpose may be subject to a right of way. (127)

Harris provides the context in which I wish to read Wordsworth's curious representation of copyright as a kind of national trust. Though he also considers copyright as a kind of life insurance, that money-form of speculation on death, the fact that Wordsworth defends *perpetual* copyright rather than its mere extension suggests how the *model* for the writer's "property" in his work will be the pauper's freehold property in the churchyard.

In his letter on copyright, Wordsworth upholds the *sanctity* of author's rights. As Mark Rose has argued in his essay on the genealogy of modern copyright law, the propositional quality of the statute may effectively supplant the previous operation of common law: although proponents for extension in the battle over copyright waged in 1774 tried to argue that the copyright statute known as the Statue of Anne (1709) merely extended or reinforced a common-law right ("provided a further basis of protection, a supplement to the underlying common-law right" [Rose, 58]), eventually the courts decided that common-law copyright (which would, in principle, be a right in perpetuity), if it did exist, was superseded by the statutory limitation of copyright. In the case of copyright, the right of the author or publisher to property interferes with the need of society to "maintain the circulation" of ideas; trying to maintain circulation, statutory law aims at a *perpetuum mobile* whose final form, according to Marx, is capital itself. The effect of statutory law – placing common law "on the books," as it were, though in truncated and rationalized form – therefore unsurprisingly will conform to the logic of the double-entry. In this context, both the formal and the thematic dimensions of Wordsworth's *Lyrical Ballads* – I refer to the 1800 edition, to which Wordsworth affixes a name and an argument (the "Preface") claiming originality as well as indebtedness to a "common" language – foreground the problematic of property in capitalism and democracy.

Wordsworth insistently calls attention to the way in which his position goes beyond that advocated by those supporting the *extension* of copyright to the term of sixty years, and he almost disdains petitioning Parliament for "what in equity I consider to be the *right* of a class, and for a much longer period than that defined in your Bill

– forever" (*PrW* III, 313). The contest between Acts of Enclosure and customary rights had been staged in terms of a similar opposition, between statute and equity law; opponents of Enclosure in 1793 claimed that "the most liberal recognition of the right to pasture a cow, in the form of a cash payment to an individual, cannot compensate for the calamities that a society suffers in the permanent alienation of all its soil" (Hammond and Hammond, 40). They represented rights of common as "incommensurable" within a single generation in a way that corresponds with Wordsworth's argument in favor of extended (in default of perpetual) copyright. Insofar as Wordsworth might regard authorship as a "corporate" entity, the extension of copyright might be conceived as an attempt to protect, rather than to evacuate, rights of common.

Wordsworth's opponents in the battle to extend copyright claimed that "every book, after its author has received from the public an adequate remuneration, becomes the property of the public, who, by affording such remuneration, have purchased it" (*PrW* III.310–11). Wordsworth rejects the equation between the literary work and the commodity; he therefore tends to represent his poetry not as a product but as a domain, the poem as a thing which may be heritable, but cannot be exchanged, for no adequate remuneration could be found. What Simmel describes as the ideological superiority of land to money – "it was value as such, the immovable ground above and beyond which real economic activity was carried on" (241) – cannot be achieved by the book if it is merely a commodity subject to exchange, with no intrinsic value but that determined by the market. But this seeming nostalgia for land-based (also, implicitly, labor-based) value must be regarded as a rhetorical tactic when we consider the extent to which the very poems he wishes to defend repeatedly represent the *subjection* of land to the money-form.

What is of even greater interest than Wordsworth's equation of the text with land is his defense of copyright in terms of *neighborhood*, a concept which, like "common" land, was acquiring an increasingly metaphorical or ideal sense. Wordsworth's fullest defense of copyright appears in a letter addressed to the editor of the *Kendal Mercury* (12 April 1838). Significantly, Wordsworth's only entirely *voluntary* public advocacy of the extension of copyright (rejecting the statutory framework of the Parliamentary petition, Wordsworth only grudgingly writes a solicited letter of support) takes the form of a *local* address – to the inhabitants of Kendal – and frequently invokes the figure of the *neighbor*. Indeed, this is the *only* identity Wordsworth cites; he remains anonymous, signing himself "A.B." and referring to himself in the third person. The letter is prompted by a report that local "letter-press printers" had expressed opposition to the Bill.[37] Wordsworth urges that the Kendal petitioners against the Bill "look[ ] with care no further than their own neighbourhood" (*PrW* III 310) in order to discover evidence against the specious claim that authors receive adequate remuneration through the copyright provision then current. Coleridge, his son Hartley, and Southey are all cited as examples of a disinterested authorship which calls into question the possibility of "an *equitable* remuneration" (311) – a phrase which returns to our consideration Wordsworth's distinction between equity or *right* and the statutory provision limiting copyright which he sees as its infringement.

Repeatedly, Wordsworth seeks to distinguish the author's property from intellectual property in "mechanical inventions and chemical discoveries" (312). To explain why he rejects such a comparison, logically predicated on the common *intellectual* nature of the property, we may turn to Wordsworth's characterization of the kind of production and circulation he values. He argues, for example, that "what we want in these times, and what we are likely to want still more, is not the circulation of books but of good books" (*ibid.*), and good books are intended for future generations. In characterizing the kind of works he has in mind, Wordsworth cites two of Southey's: "his 'Life of Nelson' and his 'Book of the Church'" (311). These choices are significant because their subject matter is identified as *national*; they encourage, according to Wordsworth, both patriotism and "enlightened attachment" (*ibid.*) to the church. Wordsworth's Parliamentary advocate, Talfourd, cited another example of the kind of "national" enterprise undertaken by a *good* book, referring to one Archibald Alison, who "calculated that by the time he finished his history of Europe during the French Revolution he would have spent £4000 on research, an expenditure that he would need the full term of copyright to recover" (Eilenberg, 265 n.). This latter example recalls Wordsworth's distinction between the *good* (or literary) and the *popular* book in the 1815 "Essay, Supplementary": the popular is that which incites a "local acclamation" and "transitory outcry"; the good, by contrast, is associated with the *national* and *permanent*. The idea of nation here is not only that of a generalized scope, but also of an extended duration; it is this scope and duration that render the question of adequate remuneration a Gordian knot: for while "a more than adequate remuneration comes in the course of a season to works intended only for the season" (*PrW* III 311), no such adequation is possible, according to Wordsworth, for works produced on a more sublime scale.

Consider the "account" of the two-volume second edition of *Lyrical Ballads* Wordsworth appended to a letter written by Dorothy to Sara Hutchinson in 1801, the most explicit evidence of Wordsworth's familiarity with the double-entry form:

For Coleridge's entertainment I send the following harmonies of criticism –

|  |  |
|---|---|
| *Nutting* | *Nutting* |
| Mr C. Wordworth worth its weight in gold. | Mr Stoddart can make neither head nor tail of it. |
| *Joanna* | *Joanna* |
| Mr John Wordsworth the finest poem in its length you have written. | Mr Stoddart takes the description of the echoes as a thing regularly and permanently believed, of course can make nothing of the poem. |
| *Poet's Epitaph* | *Poet's Epitaph* |
| Mr Charles Lamb the latter part eminently good and your own. | Mr Stoddart The latter part I dont like, it is very ill written. |
| *Cumberland Beggar* | *Cumberland Beggar* |
| Mr John Wordsworth Indeed every body delighted with Cumberland beggar. | Mr Charles Lamb The instructions too direct. You seem to presume your readers are stupid, etc., etc. |
| *Idiot Boy* | *Idiot Boy* |
| Mr John Wordsworth To a Lady, a friend of mine I gave the 2 vol: they were both new to her. The Idiot Boy of all the poems her delight; could talk of nothing else. | Mr Stoddart Thrown into a *fit* almost with disgust, cannot *possibly* read it. |

But here comes the Waggon! (*EY* 276–7)

Perhaps it is appropriate that the first judgment of poetic value offered by Wordsworth in this double-entry account should enact the implicit economic metaphor: the poem "worth its weight in gold." But Wordsworth's *balancing* of judgments indicates a more sophisticated economic understanding, or instantiates the transformation of the "monetary unit" into the "unit of account." Moreover, the "balancing" Wordsworth achieves – the left-hand column entries "crediting" the poem, the right-hand entries recording a "deficit" (usually of understanding) – corresponds with the "rhetorical" advance over the purely anecdotal account that the double-entry form offered. The "harmonies" of criticism Wordsworth offers for Coleridge's perusal establish the poems' value by effectively *negating* the criticism; the harmonies are such that they add up to zero but, far from negating the poems' value, they suggest that value is beyond measure. *Unlike* the weight of the gold coin, to advert to Christopher Wordsworth's assessment of "Nutting," the value of the poems does not fall as a consequence of circulation; rather, that circulation serves to demonstrate the way in which the poems fail to be consumed, and (like capital) themselves attract investment and encourage the reader's labor.[38]

But the best explanation of Wordworth's impassioned defense of copyright is found in another "public" document published, like the letter on copyright, in the 1830s: the "Postscript" to *Yarrow Revisited*. The "Postscript" to *Yarrow Revisited* concerns matters apparently unrelated not only to the question of copyright, but also to the volume of poems to which it is appended. Moreover, the two issues it *does* take up – Poor Law (economic) reform and the (spiritual) reform of ecclesiastical tenure – are themselves apparently unrelated to one another. But the doubled context is crucial to understanding the "spiritual economics" (the phrase is Levinson's) of copyright that Wordsworth articulates. First, as with the letter on copyright, Wordsworth distinguishes his own view from those that prevailed with the passage of the New Poor Law, blaming critics for their failure to challenge its fundamental assumption that the able-bodied had no *right* to relief (or to wander: all relief of the able-bodied was thenceforward restricted to "well-regulated" workhouses). Wordsworth insists on this *right* to relief with the same ardor that inflects his defense of copyright as a "matter of equity": "the point to which I wish to draw the reader's attention is, that *all* persons who cannot find employment, or procure wages sufficient to support the body in health and strength, are entitled to a maintenance by law" (*PrW* III.240). This right is identified not only as "one of the most precious rights of the English people," but also "one of the most *sacred* claims of civilized humanity" (*PrW* III.241; emphasis mine). This coupling of "matters of equity" with the sacred must remind us somewhat of the coupling of Law and God in the discursive trajectories of "trespass" in "Goody Blake and Harry Gill."

By linking the discourse of rights with sacred authority, Wordsworth identifies the rhetorical structure of liberalism's "self-evident truth," analyzed persuasively by Hannah Arendt. Arendt examines an "incongruous phrase" that has drifted into oral memory and the liberal imagination: " *We hold* these truths to be self-evident" (193). Her contention is that two competing economies are at work: the phrase

combines in a historically unique manner the basis of agreement between those who have embarked upon revolution, an agreement necessarily relative because related to those who enter it, with an absolute, namely with a truth that needs no agreement since, because of its self-evidence, it compels without argumentative demonstration or political persuasion. (192)

The model for the axiomatic or self-evident truth is the mathematical law; Arendt quotes Grotius to illustrate: "even God cannot cause that two times two should not make four" (192). According to Arendt, Jefferson "knew very well that the statement 'all men are created equal' could not possibly possess the same power to compel as the statement that two times two make four" (193); hence the prefatory invocation of truth as a kind of negative faith: "we hold." The liberal declaration of authority, in other words, has the rhetorical marks of the double-entry: what is in one column asserted as an ontological necessity is in the other represented as a convention, a fiction. By an extension of Arendt's logic that this chapter has tried to articulate, we can see this double-entry logic even in the operative equation, "all men are created equal": the double-predication ("are" and "equal") suggests that two different truths are being asserted at the same time, first that men are equal (by "nature") and second that this equation, man = man, is itself a product, a creation and a speculation.

Wordsworth's version of the double-predication of rights is even more revealing, for it exposes that logic as a congealing of surplus and dearth once again. In the same "Postscript" that defends the "sacred" right of the poor to relief, Wordsworth defends the rights of church dignitaries to "pluralities"; he opposes the "cry" of church reformers: "Abolish pluralities, have a resident incumbent in every parish" *PrW* III.250). Wordsworth composes an "incongruous" essay analogous to Jefferson's preamble; but in fact, his justification of the *interest* of a minister in "temporalities" (the ecclesiastical term for church property and/or income) depends for its persuasive force on the analogy to the rights of the poor.

The analogy is forged as follows: after having doubly justified the right of the indigent to worldly "maintenance" (the right is both sacred and a matter of equity), Wordsworth considers the "salutary and benign" effect of relief. This salutary and benign effect has a strongly religious – pietistic – dimension, for Wordsworth attributes *im*piety to destitution. Adam's famous lamentation in *Paradise Lost* (and the epigraph to *Frankenstein*) – "Did I request Thee, Maker, from my clay / To mold me man; did I solicit Thee / From darkness to promote me?" is cited as if to indicate how the outlawing of less metaphysical forms of request and soliciting will result in a collapse of the moral domain:

under how many various pressures of misery have men been driven thus, in a strain touching upon impiety, to *expostulate* with the Creator! and under few so afflictive as when the source and origin of earthly existence have been brought back to the mind by its impending close in the pangs of destitution. (*PrW* III 242; emphasis mine)

We have here an image of subject-construction based on vagrancy: the destituted subject is the referent of being in the abstract. In this context Wordsworth sees fit to invoke many of the indigents of *Lyrical Ballads*, quoting lines from "The Female Vagrant" and referring to the condition described in "The Forsaken Indian Woman." Later he will justify taxes that support  church "temporalities" and argue against a system of "voluntary" support for the Church of England by suggesting that what is being "paid" for is not the comfort of the curate or minister but that of the indigent, although indigency is now figured as "religious exigency" (*PrW* III 255). The comfort of the curate and the relief of the indigent become the same thing, a "sacred" (or sacralized) right.

Two stories further the analogy between destitution (empirical deficit) and spirit (transcendental surplus). One describes a homeless mother who, unable to afford a proper burial, transports her dead child from residence to residence; here the full pathos of the mother's indigency depends on the invocation of a spiritual exigency.[39] The second story too curiously conflates the vagrant and the soul:

There is a story told, by a traveller in Spain, of a female who, by a sudden shock of domestic calamity, was driven out of her senses, and ever after looked up incessantly to the sky, feeling that her fellow-creatures could do nothing for her relief. Can there be Englishmen who, with a good end in view, would, upon system, expose their brother Englishmen to a like necessity of looking upwards only; or downwards to the earth, after it shall contain no spot where the destitute can demand, by civil right, what by right of nature they are entitled to? (*PrW* III 243)

In a manuscript draft of the "Postscript" (reprinted in *PrW* III as its appendix), Wordsworth elaborates on the two possible trajectories of relief, vertical (to heaven and the grave) and horizontal: "Shall other shapes of wretchedness be wilfully placed under a like necessity, *never to look sideways*, but always upwards and downwards...?" (*PrW* III 262; emphasis mine). It is as if, in this single anecdote, Wordsworth has captured the doubling and collapse of vagrancy: on the one hand, the vertical absolute, the achievement of transcendence by means of an absolute deprivation or destitution that approximates death; on the other, the horizontal modality of wandering. But destitute wandering – transformed by law into trespass – is also afforded a sublime power; Wordsworth quotes a proverbial "saying" that renders a more pathetic version of Wordsworth's Whiggish or liberal sympathies displayed in the epigraph to this chapter: "Hunger, as the saying is, will break through stone walls" (*PrW* III 262). (Wordsworth *is* on his way to dinner.)

Wordsworth's wish to look to the future for an "adequate remuneration" of his poetic labors appears to be a negotiation of these trajectories, but this metaphorically spiritual (and literally financial, or "temporal") reduction of the afterlife to an insurance policy (in the form of copyright) nonetheless depends upon the figure of vagrancy. Once this resonance is established, the "incongruous" elements of the "Postscript" and the "Letter on Copyright" are made congruent.

What, for example, is the significance, in his letter to the *Kendal Mercury*, of the repeated insistence on "neighbourhood" and the implication that it is the essential unit of the (abstract) nation? By frequently invoking the image of writers residing in a neighborhood, Wordsworth challenges the notion of the author as an unusually greedy owner, instead giving evidence of the "liberality" (to use the language of Farwell's Salisbury Plain decision) he has shown toward those who would "glean" from his books:

Still confining ourselves to this neighbourhood, what is the fact? There is lying before me a book entitled "Gleanings in Poetry," the preface to which compilation is signed "Richard Batt," and dated "Friends' School, Lancaster." This book extends with its notes to 612 pages, of which 25 are from the poems of Mr. Wordsworth. Did Mr. Wordsworth ever complain of these extracts, which were made without application of his consent? Or did any other writer, from whom copious extracts are taken, utter such a complaint? Again – there was lately published by Mr. Housman, of Lune Bank, near Lancaster, a Collection of Sonnets, from different authors, filling 300 pages, of which pages not less than 57 are from the same author. Did Mr. Wordsworth complain of this liberty being taken? On the contrary, when the editor informed Mr. Wordsworth that the publisher of his works had threatened him with an application to the Court of Chancery for an injunction, Mr. Wordsworth's immediate reply was that he found no fault whatever, and the thing was dropped...and what is thus true of one individual, it may be confidently affirmed, would have been equally so, if a like liberty had been taken with the works of any other distinguished author, who resides, or has resided in this neighbourhood. (*PrW* III 310)

Note the consistency with which Wordsworth attaches to the names of the anthologists the *place names* of their residences, as if to suggest that property law in the republic of letters is mediated by the principles of neighborage, and supplemented by a disputed *jus spatiandi*, the right to wander for pleasure not conceived of by the traditional rights of common.

So: on the one hand, the defense of copyright takes the form of Wordsworth's defense, in the "Postscript" to *Yarrow Revisited*, of church temporalities. Although the parish is still the symbolic (and spiritual) correlative of the neighborhood, it is also the representative of a *national* institution, and a national surplus, as Wordsworth's defense of pluralities suggests. He insists that the church "exists for the benefit of all...whether of her communion or not" (*PrW* III 256); this logic of inclusion clearly extends beyond the concept of neighborage or the parishioner's freehold interest in the churchyard and his right to be buried there. Wordsworth argues that "greedy" landowners who have benefitted by a certain "nationalization" (the dissolution of the monasteries) must return the favor by supporting the "mitigated feudal institution" of the church:

a claim still stronger may be acknowledged by those who, round their superb habitations, or elsewhere, walk over vast estates which were lavished upon their ancestors by royal favouritism or *purchased at insignificant prices after church-spoliation*; such proprietors, though not conscience-sticken (there is no call for that) may be prompted to make a return for which their tenantry and dependents will learn to bless their name. (*PrW* III 257; emphasis mine)

An acknowledgment of the right of anthologists to "glean" from his extensive textual property is Wordsworth's implied acknowledgment of the extent to which his poetic achievements emerge from the "great national events" famously cited in the 1800 Preface. (The first paragraph of MS B of the "Postscript" acknowledges this "debt" more explicitly: Wordsworth there makes reference to his tendency "to express in verse" his interest in public affairs, and specifically to his youthful enthusiasm for the French Revolution [*PrW* III.260].)

On the other hand, the structural consistency of the letter on copyright depends on the identification of the poet not with the great landowner but with the indigent, and his sacred right to demand relief (transposed as the question of "adequate remuneration"). I have already catalogued the examples Wordsworth cites of Lake District authors whose entirely *in*adequate remuneration by publishers threatens to beggar their descendants. In the same way that his Yorkshire "neighbors" acquire the right to glean from his stock, Wordsworth claims the right to petition his Kendal neighbors for a charitable response. In registering the destitution of Coleridge's "pauper's death" ("as to his opulence, if the income tax had continued to the day of his death, the collectors of it would have had a sorry recompense for the trouble of calling upon him for his return" [*PrW* III.310]), Wordsworth forges an implicit correspondence between the Kendal publishers' petition to Parliament against the extension of copyright and the reprehended tendency of France to show disrespect to the pauper's body:

in France, there is no universal provision for the poor; and we may judge of the small value set upon human life in that country by merely noticing the disrespect which, after death, the body is treated, not by the thoughtless vulgar, but in schools of anatomy, presided over by men allowed to be, in their own art and in physical science, among the most enlightened in the world... Irreligion is, no doubt, much concerned with this offensive disrespect, shown to the bodies of the dead in France; but it is mainly attributable to the state in which so many of the living are left by the absence of compulsory provision for the indigent so humanely established by the law of England. (*PrW* III 247)

Wordsworth's corpus is the pauper's dead body, and copyright the "proper" respect shown to that body. Thus the poem is, to use Thomas Laqueur's description of the parishioner's right to a respectable funeral, "the last of the old *communal rights*" (121). The graveyard, like the anthology, is the last vestige of the common.

That, I would conclude, is what Wordsworth wishes copyright might afford the author – *and* the reader. Enabling the author to resist reduction to or identification with a commodity, copyright would *localize* the text. The easement, the footway that runs along the fields to the brook in "The Brothers" that makes visible and tangible the moral relation of "neighbourhood," and "neighbouring" (as an activity, as well as a relational position), is "dead and gone," like the "brother" fountain. For Wordsworth, copyright is its substitute: unlike the Bible that is subject to the Priest's sacrilegious speculations, the copyrighted text may be "gleaned" with permission – or without, provided that the reader's interest is in pleasure rather than profit. But Wordsworth's "petition" in favor of copyright is in the end the expression of a beggar rather than a plaintiff, exposing as it does the tautology of "private property:" as in the account given of "Goody Blake and Harry Gill" in the 1800 Preface, pleasure is not susceptible to enclosure.

CHAPTER 3

# *Walking and talking at the same time: the "two histories" of* The Prelude

## I: THE "TWO HISTORIES" OF *THE PRELUDE*

> No shock
> Given to my moral nature had I known
> Down to that very moment – neither lapse
> Nor turn of sentiment – that might be named
> A revolution, save at this one time:
> All else was progress on the self-same path
> On which with a diversity of pace
> I had been travelling; this, a stride at once
> Into another region. (*The Prelude* [1805], x.233–41)

He must have lived this war, in himself, according to two temporalities or two histories that were at the same time disjoined and inextricably associated. On the one hand, youth and the years of Occupation appeared there as a sort of prehistoric prelude: more and more distant, derealized, abstract, foreign. The "real" history, the effective and fruitful history, was constituted slowly, laboriously, painfully after this rupture which was also a second birth. But on the other hand and inversely, the "real" events (public and private), the grave, traumatic events, the effective and indelible history had already taken place, over there, during those terrible years...His "living present," as someone might put it, was the crossroads of these two incompatible and disjunctive temporalities, temporalities that nonetheless went together, articulated in history, what was *his history*, the only one.[1]

In the ideal exchange imagined for this essay, readers quickly scanning their memories for the moment to which Wordsworth refers in the passage above would be inclined to nominate "the French Revolution," or perhaps, "the Terror"; our tendency to regard Wordsworth's *proper* region as the English Lake District might be responsible for this desire to construct Wordsworth's "Residence in France" as the literal referent for his unhappy stride into another region. Similarly, the context that the first passage seems to supply for the second would encourage readers to read the latter passage as an interpretation of Wordsworth's "two consciousnesses" and their structuring effect on *The Prelude*, an understanding reinforced both by the reference to youth as a "prehistoric *prelude*" and the apparently symmetrical association of trauma with a distant place, "over there." These apparently common-sense intuitions or deductions might quickly be followed with the shock of misrecognition: we recall that Wordsworth identifies his coming-of-age with the French Revolution in the "Bliss was it in that dawn" passage from book x, and that the "shock" so misleadingly identified as initiating a "revolution" is in fact England's declaration of war on France. In rereading the second passage, we notice a referential trace temporarily effaced by the *Gestalt* of analogy; the years are those of "Occupation." This is Derrida talking about de Man.

I have attempted to induce these misreadings and their rapid correction in order to make several claims. First, I will argue that Wordsworth's poetic in *The Prelude* is designed to induce similar misreadings, so that whenever a reader rushes toward a conclusion or solution to a referential opacity, s/he is required, like the represented speaker of the poem, to "measure back his course – far back, / Towards the very regions which he crossed / In his first outset" (IX.5–7). Reference becomes a kind of crossroads, and enables the "shock" of wrong-turning. In this argument I therefore follow the lead of Alan Liu, who claims that "The true apocalypse for Wordsworth is reference. What now shocks us most about Wordsworth's poetry, after all, is its indelible stain of referentiality, its insistent mundanity" (*Wordsworth*, 35). If, as Steven Goldsmith has recently contended, apocalypse is a modality that aspires to collapse history into text, it is not surprising that apocalyptic referentiality in Wordsworth has the effect, here demonstrated, of collapsing past and present, the late eighteenth and the mid-twentieth centuries, the time of the poem's reading as well as of its writing. Second, by the fact that the two misreadings involve the difference between the proper and the common name, I wish to suggest that Wordsworth exploits as one of his apocalypse-inducing techniques that dimension of language de Man calls the "materiality" and Lacan the "agency" of the letter, a dimension knowable to Wordsworth through (of all unlikely sources) William Godwin. Because "revolution" in the first passage is not *capitalized*, we are in one sense mistaken if we read as its signified *French* Revolution, although Wordsworth clearly encourages such an application. Conversely, because the "Occupation" of the second passage *is* capitalized, we cannot (or ought not, by the rules governing proper reading) make it cohere with the Wordsworthian biography as "occupation" in the sense of overriding concern with politics or in the sense of "residence" – occupation of space – in France. I therefore depart from Liu's argument by including in the domain of referentiality those elements of spoken and written language exploited by Wordsworth to produce the effect we call "literature." I do not mean that this apparently self-reflexive referentiality should remain apart from the mundane, or the historical, but rather that it should not be overlooked as we search to develop an historical method adequate to the patterns of Wordsworthian displacement. To my mind, the numerous passages of self-quotation and reference to the process of writing and being read in *The Prelude* tend to validate recent attempts by Liu, Levinson, Simpson and Chandler to *relocate* the referent, insofar as they ground their meanings elsewhere (over there, back then). Rather, my attention to the materiality of the letter emerges from an admiring resistance to the phenomenological Wordsworth produced by Hartman, a Wordsworth whose "meditative consciousness" is emblematized in the imperative *Siste, viator* and the figure of the poet as halted traveler.

In *The Prelude*, a pattern of doubled reference is written into the poem by Wordsworth's inclusion of its compositional history, whose major disjunctions are structured by the doublet here/there. Thus the self-reference of *The Prelude* works, according to my argument, not to produce the poem as "transcendent to all local patrimony," although this condition may be the poem's occasional aspiration; rather, because the position of the speaking subject is perpetually destabilized, the poem offers to translate or expose such a condition – the transcendence of here and there – as vagrancy. Vagrancy – like transcendence or sublimity a condition of being neither here nor there – suggests that the absence of "local patrimony," either in the linguistic aspect of the proper name or in the social aspect of estate within a community, is an impoverishment and an alienation, which my argument will name, after Marx, the condition of the tatterdemalion. Moments of apparently methodological or formal inquiry which might otherwise function as a refuge from such contextual determinations thus free the subject from the geography of place and the place-name, from the history of revolutions (industrial, French, moral) only to reconstitute that subject as a vagrant.

The third and central point of my argument is that Wordsworth's conception of what we may call the "here/there problem" as a problem of *embodiment* dissociates his materialism from the restrictively formal sphere of linguistic materialism and demands its historicization. Wordsworth's obsessive representation of the poet as one who talks and walks at the same time may be regarded as shorthand for an implicit argument that the determinant contingencies of time and place (also coordinates of here and there) disrupt, intersect, and rupture the desire for formal completion and autistic self-enclosure that the poem may thematically represent. Wordsworth's project is important because his embodied speaker attempts to mitigate the opposition between formal destiny and actual contingency – the work and the real – by inventing an infinitely mobile subject who bears more than a passing resemblance to the postmodern subject for whom identity is rather a tactic or performance than an investment. In *The Prelude*, the very techniques whereby a verbal artifact is considered to construct its formal completion – the stationing of *sujet d'énoncé* and *sujet d'énonciation*, verbal echo, reproduction in the tonal register of the thematic register – techniques summarizable as repetition – instead compulsively inscribe the *difference* between this time and that time, here and there, and thus the impossibility of station.[2] In contrast to the "integrity of mind" which Hartman proposes as both aim and achievement of *The Prelude*, my argument traces the indecisive body of the poem (that is, both the body that is narrated and the "corpus" of the poem itself). Indecisiveness is, of course, like fatigue, a primary cause for the traveler's halting, especially at a crossroads. My presumption is that Wordsworth's representation of freedom as the ability "to pause for choice" figures the problematic conjunction of materiality and intentionality as a binary either/or, but that the walking and talking body problematizes this reduction, makes choice impossible, and reproduces an artifact likewise impossible to "determine" precisely because of the instability of reference – of here and there – he helps to mark out. The pattern of reference reproduces a similar freedom – and consequent indecision – for the reader. Reminded by Sebastiano Timpanaro of the difference between indeterminacy and self-determination, we may suspect that this simulation of referentiality produces the psychic equivalent of fatigue, like the old Femiron commercials which displayed a woman wearied by choice as she walked down supermarket aisles. Were readers able to finalize their relation to any of the problems Wordsworth encounters, which in their ideal or philosophical register read as authority, subjectivity, and community, they might decide, and move on. But in their effective historical determination, those problems are encountered as issues of the discourse of democracy and law (authority), education (subjectivity), urbanization, homelessness and poverty, economic development and redevelopment, and nationalism (community). Such problems have a life or *afterlife* of their own not always apparent in the philosophical register, and demand a retrospective and introspective practice inconsistent with moving on. Thus I attribute my own imitative methodological vagrancy, whereby the referential frame shifts among competing discourses, to my unavoidable "stationing" within a regime of texts that Wordsworth helped to install as the condition of the bourgeois liberal subject. This textual positioning tends to produce the effect of the undecidable, and to recreate this effect as (the simulation of) freedom. Rather than regarding that situation as either disabling or delegitimizing, however, I claim for it a provisional value – which is all, as we know, Wordsworth claimed for *The Prelude* itself. It registers not so much an "integrity of mind" as the limitations of mind, the array of prejudices, predilections, and external compulsions involved in contextualization – in general, the subjection of mind to structures of power most abstractly represented in the mechanisms that produce the "arbitrary" freedom of language, and most pressingly, in the redefinition, within the regime of texts that is liberalism, of freedom as social mobility.

## The Patterdemalion

To walk and talk at the same time is also to destabilize or resist the deportment of the classically bourgeois subject, whose "bodily properties" Pierre Bourdieu describes as "a certain breadth of gesture, posture, and gait, which manifests by the amount of physical space that is occupied the place occupied in social space; and above all by a restrained, measured, self-assured tempo" (218). In a sense, the "measured" aspect of this gait resurrects Zeno's paradox, for the measurement must seem infinitely to extend the distance to be traveled; it is a mobility that, through self-reference, so seeks to "occupy" space. To walk and to talk at the same time, by contrast, is to parody the social display and the production of the "body for others" that bourgeois deportment strives to conceal. Like the "pedlar's French" or "patter" of the London poor later chronicled by Mayhew, walking and talking at the same time suggests a certain urgency and lack of self-possession; a rapidity of speech determined by a necessary rapidity of motion. When the "gait" or "tempo" is more measured or restrained, as in the case of the walking and talking poet, it may still strike the witness as an exercise in showing off that displays a *lack* of self-assurance. Moreover and more importantly, it maps onto the "practice" of another, antithetical social "group": the deinstitutionalized (or not yet institutionalized) *Lumpen*. Wordsworth and Coleridge hissing and muttering as they roamed the Quantock hills resemble none so much as those who, *permanently* "out for a walk," are unable or unwilling to differentiate the voluntary from the involuntary, the public from the private. This indecision or indifferentiation produces a certain automatism of speech – "echolalia, the uttering of odd sounds, or sudden irrational outbursts" (Deleuze and Guattari, 22)[3] – that the poet may wish to confine to the thematic dimension of his production, as if they were issued from the lips only of a Christabel or a Martha Ray – but which only the disavowals that constitute the aesthetic as such preserve from identification with and as the speaking subject himself.

A rhetoric of disavowal structures identity in *The Prelude*, but in a way that suggests precisely the crucial opposition between, on the one hand, the self-representations compulsively performed by the poet–subject, and, on the other, the "strange half-absence" of the vagrant who, without relation to social institutions, no longer expresses or communicates an identity. Both groups – philosophers and schizophrenics, to use Freud's categories – "mistake words for things" (Deleuze and Guattari, 23). A related offshoot of this "mistake," it would seem, is the conflation of walking and freedom, the material practice with its symbolic referent. This confusion between the thing and its symbolic dimension, in both cases, is historically specific. The normativized subjectivity of the conversational but solitary walker and its pathologized twin, schizophrenia, both depend on a conflation of identity with property that, according to my argument, is the consequence of a logic of equivalence that freely substitutes thing and referent. At the extremes of this conflation are the materialization of identity, wherein all mental and bodily action is reproduced as motion, automatic or mechanical (the concept of labor-power), and the dematerialization of property, the symbolic form of which is money.[4]

A related contention is that the *apractical* materialism (henceforth, *apraxia*) of the vagrant, rather than what Bourdieu identifies as the "practical materialism" of the working class, is the true antithesis of the practical idealism that structures the institutions of liberalism and the behaviors of its subjects. Bourdieu describes as "erudite" the goals that appear to measure the gait and progress of the bourgeois subject; if walking and talking indicate energies directed on a practical plane forward or outward, the erudite goal mediates those energies, or, one might say, introduces a certain formal constraint, since what is important is not only the literal "way," but equally the "way" as method. This formal constraint thus corresponds to the disciplinary aspect of liberalism's political and social institutions; the rule of law insinuates itself between practice and goal and constitutes itself as ideal, or the formal substitute for that goal.

The practical materialism of daily life, exemplified for Bourdieu in the expression "That's the way it is," rebuts this formal idealism by restoring primacy to the real, hypostatizing a "way" or method now regarded as inherent in things, rather than determined by a freely choosing subject. Nike's enormously successful advertising slogan "Just do it" offers a suggestive example of the way in which practical materialism tends to dissolve the space made infinite by Zeno's paradox of analysis: the infinitely extensive referentiality of "it" is contravened or diminished by mere decisiveness. Although Bourdieu wishes to associate such "practical" materialism with a certain social stratification, it seems to be a dialectical feature of social life under the regime of texts, where decision continually takes place despite the undecidability of those texts.

By contrast, what Paul Virilio calls "the wandering body's inability to decide" (87) disables the *use* of those things that are words, or the walking that is freedom. Our contemporary tendency to conflate vagrancy or homelessness and schizophrenia suggests that we may read the classic sociological description of schizophrenia as an "alienated" body with a Marxist inflection. This would suggest that schizophrenics do not use language for expression or walk where they will because language and space are "out there"; the involuntary manner of their address and movements exhibits the absolute condition of their privation. By contrast, the poet/

philosopher's mastery of the same elements tends to deny the dependence of language and freedom on things "out there." Instead, their social production is internalized as phenomenal reproduction. Hence the emphasis on style and carriage; according to Bourdieu, the primacy given to form masks the interest in function, "so that what people do, they do as if they were not doing it" (200); one walks, but not really to *get* anywhere.

This explains why the text of liberalism is Romantic in nature, "Romantic" here indicating a text characteristically "folded" in a manner visible throughout *The Prelude*. For example, in book VI, which narrates a literal "turning point" – the missed crossing of the Alps in Wordsworth's 1790 pedestrian tour – Wordsworth appends a sort of afterword (a "parting word") that both closes and opens the poem. He issues a passionate disavowal with important repercussions for (re)reading the opening book's "glad preamble" (named as such at the beginning of book VII):

> But here I must break off, and quit at once,
> Though loth, the record of these wanderings,
> A theme which may seduce me else beyond
> All reasonable bounds. Let this alone
> Be mentioned as a parting word, that not
> In hollow exultation, dealing forth
> Hyperboles of praise comparative;
> Not rich one moment to be poor forever;
> Not prostrate, overborne – as if the mind
> Itself were nothing, a mean pensioner
> On outward forms – did we in presence stand
> Of that magnificent region. On the front
> Of this whole song is written that my heart
> Must, in such temple, needs have offered up
> A different worship. Finally, whate'er
> I saw, or heard, or felt, was but a stream
> That flowed into a kindred stream, a gale
> That helped me forwards...                    (VI.658–75)

This passage might easily conclude *The Prelude* as a whole; it is equally appropriate to several other books, and therefore threatens to suspend the narrative progress of the poem in the same manner that Locke lamented in relation to the printing of the Bible in chapter and verse.[5] Yet the suspension or punctuation of narrative progress (which appears to motivate the odd architectonic rendering of Wordsworth's pedestrian tour as a "temple") is necessary to the disavowal: the knowledge a conclusion offers cannot be attributed to an event or place as effect to cause, for that would reduce knowledge to an accidental or contingent condition. Rather, knowledge must inhere in method, in the consistency of the subject's deportment. It is a supremely democratic disavowal, for although the opposition between the autonomous subject and the "mean pensioner" is assuredly a class differentiation, the differentiation is justified by means of a universalizing logic in which the subject displays ownership of self, a proprietary and ultimately appropriative power, by controlling speech and movement. One "stands," refraining from another step, or utters a "hollow" sound in order to render immobility and silence *willful*; this is the lesson taught us by the ice-skating scene and the Boy of Winander. Thus the "Growth of the Poet's Mind" chronicled in *The Prelude* is also the development of the silent majority. Wordsworth *recalls* the "front" of his song here in the double sense exploited by Shelley's *Prometheus Unbound* when Prometheus recalls his curse: an invocation of the past that is also its revocation. The license to walk and to talk celebrated in the glad preamble, its straightforward declaration "Now I am free," is retroactively regarded as an inalienable and permanent – because entirely interior – condition, that requires neither travel to sublime regions nor even expression (exultation). What originally looks like a delineation of actual conditions of liberation in the glad preamble (allusion to the "City," the deictic "Now") here becomes the space of the poem itself – hence the oddly architectonic reconfiguring of the "space" of liberation as a "temple." In this context it is worth recalling Wordsworth's original motivation for writing the earliest versions of *The Prelude*; socially and linguistically isolated or cut off in Goslar, he finds himself without resources, and writes to Coleridge of the poem as an exercise in self-maintenance, self-support: "As I had no other books I have been obliged to write in self-defence" (*EY* 236).

The poet's rejection here of "outward forms" is not only a "Protestant" attitude (note how the "temple" is in fact the text, the poem); it is also a liberal–democratic one, in which the regime of texts is always regulated by their (historical) reinflection. The "preamble" to the self-constitution that is *The Prelude* thus must be written over by a ("parting") *afterword* disclaiming the "hollow exultation" with which the poem opens. The afterword, which purports to be a repetition, a reminder, of the original and controlling intention, by validating the importance of form rescinds (Latin *rescindere*, "to cut off, abolish") the particular referential content of the preamble. In the conclusion to book VI, Wordsworth redirects attention away from the actual (the Alpine regions directly present to the represented subject and indirectly – through imagination – present to the speaking subject) and toward the preamble; the subject of celebration is not the grandiosity of nature, and by implication is never the "matter" of the poem's chroniclings. All such narrative components become mere occasions for the mani- festation of originary power (authority) most immediately visible in the poem's opening words (also "parting" words, at least figura- tively: the poet speaks of his departure). But here the aspect of departure is textual rather than kinaesthetic: the space traversed is that of the "book," that macro-paragraph segmenting the narrative, rather than a landscape.

Hannah Arendt's analysis of the twofold aspect of the democratic constitution – as foundational act and as contigent text – has im- mediate relevance to the structure of *The Prelude*:

> In view of the strange fact that constitution-worship has survived more than a hundred years of minute scrutiny and violent critical debunking of the document as well as of all the "truths" which to the founders carried self- evidence, one is tempted to conclude that the remembrance of the event itself – a people deliberately founding a new body politic – has continued to shroud the outcome of this act, the document itself, in an atmosphere of reverent awe that shielded both event and document against the onslaught of time and changed circumstances. And one may be tempted even to predict that the authority of the republic will be safe and intact as long as the act itself, the beginning as such, is remembered whenever constitutional questions in the narrower sense of the word come into play. (204)

*The Prelude* has been subject to similar critical debunking, and certainly when placed in the context of democratic discourse, its self- serving tact (Wordsworth's erasure of Annette Vallon and their illegitimate daughter Caroline from his autobiography) and its apparent ideological tergiversations (Chandler's account of the address to Burke appended to book VII is one example) seem to indicate a failure to sustain its democratic vision. But Arendt's argument that the Constitution is sanctified by its *formal* protocols helps to explain the obsessively revisionary structure of Wordsworth's poetic as the true locus of its politics. The glad preamble inscribes on the front of his whole song the right of revocation, implicitly constituting the vacillating subject as representative of freedom.

This contradiction established between preamble and afterword crucially anticipates what Marx identified in *The Eighteenth Brumaire* as the formal structure of the liberal democratic constitution, and that analysis too offers us a "reading" of *The Prelude*:

For each paragraph of the Constitution contains its own antithesis, its own Upper and Lower House, namely, liberty in the general phrase, abrogation of liberty in the marginal note. Thus, so long as the *name* of freedom was respected and only its actual realization prevented, of course in a legal way, the constitutional existence of liberty remained intact, inviolate, however mortal the blows dealt to its existence *in actual life.* (31)

The French bourgeoisie of 1848 maps onto the English Wordsworth of 1793: this bourgeoisie, unable to "undo" the historical "accident" by which it is brought to power "not as it had dreamed...through a liberal revolt of the bourgeoisie against the throne, but through the rising of the proletariat against capital" (29), resorts (for example) to "adding the limiting proviso" of a six-month's residence to the Constitutional guarantee of universal suffrage. Wordsworth initially dreams of the Revolution as instituting a new property relation; all of earth becomes "an inheritance new-fallen" (x.728). But the "shock" of the declaration of war between England and France undoes the literal possibility of this dream, since it essentially sets the principle of property and the progress of capital (England) against the "progress" of the people and Liberty (France). The effect of this opposition is a "whirlwind" and a rupture ("I, who with the breeze / Had played...Now from my pleasant station was *cut off*" (x.253-4; 257) whose only difference from the afterword of book vi ("here I must break off") is agency or will: here the *coup* is performed by an external (naturalized) agency; there, it is refigured as a self-disciplinary masochism – it is the poet's decision to cut himself off.

How are we to read this "here" and "there": is it a strictly historical distinction (1793 vs. 1804), a moral distinction, or a grammatical one, the difference between *sujet d'énoncé* and *sujet d'énonciation*? We see in the structural similarity of the constitutional "paragraph" evidence that, in the process of iteration, contradictions become identifications by means of a formal resonance. In this sense, the various revisionary incarnations of the French Constitution only play out a structure already at work in the title of the "Declaration of the Rights of Man and Citizen," where the rights of the

preambulary "Man" undergo immediate alteration (indeed, abrogation) by his reconstitution as "Citizen." Wordsworth's attempts
to preserve or *recoup* the "general phrase" of liberty as a democratic
*form*, as a property only in a metaphorical sense, suggest not only how
the textual dimension of liberalism is its defining characteristic, but
also why the bracketing of content that Wordsworth's formalism
demands brackets so distinct, and so distinctively repetitive, a content
– that of vagrancy.

### Paragraphs and paupers

When Marx critiques the Napoleonic Code (that "classic law code of
bourgeois society," according to Engels) later in *The Eighteenth
Brumaire*, he does so in a manner that suggests the method undertaken
here. He notes the same structure of contradiction: universal "rights"
of property ownership in the (Napoleonic) Code proper are rescinded
in the "codex" (codicil, amendment, postscript) which mortgages
property ("inalienable rights") to capital, euphemized as "public
safety" or "the general welfare." Here, the "codex" is identified not
with the "small print" or "Lower House" of the Code's paragraphs,
but with a changing historical reality:

> The "Napoleonic" form of property, which at the beginning of the
> nineteenth century was the condition for the liberation and enrichment of
> the French country folk, has developed in the course of this century into the
> law of their pauperization... Feudal lords were replaced by urban usurers;
> the feudal obligation that went with the land was replaced by the
> mortgage... The small holding of the peasant is now only the *pretext*
> [emphasis mine] that allows the capitalist to draw profits, interest and rent
> from the soil... The mortgage debt burdening the soil of France imposes on
> the French peasantry payment of an amount equal to the annual interest on
> the entire national debt. Small-holding property, in this enslavement by
> capital to which its development inevitably pushes forward, has transformed
> the mass of the French nation into troglodytes... The *Code Napoléon* is now
> nothing but a *codex* of distraints, forced sales and compulsory auctions. To
> the four million (including children, etc.) officially recognized paupers,
> vagabonds, criminals and prostitutes in France must be added five million
> who hover on the margin of existence and either have their haunts in the
> countryside itself, or, with their rags and their children, continually desert
> the countryside for the towns and the towns for the countryside. (*EB* 127–8)[6]

"Condition of liberation" to "law of pauperization": this is exactly
the history that Wordsworth resists when he attempts to rewrite the

front of his whole song as if the property rights it dreamed as a future were never imagined as substantive. When Hartman notices "something peculiar in the way his text corrupts itself: the freshness of the earlier versions is dimmed by scruples and qualifications" (xvii), he draws attention to a feature of *The Prelude* belonging to all of its incarnations. Wordsworth's revisionary schema, which demands that he, like Rousseau, live off his own substance, reproduces the reduction of text to pretext that history accomplishes in relation to the Napoleonic Code. In both cases, the effect is to recast the law of pauperization (being "cut off" from an entailment) as a condition of liberation, and so to recast the citizen as the vagabond, and the right to property as the cave of the troglodyte.

But we must not invest history with so much power without attempting to render its operations less abstract. By what technique, operation, or method does a text that guarantees property become a pretext for its forcible alienation? Marx's analysis of the constitutional paragraph, that semantic unit of the philosophy of right, suggests that history's operation is visible in its discursive regimes. Consider, for example, the "terms of art"[7] that legitimize the regime of texts, or law, in liberal democracy: their repetition creates the effect of "precedents" that ground authority in time immemorial. They achieve their legal authority, wherein they seem to "speak for themselves," however, precisely as their extratextual referentiality is diminished: "in good faith" no longer describes a social or moral relation, but echoes a previous phrase. This is one sense in which we may understand Marx's description of the language of the French Revolution: "there the phrase went beyond the content" (*EB* 18). Reference to "public safety," that ground for deciding between the "higher" and "lower" of a given paragraph, is self-referential; the "public" has no other determinable referent than the speaking subject, and the safety of those in power becomes the principle of decision.

This increasing self-reference may also be read as an impoverishment, one which Wordsworth's poetic marks in the 1800 *Preface* as the necessary difference between impassioned utterance and its metrical recreation by the meditative poet. The structure of revision given to liberalism's text becomes the means of its devaluation; the Enlightenment logic of the Constitution, opposed to superstition, allows for its effective dissolution by the autocrat, who asks: "was not its whole policy based on the subordination of the paragraphs of the

Constitution to the decisions of the parliamentary majority? Had not it left to the democrats the antediluvian superstitious belief in the letter of the law, and castigated the democrats for it?" (*EB* 101). Decontextualization is at once a "condition of liberation" whereby the text may promise to speak for the Other (Martin Luther King Jr.'s startling inflection of the Declaration's subject-position – "We hold these truths to be self-evident: that ALL men are created equal" – *reverberates*, demonstrates the democratizing potential of decontextualization, even as the implicit gender exclusion suggests the continued operation of a codex of distraints) and the law of pauperization. For if *identification* is the defense that may be mounted against exclusion from power, the logic of equivalence here working to affirm right, this same logic of equivalence justifies Louis Napoleon's usurpation of the subject-position. Identity is abrogated when the proper becomes common (noun).

Volosinov also suggests how the formal features of the paragraph may inscribe this historical "progression" by which the condition of liberation becomes the law of pauperization. He writes, "very commonly, we make our own speech or some part of it (for example, the preceding paragraph) the object of discussion. In such a case, a shift occurs in the speaker's attention from the referent of the speech to the speech itself" (111). With "freedom of speech," it is indeed "the speech itself," rather than its reference, that becomes the object. We are therefore justified in regarding the structure of the Constitutional paragraph as a formal determination of the liberal idea of freedom, an idea concisely indicated by the Kantian requirement, shared by Marx, that activity be "free from" bodily necessity in order to belong to "the humanity in our person" (*CJ* 101). By this logic, finally, the "Spirit" of the Law is valued over that banal materialization, the Constitution (and the poem) itself.

But the formalization of freedom in the democratic constitution also makes possible a subversive *play* on the material residue of the concept that is the word or the text. "Terms of art" may also become what Marx calls "catchwords" (*EB* 38) *when* they are "superstitiously" regarded as containing the true "sense" of the phrase. Since, according to Adorno, language is the primary tool by which Enlightenment reason claims to exercise its imperial sway over the material world, to imagine the contamination of the word by the thing it purports to represent "objectively" (and arbitrarily) is to expose the illusory mastery of reason, to "embarrass" it. The more the concept attempts to distinguish itself from the object it describes, the more it is compelled to mimic its own contours as object: "In [articulation] thinking fulfills the mimicry of the spell it had itself cast on things" (quoted in Jameson, *Late Marxism*, 65). The material dimension of the concept, the word, exposes what Marx calls "the real Bonaparte, Bonaparte *sans phrase*" (*EB* 75): "The respectable, hypocritically moderate, virtuously *commonplace* language of the bourgeoisie reveals its deepest meaning in the mouth of the autocrat [Louis Bonaparte]" (80; emphasis mine). This real Bonaparte, moreover, is not the instantiation of subjectivity, autonomy, and property that the speaking subject had been thought to represent, but rather its antithesis: Louis Napoleon is a *vagabond*, and "a long life of adventurous vagabondage had endowed him with the most developed antennae for feeling out the weak moment when he might squeeze money from his bourgeois" (73). Recontextualized by a radical displacement enabled by the nomadism it substitutes for determination, the "common" or universal language of the Constitution legitimates usurpation.

The significance of Louis Bonaparte's vagabondage is only fully apparent when we understand that, for Marx, the Napoleonic Code, like the French Constitutions that preceded it, is the "literary" form of what in *The German Ideology* he calls "the language of property" (*GI* 100). Destutt de Tracy's famous justification of private property – "Nature has endowed man with an inevitable and inalienable property, property in the form of his own individuality" – is conducted, according to Marx, by means of that historicist play on words, etymology; de Tracy makes private property and personality identical "with a play on the words *propre* and *propriété*" and concludes that "by abolishing my existence *as a bourgeois* you abolish my existence *as an individual*" (*GI* 100–1). Marx's method of exposing the false Nature underlying this "language of property" is a symmetrical etymological play on words:

In reality, of course, the situation is just the reverse. In reality I possess private property only insofar as I have something vendible, whereas what is peculiar to me [*meine Eigenheit*] may not be vendible at all. My frock-coat is private property to me only so long as I can barter, pawn or sell it, so long [as it] is [marketable]. If it loses that feature, if it becomes tattered, it can still have a number of features which make it of value *to me*, it may even become a feature of me and turn me into a tatterdemalion [*zerlumpten Individuum*]. But no economist would think of classing it as my private property, since it does not enable me to command any, even the smallest, amount of other people's labour. (*ibid.*, 101–2)

The verbal mimesis of the language of property achieves its apotheosis in the word "tatterdemalion," a wonderful translation of Marx's critique of the etymological collapsing of *propre* and *propriété*. By virtue of this collapsing, the pronominal referent shifts from "I" to "it" – similar to the manner in which the "quotation" of a paragraph effectively formalizes its subject matter. Through sheer repetition, "it," like a frock-coat, gets worn down, an overuse which contributes to its final condition as "tattered." The originally "proper" name of the frock-coat becomes, by dint of repetition and the logic of equivalence, a "commonplace" – "it" – which finally usurps the position of the subject altogether. That subject is no longer a bourgeois property-owner, but rather a beggar, a vagabond. Marx's play on words works not only by demystifying etymology as an ideological tool, but also by suggesting that the liberal subject is a purely verbal construction, that his "rights" exist only in the general phrase, and are only as inalienable as rags are from a beggar. The critique is accomplished by a methodological mimicry that seeks meaning in the forms of thought in addition to its ostensible *content*, since the form/content split is the ruse of the ideology in question.

Given that the form/content split is precisely the ruse put in question, it must strike us as worthy of more than casual attention that Marx's interest in the "pure form" of liberalism should force his frequent return to the figure of the tatterdemalion/vagabond/ troglodyte. Implicitly, he argues that the reconstitution of the subject as citizen in the various declarations and constitutions of the late eighteenth and early nineteenth centuries *strips* the subject of substantive identity. Wordsworth imagines a similar disfigurement in a passage from the *Essay on Epitaphs* already cited:

If words be not (recurring to a metaphor before used) an *incarnation* of the thought but only a *clothing* for it, they surely will prove an ill gift; such a one as those poisoned vestments, read of in the stories of superstitious times, which had power to consume and to alienate from his right mind the victim who put them on. (*PrW* II, 84–5)[8]

Language again is the instrument that produces the tatterdemalion, that figure whose clothes alienate his previous identity. This difference between the incarnate and what we might call the "tatterdemalion" word is Wordsworth's version of the difference between *propre* and *propriété*, a difference which threatens to collapse in two figures: the poet and the vagrant. Their property is very nearly immaterial.

The opposition between the incarnate and the tatterdemalion word is neither "purely formal" nor "also political"; it is social. The self-completeness and self-reference of the incarnate word, which represents the monadic condition toward which the Romantic text may be said to aspire, is necessarily monological, whereas the figure of the tatterdemalion, or of the "real Bonaparte" who knows how to squeeze money out of his bourgeois, reinscribes the social dimension of the speech act (of *exchange*) away from which the written form orients itself, as if to repress its originating conditions. In this sense it is fitting that the characteristic form of the mature Wordsworth, the form he adopts for *The Prelude*, is the "Conversation" poem,[9] itself borrowed from Coleridge, who thus serves appropriately as the poem's addressee. The Romantic "conversation" poem is notoriously monological, and for some time the silencing of the purported interlocutor has been regarded as a necessary "depopulation" of the sublime landscape (see Ferguson, *Solitude and the Sublime*).

The philosopheme of the conversation poem in the blank verse style practiced by Coleridge and perfected by Wordsworth is the verse *paragraph*. With the intended auditor either silenced or elsewhere, s/he is marked primarily in the indentation which appears to motivate a revisionary articulation. Volosinov identifies this as a feature of paragraphs more generally: "The paragraph is something like a *vitiated dialogue worked into the body of a monologic utterance*" (111; emphasis mine). Thus although Marx's description of the liberal–democratic paragraph suggests a structure *containing* a revisionary vitiation of its apparent inclusions, whereas for Volosinov and in the conversation poem the space between paragraphs or the indentation reveals the actual exclusion, nonetheless for each the paragraph is a monological "unit of utterance." Units of utterance differ from strictly "linguistic" units because they take place in what Marx calls "actual life," not in "the abstract system of language" (Volosinov, 111). Acknowledging that paragraphs have been considered as purely linguistic units analogous to sentences, defined as a "complete thought," Volosinov points to the varied length and logic of paragraphs to suggest that the partitioning of paragraphs is effected by an element outside the system of language; namely, the imagining or calculation of the reader's or listener's response (or the writer's, *post hoc*). Paragraphic punctuation, which originates in the transition from oral to silent performance of a text, preserves only the appearance, or *representation*, of the interlocutor; yet this representation, however factitious, is entirely necessary to motivate continuation once a "thought" has been completed, or the text has come to a halt.

If Wordsworth's verse paragraphs diverge from the Coleridgean model of conversation, they do so in a manner I have suggested: the imagined interlocutor/reader/listener is the poet himself *post hoc*. This formal tendency more forcefully suggests the ouster of the Other that Marx and Volosinov discover operating in the paragraph generally, defined here as the formal unit of discursive utterance in a liberal regime. The aim of the Wordsworthian verse paragraph is to represent the lapses or turns in argument as the formal dimension of autarchic thought. Within the frame of the monologue, the verse paragraph appears to represent the movement – subjectively determined – of thought. However, although the paragraph thus represents an attempt to formalize and so to evacuate the position of the interlocutor whose responses might propel the argument or thought forward, that formalization itself threatens the represented autonomy of the subject. Split not only from an interlocutor but also from any "subject" (object) but its own thought processes, the speaking subject can no longer appeal to the contours or "outward forms" of things except to figure those things as pure contingencies which cannot affect the interior movement of thought. If the "law of pauperization" is the socioeconomic effect of the precedence given the regime of texts, this "law" has the effect of reproducing the class relation of the Constitutional paragraph in a new "subjective" split: "The surplus of the transcendental subject is the deficit of the utterly reduced empirical subject" (Adorno, 178). Adorno contends here that the systematic uprooting of the subject from any determination, ostensibly a liberation and an identification of subjectivity as that which goes beyond such determination – the Kantian continuity of "I think" (no matter where I am) – is an impoverishment, which disallows resistance to the pure form it has elevated to a position of dominance.

If the changes wrought by the liberal–capitalist regime were most visible to the writers of the early nineteenth century who chronicled its point of departure in the spectral form of the "utterly reduced empirical subject" – the horde of vagrants haunting public roads – this spectral form had its invisible double in the poet's inability to find a subject or "goods" to communicate or exchange. Wordsworth's solution – to talk about himself – effectively reveals the poet as tatterdemalion, and his rags as the *forms* of thought.

Wordsworth's attempt to conjure as subject "the growth of his own mind" always ends with – has for its postscript – not the transcendental surplus but the empirical deficit. Even as Wordsworth attempts to represent the forms of thought as free and independent of those vectors of the Wordsworthian context that are represented in the poem as so many *residences* – the cultural heritage of Cambridge, the landscape of nation, finally, the historical field of the French Revolution – to that extent the site of that freedom is a body undifferentiable from the vagrant's. The mind which develops its capital independent of those institutional forms which confer an external identity has as its "place" only the public road ("In the public roads at eventide / I sauntered, like a river murmuring / And talking to itself" [IV.109–11]). Vagrancy becomes valuable as a transhistorical, transcultural (the Arab as Bedouin, France as a half-starved peasant girl) phenomenon, as that which resists history, even as the tatterdemalion locates a defensive identity in the forms of his alienation.

If we are to take seriously the claim that "thinking fulfills the mimicry of the spell it had itself cast on things" – which seems to me the axiom of any method that aspires to a truly dialectical materialism – this conjunction of the philosophical subject and the vagrant requires a symptomatic reading. Wordsworth's example, like Rousseau's, argues that the relation between philosopher and vagrant is peculiar to bourgeois liberalism. Insofar as the philosopher takes on the attributes of the vagrant, the somatic dependencies he was wont to repress reemerge as the determining conditions of his thought. I will begin with Kant and end with Adorno in summarizing this relation. In the section of the *Critique of Judgment* concerning the sublime, the Kant performs the division of humanity and person to which I had earlier alluded: even as the "dynamic" in nature attacks the senses, the "rational faculty" enables self-preservation. In fact, the experience of the sublime functions as an "inspiriting satisfaction" precisely by enabling the split of the physical from the rational, the realignment of identity toward the rational and away from the physical. In a sense, the continuity of thought in the face of the threatening *mobility* of nature (Kant's rendition of the sublime landscape as comprised of "threatening" and overhanging rocks, clouds "moving... with lightning flashes," hurricanes "with their track of devastation," "boundless oceans" and "lofty waterfalls" [*CJ* 100] is familiar to any reader of *The Prelude* and its criticism) is what "elevates" the mind over nature. But insofar as "nature" in the analytic of the sublime includes the somatic element – what Kant calls "our own physical impotence, considered as beings of nature" – the "elevation" is only metaphorical, for it requires a certain *situation*. Kant identifies this situation as (public?) *safety*: "we must regard ourselves as *safe*" (101). In other words, Kant does not deny that the achievement of a contemplative autonomy requires a certain freedom from exigency or want – a negative freedom. What about positive freedom to act? Kant replies: "the tendency to this destination lies in our nature, while its development and exercise remain incumbent and obligatory" (102).

Thus we are not surprised when Adorno reminds us that, elsewhere in Kant, the introspective method for proving freedom chooses as its example "the decision to rise from a chair" (Adorno 223). The contemplative autonomy Kant renders as the condition of judgment is implicitly associated with a *somatic* situation; the body seated ceases to represent desire (Adorno: "Woe speaks: 'Go'"). Adorno sees in Kant's representation of freedom the requirement that "situations must be rigorously cleansed of their empirical content" (223); otherwise, decision, the exercise of freedom, will appear to be determined by its conditions. The effect of this requirement is to reduce proofs of freedom to the "inanity" that is this ascription of freedom "to an ass." But this ascription might also be regarded as the mimicry that reverses the spell the contemplative "stance" (rather, "situation") casts on human nature. Domination of the body by the mind ends with the location of freedom in the gluteal muscles.

A similar paradigm of freedom operates in *The Prelude*. As if in imitation of the Kantian experiment, Wordsworth in *The Prelude* must continually "exercise" his sovereignty by moving from places of residence – situations – thereby depriving those situations of any status as determining conditions. But even as this movement operates to erase the referential vectors which might subject the poet to determination by history, the somatic content that a situated posture renders invisible is made manifest in the poet who insists on walking while he talks. Condition of liberation to law of pauperization: the "inspiriting satisfaction" of the Kantian sublime is mimicked in the "breathing spell" that marks the intervals of compulsory mobility in *The Prelude*.

For Adorno, and, I would argue, for Wordsworth, the somatic element that infects forms of thought and so dooms the experimental proof of mental freedom to failure also appears to be the salvation of thought in relation to freedom, for the reappearance of the body in thought, whether in the thematic form of the beggar or in the formal theme of the mobile subject, preserves the concept of *practical* freedom. The dilatoriness of thought, although in one sense a procrastination of practice, can also, in a context where practice has been abstracted into automatism, preserve the subject's freedom from complete identification with functionality or the law. This preservation operates as irony, that rhetorical form of mimicry: the homeless rest and sit down in places functionally (and legally) identified as "for transportation." Adorno reminds us of Benjamin's claim: "While there is a beggar, there is a myth" (203). Loitering, that characteristic activity of the Romantic knight-at-arms, works to expose the material effects of *laissez-faire*, and the distinctive historical cast of freedom's failure. Adorno: "Paradoxically, it is the desperate fact that the practice that would matter is barred which grants to thought a breathing spell it would be practically criminal not to utilize" (245). And the procrastination of/as practice that is loitering has its equivalent in the poem as it defines the emergent category of the literary – an articulation with no place to go.

In the spirit of Adorno's *double entendre*, we may understand the privilege conferred upon the interval in (and as) the poem as a "breathing spell" – as both an enchantment and a respite from enchantment. The verbal iteration that "spell" and "enchantment" indicate corresponds to the empty formalism of the regime of texts. But iteration also implies the temporalization of the text, a temporalization likewise indicated by the rhythm of breathing that now is heard to punctuate the apocalyptic silence that Wordsworth envisions as the incarnate form of the transcendent subject. Wordsworth's turn to the rhythm of breathing, a turn compelled by the requirement that his mental capital (imagination) develop independently of socially determining forms, has the effect of rendering language as a kind of echolalia. In practice it reverses the normative understanding of breath as automatic, involuntary, and language as an intentional (mental and social) domination of the somatic condition. Rather, the pause for breath operates as a defense against the demand, legislated by the forms of language and of thought (ideology), to move on. If the privative dimension of this practice is indicated when we think of the pause for breath as a gasp for air – the breathing spell as a defense mechanism triggered by that demand – still, breathing establishes an economy or exchange beyond legislation. As Adorno contends, the "somatic element …lives on in knowledge as the latter's unrest, that it sets in motion and continues to reproduce, unassuaged, in its progress" (203).

## II: A "BREATHING SPELL": THE "GLAD PREAMBLE" OF THE 1805 *PRELUDE*

Oh there is a blessing in this gentle breeze,
That blows from the green fields and from the clouds
And from the sky; it beats against my cheek,
And seems half conscious of the joy it gives.
O welcome messenger! O welcome friend!
A captive greets thee, coming from a house
Of bondage, from yon city's walls set free,
A prison where he hath been long immured.
Now I am free, enfranchised and at large,
May fix my habitation where I will.
What dwelling shall receive me, in what vale
Shall be my harbour, underneath what grove
Shall I take up my home, and what sweet stream
Shall with its murmurs lull me to my rest?
The earth is all before me – with a heart
Joyous, nor scared at its own liberty,
I look about, and should the guide I chuse
Be nothing better than a wandering cloud
I cannot miss my way. I breathe again –
Trances of thought and mountings of the mind
Come fast upon me. It is shaken off,
As if by miraculous gift 'tis shaken off,
That burthen of my own unnatural self,
The heavy weight of many a weary day
Not mine, and such as were not made for me.
Long months of peace – if such bold word accord
With any promises of human life –
Long months of ease and undisturbed delight

Are mine in prospect. Whither shall I turn,
By road or pathway, or through open field,
Or shall a twig or any floating thing
Upon the river point me out my course?

Enough that I am free, for months to come
May dedicate myself to chosen tasks,
May quit the tiresome sea and dwell on shore –
If not a settler on the soil, at least
To drink wild water, and pluck green herbs,
And gather fruits fresh from their native bough.
Nay more, if I may trust myself, this hour
Hath brought a gift that consecrates my joy;
For I, methought, while the sweet breath of heaven
Was blowing upon my body, felt within
A corresponding mild creative breeze,
A vital breeze which travelled gently on
O'er things which it had made, and is become
A tempest, a redundant energy,
Vexing its own creation. 'Tis a power
That does not come unrecognized, a storm
Which, breaking up a long-continued frost,
Brings with it vernal promises, the hope
Of active days, of dignity and thought,
Of prowess in an honorable field,
Pure passions, virtue, knowledge, and delight,
The holy life of music and of verse.

Thus far, O friend, did I, not used to make
A present joy the matter of my song,
Pour out that day my soul in measured strains,
Even in the very words which I have here
Recorded.　　　　　　　　　　　　　　(1.1–59)

## Place and the pedestrian; time and the traveler

Kenneth Johnston has concisely and persuasively explained the
organizational plan of the expanded *Prelude* for which the first fifty-
four lines of the poem, known as the "glad preamble," were
composed. Johnston argues that the expansion of the five-book to the
1805 thirteen-book *Prelude* is structured by "residential units"
(Cambridge, London, and France): "each new residence initiates a
crisis that is partially resolved before the next residence is established"
(120). This model seems to offer a fitting structure for the

autobiographical representation of a poet whose "history" is so frequently considered in terms of a greater series of residences. We might glance at the chapter headings of Mary Moorman's still classic biography:

| | |
|---|---|
| II. | Hawkshead I, 1779–83 |
| III. | Hawkshead II, 1783–7 |
| IV. | St. John's College, Cambridge, 1787–90 |
| V. | The Alps, London, and Wales, July 1790–Sept. 1791 |
| VI. | France, 1791–2 |
| VII. | Racedown, Sept. 1795–June 1797 |
| IX. | Alfoxden, 1797–8 |
| XIII. | The Beginnings of *The Prelude*: Germany, 1798–9 |
| XIV. | Sockburn-on-Tees, May–December 1799 |
| XV. | 'A Poet Living in Retirement.' Grasmere, December 1799–December 1800 |

Like the "books" of the *Prelude*, Moorman's chapter headings suggest that the construction of a subject depends at least as much on *geography* as on the "history" so recently the focus of Romanticist inquiry. Or, more precisely, they suggest that the "real" of history inheres in the local instance. Here, of course, I invoke Wordsworth's own representation of personal history as "spots" of time. The concept of such "spots" has for some time (since Abrams, at least) been thought consistent with the "retirement" toward which the circuitous Romantic journey ostensibly aspires; in a way, the spot of time seems to distance itself from history, like an island in a stream (or a deluge); the genitive "of" might equally be read as "from" – the spot taken, or saved, from time. The spot of time is a place in which the subject might stand so as, in Coleridge's famous instructions for Wordsworth's *The Recluse*, "to deliver with authority upon a system of philosophy." Here we notice the odd logic by which authority or subjectivity seems to require a *residence* – a logic ostensibly at odds with the practice readable in the glad preamble. Although Wordsworth looks forward to the establishment of residence, we nonetheless must register the central fact that that represented speaker is a *transient*. His transience is what requires the "geographical," even topographical, structure of the poem; were he stationed, established in one position, that position would not have to be written into the text.

One might explain Wordsworth's representation of subjectivity as a walking body in several ways, all of which will be considered in the argument to be advanced below. From a sociopolitical perspective, it appears that Wordsworth's is a "rentier's vision." Because he lacks the traditional authority accorded to landed estate, he must locate his authority in a different form of cultural capital, most visible in the public signature attached to his first publication: "Fellow of St. John's College, Cambridge." From a literary-historical perspective, Wordsworth's appearance *in medias res* is part of the locodescriptive tradition which John Barrell has persuasively allied with the emergence of the middle class, the picturesque "station" in the middle ground suggesting an analogous social station. Similarly, Wordsworth's epic ambitions make the "travel" motif appropriate, although adopting a *pedestrian* mode of travel is Wordsworth's crucial attempt to create his own rather than to draw on his culture's capital. The pedestrian motif offers a locomotive equivalent of the "innovation" Wordsworth wrought on poetic diction; ironically or at least paradoxically, the claim to greatness and originality lies in the versified representation of the most common practices, "speaking" ("a man speaking to men") and walking. Finally – and crucially, I believe – noting the observed invariance with which philosophy registers its dependency on the practice of walking (Socrates, Rousseau, Kant, Nietzsche, Wittgenstein) one would notice how all thought is in this sense a geography. We are used, perhaps, to recognizing that the very materiality of language requires for it a place or space, and its reading a traversing of that space. The line of a poem may be regarded, in this view, as the ur-text of writing, since its geography or mapping of the page foregrounds the necessarily tropological character of language.

In a sense, the reader's relation to the text is analogous to the situation of the subject in relation to the sublime: the reader's sedentary position enables submission to the extraordinary procrastination of the single line that constitutes the book. But submission to the law of residence which defines both the epistemological and the political subject is mitigated by Wordsworth's contribution to the ideology of the aesthetic. The "breathing spell," or rather, perhaps, the "breathing spelled," like the footpath, mitigates the absolute determination of the subject in relation to residence; that is, the determination of the subject by social and economic coordinates. The "breathing spell" rebels against a "necessary" tropology – the infinite deferral of meaning and value until the end is reached – by instituting, through enjambments ("anti-iambic" encroachments or trespasses upon the bounding line) and caesurae (of poetic units of thought as well as rhythm), opportunities to "pause for choice." The very lexicon of poetics here helps to underscore the effect produced by Wordsworth's representational strategy in *The Prelude*; if the relation between form (poetic feet) and content initially appears to be analogical, Wordsworth's insistent materialization of the formal dimensions of the poem suggests a closer or more determinate relation between form and content, one which reverses (or allows for the reversal of) hierarchies of mind and body, the rational and somatic faculties. Like a verbal pun, the formal puns of walking and breathing in *The Prelude* lay stress upon, and potentially *dis*tress, the illusion that the forms of thought are uncontaminated by their materials.

This said, one should note that the "glad preamble" seems to obfuscate precisely the dimensions of human (and personal) experience we associate with the pedestrian body: the historical, the economic, the social. Much as critics might try to locate the spot upon which Wordsworth stands (or across which he moves), or to name "yon City" from which he makes his escape, they have produced only a multiplicity of possible referents, both literal and metaphorical. If one critic claims that identification of the city as Goslar "is surely wrong," others admit that London, Bristol, and Goslar are equally plausible referents, as are the literary allusions to Milton and to Exodus.[10] If we resist the impulse to identify the referent of the deictic with the place of composition (following, therefore, the lesson of "Tintern Abbey," whose compositional history directly contradicts the "geography" of the titular inscription, since the lines were neither composed a few miles above the Abbey, nor in the "station" indicated by "here I stand," but rather on the walk back to Bristol, and written that evening at an inn), our failure to identify *place* means a concomitant failure to locate in time. This has potentially more serious repercussions for reading the poem; without the name of the city, we cannot authoritatively identify the year nor the (political) "moment of consciousness" indicated by the deictic "now." Does the glad departure coincide with Raisley Calvert's offer of a legacy, probably in mid-May of 1794?[11] This identification is problematized by the fact that Wordsworth was visiting the Calverts in the Lakes at the time, and that the legacy "excused Wordsworth from London," as Liu puts it (*Wordsworth*, 335), only by freeing him from the obligation to *return* there in order to make a living as a man of letters. But the temporal location is crucial: are we to identify Wordsworth's "present joy" with a lingering revolutionary enthusiasm (he writes the Paine-inspired "Address to the Bishop of Llandaff" in 1794) or with the poetic resources to which he resorts when that enthusiasm is depleted? Since, as we are immediately reminded when the first fifty-four lines become identified as a "glad preamble" to the poem proper, Wordsworth is "not used / To make a present joy the matter of a song," its performative character ("to the open fields I told / A prophecy" [1.59–60]), the poetic *declaration* of independence, might be regarded as an inscription of error (as the allusion to Milton's exodus would seem to indicate) parallel to that impersonal time of the French Revolution and the performative encouraged by revolutionary enthusiasm:

> The state, as if to stamp the final seal
> On her security, and to the world
> Shew what she was, a high and fearless soul –
> Or rather in a spirit of thanks to those
> Who had stirred up her slackening faculties
> To a new transition – had assumed with joy
> The body and the venerable name
> Of a republic. (x.24–31)

"Stirred up... to a new transition" and thankful to the breeze which consecrates his liberation, the represented speaker of the glad preamble walks in a spirit that can be plausibly allied with this "republican" fervor criticized elsewhere in the poem as the "overlove of liberty" prompting Wordsworth's first "truant" travels in France and the "march of military speed" which was its method. But the preamble's representation of walking and talking at the same time, addressed to Coleridge, also forecasts and mirrors Wordsworth's representation of the compositional history of *Lyrical Ballads*, the walking and talking that *will have taken place* in 1798. I use the future anterior here because it offers a rhetoric of temporality suitable to the represented geography of the following passage:

> having given this record of myself,
> Is all uncertain; but, belovèd friend,
> When looking back thou seest, in clearer view

> Than any sweetest sight of yesterday,
> That summer when on Quantock's grassy hills
> Far ranging, and among the sylvan coombs,
> Thou in delicious words, with happy heart,
> Didst speak the vision of that ancient man,
> The bright-eyed Mariner, and rueful woes
> Didst utter of the Lady Christabel;
> And I, associate in such labour, walked
> Murmuring of him, who – joyous hap – was found,
> After the perils of his moonlight ride,
> Near the loud waterfall, or her who sate
> In misery near the miserable thorn;
> When thou dost to that summer turn thy thoughts,
> And hast before thee all which we then were,
> To thee, in memory of that happiness,
> It will be known – by thee at least, my friend,
> Felt – that the history of a poet's mind
> Is labour not unworthy of regard:
> To thee the work shall justify itself.          (xiii.389–410)

This passage, effectively an afterword to *The Prelude*, since it follows the completed "record," offers as its prospect – the landscape which now stands before the reader as the equivalent of the prospect of green fields confronting the glad preamble's represented speaker – a recollection, or looking back that will *justify* the claims of the poem. But unlike Milton's theological or moral justification, *The Prelude* is *formally* justified, by self-reference.

One implication of this passage is that "speaking," the verbal practice that serves for Wordsworth as an equivalent to walking, may also have the effect, when represented in writing, of displacing the referent. This effect is most visible in the operation of deixis. It is the difference, in the lines quoted above, between the referential field established by "Quantock's grassy hills" and "the loud waterfall" or "the miserable thorn"; the fact that Wordsworth registers this difference in the conclusion to a poem that has been so heavily topographical should alert us to suspect that it is a question of central concern. "Quantock" is a place that for most of Wordsworth's readers today may have the effect of a purely literary reference; nonetheless, the capitalization, indicating that it has a "proper" name and belongs in real space, specifies the place in a way that the latter two descriptive phrases do not. No matter how steadily the poet might look at these objects, detecting qualities of sound and even less tangible emotional moods or the "inner life" of things, without the symbolic register of proper names, readers come no closer to identifying them. It does not matter either that readers *familiar* with Wordsworth, like the friend to whom the *Prelude* is addressed, Coleridge (in the 1850 edition "friend" becomes "Friend", the capitalization marking explicitly the reader's exclusion from the adjudicating positions of the glad preamble's "now" and Quantock's "then"), can point to the proper names "The Thorn" or "The Idiot Boy" as the *places* in which thorn and waterfall are located, since those poems only frame the referent in a *mise en abîme*. Moreover, the apparent reference of the passage is not to specific objects in the landscape but to "that summer" (time rather than place) and to the wandering and murmuring (direction and articulation both carefully obscured) that "took place," so to speak. The effect of the passage is that of deixis writ large: simply put, you had to be there. When we recall that the passage is a final attempt at justifying the autobiographical project of the *Prelude*, and reflect on the indeterminacy of the poem's earliest beginning ("Was it for this?") – when, in other words, we find ourselves left neither "here" nor "there" – then we discover how appropriately emblematic is the posture of the represented speaker in the glad preamble. Walking, the poet too is neither here nor there.

### *The commonplace and the placeholder*

What is accomplished by the indeterminate character of Wordsworth's referentiality? Left unable to know whether the "measured strains" that constitute the glad preamble are a declaration of independence that may require the corrective disavowal constituted by *The Prelude* proper or the "mutterings" of a poetic process patented by Wordsworth and Coleridge; left with a speaking practice strictly frameable neither as a political (public) nor aesthetic (established by its opposition as private) discourse, readers are cut off from decision. The contest between "here" and "there," whatever is implied by this opposition that marks the space of the glad preamble, is conducted within or extends into the regime of the word.

Let us then begin with the first word, "Oh." (It is rendered "O" in the 1850 text.) "Oh" will be an epitome of the contest the poem will wage between "measured strains" and "mutterings," and their

pedestrian equivalents, a determined pace and wandering. Can such
a word – really more a *sound* than a word – bear the indelible stain of
referentiality? What, in the context of the line, does the word or
sound "signify"? In contradistinction to that word nominated by
Rousseau for consideration as first word, the metaphorical "Giant,"
"Oh" does not appear to represent or misrepresent any object at all;
it is merely the gesture of invocation itself. What distinguishes this
invocation as particularly Wordsworthian, however, is the insistently
physiological inflection: this "Oh" does not *call*, since the only other
presence, "this gentle breeze," is emphatically *not* addressed until
line 5. We are left to consider the function of the "Oh" in monologue.

A monologue in iambic pentameter. This feature of the fictive
utterance is, of course, both visible and invisible: iambic pentameter
operates, as Antony Easthope has persuasively demonstrated, to
naturalize its formal determinations, in two significant ways. First,
iambic pentameter differs from older forms of strictly accentual verse
by its greater regulation: "Relative to accentual meter whose
requirement of four stresses admits a wide variety of line lengths, the
abstract pattern of pentameter...represents a systemic totality, an
explicit preconception legislating for every unit of stress and syllable"
(66). Even though the form is thus more greatly "legislated"
(Easthope offers Saintsbury's appropriately political description of
pentameter: "the claims of Order and Liberty are jointly met as in no
other metrical form" [67]), pentameter introduces a compensatory
mitigation of regulation in the form of intonation: "Since syllable
prominence [in spoken English] is relative, it follows that the abstract
pattern...is never *actualized*" (63). Second, in the case of blank verse,
or Wordsworth following Milton rather than Pope, extended
syntactic units form a counterpoint to the arbitrary line ending. As
we will see, Wordsworth is exemplary in resisting a correspondence
between phrasal units and the line; the *Prelude*, like "Tintern
Abbey," is an exercise in enjambment. Wellek and Warren's
summary of these mitigations, quoted by Easthope, will help in
producing a new reading of the famous "correspondent breeze"
passage and its relation to the "measured strains" of the glad
preamble: "English verse is largely determined by the counterpoint
between the imposed phrasing, the rhythmical impulse, and the
actual speech rhythm conditioned by phrasal divisions" (61). We
note here that both "rhythms" are conditioned, one by the technical
referent (the metrical pattern), the other by the historical (actual

speech rhythm), and the tension established between the two orders of determination produces the appearance of nature. Like Rousseau's imagining of the state of nature, an antithetical structure produces the effect of a "common" or "natural" language.

A related observation: such a state of nature can only be represented through – indeed is conceptually tied to – the technology of writing. Its discursive nature is that of the paradox of written speech. Poetry is the "natural" form of a man speaking to men for Wordsworth because its artificial rhythm induces by counterexample the rhythms that accompany speech, rhythms that are lost in the silence and stationariness that characterize the (modern) practice of reading. Hence Wordsworth contends in the 1800 Preface that "the language of a large portion of every good poem, even of the most elevated character, must necessarily, except with reference to the metre, in no respect differ from that of good prose" (*PW* 736), and mounts a spirited defense of meter as more important to "regularity" than a conventional "phraseology." The difference between meter and other "superadded" devices is, according to Wordsworth, a political one: diction is

arbitrary, and subject to infinite caprices, upon which no calculation whatever can be made. In the one case, the Reader is utterly at the mercy of the Poet, respecting what imagery or diction he may choose to connect with the passion; whereas in the other, the metre obeys certain laws, to which the Poet and Reader both willingly submit because they are certain. (*PW* 739)

The difficulty in reading an involuted syntax with the proper inflection without resort to an overview of the whole – the way, in other words, that such a syntax trips us up – may be contrasted with the measured motion of metric regulation. On the other hand, as Easthope points out, a "proper" reading of blank verse naturalizes the effect or makes the regulation disappear:

Pentameter *can* be performed as though it were accentual meter; that is, thumped out as doggerel so that the abstract pattern and intonation coincide. This is how children and the inexperienced, used mainly to accentual metre...generally speak pentameter. (63–4)

Oral performance of the poem that aspires to the natural, in other words, requires an assimilation of the extended semantic unit as well, but meter provides a breathing spell.

Wordsworth's dual insistence that meter offers to regulate or temper the extemporaneity of the passionate language of "real life" even as it restores passion or the appearance of extemporaneity to the written text – breathes life into it, so to speak – is the crucial thesis of the "correspondent breeze" passage. There, the internal and the external, or sense and meter (we recall that meter is a superaddition), are represented as crosswinds, which suggests the opposite purposes to which meter may be put. The "mild creative breeze" represents meter, whose important feature of regularity is evoked as *correspondence* – that is, an analogical relation to the "natural" breeze. Hence the representation of this "internal breeze" by means of a metaphor of travel – "A vital breeze which travelled gently on / O'er things which it had made" (44–5), which invokes the analogy between versification and pedestrian travel at work in the common designation of metrical units as "feet," and the etymology of "iamb," an analogy reinforced by the more literal "travel" narrative of the preamble, in which the poet adopts a "gentle" pace in traveling. However, this "breeze," like the poet's character in the Preface, is not *dependent* on external excitement, but rather represents a mental domination – the "internal echo of the imperfect sound" of the poet's own voice.

We may further compare Wordsworth's poetic theory of metrical regulation of speech patterns with his elaboration of that theory in the "Essay, Supplementary to the Preface" of 1815. This essay, marking an attempt resisted in the earlier "Advertisement" and Preface to *Lyrical Ballads* to "reason the audience into approbation," grounds its rationale for approbation of Wordsworth's experiments in a conception of the "*Vox populi*" that has much in common with the peculiarly modulated rhythms of pentameter. First, he criticizes as false the identification of this "voice of the People" with "popular opinion," associating the latter with the "senseless iteration" that describes doggerel: "Away then, with the senseless iteration of the word, *popular*, applied to new works in poetry, as if there were no test of excellence in this first of the fine arts but that all men should run after its productions, as if urged by an appetite, or constrained by a spell!" (*PW* 751). Accentual meter common to the ballad and the "spell" of iteration had already been related in Wordsworth's account of "Goody Blake and Harry Gill" in the 1800 Preface. Far from denying the power of iteration, therefore, it would seem rather that Wordsworth argues here for the necessity of intonational counterpoint, or phonetic iteration modulated by reference to sense, meaning, syntax. Moreover, in his reference to the *speed* of senseless iteration ("running"), we hear an implicit preference for the "proper speaking" of blank verse, and its "gentle" (also "gentlemanly") pace. To read blank verse (silently or aloud) is effectively to reduce the speed of actual speech, "because it legislates for the number of syllables in the line and therefore cancels elision, making transition at different word junctures difficult" (Easthope, 68). That speed, like the "eager" or brisk pace of the petit bourgeois man of business, is a side-effect of a preeminently communicative intent. By contrast, Wordsworth's own compositional practices, made familiar to his contemporaries through the anecdotes of Hazlitt and DeQuincey, suggest an entirely hypothetical intent, as if literalizing the "state" of nature. Hazlitt remarks:

Coleridge has told me that he himself liked to compose in walking over uneven ground, or breaking through the struggling branches of a copse-wood; whereas Wordsworth always wrote (if he could) walking up and down a straight gravel-walk or in some spot where the continuity of his verse met with no collateral interruption. (*CW* xvii.119)

Wordsworth's practice entirely eliminates the potentiality of the external goal implicit in the "struggling" and "breaking through" of the Coleridgean model, and all impediments to perfect regularity of meter must therefore (apparently) originate in thought. Despite the artificial constraint of the landscape of composition, therefore, Wordsworth's habit of walking out his lines of poetry seems *only natural* – that is, unmotivated by the cultural imperatives we hear in "appetite" and "spell."

Second, Wordsworth suggests that to hear the *vox populi* accurately requires the temporal and spatial distance that characterize his indeterminate deictic referents, "here" and "now":

The voice that issues from this Spirit, is that of the Vox Populi which the Deity inspires. Foolish must he be who can mistake this for a *local acclamation*, or a *transitory outcry* – transitory though it be for years, local though from a Nation. (*PW* 751; emphases mine)

For Wordsworth, the people thus "philosophically characterized" are distinct from the "Public" and its "clamour." As distinguished from the impassioned utterance that describes acclamation and outcry, the voice of the people, like Wordsworth's voice in the glad preamble, must be imagined to issue forth in "measured strains." Only speech rendered as poetry enables the communication of its language across time and space. In this sense, poetry is the only language of *writing*.

How curious then, that the "Oh" with which Wordsworth begins his attempt to communicate across time and place – not only to Coleridge, but also and especially to future generations, an intention especially registered by the fact that Wordsworth planned for the posthumous publication of the *Prelude* – should begin with an iconic intonation, and thereby effectively erase the "arbitrary" but also creative nature of the sign.[12] Because, in the absence of an other to whom the "Oh" might refer in an apostrophic modality, we tend to regard the "Oh" as the pure sound produced by exhalation (the physiological mark of *release* narrated subsequently). "Oh" denotes primarily exclamation or outcry, according to the *OED*. However, because the "Oh" without referring to is nonetheless followed by a statement, "there is a blessing in this gentle breeze," and *not* a diacritical mark of exclamation or "clamour," its signification is seemingly transformed; through a retrospective movement, it becomes the correspondent of the breeze. As exhalation, the "Oh" is an internal echo of "the sweet breath of heaven" (line 41); however, it is not *determined*, but determinative, in that relation, since the rendering of the breeze as "breath" (metaphor, personification) is itself the product of the authorial voice or "creative breeze."

The "Oh" is also a place-holder in the abstract pattern of iambic pentameter: it functions as a kind of rest stop in music. By beginning his utterance in this way, Wordsworth at once calls attention to and obscures the way in which writing is an imitation of speech, and speech itself a modulation of sound. The "Oh" suggests that utterance requires a previous intake of breath and so corresponds to the world of objects. It also forces consideration of the way in which inhalation and exhalation are prior to and may suggest the artifice of the iambic foot, stress corresponding with exhalation (hence the extended pause of the line break – time for a breath – follows a stressed syllable). We can further imagine, as the glad preamble implicitly asks us to do, the coincidence of breathing (and speaking) with bipedal locomotion, noting how in breathing and in talking, exhalation and stress will naturally accompany the footfall (see Holmes, "Physiology of Verse").

Wordsworth's practice both obscures and exposes because, although the association of poetic utterance with breathing and walking works to naturalize metrical verse, and therefore to establish what Easthope describes as "unruffled smoothness, flowing eloquence, poise" (67), the technical apparatus of this naturalization – iconic intonation – foregrounds the non-syntagmatic elements of the meaning-structure. Notably, walking itself is an activity unrepresented in the glad preamble, as if the rhetorical convention alone ("preamble") must suffice to establish the connection between a "prelude" to the main song and "ambulation." (Its identification as "preamble" is, of course, entirely retrospective.) And although breathing *is* foregrounded ("I breathe again" [1.19]), it is given a metaphorical cast. The evidentiary basis for our resisting a common misperception that Wordsworth's speaker here is necessarily a *halted* traveler[13] comes mostly from the narrative aftermath of the glad preamble:

> Whereat, being not unwilling now to give
> A respite to this passion, I paced on
> Gently, with careless steps, and came erelong
> To a green shady place where down I sate
> Beneath a tree, slackening my thoughts by choice
> And settling into gentler happiness.     (1.68–73)

The 1850 revision of a single line helps us to understand the relations and oppositions Wordsworth intends to set in place. In 1850, "gently, with careless steps" becomes "with brisk and eager steps." In both cases, the decision to give passion a respite, to seek a calming balance to a "present joy" and its associate exclamation, is rendered as a deceleration that is also a delay, or an intentional downshifting. In the first version, this deceleration has already occurred and is readable in the "gentle" pace of the poet; in the 1850 version, the "brisk and eager steps" continue the movement of the preamble and the downshifting only occurs when the poet sits. It is difficult to judge which version accomplishes more successfully the desired effect, which is a conflation of mental and physical motion, so that a "slackening of thoughts" accompanies a slackening of pace. Although we are able and in fact required to register this slackening as a volitional act ("by choice"), so close is the correspondence between mind and act, so parallel their rates of speed, that it is unclear to what extent the slackening of pace and the meditative frame of mind it indicates *require* a decrease of speed (and an increase of leisure) –

whether, in other words, halting is a cause or a symptom of volitional experience. I would suggest that this confusion is central to the structure of the first book, which laments the poet's inability to distinguish determination from determinism (restrained volition from passivity), and ends in celebrating the revised scope of the poem ambiguously as "a theme / Single and of *determined* bounds" (1.668–9).

Readers who wish to decide whether (and why) the "eager" spirit of enthusiasm of the preamble is presented as requiring a calmly reflective correction or as a model of self-authorizing utterance to which the Poet continually aspires are put in a similar quandary by the act of self-quotation that line 55 initiates. That line, which turns the breathy "Oh" of the opening into the conventional apostrophe ("Thus far, O friend"), creates or reveals one final aspect of the dichotomies Wordsworth manages to set in play by his technical mastery of the "regulations" of iambic pentameter. The initial declaration (the first line of the poem is a simple declarative, "There is a blessing in this gentle breeze," except for the superadded "Oh" whose function in this context is primarily to mark a certain passion or inflection) introduces utterance as monological, but Wordsworth's subsequent prosopopoeia ("O welcome messenger! O welcome friend!" [1, 5]) exploits the figurative dimensions of language to enact an imaginary dialogue; the breeze is his "correspondent." However, the phonetic register suggests that the breeze "blows" only by virtue of the poet's technical mastery; as Wordsworth puts it later, the preamble is an exercise in ventriloquy:

> My own voice cheared me, and, far more, the mind's
> Internal echo of the imperfect sound –
> To both I listened, drawing from them both
> A chearful confidence in things to come.                    (1, 64–7)

The "Oh" with which the poem opens confirms Wordsworth's representation of the breeze as a mental or linguistic "echo" of the "imperfect sound" of his own voice, since the intonation or voicing of the sound "oh" requires an exhalation that is the phonetic equivalent of a breeze, and the alliteration with which he registers the description of the breeze in the first four lines (blessing/breeze/ blows/beats) consists of a series of bilabial stops which close rather than open the mouth. If breathing represents involuntary motion, then the *representation* of breath by this alliteration designates the control of that "glad *animal* movement" ("Tintern Abbey") by the mind and will. Although the later personification of the breeze as the "sweet breath of heaven" would suggest a literal inspiration, Wordsworth does not represent the inhalation that must have preceded his own utterance, as if to erase any suggestion of the debt language might owe to nature or to physiology.

On the most general level, then, the problematic of the glad preamble involves the mapping of signs of will onto apparently natural practices, although in so subtle a manner that volition itself is rendered equivalent to the automatism of breathing or walking. Such is the effect of the preamble's largest identification, of escape from the city's walls with breathing, and a return to a "natural" self. Wordsworth's escape from this walled (though unnamed) city must remind us, in addition to the other geographical and literary allusions catalogued by critics, of Rousseau's "escape" from the walls of Geneva; as I have argued, the symbolic dimension of the geographical here represents entry into the open space of the preamble as the adoption of a *stateless* condition.

## *The (Godwinian) politics of walking and talking*

But it is less the specter of Rousseau than that of Godwin which most immediately confronts Wordsworth in the preamble. Although the name of Godwin appears frequently in studies of *The Prelude*, he is cited almost exclusively in relation to the political philosophy of the French books, and never as a formal model for the aesthetic experiment of *The Prelude* (except, perhaps, insofar as critics have read *The Prelude* in the context of associationism and its critique). In my own account of the poem, which attempts precisely to refuse the critical separation of autobiographical "integrity of mind" from political digression (and tergiversation) by reading the poem's unifying "method" *as* its politics, Godwin's political theory figures in Wordsworth's text most prominently when *The Prelude* is at its most self-reflexive; that is, when it is least apparently political. This is the case because Godwin's theory is primarily a political *philosophy*; its practical politics derive from his investigation of mental organization. For Godwin, the representation of thought in language may be fairly held to demonstrate the problems of representation generally.

Godwin's chapter "Of the Mechanism of the Human Mind" in

the *Enquiry Concerning Political Justice* attempts to prove the possibility
of human perfectibility by demonstrating how an antecedent mental
operation is responsible for all apparently (glad) animal spirits, and
his primary example, walking, is itself preceded by a consideration of
two primarily mental operations – reading and listening – which
also map on to what I have suggested is the self-conscious poetics of
the preamble. Walking (bipedal locomotion) is identified as a
characteristically human or "percipient" form of motion:

An example of one of these classes suggests itself in walking. An attentive
observer will perceive various symptoms calculated to persuade him that
every step he takes, during the longest journey, is the production of thought.
Walking is, in all cases, originally a voluntary motion. In a child, when he
learns to walk... the distinct determination of mind, preceding each step, is
sufficiently perceptible. It may be absurd to say that a long series of motions
can be the result of so many express volitions, when these supposed volitions
leave no trace in the memory. But it is not unreasonable to suppose that a
species of motion which began in express design may, though it ceases to be
the subject of conscious attention, owe its continuance to a continued series
of thoughts flowing in that direction, and that, if life were taken away,
material impulse would not carry on the exercise for a moment. We actually
find that, *when our thoughts in a train are more than commonly earnest, our pace
slackens*, and sometimes our going forward is wholly suspended, particularly
in any less common species of walking, such as that of descending a flight of
stairs. In ascending the case is still more difficult, and accordingly we are
accustomed wholly to suspend the regular progress of reflection during that
operation. (374–5; emphasis mine)

According to this account, the pace of walking would almost
certainly diminish were it accompanied by the more obviously
voluntary exercise of speech; or at least, there would have to be an
alternation between the willed contraction of leg muscles and
deliberate articulation. But Godwin's analysis of habituation, whereby a certain "flow" of thought replaces conscious attention (so that,
to adults, walking appears automatic rather than willed), allows us to
imagine that talking too may take the form of "material impulse," so
that what directs speech seems not so much the mind of the poet as
the ravinated paths of sound and rhythm.

   Walking had been a crucial example in Godwin's demonstration of
philosophical necessity. Admitting that walking functions in the
"popular" imagination as a primary instance of human liberty
("Liberty, in an imperfect and popular sense, is ascribed to the
motions of the animal system, when they result from the foresight and

deliberation of the intellect, and not from any external compulsion"
[346]), Godwin argues that we ought to regard motion as engendered
from a larger series of antecedents and consequents, that walking is
always caught up in this larger chain:

Power, in the sense of the hypothesis of liberty, is altogether chimerical...A
knife has a capacity of cutting. In the same manner a human being has a
capacity of walking: though it may be no more true of him than of the
inanimate substance that he has an option to exercise or not to exercise that
capacity. (353)

According to this explanation, only "popular" opinion would regard
walking as intrinsically an exercise of freedom, since we can imagine
not only a case in which external constraint prohibits this exercise
(the "City" of Wordsworth's imagination), but also a case in which
the subject is constrained or *compelled* to walk – for example, the case
of the truant "fugitive," the "march of military speed," and even, to
a lesser extent, the "pilgrim resolute" – all representations of
pedestrian mobility Wordsworth uses elsewhere in *The Prelude*. Fully
to identify walking with freedom, one would have to demonstrate a
capacity *either* to rest *or* to walk – a demonstration that occurs with
Wordsworth's narrative representation of slackening pace. Obviously
the corollary to this demonstration of pedestrian freedom in language
would require an alternation between speech and silence, or a
"speaking" silence such as that represented in the controlled,
articulated exhalation "oh."
     As the "oh" of breathing modulates into the "O" of address, we
read in the glad preamble an implicit equivalent to Rousseau's myth
of the social contract. Rousseau had argued that language was the
means by which natural man exchanged "independence" – represented as a nomadic culture – for civil freedom. The modulation of
monologue into conversation, first in the refiguring of the breeze in
line 5 ("O welcome messenger! O welcome friend!"), and then with
the inclusion of Coleridge (and reader) in the field of reference in line
55, in both cases suggests that the inalienable freedom to breathe
establishes a kind of physiological basis for a political right whose
chief form is (free) speech. "Friend" is a designation that even as it
invokes the idea of a "natural" man[14] devoid of titles also suggests
the voluntary constitution of society or social bonds (that this
constitution is essentially *fictive* is registered by the prior figuration of
the breeze as such a "friend"). Unlike kinship, friendship constructs

its relation without reference to a determining Nature. The *abstract* quality of friendship allows for an infinite substitution as well, so that any reader may potentially take up the position inscribed by the poem as correspondent or friend. The address of the "glad preamble" is thus sharply distinguished from the constraining, regulated practice of social address Wordsworth had criticized in the *Letter to the Bishop of Llandaff*:

Are you disgusted with the hypocrisy and sycophancy of our intercourse in private life? You may find the cause in the necessity of dissimulation which we have established by regulations which oblige us to address as our superiors, indeed as our masters, men whom we cannot but internally despise. (*PrW* I, 18).

If it seems plausible that doctrines of the social contract associated with Rousseau and Godwin are invoked by the representation of walking and talking in the glad preamble, such referentiality is no more determining than a more topographical or historical location might be. Wordsworth's general relation to Godwin – a revisionary one – is summarized in the language of book x, when he indicates his initial enthusiasm for the Godwinian doctrine of perfectibility in a manner that ironizes the "dithyrambic fervour" (VII, 5; "fervour irresistible / Of short-lived transport" [1850]) of the glad preamble. Exclamations – "What delight! – / How glorious!" (x.18) – precede his representation of "liberation" into Godwinian philosophy:

> with a resolute mastery shaking off
> The accidents of nature, time, and place,
> That make up the weak being of the past,
> Build social freedom on its only basis:
> The freedom of the individual mind.                    (x.821–5)

The opposition of freedom to "accident" here is purely Godwinian; Wordsworth's particularization of accident as the axis of reference (time, place, and "nature") thus offers to refigure the ambiguity of reference in the glad preamble – a discursive representation of Wordsworth "shaking off" the "unnatural" (i.e., historical or actual) self – as a Godwinian argument. If we read the poem as renouncing Godwinian doctrine, then the ambiguity of reference, which in the glad preamble is what appears to assure the sovereignty of the subject, functions instead to ironize that sovereignty and to associate the subject with Wordsworth's representation of French

Revolutionary enthusiasm in the *Letter to the Bishop of Llandaff*: "The animal just released from its stall will exhaust the overflow of its spirits in a round of wanton vagaries" (*PrW* 1.38). Only the careful modulation of the "overflow of spirits" which the Preface famously identifies as the originating source of poetry suggests that even before the "recollection" of the glad preamble in line 55, Wordsworth seeks to identify the preamble's (revolutionary) enthusiasm as more than an automatic expression of animal impulse; hence the controlled, *anti*-exclamatory "Oh."

However, the echoes of Godwinian argument visible in both the rhetoric and the narrative content of the glad preamble and its aftermath problematize any reading which would render its articulations as the simple equivalent of the dithyrambic "Ça ira" of the French Revolution, and reprehend them as such. Godwin himself had already criticized the kind of abstraction that would simply correlate such mere "going" (talking as well as walking; hence the modern slang, "I go" for "I say") with freedom. Godwin insists that it is not merely the internal mechanism of mind – the tendency to habituation of all voluntary action – that threatens the politics of walking. If "popular opinion" mistakes walking for freedom because of an abstract correlation, political theory makes the opposite mistake, holding that not only silence but also stationariness means consent (and assures freedom). The doctrine of consent informing all versions of social contract is built on such a falsely abstract correlation: as "silence means consent," then residence too indicates acquiescence and consequent obligation to the structures of power. As Godwin remarks, "It is usually said 'that acquiescence is sufficient; and that this acquiescence is to be inferred from my living quietly under the protection of the laws'" (213). Godwin, however, criticizes such an inference by discriminating the class-determined limits to locomotive trajectory:

Acquiescence is frequently nothing more than a choice on the part of the individual of what he deems the least evil. In many cases it is not so much as this, since the peasant and the artisan, who form the bulk of the nation, however dissatisfied with the government of their country, seldom have it in their power to transport themselves to another. (213)

Pierre Bourdieu's analysis of the continuing significance of walking as the recreational activity of a specific class (the "culturally richest fractions of the middle class and the dominant class") helps to update our understanding both of the *abstract* correlation between walking and freedom that Godwin criticizes and of Wordsworth's compositional practices. Describing recreational activities in general, Bourdieu writes,

> Generally speaking, they are meaningful only in relation to a quite theoretical, abstract knowledge of the effects of an exercise which ... is itself reduced to a series of abstract movements, decomposed and organized by reference to a specific, erudite goal (e.g., "the abdominals") entirely opposed to the total, practically oriented movements of everyday life. They presuppose a rational faith in the deferred, often intangible profits they offer ... It is therefore understandable that they should find the conditions for their performance in the ascetic dispositions of upwardly mobile individuals who are prepared to find satisfaction in effort itself and to take the deferred gratifications of their present sacrifice at face value. (214)

Not only does the language of this description evoke Wordsworth's relocation of pleasure in "effort" and goals in "infinitude" that follows the crossing of the Alps; but more importantly, Bourdieu identifies the technology which enables such a relocation. Here Bourdieu suggests that the opposition between (the "breathing spell" of) recreation and (the automatism of) "everyday life" is not strictly a matter of "practical" orientation; after all, the achievement of muscle tone too requires "practice." The difference is produced by the interposition of analysis, the "decomposition" and (re)"organization" of what, without such a process of reflection, would be experienced as a continuity.

Were we for purposes of comparison to regard the difference between a literary and an "everyday" use of language in similar terms, the literary would consist in the reconstitution of parts by reference to the whole, and its "practice" would involve repetition of abstracted units of speech – that is, the replacement of "actual speech rhythms" by the metrical unit. Godwin implies just such an analogy when he considers, in proof of his contention that thought is essentially *serial*, and that we can attend to only one thought at a time, rational comprehension of the complex sentence, capable of "containing twenty ideas," yet apprehended as a unit – or unity. This unity is produced in two ways: first, as "the unity of uninterrupted succession, the perennial flow as from a stream," a flow which the period both originates and brings to a close; second, by "unity of method" (368). These unities, however, are constructed:

an accurate attention to the operations of the mind would show that we scarcely in any instance hear a single sentence without returning again and again upon the steps of the speaker and drawing more closely in our minds the preceding members of his period, before he arrives at its conclusion. (369)

Godwin's representation of the production of unity as the repetition of steps is more than fortuitous, certainly when read in the context of *The Prelude*; as Andrew Bennett has claimed in an essay about the paronomastic use of "scan" and "measure," Wordsworth conceives an intrinsic relation between bodily disposition in space and literary movement. In Wordsworth, as in Godwin, the movement of reading, imagined as bodily movement – the mobile eye – differs from the practical orientation of "everyday life" by its repetitive nature, its backward (and forward) glance. The orientation toward unity produces the "erudite" goal of tautology (in the sense tautology might be employed to describe the "tatterdemalion" identity of the commodity form, where effect is identified with cause through repetition), or method.

"Methodical discourse," exemplified (appropriately for our purposes, since Burke will be celebrated as a "literary" orator in the 1850 *Prelude*) in Godwin's text by Burke's Speech on Oeconomical Reform, allows an anticipation of the whole to mitigate the condition of seriality both listening and reading impose upon thought, as if providing temporary succor – a kind of "breathing spell" – or relief from the imposed delay of the period. Thus method is the equivalent of "gait" and distinct from goal; even in Descartes, the empirical method, imagined as walking in a straight line, is as important for the consistency and order it imposes (the elimination of any need to "pause" for choice) as for the result it promises (see Zizek, *SO*). We might thus revise Bourdieu's estimation of the satisfaction or gratification derived from such recreational practices as walking to claim it as a necessary compensation for the rigors of denial set in play by the abstraction in general of practice for which capital, like the sentence's period, is both origin and end. The dismantling of recreation follows the procedure by which the "know-how" that had characterized labor is replaced (for example, in Adam Smith's description of pin-making manufacture) by discrete operations whose control by abstraction makes them no longer constitute a "practice," since their infinite repetition is linked to no actual or tangible product except by an equally infinite serialization. In this context

Wordsworth's decision to append the "genius of Burke!" passage to the catalogue of London recreations, whose discursive form – "words follow words, sense seems to follow sense" (vii.540) – mirrors the practice of urban walking ("The endless stream of men and moving things, / From hour to hour the illimitable walk / Still among streets" [vii.158–60]), is far more comprehensible. Burke's oratory, whose form itself indicates the importance to understanding of "Custom," or repetition, offers (retrospective) relief from the effective suspension of "All laws of acting, thinking, speaking man" (vii.606), the endless seriality that the capital city sets in motion. When Wordsworth "see[s] him... / *Stand*" in his mind's eye, Burke quite clearly functions as a literary figure, equivalent to the blind beggar. In both cases, the spectacle of discourse effects a mental (in the case of Burke, also a political) tergiversation: at the sight of the Beggar's "written paper," Wordsworth reports, "My mind did at this spectacle turn round" (vii.616). Here mental and potentially political revolution are allied with the stationary text, over whose dimensions the subjective I/eye travels. If London paralyzes Wordsworth's imagination because its society represents an excess of mobility and paucity of purpose, the reduction to *form* of this conjunction in the blind beggar (and in general in the literary or rhetorical figure) appears to prove a certain transcendental mastery.

We cannot ignore the apparent consanguinity thus established between Burke, the poet, and the beggar, between "Wisdom" (Burke's discourse), literature, and the beggar's "written paper," for if the "standing" position of the first two figures appears to represent a self-sufficiency that lends the text authority by distancing its content from conditions of emergence (and emergency or exigency), the position of the beggar recalls precisely those conditions. Rather than representing self-sufficiency, he is "propped against a wall" (vii.613) and so recalls the figure of the discharged soldier; given the reference to that figure, his written paper may be construed to "tell in simple words a [beggar's] tale." Wordsworth's former insistence that his is *not* the tale of a "mean pensioner" takes on a strange or ghastly aspect in this context: he has merely waived his social guarantee, and appears as a beggar rather than a pensioner. This is the right of man and citizen defended in *The Prelude*.

The truly revolutionary aspect of Wordsworth's foregrounding of method through the figure of the vagabond/beggar is, according to my argument, the conjunction of form and content to which this figure so powerfully draws our attention. The emergency conditions of utterance governing the beggar's written paper which produce or demand its cursoriness become, through the very typological weight Wordsworth lends to the figure, the conditions of utterance for *The Prelude* as well. If we now have to explain the extraordinary *prolixity* of *The Prelude* in relation to the "simple tale" of beggars and discharged soldiers, we nonetheless are in a better position to understand why those figures and their tales function so frequently as spots of time, or breathing spells, in its narration.

Slavoj Zizek's work on the chiasmus of form and content in philosophical ("methodical") discourse since Kant is useful here; Zizek contends that Hegel's major contribution to the critique of the philosopheme of the Enlightenment is an analysis that regards the formal elements of thought as constitutive:

> When Hegel reproaches Kant with "formalism," it is because Kant *is not* "*formalist*" *enough*; that is to say, because he still clings to the postulate of an In-itself supposed to elude the transcendental form and fails to recognize in it a pure "thing-of-thought." (*KN*, 163)

For Zizek, Hegel's contribution is to suggest that "the 'unthought' of a thought is not some transcendent content eluding its grasp but its form itself" (164).

In this sense, formalism is *both* the transcendental surplus *and* the empirical deficit. I contend that this is the version of formalism that Godwin's account of methodical discourse unwittingly offers to Wordsworth. Godwin's discussion of the problem of talking and thinking at the same time, like Wordsworth's representation of walking and talking at the same time, occasions a reflection on method:

> While I am speaking, no two ideas are in my mind at the same time, and yet with what facility do I pass from one to another? If my discourse be argumentative, how often do I pass in review the topics of which it consists, before I utter them; and, even while I am speaking, continue the review at intervals, without producing any pause in my discourse? How many other sensations are experienced by me during this period, without so much as interrupting, that is, without materially diverting the train of my ideas? My eye successively remarks a thousand objects that present themselves. My mind wanders to the different parts of my body, and receives a sensation from the chair on which I sit, or the table on which I lean; from the pinching of a shoe, from a singing in my ear, a pain in my head, or an irritation of the breast. (369)

The figural contradiction between physical and mental activity, the sedentary body and the wandering mind's eye, bears witness to the contradiction Godwin sees at work in discourse, where seriality achieves its formal unity by means of invisible "intervals" of prospective and retrospective review – the equivalent, of course, of the halted traveler. In fact, the paragraph is structured by a number of contradictions, and the formal structure of contradiction undermines the claim that "the mind can only apprehend a single idea at once" (366). Purporting to illustrate the process of thought as a continuous passage, the paragraph posits an hierarchical relation between the "train of thought" and objects of distraction, which are categorized as heterogeneous, or non-determining, elements. And yet the procedural development of the paragraph suggests a more complex interaction than Godwin wishes to allow: the reporting of apparently unrelated sensory input causes the subject matter of the paragraph to shift from the philosophical argument with which he began to the somatic disturbances affecting the philosopher–subject. The "train of thought" is thus effectively derailed by the mind that "wanders," even (especially) at the moment when Godwin attempts to deny the import of these "petty irregularities" (371). The fact that we see Godwin sitting as we read the prose produced in that situation (a situation which is doubled by the probability of our being seated ourselves; sitting is, *pace* Adorno on Kant, the foundation of philosophical argument) indicates the collapse of knowledge into its articulation and the ability of the mind to be "distracted" as it passes from the "universal" thesis to the petty irregularity of its exemplification. If it is true that this mental vagabondage produces no cognitive "pause" such as might be indicated by the "breathing spell" of a paragraphic period, it is also the case that the consistency of the paragraph depends on a supplementary logic legible in the necessity of "returning again and again."

Coleridge's *Biographia Literaria* is the discursive form which most closely reproduces, out of the configuration established here by Godwin between philosophical consistency (or method) and distraction, a new form (and formalism). But Wordsworth in *The Prelude* demonstrates the exigency of a literariness which, by foregrounding its distractions (Macherey: literature as "a procrastinated anecdote"), itself evades acknowledgment of the conditions from which diversion is sought. Philosophy refuses to acknowledge thought's dependency on that which it constructs as external to its procedures, in other words, its *improvisational* nature; literature, as Wordsworth defines it in *The Prelude*, similarly refuses, on the face of it (on the front of his whole song), to assume the position of the "mean pensioner on outward forms." But by seizing in defense upon the "inner" form of method, literature is thrown back into an identification with the very figure of improvisation (here connoting improvidence) it had sought to avoid. Again Zizek may serve to gloss the dialectical effect put in operation by the kind of reading Wordsworth will suggest is "proper" to *The Prelude*:

one does not compare the universality of the "thesis" with some Truth-in-Itself to which it is supposed to correspond: one compares it to *itself*, to its concrete content. One undermines a universal "thesis" by way of exhibiting the "stain" of its constitutive exception – let us just recall Marx's *Capital*: the inherent logic of private ownership of the means of production (the logic of societies where producers themselves own their means of production) leads to capitalism – to a society where the majority of the producers own *no* means of production and are thus forced to sell on the market themselves – their labour – instead of their products. (*KN*, 160)

*The Prelude*, which has only itself to talk about, is the "constitutive" paragraph of liberalism, and the "propriety" of its subjectivity is exposed as the tatterdemalion's.

Because liberalism is a form of thought that does not end with Romanticism, it may be valuable to place this emergent philosophical conflict between form and content within the larger context of intellectual history Frances Ferguson has recently outlined. In *Solitude and the Sublime*, she constructs a debate between empiricism and formalism originating with the category of the aesthetic in Burke and Kant. She regards Burke and his successors as linked by the production of interpretation as an infinite regress, "in which the representation of sensation produces representation as always something additional to be responded to" (viii); historical materialism and deconstruction, those two privileged forms of Romanticism, are Burkean, and therefore "crypto-empiricist" in orientation. In other words, they are overcome by the "petty irregularities" affecting even the most sedentary philosopher. Relevantly, Ferguson includes as an example of the effect of discursive representation an anecdote by Paul de Man:

We can all remember personal versions of such a fall from grace, of such a loss of innocence. (I for one remember trying to drive down a Swiss street after having just read, in a local newspaper, that for every 100 metres one drives one has at least thirty-six decisions to make. I have never been able to drive gracefully since.) (35)

Here, discourse intervenes and forms an obstacle to thought's transcendental prowess, its ability to get from here to there. De Man's anecdote, however, is especially appropriate in relation to *The Prelude* because of a suppressed context; Italo Svevo's *The Confessions of Zeno*.[15] There, the eponymous subject experiences a "shock" to his nervous system whose agency is discursive:

Tullio and I began talking again about his illness, which was his principal distraction. He had studied the anatomy of the leg and foot. He told me with amusement that when one is walking rapidly each step takes no more than half a second, and in that half second no fewer than fifty-four muscles are set in motion. I listened in bewilderment. I at once directed my attention to my legs and tried to discover the infernal machine. I thought I had succeeded in finding it. I could not of course distinguish all its fifty-four parts, but I discovered something terrifically complicated which seemed to get out of order [an equivalent in French: *désœuvrer*] directly I began thinking about it.

I limped as I left the cafe, and for several days afterwards walking became a burden to me and even caused me a certain amount of pain... Even today, if anyone watches me walking, the fifty-four movements get tied up in a knot, and I feel as if I shall fall down. (98)

Beginning with a dream of locomotion (the dream of sitting in a train being itself an allusion to Freud's description of free association) and ending with a Rousseauvian lamentation that the "machine" has robbed humanity of health ("Health can only belong to the beasts, whose sole idea of progress lies in their own bodies" [415]), Svevo implies that *human* progress, even in its most physiological register – the "glad animal movements" of walking – is infected by a machine which the passage above decidedly renders as thought itself. The confessional prolixity of the crypto-empiricist walker will mark him as a descendant of Zeno: "what the consciousness took only for a path to the truth, and as such external to it (Zeno's argumentative procedure, for example), *is already truth itself*" (*KN*, 163).

If we are not surprised to discover a certain affinity between Zeno and de Man, it is because the "fall from grace" de Man describes in his anecdote enacts the paralysis or "limping" effect we associate with the interaction of theory and practice. Gracefulness in de Man's anecdote corresponds to Bourdieu's description of the bourgeois gait, and distinguishes itself from the odd consciousness set in play by talking about walking in *The Confessions of Zeno*. Lack of this grace is then characteristic of the critical gesture, a gesture which, if effective, must interrupt the know-how of thought. Both deconstruction and the saturation of the historical context are articulations of reading practices which emulate this fall from grace; readers become aware of "at least thirty-six decisions to make" (or fifty-four movements made) for every hundred or so metrical units of a Wordsworth poem. What is peculiar – and valuable – about the Wordsworthian instance is the attention he draws to this problem by writing – in absence of sufficient knowledge or purpose – on know-how or procedure itself.[16] *The Prelude*, despite its canonization, has never functioned as an adequate substitute for the projected epic project of *The Recluse* because of its lack of any subject matter other than the "petty irregularities" that continually derail the train of poetic thought.

### III: THE MEASURED GESTURE AND THE COUP

### *The Eighteenth Brumaire of William Wordsworth*

One history of *The Prelude* has been written by Alan Liu, who persuasively demonstrates in *Wordsworth: The Sense of History* the extent to which Napoleon Bonaparte figures as a ghastly presence in the spaces opened to Imagination in the poem. In according to Napoleon the status of privileged historical referent, Liu displaces the poem's explicit referent: the course of the French Revolution from the Fête de Fédération in July 1790 to the execution of Robespierre in 1794. The relevant aspects of Napoleon's career – the Egyptian campaign, the *coup* of 18 Brumaire, 1799, his crowning as emperor in 1804 – take place during the composition of *The Prelude*, according to Liu's argument intervening to reshape Wordsworth's imagination or memory of earlier events. Thus even in his figurative dimension, Napoleon functions as usurper.

In lieutenant-like fashion, Napoleon can "stand in" for history in Liu's argument and in Wordsworth's poem by virtue of a certain formal equivalence. The military *coup de force* with which he came to be associated was a stroke of supreme ambivalence, regarded by some as the culmination, by others as the travesty, of the politics of liberalism. An epitome of the various *coups d'état* (and *coups de tête*) by which the French Revolution had proceeded, it similarly summarized the nature of various legislative measures enacted by the "republican" government – for example, the decree of 23 August in Year I (1793) ordering the *levée en masse* ("full conscription"), which made every citizen a (potential) soldier. The "Defender of Liberty" become its enforcer; freedom from unjustified restraint transformed into the march of military speed: these are the equivalences established by the *coup* of Napoleon Bonaparte and by legislative measures which preceded and may be said to have determined its enactment.

For another historian, however, not Bonaparte but his nephew, Louis Napoleon, functioned at once as the culmination and the travesty of liberalism. Marx's historiographical method in *The Eighteenth Brumaire* may be regarded as a model for Liu's reading of *The Prelude*, for Marx's text suggests a precedent for a referentiality of the future anterior. By identifying Louis Napoleon as "the real Bonaparte, the Bonaparte *sans phrase*," Marx means, of course, to suggest that force has replaced Parliament, and Parliamentary procedure. But he also suggests that this re- or displacement reveals the double nature of liberalism: what initially appears as an opposition – the difference between right and force, between the decree and the *coup* – is not an ontological difference but a temporal one. The decree, or phrase, is enacted by the *coup* of force. Moreover – and this is precisely *why* Marx chooses to attach to Louis Bonaparte a representative significance – this "real" Bonaparte, who does not bother to address the Parliamentary body except after the fact, gives to the "general phrase" of liberty a particular content: the vagabond's solicitation for funds.[17] Marx describes the final enactment of the "absolute liberty" that is the "general phrase" of liberalism: on 2 December 1851, Napoleon's nephew (his second self), Louis Napoleon, dissolves Parliament by a *coup*. It is a supremely parodic enactment, of course; Louis Napoleon, the (political) vagabond interested only in the continuing increase of his salary (or pension), usurps absolute power *in the name of* restoring universal suffrage.[18] What had appeared in its initial "phrase" as the pure form of representation – the self-authorized declaration, the claim to being of the third estate – is now marked by a certain social inflection, a different kind of claim: "Give money." By establishing a formal resonance between the two figures, Marx refuses the separation of the political and the social that constitutes the philosophical *coup* of liberalism. His historiographical method teaches us to expect that the political address has an *ulterior* (subsequent) content, or referent. The *charitable gesture* of liberalism, the offer of the bourgeoisie to represent the whole People, is given the aspect not of the legislative *measure*, that unit of the poetic phrase, but of the *coup*: a stroke, or stress, whose repetition dismantles or abrogates the semantic content of that phrase.

I wish to read Wordsworth's representation of the encounter with the discharged soldier as containing the ulterior content of the pure form of liberation – liberalism – represented in the poem's glad preamble. Although the example of Louis-Napoleon could have served only by a remarkable foresight as an historical referent for *The Prelude*, Marx's analysis of the situation and the style of his speech allows us to recontextualize the poem's record of the encounter between the vagabond and the bourgeois in light of the space opened in *The Prelude* between the origins and ends of liberal democracy. That space, to which Wordsworth gives an aesthetic shape, is consistent with the character of the liberal text, which couches its decrees in ambiguity in order to legislate the future. One project of *The Prelude* is to refuse priority to historical time by regarding the formal time of composition as capable of usurpation; the famous apostrophe to imagination in book VI – "Imagination! – lifting up itself / Before the eye and progress of my song" (VI.525–6) – represents this constituted time of composition as a *mise en abîme*, wherein the present (and presence) appears as an interstitial function, a *coup* separating prospect and retrospect, or past and future. We may regard the apostrophe as Wordsworth's version of a revolution in which the phrase goes beyond the content. Read large, the apostrophe thus suggests that Wordsworth intends the structure of *The Prelude* to include not only events that may have intervened between the narrated and narrative time, but also those that have intervened between the time of its composition and its rereading, for its end is infinity. But if imagination here functions as a proactive riposte to the earthly and mortifying spectacle of politics, nonetheless the form of its representation must suggest an alliance with the very spectacle upon which it had thought to obtrude: the Napoleonic *coup*, which is itself a formal repetition of the revolutionary rupture.

Marx notes that Louis Bonaparte was a *vagabond*, and characterizes the vagabond as one whose speech is shaped to extract the last penny from the bourgeois. If actions speak louder than words in the *coup* of 1851, they are nonetheless accompanied by a certain *style* of speech.

Marx describes a characteristic message sent by Louis Bonaparte to the National Assembly as one of "American prolixity": "overloaded with detail, redolent of order, desirous of reconciliation, constitutionally acquiescent, treating of all and sundry, but not of the *questions brûlantes* of the moment" (*EB* 79). Thus the *coup de force* has a poetical accompaniment, notably destitute of a particular political agenda or affiliation with a party.

The style of speech characteristic of Marx's political "vagabond" is elsewhere characterized as "regular *chantage*" (*EB* 73). The *Littré* defines *chantage* as an "action de faire chanter quelqu'un, c'est-à-dire de lui extorquer de l'argent en le menaçant de révéler quelque chose de scandaleux, ou de le diffamer, etc." ("the act of making someone 'sing,' that is to say, to extort money from him by threatening to reveal some scandal, or to defame him, etc."). What kind of dirt does the political vagabond have on the bourgeois? In the historical instance cited by Marx – here to be expanded into a more general paradigm – he has witnessed the bourgeois repeal of universal suffrage: an electoral law which disenfranchised the vast majority of those from whom the electors derived their authority. On 31 May 1850, the parliamentary majority, in temporary ascendancy, enacts a law

by which universal suffrage was to be abolished, a residence of three years in the locality of the election to be imposed as a condition on the electors and, finally, the proof of this residence made dependent in the case of workers on a certificate from their employers. (*EB* 70)

Thus by a stroke of the pen – a "coup" given legitimacy by the discursive form of the legislative "measure" – the Parliamentary majority produces on a formal level what Marx argued the Napoleonic Code had wrought economically: a transformation of the mass of the French nation into troglodytes, vagabonds. All who might travel in search of employment – and Hufton has demonstrated the extent to which the seasonal nature of agricultural employments necessitated such travel – as well as all those who, as a consequence of the economic contractions and expansions induced by the debt-structure of the French state faced periodic unemployment, were excluded from political suffrage.

In a way this repeal of universal suffrage, which merely reenacts the Abbé de Sieyès' distinction between the active and the passive citizen, reduces the Parliament to the passive double of the French people it purports to represent; in Marx's phrase, the Electoral Law "was the leaden ball chained to the feet of [the National Assembly], which prevented it from walking – so much the more from storming forward!" (*EB* 80). To *act* against the threat of usurpation, the National Assembly "would give the nation its marching orders, and it fears nothing more than that the nation should move" (*EB* 83). By means of an appropriately literary allusion, Marx indicates the *jacquerie* ("joke") by which the National Assembly becomes the spectral double of the passive citizen: "no longer the representative of the sovereign nation, *sans* eyes, *sans* ears, *sans* teeth, *sans* everything" (*EB* 89), the Assembly replicates the political identity it retroactively assigns to the people from whom it had derived its authority. The *negative litany* with which democratic politics begins (the invalidation and abrogation of titles, those "phrases" of identity, may serve as an example) becomes a means of disenfranchisement, but not only of the peasant "sans biens." It also proves the final undoing of his *representative*. A National Assembly more meager was never seen abroad by night or day.

As I have suggested, this measure merely repeated the distinction, made by the Abbé de Sieyès precisely one week after the storming of the Bastille, between the active and the passive citizen, a distinction based not on the degree to which citizens had taken part in "liberation" (one way to construe "active" citizenship) but rather on their ability to pay "a direct tax that amounted to triple the daily wage for unskilled labor in the locality."[19] Money, that congealed form of activity, performs an essential *transmutation*, giving to the apparent immobility of "estate" a certain *potential energy*. Sieyès' aim was to differentiate between the right to vote and the "ordinary" civil rights – "for instance, freedom from unreasonable imprisonment" (4). But by May 1796, even the right to petition had been denied to the ranks of citizens designated "passive" – "men over the age of 25 with little or no property and also unknown numbers of vagrants and domestic servants" – thereby confining those ranks, if not to prison, then certainly to a subjection which their enforced silence and exclusion from the political field appeared to render permanent. The encounter between beggar and bourgeois, where the form of petition is not political but economic – "give money" – is the exposure of this silencing and immobilization.[20]

As if instantiating the return of the repressed, rationales against universal suffrage returned compulsively to the spectacle of vagabondage – in England as well as in France. The vagabond and vagrancy suggest the impotency of the enforced distinction between public and private, since the beggar's appeal, while directed toward private needs-satisfaction – the measure of ale or food – is made toward the public, rather than the private, unit. His petition destabilizes the distinction between private interest and public (dis)interest, thereby revealing the "sheer egoism" Marx attributes to the tendency of the bourgeois "to sacrifice the general interest of his class for this or that private motive" (90).

By representing the relation between president and Assembly as the relation between a vagabond and his bourgeois (or, in Cowper's phrase, the leech and his spendthrift; see below), Marx also allows us to see as *political* the importunate address of the many vagrants whom Wordsworth encounters in *The Prelude*.

The vagabond makes the bourgeois "sing" because the petition is accompanied by a *coup*, or its threat. It is not insignificant that the vagabond's *chantage* takes place in proximity to the specter of military force; thus Louis Napoleon's political model, Napoleon Bonaparte, in 1799 addressed the Council of Ancients in the guise of a soldier. According to his secretary, "only the words 'brothers in arms' and the 'frankness of a soldier,' were heard" (Liu, *Wordsworth*, 450). This characteristic may be more telling than the apparent stylistic difference between Napoleon and his vagabond nephew: whereas Louis Napoleon is prolix, Napoleon Bonaparte's speech was notoriously confused and poorly expressed, even if the written versions of the speech that appeared in the press shortly thereafter were generally more polished (*ibid*, 450). Marx comments: "Napoleon, smaller than his prototype [Cromwell], at least betook himself on the eighteenth Brumaire to the legislative body and read out to it, though in faltering voice, its sentence of death" (*EB* 115).

In the case I wish to propose as a third instance of this discursive encounter between the vagabond/dictator and the bourgeois – or, put more abstractly, the collision between the social and political dimensions of liberalism – a third "style" of presentation will be enacted: the murmur. As a disarticulation of speech, murmuring in fact may capture the effect of both Napoleonic modes of address, since in both instances the threat of usurpation renders the variously flattering and faltering words of the dictators ultimately meaningless and reduces language to the status of so much background noise. But in the third instance I propose, this rendering or reduction will be foregrounded as the utopian *common* language dreamt of by philosophy.

## The beggar and the bourgeois

While thus I wandered, step by step led on,
It chanced a sudden turning of the road
Presented to my view an uncouth shape,
So near that, slipping back into the shade
Of a thick hawthorn, I could mark him well,
Myself unseen. He was of stature tall,
A foot above man's common measure tall,
Stiff in his form, and upright, lank and lean –
A man more meagre, as it seemed to me,
Was never seen abroad by night or day.
His arms were long, and bare his hands; his mouth
Shewed ghastly in the moonlight; from behind,
A milestone propped him, and his figure seemed
Half sitting, and half standing. I could mark
That he was clad in military garb,
Though faded yet entire. He was alone,
Had no attendant, neither dog, nor staff,
Nor knapsack; in his very dress appeared
A desolation, a simplicity
That seemed akin to solitude. Long time
Did I peruse him with a mingled sense
Of fear and sorrow. From his lips meanwhile
There issued murmuring sounds, as if of pain
Or of uneasy thought; yet still his form
Kept the same steadiness, and at his feet
His shadow lay, and moved not. In a glen
Hard by, a village stood, whose roofs and doors
Were visible among the scattered trees,
Scarce distant from the spot an arrow's flight.
I wished to see him move, but he remained
Fixed to his place, and still from time to time
Sent forth a murmuring voice of dead complaint,
Groans scarcely audible. Without self-blame
I had not thus prolonged my watch; and now,
Subduing my heart's specious cowardice,
I left the shady nook where I had stood
And hailed him. Slowly from his resting-place
He rose, and with a lean and wasted arm
In measured gesture lifted to his head
Returned my salutation, then resumed

His station as before. And when erelong
I asked his history, he in reply
Was neither slow nor eager, but, unmoved,
And with a quiet uncomplaining voice,
A stately air of mild indifference,
He told in simple words a soldier's tale:
That in the tropic islands he had served,
Whence he had landed scarcely ten days past –
That on his landing he had been dismissed,
And now was travelling to his native home.        (IV.400–49)

To this point, the narrated encounter between the vacationing
student and the discharged soldier in book IV of *The Prelude* seems
designed precisely to erase the social context of the two figures – one
a bourgeois, the other a vagabond – from the horizon of meaning, or
at least to refuse to that context a determinative status. The soldier
appears as an emblem of resolution and independence, his "measured
gesture" and "stately air" being equivalent to the leech-gatherer's
"courteous" and "stately" speech, the "solemn order" and "measured phrase" of the latter's "lofty utterance." His articulate speech
is represented as – indeed, identified with – the very language of *The
Prelude*; the "simple tale" is repeated as if verbatim, yet without
quotation. Even his figure, in such apparent contrast to his speech,
connects him with literature; as Hartman and others have pointed
out, he emerges "ghastly" as if from the torn pages of the children's
books that Wordsworth read.

As in "Resolution and Independence," however, Wordsworth
characterizes the "measured phrase" of these "poets of nature" in
such a way that the context of *chantage* reemerges.[21] The rude,
repetitive interrogation to which the poet subjects the leech-gatherer
after their initial greeting appears to produce the very form of his
autobiography; if the vagabond is forced not only by the poet, but
also by others – both police and potential benefactors – constantly to
"his words repeat," it is small wonder that his autobiography is
rendered thus: "from pond to pond he roamed, from moor to moor"
(103). The apparent independence of the leech-gatherer may owe as
much to the interviewer's obtuseness as to fact; recall that the initial
question – "What occupation do you there pursue?" – already
frames the encounter within the discourse of employment, of the
deserving and undeserving poor. The leech-gatherer may thus be
understandably anxious to represent himself as pursuing "honest

maintenance." Or, rather than anxiety, his responses suggest the formulaic air of the mnemonic murmur, the alienation that comes with (false) representation. In Dorothy Wordsworth's account of their actual conversation, a different answer to the second question – "How is it that you live, and what is it you do?" ("Resolution and Independence," line 119) – is offered. "His trade *was* to gather leeches, but *now* leeches are scarce and he had not strength for it. He lived by begging and was making his way to Carlisle where he should buy a few goodly books to sell" (*DWJ*, 42; emphases mine).

Thus Wordsworth's later description of the discharged soldier's responses to his similarly repetitive questions:

> Solemn and sublime
> He might have seemed, but that in all he said
> There was a strange half-absence, and a tone
> Of weakness and indifference, as of one
> Remembering the importance of his theme
> But feeling it no longer. (IV.473–8)

Here sublimity and especially the "demeanor calm" or *composure* of the discharged soldier seems attributable to the necessity, to which he has apparently been subject, of repeating his tale. The intonation or oral performance of the tale approximates the language of poetry precisely to the extent that it is distanced from the "impassioned utterance" Wordsworth identifies as the source of poetry in the Preface to *Lyrical Ballads*. The soldier himself has become a type of the Romantic ventriloquist; the *sujet d'énonciation* has split by dint of repetition from the *sujet d'énoncé*. His style of utterance now represents, in a potentially mocking way, the structural divide between (to use Adorno's terms of analysis) the transcendental subject and the utterly reduced empirical subject.

Despite the absence of passionate importunity in the self-descriptions of the leech-gatherer and the discharged soldier, questions of "worldly maintenance" obtrude upon the consciousness of the interlocutor, and, if in neither case is the vagabond figure successful at extracting "de l'argent" from the bourgeois poet (one is reminded of De Quincey's response to "The Ruined Cottage": "Pray, amongst your other experiments, did you ever try the effect of a guinea?" [*CW* II.305]), their style of address does make the poet "sing." In both cases, the poet's anxiety about the subject's worldly maintenance derives from the spectacle (or its auricular equivalent) of the speech itself, where an absolute destitution (desolation) seems responsible for producing the loftiness of utterance. It is not, in other words, that Wordsworth necessarily gains strength by witnessing the perseverance of the literary despite destitution; rather, now the quality of literariness seems indistinguishable from, is identifiable as, that empirical deficit. The tone of the retrospective narrative in book IV is, after all, one of gentle self-accusation, as if the youthful poet's pursuit of detail, fact, context, demonstrates an inappropriately historical, social, political, even economic interest in the essentially figural or literary dimension of the soldier. Each of the questions and actions undertaken by the poet seems governed by an overriding desire: "I wished to see him *move*" (429). When, after the "measured gesture" of the initial greeting, the soldier remains "unmoved" by the reiteration of his own history, Wordsworth performs a severer intervention, analogous to the demand of the police to the vagrant: "Move on."

> At this I turned and looked towards the village,
> But all were gone to rest, the fires all out,
> And every silent window to the moon
> Shone with a yellow glitter. "No one there,"
> Said I, "is waking; we must measure back
> The way which we have come. Behind yon wood
> A labourer dwells, and, take it on my word,
> He will not murmur should we break his rest,
> And with a ready heart will give you food
> And lodging for the night." At this he stooped,
> And from the ground took up an oaken staff
> By me yet unobserved, a traveller's staff
> Which I suppose from his slack hand had dropped,
> And lain till now neglected in the grass. (450–63)

Wordsworth's deictic inference – that "there," the village in prospect, is the soldier's "native home," and as such, the object of his journey – seems in keeping with the general prosaism of his reading practice, since the ghastliness of the apparition suggests that the soldier is from another world entirely. In any case, however, he suggests a walk directly the reverse of what he ascribes to the soldier's intention, and thus – as with the demand of the police – we recognize this "obligation to mobility" as also a constraint placed upon the abstraction of freedom which, here and elsewhere in *The Prelude*, is associated with *elective* wandering or halt.

In fact, one way we recognize the "specious cowardise" of the youthful poet as continuing to govern his actions long after he abandons his place of hiding and confronts the soldier is by the evidence of his own *dis*composure. A discomposure that seems contagious: although his first representation of the soldier is strictly visual – a "mute" depiction – Wordsworth's voyeurism appears responsible for the reproduction of the *privacy* represented by the solitary figure as *privation*. His characterization of the "murmuring" sounds that issue from the soldier's lips as evidence of "pain," "uneasy thought," or "dead complaint" seems almost to be an instance of pathetic fallacy, for elsewhere "murmuring" is represented as the language of Nature; Wordsworth describes "the brook / That murmured in the valley" (IV.374–5) as having a "peaceful voice." Even more important, book IV begins by recounting episodes that feature the youthful poet under an aspect clearly foreshadowing the figure of the discharged soldier; there, however, murmuring is the sound of verse. We know from the narrative of these walks, for example, why Wordsworth notes that the soldier stands with "no attendant, neither dog, nor staff, nor knapsack"; such props would enable a certain self-recognition and thus diminish the strange otherness of the figure, for the youthful poet's own dog "was used / To watch me, an attendant and a friend, / Obsequious to my steps early and late, / Though often of such dilatory walk / Tired, and uneasy at the halts I made" (IV.96–100). If there is a difference between the poet and the soldier, it is that the soldier is found at a standstill, whereas the poet murmurs while he moves:

> And when in the public roads at eventide
> I sauntered, like a river murmuring
> And talking to itself, at such a season
> It was his custom to jog on before;
> But, duly whensoever he had met
> A passenger approaching, would he turn
> To give me timely notice, and, straitway,
> Punctual to such admonishment, I hushed
> My voice, composed my gait, and shaped myself
> To give and take a greeting that might save
> My name from piteous rumours, such as wait
> On men suspected to be crazed in brain. (IV.109–20)

In comparing his "measured" murmurs ("the toil of verse" [102]) with the river, Wordsworth establishes a principle of correspondence which effaces that of communication. Approximate to the language of nature, murmuring achieves a certain self-sufficiency; it is the language of "no mean pensioner." Thus it precedes, but does not accompany, the social gesture of salutation, as if the hushed "voice" were a different organ from that of speech – one which may be shaped, as gait may be "composed."

Because of this opposition between private and public language, the language of poetry and the language of society, Wordsworth appears to cast the encounter with the discharged soldier in the context of Rousseau's "Essay on the Origin of Languages." Alan Bewell has noted the way in which Rousseau's account of the formation of language and society appears to anticipate the emblematic account offered in the encounter with the discharged soldier.[22] By attributing his secretive observations to a "specious cowardice," Wordsworth foregrounds issues of representation and translation also at work in Rousseau's essay. There, "fear" had prompted the metaphor/misnomer of the Other as "Giant"; later, after the application of "measure," or the language of the geometer, the "literal" corrective name "man" will render the first metaphor erroneous:

A savage, upon meeting others, will at first have been frightened. His fright will have made him see these men as larger and stronger than himself; he will have called them *Giants*. After much experience he will have recognized that, since they are neither bigger nor stronger than himself, their stature did not fit the original idea he had formed of the word Giant. He will therefore invent another name common both to them and to himself, for example the name *man*, and he will restrict the name *Giant* to the false object which had struck him during his illusion. That is how the figurative word arises before the proper [or literal] word does, when passion holds our eyes spellbound and the first idea presented to us is not that of the truth. (*OR*, 246–7)

In the encounter with the discharged soldier, similarly, the "giant" comes before the man. Wordsworth estimates the "uncouth shape" as "a foot above man's common measure tall"; our suspicion that his estimate may be an exaggeration of the "literal" fact is suggested when Wordsworth registers the surprising detail that the soldier is not even fully erect: "his figure seemed / Half sitting, and half standing" (IV.412–13). Other minutiae of representation reinforce our understanding of the way in which the episode reenacts Rousseau's narrative of the giant/man: the initial spectacle lacks substance – "A man more meagre... / Was never seen abroad by night or day," and appears altogether "ghastly." Here Wordsworth allows us to regard the distension of the figure as an effect of moonlight (and romance); the figure is a shadow, and therefore has an *illusory* priority, the shadow being in fact derived from, dependent on, the second, substantial figure – of "man."

Given the soldier's half-seated posture (may we read this as an ironic commentary on the liminality of freedom, freedom as the moment of poise between the sedentariness of the philosopher, dependent upon social safety, and the vagrancy of his afterlife?), his "upright" form seems less a literal than a figurative description, whose purpose is to evoke other, related "figures" which confront or are imagined by the poet elsewhere in *The Prelude*: the crag that "upreared its head" in book I's boat-stealing scene; the drowned man of Esthwaite, who "bolt upright / Rose with his ghastly face"; and the blind beggar with "upright face" similarly "propped," against a wall, in book VII. More importantly, these figurations of uprightness – that distinctive carriage of moralized or socialized "man" – insist upon an actual *immobility* (the blind beggar is "that unmoving man") inconsistent with the apparently "natural" desire for freedom-as-agency: "I wished to see him move." These forms thus presage Wordsworth's most general representation of figuration, the apostrophe to imagination in book VI. There "imagination" functions as the "dead" nonetheless "lifting up itself." In Hartman's reading, this ascription of agency to imagination accomplishes the poem's "halt":

There is no more "eye and progress"; the invisible progress of VI-a (Wordsworth crossing the Alps unknowingly) has revealed itself as a progress independent of visible ends... Any further possibility of progress for the poet would be that of song itself, of poetry no longer subordinate to the mimetic function. (47)

What for Hartman is *The Prelude*'s crucial validation of a poet's "integrity of mind" antithetical to the mean pensioner's dependence on visual perception (and hence on the object-world) correlates with the distinction between the "murmur" and the "soldier's tale." That murmuring which is inarticulate ("groans scarcely audible") represents a condition of independence: the self-sufficiency, at once monological and conversational, of the river talking and murmuring to itself. The youthful poet's demand for articulation within defined narrative conventions – a soldier's tale – is what infects the identity between the two "murmurers" with the dimension of politics registered as class.

The interruptive aspect of the apostrophe to imagination in book VI, a sort of chiasmus, or *formal* "crossing," in which the address to imagination takes precedence over the narrative of the journey, thus replicates the formal dimension of the discharged soldier narrative. The murmuring evidence of the soldier's self-sufficiency, his ability to produce poetic "measure" despite (also because of) material destitution, has the immediate effect of arresting not only Wordsworth's attention, but also the reader's. In addition, we find the same motif of the interrupted (literal) journey; if by the Alpine peasant's instructions Wordsworth and his friend Jones learn "that to the place which had perplexed us first / We must descend" (VI.514–15), the youthful poet similarly instructs the discharged soldier: "We must measure back / The way which we have come" (IV.455–6). Why, in both cases, does the poet recommend as a necessity this kind of retrospective progress? Precisely because it mimetically represents the triumph of the formal over the "objective" dimension. Wordsworth signals this by foregrounding the "measure" of the way, the way as *method* rather than road, suggesting that walking is purely motif in *The Prelude*. The ostensible goal, the soldier's "native home," is abandoned or crossed over; it is, after all, part of the "soldier's tale," whose prosaism appears to *mis*represent the figural dimension of the giant/man. If Wordsworth corrects an initial misapprehension, therefore, he proceeds not by reassessing the dimensions of his initial estimate of the soldier's size through the application of a *geometer's* measure, but by reassessing the soldier's apparent discontent as a kind of literal dys-content, and murmuring as the pure form of the *poetic* measure.

### The methodological injunction against soliciting

As if in proof of my contention here, the final three lines of the 1850 manuscript of book IV stand athwart any other reading:

> This passed, and he who deigns to mark with care
> By what rules governed, and with what end in view,
> This work proceeds, *he* will not ask for more.[23]

These concluding three lines recommend that the reader attend to the rule or method by which *The Prelude* as a whole is constructed in order to understand the composure of (1) the discharged soldier, and

(2) the narrative of his encounter. Given that the lines occur prior to the narrative of what has come to be regarded as the *major* digression of the poem – Wordsworth's experience of the French Revolution – it seems difficult to account for the appearance and somewhat reproving tone of the authorial intrusion here. This difficulty may itself account for the unauthorized editorial exclusion of the lines from the first edition of the poem, and the repeated query of the copyist in the manuscript versions: "NB Q. as to the omission of these three last lines?" It may also be the case that the copyist (Mary Wordsworth), familiar with the 1805 version (MS A) which included no such reproof, regarded the interruption of narrative as unnecessary – especially since in book IV of the five-book *Prelude* there was no punctuation at all of the discharged soldier narrative, but rather what editors of the Norton *Prelude* call a "transition-piece" that "carried Wordsworth from the personal sufferings of the poor unhappy man, through to more general reflections" (152).

What must have prompted the belated authorial interruption? Why did Wordsworth, elsewhere so confident of a receptive audience to the extent that he can ask "Yet wherefore speak? / Why call upon a few weak words to say / What is already written in the hearts / Of all that breathe?" (v.183–6 [1850]), feel compelled to silence objections to the matter-of-factness of the episode? For evidence we may turn to Wordsworth's knowledge of the reception of that related poem, "Resolution & Independence." The early audience for *that* poem, Mary and Sara Hutchinson, apparently objected to the poem's latter focus on the speech and history of the leech-gatherer, which, according to Mary Moorman's reconstruction, was regarded as a falling-off from the first stanzas' representation of subjectivity. In responding to the general tendency of this criticism, Wordsworth refuses to accept praise for the first part as long as criticism of the second part is attached to it:

You say and Mary (that is you can say no more than that) that the Poem is *very well* after the introduction of the old man; this is not true, if it is not more than very well it is very bad, there is no intermediate state. You speak of his speech as tedious; everything is tedious when one does not read with the feelings of the Author... It is in the character of the old man to tell his story in a manner which an *impatient* reader must necessarily feel as tedious. (Alan Hill, 56)

As Moorman points out, Dorothy Wordsworth's postscript helps to clarify the nature of the Hutchinsons' objections when she recommends to Sara, "ask yourself in what spirit it was written – whether merely to tell the tale and be through with it, or to illustrate a particular character or truth etc." (543). In the final three lines, then, Wordsworth appears to repeat this injunction, which resists the time-saving utilitarianism or orientation toward *straightforwardness* responsible for the experience of tedium that comes (as Wordsworth himself acknowledges in book VI) with the realization that we must "measure back our way." For, despite an emphasis on forward motion, or progress, given to the concluding lines of the methodological injunction by attention to the "end in view" and the procedure of the poem, the actual narrative conclusion of the episode suggests a different orientation:

> Back I cast a look,
> And lingered near the door a little space,
> Then sought with quiet heart my distant home.          (IV.502–4)

And although both concluding passages highlight primarily visual motion (in the MS D lines, Wordsworth recommends a review of the text), the backward glance, in echoing the backward glance of the glad preamble, suggests as well that we regard the destination of the poet as having been altered.[24] Prior to the encounter, perhaps, the youthful poet had regarded his "native home" as his goal; certainly that is the sense of the "preamble" to book IV, which narrates Wordsworth's glad return from Cambridge to "that sweet valley where I had been reared" (IV.11). Such an orientation determines the gait and trajectory of the youthful poet as he approaches the Windermere ferry: "Thence right forth / I took my way..."; "'twas but a short hour's walk" (IV.9–10, 12). When he recasts his home as "distant" after this second approach to the Windermere ferry (the walk that Wordsworth "single[s] out" and which includes the accidental encounter with the soldier is up Briers Bow, likewise above the Windermere ferry), he appears to measure the distance in a different manner. Now, that home is "distant," and apparently realigned with the "infinitude" of book VI ("Our destiny, our nature, and our home, / Is with infinitude – and only there" [VI.538–9]). On such a scale, tedium has no measure.

But when Wordsworth responds to Sara's objections, he attributes her experience of tedium and her reluctant approbation of the representation of the leech-gatherer to something besides a prosaic disdain for the tedious murmur of poetic measure. His prose explanation of the logic of the poem, turning upon the appropriateness of the old man as a figure for imagination, suggests that hers is a class bias. At the conclusion of the letter, he offers a strong moral reproof:

My dear Sara, it is not a matter of indifference whether you are pleased with this figure and his employment; it may be comparatively so, whether you are pleased with *this Poem*; but it is of the utmost importance that you should have had pleasure from contemplating the fortitude, independence, persevering spirit, and the general moral dignity of this old man's character. Your feelings upon the Mother, and the Boys with the Butterfly, were not indifferent; it was an affair of whole continents of moral sympathy. (Alan Hill, 56–7)

Wordsworth implies that Sara has liberal sympathies for beggars who are women and children ("the Mother, and the Boys with the Butterfly" appears to refer to Wordsworth's poem, "The Beggars"), but criticizes her failure to extend this sympathy to the old man (in fact also a former soldier; Dorothy's journal records that he "had been born in the army" [*DWJ* 42]).[25] Of course, the poem as we now have it erases the leech-gatherer's identity as beggar. But the distaste one might have for such a figure is at least in part attributable to our metonymic identification of his occupation as parasitic; and as early as Cowper's *The Task* (an important literary precedent for Wordsworth's experiment with the structure of the literary excursion) that metonymic identification had an extended social connotation, applicable to the relation between the beggar and the bourgeois: "the spendthrift, and the leech / That sucks him" (III.817–18). Thus the leech-gatherer's *actual* occupation, the self-evidence of which conditions his "mild surprise" at the poet's questioning, is very much central to Wordsworth's conception of the poem – a fact reinforced by his suggestion to Sara that "The Beggars" is its closest parallel.

Moreover, the letter's explanation of the poem suggests that it is structured to turn precisely on the identification of the leech-gatherer as a beggar. Crucial to this explanation is Wordsworth's underscored affirmation:

but this I can *confidently* affirm, that, though I believe God has given me a strong imagination, I cannot conceive a figure more impressive than that of an old man like this, the survivor of a Wife and ten children, travelling alone among the mountains and all lonely places, carrying with him his own fortitude, and the necessities which an unjust state of society has entailed upon him. (Alan Hill, 56)

The testimony to a "strong faith" in the power of his imagination parallels *The Prelude*'s methodological reminder, in book VI, that the poet is no mean pensioner on outward forms. Here, however, Wordsworth claims that his imagination is outdone altogether by the figure of the old man, product of "an unjust state of society." Within the narrative of the poem, we see the logic of this explanation repeated, when, in Wordsworth's words, "I consider the manner in which I was rescued by my dejection and despair *almost* as an interposition of Providence" (56; emphasis mine). But the interposition is *not* providential; the leech-gatherer, like the discharged soldier, is in the road and athwart the poet as a consequence of purely social coordinates, statistically verifiable by criminologists as well as geographers. As Liu notes in the context of his reading of *The Borderers*, "the upsurge in crimes by veterans would help explain the dangerous side of such characters as the Sailor in the *Adventures* and the Discharged Soldier in *The Prelude*" (*Wordsworth*, 581).[26] Why *does* the discharged soldier appear in the middle of the road, at night, propped by a milestone? It *will have been* because of social legislation.[27]

On 24 June 1803, Parliament enacted a vagrancy statute (43 Geo. III c. 45) which justified and legitimated the temporary mendicancy of veterans:

Soldiers and Mariners, and Sailors, or Persons discharged from such, having Occasion to return to their respective Homes in England, which are frequently at a considerable Distance, are under the necessity of soliciting alms for their Relief.

This statute was intended to mitigate the measures of an earlier statute (32 Geo. III c. 45), designed to outlaw begging by the swelled number of pauperized veterans returning from the American war. Since the whole system of the Poor Laws in England was based upon the parochial administration of charity, whereby only those "settled" – either by birth or by a significant period of employment – within parish boundaries were entitled to seek relief, this statutory revision, by recognizing the legitimacy of an extraparochial charity, constituted a fundamental challenge to that administration. This legitimation, necessitated in part by the debt-structure of the fiscal–military state and the capitalization enabled by and enabling the American war, suggests a more implicit recognition of the "obligation to mobility" demanded by that state and its economy, and suggests as well that the apparently anomalous condition of the discharged soldier was increasingly to be the normative condition of the laborer. Evidence of this recognition appears in the literal obligation to mobility that accompanied the statutory legitimation of begging:

Every Soldier, Mariner, or Sailor carrying his Discharge out of any Regiment, Ship, or Vessel, within three Days to the nearest Chief Magistrate, shall receive a certificate of his Place of Settlement, fixing the time he is to reach it at the rate of 100 miles in 10 days and so on in proportion, on producing of which, being in his Time and Route, he shall not for asking relief, be deemed a Vagabond.

Although the statute attempts to maintain a fundamental determination of identity by "place of settlement," that identity is now attenuated, localized only as the distance between here and there. The orientation toward one's native home is all that determines the difference between the discharged soldier and the vagabond.

In this context, we may reread Wordsworth's representation of the discharged soldier's ghastliness as a symptom of this attenuated identity; at least as much as the episode premises an epistemological difficulty – the difference between "giant" and "man," or imagination and object – it constructs this social impasse: the necessary artifice, or textualization, of any difference between the soldier and the vagabond (which, in another register, may be construed as the difference between the public and the private).[28] Stationed conspicuously in front of a milestone – that measure of progress and rates of speed – the discharged soldier appears to contravene its power sufficiently to determine identity. At the same time, however, his agency is similarly suspended. The freedom from determination by the social order he represents may only be maintained by his motionless composure.

The vagrancy statute enables us also to reassess the verbal articulation of that composure. Now, the form of "a soldier's tale" seems entirely prescribed by the ordinance: he provides a record of service and the information that might enable the auditor to determine the straightforwardness of his itinerary: the date of his return to England ("scarcely ten days past") and his destination or orientation ("now was travelling toward his native home"). This account, which might duly distinguish him from the vagrant, nonetheless reinforces a certain "dys-content" we might well associate with murmuring: the *formalization* of identity that the statute sets in play makes irrelevant all (extraordinary) incident that might give to the commonplace ("*a* soldier's tale") an aspect of individuality. Hence when the youthful poet seeks just such information, asking "what he had endured / From hardship, battle, or the pestilence" (IV.470–71), the soldier's apathy seems symptomatic of his understanding that, having fulfilled his obligatory self-representations (note that the "measured gesture" by which he returns the poet's greeting appears to be a military salute) all further communication is superfluous.

These two aspects of the soldier's behavior foregrounded in the narrative – his stationariness and his quiescence – are, as I have suggested, in contrast to the moving and murmuring poet. In fact, they have the surprising effect of reversing the social relation that the encounter appears to mark out. Although evidence of the soldier's apparent conformity with the vagrancy statute would legitimate his request for relief, such a request – the articulation of desire or need – derives from a concept, bodily or psychological, of agency, which his entire passivity appears to preclude. Instead, we watch the *poet* go begging. The poet knocks on the cottager's door to gain the soldier's admission, and finally solicits the soldier himself for assurances:

> I *entreated* that henceforth
> He would not linger in the public ways,
> But ask for timely furtherance and help
> Such as his state required.        (IV.489–92; emphasis mine)

This entreaty is parallel in spirit to the poet's earlier inability to "forbear" questions that inappropriately (inappropriately according to the justifying aesthetic of the poem) attempt to contextualize the pure form of the soldier's tale, as if a fleshy detailism were required to *inspire* the compassion which the statute *enjoins*. Thus we find the youthful poet occupying the morally bankrupt position of Sara Hutchinson; unable fully to recognize humanity in the tedious form of beggarly self-representation, he wishes to effect a displacement of the figure that has arrested his attention and progress. In this desire he emulates the example of the French legislator M. Noailles du Gard, who celebrated the Napoleonic repression of mendicity by saying:

Eternal gratitude to the hero who has found a refuge for the needy and the means of life for the poor ... *Nos pas ne seront plus arrêtés par l'image dégoutante des infirmités et la honteuse misère*. ["Our footsteps will no longer be halted by the disgusting image of infirmities and of shameful misery.]" (Furet, 128)

Noailles du Gard here clarifies the double-binding logic of freedom readable in vagrancy statutes: in legislating the removal of the vagrant, the bourgeois is likewise allowed/impelled to move on.[29] Thus the citizen becomes a (not yet discharged) soldier.

The desire to move on, which the repression of vagrancy reconstitutes as an obligation, accounts for what I have noted is the oddly paradoxical language and effect of the methodological injunction with which book IV concludes, where the importance of measure and retrospect is justified as enabling the work to "proceed," even though the injunction itself functions as an interruption of the narrative: its punctuation, or arrest. Moreover, it discursively replicates the removal of the soldier to the laborer's cottage; if "a soldier's tale," dutifully rehearsed, represents a certain abstraction of identity, how much more does the generalized referentiality of " *This* passed." However, as a description of specifically aesthetic movement in *The Prelude*, the methodological injunction resists the utilitarianization of movement. Remember that the poet encourages the soldier to move in a direction entirely contrary to the spirit of the law, as, later and as if in imitation of his own consequently altered journey "home," his "overlove of liberty" will lead the vacationing student away from family duty and Cambridge and toward the Alps – where, once again, he must retrace his steps.

## *Passive panhandling*

It is the bourgeois subject, of course, who is characteristically free to walk both toward and away from his native home. This freedom even belongs to the female bourgeois; despite her aunt's Caroline Bingley-like objections to the undomestic seeming of Dorothy Wordsworth's *manie ambulante*, the courteous greetings and invitations by which she is met in her walks suggest the normative sociability of her appearances in the public road. On the other hand, the vulnerability and relative dependence of her social position (her small annuity was generously supplemented, prior to the Lowther debt-settlement, by yearly allowances from her brothers Richard and John) may account for the fact that her *Journals* record with perhaps even greater frequency than *The Prelude* encounters with vagrants which give her *pause*. A journal entry for 22 December 1801, too late to serve as the original for the manuscript version of "The Discharged Soldier," nonetheless offers an account with such interesting echoes of Wordsworth's narrative that it may well have influenced textual revisions, including the methodological injunction appended to the narrative in MS D and E. I quote material preliminary to the encounter in order fully to suggest the social dimensions of the encounter:

Wm and I went to Rydale for letters. The road was covered with dirty snow, rough and rather slippery. We had a melancholy letter from [Coleridge], for he had been very ill, though he was better when he wrote. We walked home almost without speaking. Wm composed a few lines of the Pedlar... We stopped a long time in going to watch a little bird with a salmon-coloured breast... It was pecking the scattered Dung along the road. It began to peck at the distance of 4 yards from us and advanced nearer and nearer until it came within the length of William's stick without any apparent fear of us. As we came up the White Moss we met an old man, who I saw was a beggar by his two bags hanging over his shoulder, but from a half laziness, half indifference and a wanting to *try* him if he would speak I let him pass. He said nothing, and my heart smote me. I turned back and said You are begging? "Ay," says he. I gave him a halfpenny. William, judging from his appearance joined in I suppose you were a sailor? "Ay", he replied, "I have been 57 years at sea, 12 of them on board a man-of-war under Sir Hugh Palmer." Why have you not a pension? "I have no pension, but I could have got into Greenwich hospital but all my officers are dead." (*DWJ* 71)

We could ask for no richer an account of the ways in which walking and talking might figure differentially in the paradigmatic encounter of beggar and bourgeois. For the poet and his sister, walking begins as an errand; if one were to map the trajectory of their journey from Dove Cottage to Rydale, it would no doubt follow the straightest line, as reference to the condition of the road suggests. Within this Euclidean geometry of movement, even that road appears as an obstacle intervening between the projection of the goal and its attainment. On the return journey, however, where the object is less determined – where they already carry with them the means of their self-satisfaction – the walk appears to modulate into recreation; not only does Wordsworth compose some lines of "The Pedlar," but Dorothy records with a naturalist's detail their arrest by the sight of a bird pecking along the road. The bird's indifference to their approach appears to remind Dorothy of "The Old Cumberland Beggar" ("the small mountain birds, not venturing yet to peck their destined meal, / Approached within the length of half his staff" [19–21]); or at least that is one way of accounting for her mood in the subsequent encounter with an old beggar. "The Old Cumberland Beggar" had recorded the psychological effect produced upon the public by the Beggar's slow and self-absorbed movement: indifference – "All pass him by."

If it is not "specious cowardise" that compels Dorothy to greet the beggar, implicitly asking him, in the language of the "Leech-gatherer," "How is it that you live, and what is it you do?", her "indifference" is an emotion she similarly reprobates. Even more noteworthy, we find once again that the taciturnity of the beggar produces an active solicitude in the bourgeois. Overcoming both her indifference and a "half laziness" that might identify her with the entirely passive figure, Dorothy must discursively *project* agency: "You are begging?" Wordsworth's question follows a similar pattern: less a question than a statement – "I suppose you were a sailor" – it half performs the self-representation that the old soldier's subsequent tale only completes.

An anecdote similar to Dorothy's recently appeared in *The San Francisco Chronicle*. In a column which regularly cites as evidence both of the city's economic deterioration and loss of social grace the increase in aggressive panhandling, Herb Caen reports: "André Previn has been in town all week [on business]...He even met a mendicant he liked in Union Square: His sign read 'Passive Panhandler' and he was quite dignified. We had a nice talk."[30] We may notice an attribution of solemnity and sublimity to the figure ("quite dignified") and his speech parallel to Wordsworth's report of the discharged soldier's conversation; in both cases, this attribution appears to rest on the conversation's distance from the mode of entreaty. But if we are able to regard the San Francisco panhandler as possessing the same dignity and calm of the soldier, it is worth pointing out that a San Francisco statute passed in 1992 prohibits what is called "aggressive panhandling," making the "composure" of the panhandler similarly a matter of legislation.

In effect, the San Francisco panhandler's sign is a terser version of the blind beggar's of book VII. Whereas the sign of the London beggar contains the equivalent of the "soldier's tale" or the details which the Rydale beggar provides to Wordsworth of his service ("his chest / Wearing a written paper, to explain / The story of the man, and who he was" [VII.613–15]), the self-identification as "Passive Panhandler" suggests an entire formalization of identity such that even supplicatory gestures might be replaced (and outlawed) by the written word. In the case of the discharged soldier, of course, even the written word is eliminated, since the body of the soldier is itself a figure – a figure for the muting of self-expression.

Significantly, the only part of the discharged soldier's sublime conversation directly quoted in the narrative takes the form not of entreaty or supplication but of reproof. For, although the poet characterizes his "entreaty" that the discharged soldier "move on" ("ask for timely furtherance") as a "reproof," it is in fact the soldier's response which seems to issue "apt admonishment":

> At this reproof,
> With the same ghastly mildness in his look,
> He said, "My trust is in the God of Heaven,
> And in the eye of him that passes me." (IV.492–5)

This expression of passive panhandling is antecedent to and apparently provides the conceptual model for Wordsworth's methodological injunction, which begins, "This passed." Like the soldier, the last three lines reprove not only inquiring minds, but the act of inquiry itself, as if the formalization of procedure in law or in the poem produces a self-evidence which makes such inquiry superfluous. Since the self-evidence is in each case – that of the discharged soldier, the Rydale beggar, and the San Francisco panhandler – a self-evident *impoverishment*, however, we may suspect that this formalization of self-expression cannot fully evacuate from language (Rousseau's "aimez moi" and "aidez moi") its social register.

The strong relation between the soldier's reproof of the poet's entreaty and the poet's methodological injunction against a reader's potential entreaty for "more" underscores this point. Although the three lines appear to cast the reader in an epistemological or heuristic position analogous to the social position of the beggar, and to cast Wordsworth in the position of the bourgeois who from half laziness, half indifference, might disregard his silent supplication, the narrated encounter suggests otherwise. Thus if we obey the injunction, and "mark with care" what has "passed," we discover that the poem itself performs the function of the beggar's sign and silenced figure, and its refusal directly to engage the social, political, or moral questions posed by the encounter – its quiescence, in other words – may be attributable to the drive of the poem – the aesthetic – to achieve a legitimacy politically defined as autonomy.

As I have suggested, Wordsworth's emblem for this poetic autonomy is the murmur; it characterizes both the early poetic labors of the vacationing student and the "speech" of the discharged soldier when detached from the context of social "address," reduced by law to so many forms of *chantage*. In one sense, murmuring represents the naturalization of speech; in this sense it is merely a lengthening out and modulation of the "Oh" of the glad preamble. But the ambiguity that allows the sound of exhalation to be heard as "groans scarcely audible" focuses our attention on a second, and potentially dominant, sense of murmuring. Here again, Dorothy Wordsworth's journal provides a useful gloss:

We walked on very wet through the clashy cold roads in bad spirits at the idea at having to go as far as Rydale, but before we had come again to the shore of the Lake, we met our patient, bow-bent Friend with his little wooden box at his Back. "Where are you going?" said he. "To Rydale for letters." "I have two for you in my Box." We lifted up the lid and there they lay. Poor Fellow, he straddled and pushed on with all his might but we soon outstripped him far away when we had turned back with our letters. We were very thankful that we had not to go on, for we should have been sadly tired. In thinking of this I could not help comparing lots with him! He goes at that slow pace every morning, and after having wrought a hard day's work returns at night, however weary he may be, takes it all quietly, [as a thing of course, (erased)] and though perhaps he neither feels thankfulness, nor pleasure when he eats his supper, and has no luxury to look forward to but falling asleep in bed, yet I daresay *he neither murmurs nor thinks it hard.* He seems mechanized to labor. (*DWJ* 86; emphasis mine)

In comparing her and William's lot to the condition of the bow-bent, mechanized laborer, Dorothy's attention seems particularly fixed, again, by her mental disposition previous to the encounter.[31] Although their walk to Rydale is essentially recreational in purpose, once the "end in view" has been decided, the walk to Rydale takes on the aspect of necessity, and the "bad spirits" in which the Wordsworths walk approximates the aspect of complaint Dorothy refuses to impute to the laborer. If they do not "murmur," they nonetheless appear to think it hard, imagining the consequent fatigue ("we would have been sadly tired") and expressing gratitude for its avoidance. Moreover, in receiving the letters from the laborer, again the Wordsworths in their walk unwittingly enact the logic of the "ça ira" ("Qui s'élevera s'abaissera"), reversing the normative social relation between benefactor and beneficiary. Whereas the bourgeois family regards the walk as a laborious necessity, the most taxing portion of a day otherwise spent reading and writing, the laborer has so "bowed" to its inevitability ("a thing of course") that it has become, as it were, a mere formality, unrelated (or merely a prelude and afterword) to the hard day's labor he performs at Rydale. It is also, we should note, a matter of choice, an exercise of agency, that sends the Wordsworths off on their excursion, unlike the "mechanized" deportment of the laborer.

In an entry dated four days later (12 February 1802), Dorothy compares her condition more explicitly to the beggar's or pauper's impoverishment. After a female beggar has called, she reflects:

When the woman was gone, I could not help thinking that we are not half thankful enough that we are placed in that condition of life in which we are. We do not so often bless god for this as we wish for this £50 that £100 etc. etc. We have not, however to reproach ourselves with ever breathing a murmur. (*DWJ* 89)

Again we find strong echoes of Wordsworth's methodological injunction: the encounter with destitution, properly read, *cannot help* but produce gratitude on the part of the bourgeois (the same moral lesson appended to "The Old Cumberland Beggar") and should certainly preclude the wish for "more." When we recast these reflective comparisons of class positions in the discourse of language, as Dorothy herself does in associating the wish for "more" with the murmur (of complaint), we see why Wordsworth may wish to suggest that the entire poem has been "ruled" by an injunction against the murmur of complaint, or supplication: his attempt in book 1 to free utterance from all determinations is what had required the differentiation between the "oh" of breathing and the "O" of address – now precisely identified (as "groans") with supplication and complaint.

### The Murmur and the Strike

One other connotation of murmuring – a discontent or disgruntlement recognizable in the *vox populi* – must certainly be suspected as operating in the background noise of *The Prelude*. Like the related "muttering," similarly an onomatopoeic formation, murmuring in a political context has a potentially subversive undertone. The *OED* cites Hall's *Chronicle of Henry VI*: "certain souldiors...beganne to mutter and murmur against the kyng and his consaill." Within the context of the French Revolution, murmuring indicates a dangerous and indeterminate unrest; Carlyle, writing the discursive history of the French Revolution as the "Age of Paper," nonetheless repeatedly acknowledges the role of voice, sometimes in the form of the articulated demand, "Bread! Bread!," but more often as an indeterminate murmur, as, for example, in response to the "martyrdom" of Charlotte Corday: "A strange murmur ran through the hall at the sight of her; you could not say of what character." Whereas Dorothy's suppressed murmurs are private, and privatized, the public murmur indicates a certain kinaesthetic energy, aptly represented in the figure of Charlotte Corday, whose murmur that she is "unfortunate" is a mask for murderous intent.

If the potentiality for action represented in the soldier's murmur is mutiny, when soldiers are discharged the potentiality is for the *strike*, whether we regard that strike as a *coup de force* or the cessation of labor now known as a work stoppage. We see evidence of this connection for Wordsworth in the plot of the "Salisbury Plain" poems; there, the discharged soldier, in apparent despair at his impoverishment (like the Rydale beggar, he is not given the pension to which he is entitled), suddenly commits a murder later described as a "stroke of violence" (752). The second sense of strike also was already available at the time of *The Prelude*'s composition; the 1768 *Annual Register* chronicled both a hatter's strike and a soldier's strike (the latter an action from which the usage appears to be derived: soldiers read their grievances to the commanding officers, then "struck their yards" in order to prevent ships from sailing).[32] In 1793, the *Annual Register* uses the same word to describe a political action, suggesting, perhaps, the influence of events in France: "This day the whole body of chairmen... struck their poles, and proceeded in a mutinous manner to the Guildhall, respecting the granting of their licenses." In 1803, Sir Walter Scott could even imagine a writer's strike: "I never heard of authors striking work, as the mechanics call it, until their masters the booksellers should increase their pay" (see *OED* entry).

These two connotations of the strike are no more separable than is the musical murmur from the murmur of complaint. The threat of violence accompanies the passive strike; when the chairmen "proceed[ ] in mutinous manner," they march in (parodic) imitation of the military regiment, and aggressivity seems an aspect of their sheer number. It is little wonder that such processions – in various forms, from the picket line to the protest march – should have emerged within liberalism as the standard practice of political, economic, and social dissent, for such processions – movements against the grain – derive from what I have suggested is its central tenet: *laissez faire, laissez passer*. These forms of passive resistance reveal the double-bind of obligatory mobility; as the picket line stands athwart progress and commerce, so the march reproduces workers who have ceased work in order to walk as citizens, thereby delegitimating representation (Rousseau: "in the presence of the person represented, representatives no longer exist" [*SC* 264]).[33]

Given the general population of those participants in events generally designated as popular "uprisings," as if in deference to Wordsworth's symbolization of the upright figure, we may speculate that passive resistance – the show of force through mere assembly – is the representational method of those who occupy the position of passive citizenship. E. P. Thompson and George Rudé have discussed popular organization; what I wish to highlight here, alternatively, is a kind of popular *dis*organization, the kind of representation remaining available to those who, having been effectively *discharged* from any stable place within a social order either as a consequence of military mobilization and demobilization or its industrial counterpart, belong to no *body* – no collectivity, of family, community, or class – that might serve as the basis for coordination. This condition is, in effect, the social dimension of what Merleau-Ponty describes as the condition of *apraxia*:

(i) A disorder of voluntary movement, consisting in a more or less complete incapacity to execute purposeful movements, notwithstanding the preservation of muscular power, sensibility, and co-ordination in general. (ii) A psychomotor defect in which one is unable to apply to its proper use an object which one is nevertheless able to name and the uses of which one can describe. (Translator's note, 126)

Apraxia is a psychological or phenomenological term for what Rousseau, in describing his experience of the condition of social marginality and the relinquishment of any concept of audience or address for his writing, had called *un désœuvrement du corps*, and for what Blanchot and Nancy, among others, in describing the postmodern condition have called *la communauté désœuvrée*.

This alternative terminology helps us to uncover the social etiology of what Merleau-Ponty reminds us is not a psychosomatic condition ("After all Schneider's trouble was not initially metaphysical, for it was a shell splinter which wounded him in the back of the head" [126]). Contemporary studies of homeless populations confuse the issue in determining that up to 75 percent suffer from mental illness, drug or alcohol addiction since, as critics have pointed out, these may be the effects or symptoms of having been "discharged" from jobs or evicted from homes. If we may describe the nomadic or immobile condition of occupants of the public road as apraxia, its social cause appears to be – above all – unemployment. We may refer here to Alexandre Vexliard's classic history of vagabondage for a description of the difference between pre- and postindustrial forms of vagrancy. Vexliard makes a valuable distinction between "elementary" and "structural" vagabondage, the difference between an occasional homelessness produced by earthquakes and fires and "the vagabondage of the dispossessed and the unemployed in a society based on principles of individualism and free enterprise" (20).[34] According to Vexliard, one of the great goals of social organization is protection against the calamities that produce elementary vagabondage, calamities which may randomly affect any of its members. Social engineering to protect against structural vagabondage, however, is more of a conundrum; after all, structural vagabondage (Marx's "industrial reserve army" of the unemployed) itself represents the institutionalization of one form of protection against random calamity, capital accumulation.

If *social* apraxia – or unemployment – follows the pattern described above, the unemployed would be found to suffer primarily from insufficient motivation – a loss of purposiveness – and/or from an improper utilization of objects or tools. This latter part of the syndrome might clearly include the utilization of *language*: for example, *anarthria* (loss of power of articulate speech, as distinct from the more general *aphasia*, where not only the articulation of the word but conceptualization is impaired [Merleau-Ponty, 175]). Symmetrically opposed to the condition of apraxia – the slack hand and the murmur – would be certain practices identifiable with dictatorship (here representing the full embodiment of social power): the *coup* and its verbal equivalent, the decree. This symmetrical relation allows us to extend our earlier envisaging of the encounter between the beggar and the bourgeois in a more explicitly political direction, appropriate to *The Prelude*'s thematic of liberty. We may note in retrospect that under the aspect of entreaty, Wordsworth *commands* the discharged soldier ("we *must* measure back..."), thereby restoring a measure of identity to the figure, visible in the appropriate (though proactive) salute.[35] Commanding the disappearance of the vagrant from the road, Wordsworth prepares us for understanding the similar behavior of Robespierre and Napoleon.[36]

Of the latter, Marx reports,

*Napoleon* wished to do away with begging at a single stroke. He instructed his officials to prepare plans for the abolition of beggary throughout the whole of France. The project was subject to delay; Napoleon became impatient, he wrote to Cretet, his Minister of the Interior; he commanded him to get rid of begging within a month. He said, "One should not depart this life without leaving traces which commend our memory to posterity. Do not ask me for another three or four months to obtain information; you have young advocates, clever prefects, expert engineers of bridges and roads. Set them all in motion, do not fall into the sleepy inactivity of routine office work." (Furet, 127)

Napoleon's suppression of pauperism by order – the *coup* ("at a stroke") works like the methodological injunction against begging; it means the confinement of the poor, their arrest by the police and incarceration in the *dépôts*. We might think of the *coup*'s suppression of begging as an ironization (in the sense of farcical repetition outlined by Marx) of Benjamin Constant's classic description of civil liberty: "The large states have created in our day a new guarantee: obscurity" (321). Obscurity represents the condition necessary to the exercise of private interest, an exercise now, "at a stroke," no longer subject to surveillance by the public (a feature of the *political* liberty of the ancients). But in relation to the vagrant, this obscuring can only be achieved by his confinement, for his appearance on the public roads exposes the "sheer egoism" organizing the public sphere, and, moreover, menaces the equation of self-interest and *autonomy* (since the vagrant re-presents the *absolute* condition of the individual as one of utter dependence).

But, as will be the case with Louis Napoleon's disenfranchisement of Parliament – a usurpation of state power *sans phrase* – Napoleon Bonaparte's elimination of begging "at a stroke" only imitates with greater effectiveness the logic of a similar *legislative measure* enacted by the Convention in 1793. Rhetorically suggesting the essential contiguity of the legislative measure and the dictator's *coup*, Marx describes the political response to the spectacle and spectacular increase in mendicancy in the 1790s:

For a moment the *Convention* had the courage to *decree* the abolition of pauperism, not indeed "at a stroke"... but only after instructing the

Committee of Public Safety to draw up the necessary plans and proposals, and after the latter had made use of the extensive investigation by the Constituent Assembly in the state of poverty in France and, through Barère, had proposed the establishment of the "Livre de la Bienfaisance nationale," etc. (Furet, 128)

He then reports on the effectiveness of this measure: "What was achieved by the decree at the Convention? Simply that there was now one more decree in the world and that *one* year later starving women besieged the Convention" (128). Although in Marx's narrative the Napoleonic *coup* is thus regarded as the more effective and *final* stroke (of the pen), in both cases we must note a certain intrinsic impotence in the political (whether discursive or military) strike at an (apparently) intransigent social problem. This impotence relative to the spectacle of the vagrant is based on its constitutive contradiction, expressed in the "perversity" of such figures: "They grumble about the government when it places limits on freedom and yet demand that the government should prevent the inevitable consequences of that freedom!" (130). Vexliard provides a gloss: if the traditional goal of social organization is protection against dispossession, "the era of laissez-faire called 'liberal' is characterized by a minimum of institutions capable of this function. Its ideal would have been to eliminate them altogether" (21).

In *The Prelude*, the *coup de grâce* by which Wordsworth manages the removal of the discharged soldier will be followed by the appearance of the "hunger-bitten girl" in book IX, an appearance ironically appropriate to Beaupuy's and Wordsworth's enthusiastic discussion of the abolition of the *lettre de cachet* ("Captivity by mandate without law" [IX.538]). Upon her appearance, Beaupuy exclaims, in the language of the soldier and the discourse of the *coup*, "'Tis against that / Which we are fighting'" (IX.519–20). In the critical retrospect of his narration, Wordsworth evinces a skepticism that either the political decree or the military *coup* might eliminate poverty; I would suggest that the methodological injunction of book IV is the locus of a similar criticism. Far from being an open book (*livre ... nationale*), the poem is, like the liberal state, a self-canceling phrase.

Wordsworth's nostalgia in *The Prelude* is consistently for the traditional institutions that mitigate dispossession: the endowed colleges of medieval universities which allowed impoverished scholars to "sit down"; the Grand Chartreuse, that sanctuary for pilgrims and other pedestrian travelers; and the Parisian nunnery which protected that abandoned woman, the Magdalen of Le Brun. Even his assurance that the laborer "will not murmur" though his rest be disturbed by the discharged soldier suggests reference to the "bonds of domestic feeling among the poor" rapidly disappearing along with the class of small proprietors Wordsworth calls "Statesmen" in an 1801 letter to the Whig leader Charles James Fox. But the celebration of these landmarks *is* nostalgic – or "sentimental," to use Schiller's opposition – rather than naive. *The Prelude* cuts itself off from such institutions by at once referring to and imitating the decree. Its transcendental surplus is produced by the empirical deficit, just as Republican France solves its problematic economic deficit by the appropriation of the "spiritual" or transcendental wealth represented in church lands. To juxtapose, in the figure of the discharged soldier, an embodied meagerness and a spiritual surplus (the biblical allusiveness of his remonstrance) is to call attention to the paradox attending liberal justice: freedom as dispossession, vagrants as "the inevitable consequences of that freedom."

The analogy between the *coup* and the decree is then crucial for our understanding of Wordsworth's production of a thematic unity in the form and content of *The Prelude*, a thematic unity represented in book IV's methodological injunction. The *decree* with which Wordsworth chooses to end book IV is a mitigation of the abrupt alternative (here a stylistic representation of the *coup*): ending without commentary and demanding that the reader "move on," closing book IV and opening book V. The methodological injunction is thus the equivalent of the "measured gesture" performed by the discharged soldier's "slackened hand" (both representative of an "intrinsic impotence"), and may be contrasted to another possible scenario, as for example reported recently in a local newspaper's "police blotter":

April 23, Strong arm robbery, 400 block of 51st Street, at 4 p.m. Male suspect asked for spare change; hit victim; loss of cash reported.[37]

The discharged soldier of *The Prelude* seems a "ghastly" apparition because his is the afterlife of the discharged sailor from the "Salisbury Plain" poems, the sailor executed by the "stroke" ("Adventures" 817) of capital punishment.[38] This "stroke" appears just – i.e., represents the self-canceling phrase of liberal justice – because it mimics the action of the discharged sailor earlier in the poem, during a foreshortened version of the kind of encounter (of two strangers) narrated in *The Prelude*: "he met a traveller, robb'd him, shed his blood" (97), although the criminal aspect of the encounter is suspended in book IV. Like the Rydale beggar of Dorothy Wordsworth's journal, this sailor is discharged without receiving the pension to which he is entitled; rather than grumble (according to the "perverse" behavior of those dispossessed by the freedom of *laissez-faire*), he executes a *coup*, or military strike. This strike of force is the logical outcome of what had already been foreseen by Cowper in *The Task*, when, in narrating the difference between the agricultural and the military "walk" of life, he had lamented the inability of the erect(ed) soldier to return to the bow-bent condition of the laborer: the plowshare has become a sword; the discharged and apraxic soldier misuses his tool as a weapon.

In the earlier poem, Wordsworth offers his own version of this metamorphosis – a liberation that is also a *désœuvrement* – in the embedded narrative of the poem. This narrative will sentimentally express his dissatisfaction with the prevailing modes by which the political and the social are negotiated. In the gap between the *coup* and the decree, a third measure – the literary absolute – will be enacted. This third *measurement* effaces the difference between the giant and the man, the bourgeois and the beggar, by *refiguring* both as a single, individual *absolute*.

Watched by the discharged sailor and his companion, the Female Vagrant, a homeless family, "sheltered" in the expanse of Salisbury Plain, reenacts the opposition between the *coup* and the decree:

> Her husband for that pitcher rose; his place
> The infant took – as true as heaven the tale –
> And when desired to move, with smiling face
> For a short while did in obedience fail.
>
> ("Adventures" 622–5)

Like the vacationing student, the mobilized father "wished to see him move", as it were; the child, enacting the stationariness of *The Prelude*'s soldier – a stationariness likewise apparently contravening the decree of compulsory mobility – remains in (a usurped) place. The impotence of the decree (the father's word-wish) – like the failure of the legislative measure to eradicate begging – leads to the supplementary "stroke" of force. By melodramatic narrative co-incidence, the father strikes the infant in exactly the place the sailor had struck his murdered victim. This coincidence, a formal repetition that evokes the sailor's compassion, is a recognition preceded and in fact made possible by a kinaesthetic formal repetition: the sailor "Nor answer made, but stroked the child" (540). This compassion-ating language of the body is the stroke as "measured gesture," now measured precisely to mediate the impotence of the decree and the brute force of the *coup*.

This narrative is, as I have suggested, a melodramatic version of the episode marked by the methodological injunction in book IV of *The Prelude*; the sailor's compassionate gesture contrasts sharply enough with the absolute (though mild) *indifference* of the discharged soldier. Indifference, in relation to vagrancy, is, as Dorothy Wordsworth's journal entries would suggest, often a consequence of the *proliferation* of figures – persons – seeking to elicit compassion. In *The Prelude*, which reflects on the similar proliferation of vagrants in Wordsworth's corpus, Wordsworth uses that proliferation and consequent indifference to advantage: insofar as the discharged soldier represents the poetic or figural *afterlife* of the figures foregrounded in *Lyrical Ballads* and elsewhere, he is deprived (dispossessed) of purely *social* coordinates; we must read him less in the context of social history than in the context of Wordsworth's poetic development. Hence the allusion of the methodological injunction to the "rule" by which *The Prelude* is governed may be read as an allusion to the "rule" governing Wordsworth's corpus – the first article of which is to live off its own substance – and beyond that, to the rule of the aesthetic in general.

The aesthetic rule is also the poetic measure, the repetition of strokes or stresses (recall the boat-stealing episode: "I struck, and struck again") of the poem. A tranquilizing spirit presses on the corporeal frame of the sailor when he finally speaks: "While his pale lips these homely truths disclose, / A correspondent calm stole gently on his woes" (665–6). Like the prolix repetitions of the leech-gatherer or the biblical resonances of *The Prelude*'s admonishing soldier, the content of these "*homely* truths" seems entirely inadequate to the task of reconciliation or amendment – if only because the idea of home itself seems vacated by the homeless coalition inhabiting the empty space or open field of the poem. Again Wordsworth would seem to draw attention to the form of the utterance itself. The speech act, as a continuation of the soothing stroke of kindness, produces a correspondent calm as, earlier, the poet's verbal representation of the breeze by a series of bilabial stops had generated its own "corre-spondent breeze." Violence and impotence are countered not by the explicit politics of the sailor's speech ("'Tis a bad world, and hard is the world's law" [658]) but by its tonal mitigation of impassioned utterance. In contrast to both the "Firm voice and indignation high" by which the sailor initially accosts the abusive father and the "bitter insult" with which the father responds "confident in passion" (631, 633), the soldier's homely truths are uttered with a *broken* voice ("A voice which inward trouble broke" [656]). The intonation of his social address is affected by the self-recognition he articulates "within himself," an ironic self-consciousness that is perhaps most visible in his silent and ironic pun: "The blessing this the father gives his child!" (650).[39]

## The mute sign and the tone

In his recent critique of Romantic *formal* resolution, Steven Goldsmith calls attention to a "transformation of matters of power into matters of language" that occurs in Romantic poetry and the theoretical discourses that would interrogate the implicit privileging of the literary. For example, he cites Derrida's ascription of linguistic agency to tone: "By its very tone, the mixing of voices, genres, and codes, apocalyptic discourse can also, in dislocating destinations, dismantle the dominant contract or concordat," commenting, "Surely this marks a quantum leap in the empowerment of "tone," that non-semantic component of language which, simply by going about its business as usual, produces subversive effects" (Goldsmith, 15). But Rousseau had empowered tone some time before Derrida: "In writing one is compelled to use every word in conformity with common usage; but a speaker utters meanings by his tone of voice, determining them as he wishes" (*OR*, 253). Thus the word "blessing," which the sailor murmurs to himself to evoke both the wound and its cure, has a certain representative status: in order to hear its *double entendre*, the reader must imagine alternate and potentially contradictory intonations – a *broken* voice and a strange half-absence. Only then does the (infinite) referentiality of "this" in the inward murmur become available: the "blessing," that anointment which had formerly consecrated the structural patriarchy of the *ancien régime*, is now reduced to bloody violence (the self-anointing *in blood* of the wound).

Goldsmith's point is not to deny that language practices are tools of subversion as well as domination, but rather to resist what he calls a "gravity-free textual politics without precise historical coordinates" (15). It is the goal of Rousseau's "Essay on the Origin of Languages" to provide those historical coordinates, and to historicize "tone." As Derrida points out, the "Essay" is structured by reference to the *loss* of tone that is writing (an effect of the "sedentarization" of language): it "begins in praise and concludes with condemnation of the mute sign" (*Grammatology*, 232). In the last chapter, Rousseau writes,

> Societies have assumed their final form: nothing can be changed in them anymore except by arms and cash. And since there is nothing to say to people besides *give money*, it is said with placards on street corners or by soldiers in private homes; for this there is no need to assemble anyone; on the contrary, subjects must be kept scattered; that is the first rule of modern politics. (*OR*, 294)

The vagrant, whose gesture and speech are always "measured" by this reduction of language to a single meaning – "give money" – represents this historical consummation, this "final form" of liberalism, in which the primary "measure" of legislation itself is usually the tax. If initially Rousseau had imagined an opposition between the language of poetry and the language of the geometer, between the giant and the man, finally a *common* measure is established – not the ballad but *chantage*. If the recreational return journey of the bourgeois subject may initially be contrasted to the compulsory mobility of the discharged soldier or the bow-bent laborer, we should also note that Wordsworth uses the time and space to compose portions of *The Pedlar*. There is *only* getting and spending. Perhaps this is why De Quincey, in constructing his own narrative of Wordsworth's life, ironizes the financial "luck" that attends Wordsworth's walk of life, referring to the Calvert annuity, the payment of the Lowther debt, Mary Hutchinson's small fortune, and subsequent appointments to pensioned government offices as "accesses of fortune stationed, upon his road, like repeating frigates, connecting, to all appearance, some preconcerted line of operation" (*Recollections*, 196). De Quincey is careful to represent Wordsworth as a type of the *passive* panhandler:

> At the same time, every reader will, of course, understand me to mean, that not only was it utterly out of the power or will of Wordsworth to exert any, the very slightest influence upon these cases, not only was this impossible – not only was it impossible to the moral nature of Wordsworth, that he should even express that sort of interest in the event, which is sometimes intimated to the incumbents of a place or church-living by sudden inquiries

after their health from eager expectants – but also, in every one of the
instances recorded, he could have had not the slightest knowledge beforehand of any interest at issue for himself...And yet, for all that, so true it is,
that still, as Wordsworth needed a place or a fortune, the holder of that place
or fortune was immediately served with a summons to surrender it – so
certainly was this impressed upon my belief, as one of the blind necessities,
making up the prosperity and fixed destiny of Wordsworth, that, for myself
– had I happened to know of any peculiar adaptation in an estate or office
of mine, to an existing need of Wordsworth's – forthwith, and with the speed
of a man running for his life, I would have laid it down at his feet. "Take it,"
I would have said – "take it – or in three weeks I shall be a dead man."
(*ibid.*, 196–7)

We have been witness to the Wordsworths' repeated inquiries after
the health and well-being of the incumbents of a place, though that
place is generally in the road. De Quincey may have become
convinced of an "air of purpose and design" in Wordsworth's
apparently disinterested progress as a consequence of the profit he
derives from each of these encounters. So assured is this profit that
Wordsworth need not render an account – hence the methodological
injunction. The exchange is off the books, not subject to taxation.

  These inquiries are, after all, the prelude to an act of charity. But
the more passive the panhandler, the muter the sign, the greater the
testimony to the pervasiveness with which the model of exchange
governs all social relations, all object-relations, even self-relations –
to the extent that breathing itself – that imitative murmur by which
the human body responds to its environment – becomes a form of
exchange, inhalation and exhalation the equivalent of getting and
spending. Wordsworth had claimed, in the 1800 Preface, that the
poet "binds together the vast empire of human society." We may
conclude that one method for achieving such a bond is to make the
road – that interval separating alienable labor from the person, work
from home, and also public from private (and as such, the mark
of social division) – into his home. It may seem that the road is
a nomadic space, an actual *utopia*. But as the milestone helps to
mark out, the road is, on the contrary, exactly the space wherein is
registered the extent of capitalization, and the vastness of empire.
Moreover, this road is already inhabited, by vagrants whose destitution similarly marks the extent to which the surplus represented in
the road derives from an extortion. In accounting the costs of the
laborer's self-reproduction, the interval of travel is time and energy
always charged to the worker. Vagrancy occurs when the time and

energy devoted to travel exceed the time and energy of labor, through which the worker achieves either surplus or subsistence. Even the vagrancy statute of 1803 allows that travel drains resources, and therefore requires support. Logically, therefore, the statute suggests that the *infinite* circulation of capital and expansion of empire similarly must demand a charitable assist. Vagrancy is the symptom of a production whose sole logic is expansion. Poems that echo the strange half-absence of wandering and murmuring vagrancy are its articulation.

# CHAPTER 4

# The walking cure

## I: THE THERAPEUTIC SUBJECT

I wish you would write a poem, in blank verse, addressed to those, who, in consequence of the complete failure of the French Revolution, have thrown up all hopes of the amelioration of mankind, and are sinking into an almost epicurean selfishness, disguising the same under the soft titles of domestic attachment and contempt for visionary *philosophes*. It would do great good, and might do for a part of 'The Recluse', for in my present mood I am wholly against the publication of any small poems. (S. T. Coleridge to W. Wordsworth, 10 September 1799)

Did Mr Wordsworth really imagine, that his favorite doctrines were likely to gain anything in point of effect or authority by being put in the mouth of a person accustomed to higgle about tape, or brass sleeve-buttons? (Francis Jeffrey, review of *The Excursion*)

Perhaps the image of psychological man presented here is the one most appropriate and safe for use in this age. It is the self-image of a travelling man rather than a missionary. Unfortunately for culture and good taste, the salesman always cruelly parodies the preacher – without being able to help doing so, for his cultural history has dictated to the salesman the rhetorical style of the missionary. (Rieff, "Introduction" to *Freud: Therapy and Technique*)

When Philip Rieff identifies the subject of Freudian analysis as the "isolated individual and defaulting citizen," he restores to critical attention the historical relation of the psychoanalytic subject of desire to the political subject of the discourse of rights. By describing the psychoanalytic subject as a "defaulting" citizen, Rieff suggests that the therapeutic subject emerges as a consequence of the hegemony of the private over the public sphere. His language of default also points to a significant symbolic mutation in the organization of the public sphere – the state. Describing the emergence of those modes of thought we associate with liberalism, J. G. A. Pocock describes two such symbolic mutations. Because "property – the material foundation of both personality and government – has ceased to be real and has become not merely mobile but imaginary" (112), Pocock argues that the "public" was transformed into the idea of "public credit," reducing the relation between the citizen and the state to "relations between debtors and creditors" (110).[1] These mutations, which Pocock dates more or less from the establishment of the Bank of England, are made fully public, so to speak, with the French Convention's distinction between active and passive citizens. The transformation of the public persona – the citizen – into debtor or creditor destabilizes "personality" and so produces the therapeutic subject, incapable of self-knowledge, indebted to the future and the past for what s/he will have been.

Readers familiar with the genesis of *The Excursion* will understand immediately the connection to be made between Wordsworth's project and the therapeutic moment of literature. Coleridge testifies to having suggested the larger project of "The Recluse" as a remedy for the "malaise" of postrevolutionary depression, and both parts of "The Recluse" that Wordsworth completed, *The Prelude* and *The Excursion*, contain extended representations of a mental or emotional breakdown attributable, no doubt, to a multitude of causes, but chiefly to the collapse of what recent political theorists have named "the Jacobin imaginary."[2] "Despondency," that mental condition affecting the autobiographical subject of *The Prelude* and the eponymously defaulted (e.g., privatized) citizen of *The Excursion*, the Solitary, occurs in the aftermath of the shift, much lamented by Burke, from a discourse of obligations to one of rights. The *negative* character of liberty within the regime and discourse of liberalism effectively eliminates the deontological or ethical aspect of the political; the subject no longer knows himself by virtue of what he owes to past, present, and future generations. But the discourse of rights in fact deepens the debt; "man" and "citizen" owe their being to each other.

The relation between the *political* discourse of rights and the economic discourse of debt and credit will always appear in the figure of the beggar. Consider Charlotte Corday's parodic letter to Marat, that "Friend of the People." As Mary Favret notes, David's painting makes legible the form of address: "It is enough that I be unfortunate to have a *right* to your benevolence" (2). Charlotte Corday effectively reveals the citizen as a version of Rousseau's crippled beggar, who regards any act of charity as a down-payment on a debt that can never be retired. It is this metamorphosis of citizen subject into citizen beggar, I suggest, that is neurotically represented in that therapeutic subject, the defaulted citizen. The therapeutic subject is indebted to the "subject supposed to know," thus miming the relation of the citizen to the state, according to Pocock:

Government stock is a promise to repay at a future date; from the inception and development of the national Debt, it is known that this date will in reality never be reached, but the tokens of repayment are...determined by the present state of public confidence in the stability of government, and its capacity to make repayment in a theoretical future. (112)

Coleridge's commissioning request for a long poem that would distinguish "epicurean selfishness" from "the amelioration of mankind," quoted above, is a curious commingling of two different agendas, the political and the therapeutic: on the one hand, he wishes the Romantic project to be conceived as supremely political, and classically liberal; on the other, his rhetoric – "I wish you would," "my present mood" – confers on his speculation that it "would do great good" more a therapeutic aspect than a socially meliorist one. I suggest that Coleridge's commission to Wordsworth is fulfilled in *The Excursion*, similarly split between the political and the therapeutic: the citizen whose infinite rights make him a creditor of the state is balanced by the structurally indebted therapeutic subject.

The task of finding a cure for defaulted citizenship is left in *The Excursion* to various missionaries – the Wanderer, the Poet, and the Pastor – who address themselves to that despondent subject and defaulted citizen, the Solitary. These "missionaries" emerge, respectively, from economic, aesthetic, and spiritual walks of life – not, as we might expect, from the political or the "public." The consolations of despondency work by placing the political subject in an extended network whereby the constraints placed upon absolute freedom, otherwise evidence of political failure, are reconfigured as the consequences of ecological inevitability and human fatality. As a sign of the "new ethics" that the poem will preach, doctrines do not build *from* the political or the economic *toward* the spiritual, but rather, perpetually traverse the apparent distance between them. The asymptotic structure of discourses in *The Excursion* exhibits itself in the failure of the prescription to cure the symptoms: ironically, what Wordsworth identifies as cause of despondency and default, the mistaken transformation of negative freedom (of movement) into positive right (expectation that "open" roads must yield advancement) is corrected by the recommendation *to walk*.

Because the institutions that guarantee mobility and equality to the liberal subject – liberal education and state religion are those institutions most prominent in Wordsworth's analysis – operate by the logic of credit or future promise, it is perhaps most surprising that the "spiritual economics" proposed in *The Excursion* will posit an equally important function for forms of debt, or deficit. If debt will initially be represented in the poem as the source of despondency – distress – it is nonetheless the goal of the poem to regard the structure of deficit as the paradigmatic form of a truly spiritual economics, emblematized in Simonides' epitaph: "We are all debts owed to death."

Thus, even as they are rhetorically identified with the "missionary" or creditor position of surplus knowledge, the Solitary's interlocutors will be represented by Wordsworth in a way that parodies such an identification. Each bears the marks of a certain self-division that we may attribute to the split of the social imaginary into public and private spheres. We might describe this self-division in the terms that Rieff establishes for us – as the residual effect of the cultural accident by which the salesman follows the missionary – were it not for the fact that Wordsworth imagines an opposite trajectory: for him, the missionary follows the salesman. The spiritual outlook belongs to those who have been deeply in debt.

Each figure of surplus is presented to us first as an economic agent and only later "sublimed" into the transcendental subject. We are almost too familiar with the poet's self-representation, in the opening lines of *The Excursion*, as a man traveling with hardly less effort than could be imagined were he to be, in Jeffrey's phrase, carrying sleeve-buttons and tape enough for the entire nation. Unlike the "dreaming man" he aspires to be, this Poet must labor for a living. Likewise, the apparent "leisure" which governs the Pastor's parish rounds is parodied in his own representation of his predecessor, who arrives "with store of household goods, in panniers slung / On sturdy horses graced with jingling bells" (vii.64–5), and who is first thought to be one of a band of gypsies or traveling actors – in other words, a vagabond.[3] Finally: if Jeffrey and contemporary critics, including

Coleridge, respond with skepticism or chagrin to the apparent incongruity of a missionary-cum-traveling-salesman as primary speaker of *The Excursion*, Wordsworth seems nonetheless to insist that the despondency of the defaulted citizen requires the address of such a figure. We know that as Wordsworth revised the "Ruined Cottage" fragment for *The Excursion*, the background of the Pedlar achieved ever greater prominence. Moreover, James Butler's careful work on the patterns of manuscript composition suggests that almost from the beginning, Wordsworth saw the Pedlar's history and occupation as a crucial balance to the story of that other disconsolate subject, Margaret (see Butler, 3–35). Even were this not the case, however, and "The Ruined Cottage" took the form of so many other of Wordsworth's poems, narrating an encounter between the tran-scendental subject and a (female) vagrant, we would confront the same problem. As De Quincey was the first to point out, this encounter is marred by two competing economies: Margaret's psychic decline is related to her economic condition, and the Wanderer offers her only spiritual relief. This failure of the cure to match the disease will be a repeated trope in *The Excursion*.

Implicit in the argument to be advanced here is my contention that the encounter between the missionary salesman and the disconsolate subject produces for Wordsworth the cure (which is also, as Coleridge's description of a political malaise taking the form of a division between public and private implies, the disease itself) we now call liberalism. That encounter exhibits the conjunction of surplus and *distress*, not, as one might expect, surplus and dearth, or tranquility and distress. Thus exhibited in the encounter is the split subject of liberalism. The impossible attempt to conjoin the two, however, is what allows liberalism to develop, for its institutions – a democracy populated by sovereign subjects, a system of "liberal" education that increases social mobility, and a *laissez-faire* capitalism that removed obstacles to trade – are justified by reference to "general welfare." This term, embracing the economies of surplus *and* distress, perhaps best describes the complex logic which joins classic and contemporary versions of liberalism. Consequently, I believe, one valuable if long-neglected approach to understanding the emergence of liberalism is to focus on the transformation of the practice of "liberality" as it is recorded in Wordsworth's poems. What we find is that liberalism is not itself a plan of political and social action that *responds* to perceived conditions of distress or inequity, but rather the represented conjunction of surplus and distress, the "moving spectacle" contained in the image, for example, of a man bent double by a pack of merchandise. The "revolution in manners," which Burke proclaimed as the most profound of revolutions witnessed in 1789, is the supplanting of an ethic of "liberal, plenteous hospitality" (see below) by a liberal *attitude* – in common parlance, a social conscience. Where "The Old Cumberland Beggar" envisions "liberality" as voluntary charity, "The Ruined Cottage" celebrates its spiritualization into voluntary *sympathy*.

It is in this context that we may address perhaps the most problematic questions suggested by the poem. To the series of questions by Coleridge –

Is there one word, for instance, attributed to the pedlar in *The Excursion*, characteristic of a *pedlar*? One sentiment, that might not more plausibly, even without the aid of any previous explanation, have proceeded from any wise and beneficent old man, of a rank and profession in which the language of learning and refinement are natural and to be expected? (*BL* 257)

– we may add the following: how do the narratives of loss of place and destitution inscribed in each epitaphic pronouncement of *The Excursion* describe a particularly *political* malaise? And of what avail are the two therapies – talking and walking – proposed for the subject's cure?

The anti-Freudian formula proposed by Deleuze and Guattari in *Anti-Oedipus* – "The schizophrenic out for a walk is better than the neurotic lying on a couch" – illustrates a therapeutic aesthetic initiated by Cowper's *The Task*[4] and carried to its logical conclusion in *The Excursion*. Coleridge's letter to Wordsworth suggests that passivity and sedentariness are the somatic traces of the subject's "sinking" into epicurean selfishness. The practice or therapy of walking advocated in *The Excursion* (the Wanderer insists that the Solitary "Quit your couch – / Cleave not so fondly to your moody cell" [IV.481–2]) thus appears as an antidote, a cure for the defaulted, or "passive" citizen. As one critic cavilled, its doctrine "amount[s] to little more than a prescription of air and exercise, and the contemplation of nature, whereby health of body and peace of mind may be restored!"[5] But since the liberal subject is constituted as an essentially *mobile* subject, dispossessed of local attachments, the walking cure reenacts the condition it is meant to alleviate, or rather reveals an unwitting coercion (neurosis) still at work. What Sebastiano Timpanaro, a Marxian critic of Freud, has argued concerning the Freudian analytic or "talking cure" – that the failure of explanation to eliminate neurosis produces "the interminability of the cure, which was to assume the proportions of another, substitute neurosis" – affects Wordsworth's model of "walking cure" as well.

To read Descartes' second maxim is to suspect that such a "walking cure" is identifiable with and as Enlightenment ideology.

My second maxim was to be as firm and resolute in my actions as I could be, and to follow with no less constancy the most doubtful opinions, once I have decided them. In this I would imitate travellers who, lost in a forest, ought not to wander this way and that, or, what is worse, remain in one place, but ought always to walk as straight a line as they can in one direction and not change course for feeble reasons, even if at the outset, it was perhaps only chance that made them choose it; for by this means, if they are not going where they wish, they will finally arrive at least somewhere where they will probably be better off than in the middle of a forest. (13)

Just such a maxim informs the Wanderer's apt admonishment to the Poet in book II of *The Excursion*; when the Poet sees a Mayday celebration on his way to visit the despondent Solitary and wishes to "quit our road, and join / These festive matins," the Wanderer claims that

> he, who intermits
> The appointed task and duties of the day,
> Untunes full oft the pleasures of the day;
> Checking the finer spirits that refuse to flow
> When purposes are lightly changed.          (147–51)

Although an "excursion" is a *recreational* activity, the Wanderer insists that its form mime the aesthetic virtue of "purposiveness without purpose." The formal or aesthetic pleasure that constitutes the excursion thus replaces the "old" ethics or the discourse of obligation, and bears a marked similarity to the "surplus-enjoyment" Zizek finds operating in Descartes' moral methodology:

the real aim of ideology is the attitude demanded by it, the consistency of the ideological form, the fact that we "continue to walk as straight as we can in one direction"; the positive reasons given by ideology to justify this request – to make us obey ideological form – are only there to conceal this fact: in other words, to conceal the surplus-enjoyment proper to the ideological form as such. (*SO*, 83)

This attitude – the formal equivalent of a deontological demand – is
at once a burden *and* the source of surplus-enjoyment, for it is the
infinite deferral of "actual" desire that makes surplus-enjoyment
possible.

Descartes' and the Wanderer's admonition "to walk as straight as
we can in one direction" may seem antithetical to the Freudian
talking cure, and its methodology of free association. But the
apparent antithesis dissolves when we recall that the aim of analysis
is to reveal an absolute determination of the apparently random
detail:

When I instruct a patient to abandon reflection of any kind and tell me
whatever comes into his head, I am relying on the presumption that he will
not be *able* to abandon the purposive ideas inherent in the treatment and
I feel justified in inferring that what seem to be the most arbitrary and
innocent things are in fact related to his treatment. (Rieff, 115)

To discover purpose in apparently random details offers strongest
proof of the subject's sovereignty. Unlike the sovereignty of a king,
which insofar as it is situated in a name and a body, is "given" to him
by history and by nature, postrevolutionary subjects "must 'invent'
themselves, elaborate the essence of their being by their activity"
(Zizek, "The King Is a Thing," 31). The fact of the necessary
"exercise" of sovereignty, however, does not contradict its necessary
persistence. Once the entire day is dedicated to "pleasure," the
apparent opposition between duty (tasks) and pleasure collapses. A
related opposition, between constraint and freedom, is subject to a
similar collapse. Such oppositions had enabled choice, and the *active*
exercise of sovereign decision. When this space of choice is evacuated,
left in place is a potentially frightening incapacity to distinguish self-
government from the rigorous and inescapable consistency of mere
sequence. Simmel's metaphysics of freedom has become Holmes's
physiology of walking.

The cultural capital Wordsworth accumulated from access to
liberal education similarly collapses the difference between desire
and duty, indolence and purpose, freedom and constraint – even
debt and independence. Consider, for example, Wordsworth's odd
and ultimately contradictory comparison of liberal education and
wandering in the Fenwick note on *The Excursion*. Explaining his
decision to make the Wanderer the poem's chief interlocutor,
Wordsworth writes,

But, had I been born into a class which would have deprived me of what is called a liberal education, it is not unlikely that, being strong in body, I should have taken to a way of life such as that in which my Pedlar passed the greater part of his days. At all events, I am here called upon freely to acknowledge that the character I have represented in his person is chiefly an idea of what I fancied my own character might have become in his circumstances. (*PW* v.373)

Here liberal education is represented as an asset that makes wandering unnecessary; wandering is therefore a kind of dispossession, a way of life undertaken by those without sufficient resources to be "lodger[s] in that house / Of letters" called Cambridge. Earlier in the same note, however, Wordsworth had represented wandering as a way of life unavailable to the man with only *cultural* capital at his disposal. Comparing himself to Southey, he comments that "*Books* ... were in fact [Southey's] *passion*; and *wandering*, I can with truth affirm, was *mine*; but this propensity was happily counteracted by inability from want of fortune to fulfil my wishes." In the two passages, "want of fortune" and "liberal education" respectively preclude wandering.

In fact, liberal education and want of fortune were intimately connected in Wordsworth's life; deprived of the fortune owed Wordsworth's family by Lord Lonsdale, Wordsworth became indebted to his uncles for his Cambridge fees. In a 1792 letter, Wordsworth cites this indebtedness, rather than liberal education itself, as the obstacle to William Matthews' proposal that they wander through England: "I cannot deny, were I so situated as to be without relations to whom I were accountable for my actions, I should perhaps prefer your idea to vegetating upon a paltry curacy" (*EY*, 165). The cultural capital represented by a Cambridge education would thus appear to be *negative* capital; although the Pedlar might appear to be more "burdened" by his pack than the unconstrained student on summer vacation, Wordsworth's note suggestively indicates how liberalism coalesces forms of indebtedness (gratitude as well as credit) into an uncommodifiable burden. The indebtedness that resulted both in and from his "liberal" education did little in reality to curb Wordsworth's "passion" for wandering, but it may be said to have placed that wandering under the formal equivalent of a deontological constraint.

Recall that Wordsworth publishes his first poems as if to confirm the cultural capital acquired through his Cambridge education:

it was with great reluctance I huddled up those two poems [*An Evening Walk*
and *Descriptive Sketches*] and sent them into the world in so imperfect a state.
But as I had done nothing by which to distinguish myself at the university,
I thought these little things might shew I could do something. (Alan Hill,
13)

Moreover, the content of the poems, a kind of contraband material
acquired through the wandering that liberal education ostensibly
precludes, is redeemed by subjugation to a form – the "evening"
walk, that precursor of "free" association – that produces pure
consistency. Such pure consistency is the single but also singular
demand placed upon the liberal subject, as Freud's instructions to the
analysand suggest:

Your talk with me must differ in one respect from an ordinary conversation.
Whereas usually you rightly try to keep the threads of your story together
and to exclude all intruding associations and side issues, so as not to wander
too far from the point, here you must proceed differently…say whatever
goes through your mind. Act as if you were sitting at the window of a
railway-train and describing to someone behind you the changing views you
see outside. (Rieff, 147)

Here we have another structure of debt, wherein the future anterior
of order is guaranteed by the eventual destination (of the train, or of
the analysis). The contradiction inherent in this technique is
illustrated by our ability to name as either "free" or "involuntary"
association the conjuring of details to produce a subject-for-analysis.
The analysand is incapable, according to Freud, of purely random
associations; "resistances" to free association emerge as evidence of
neurosis. More important, perhaps, the analysand is incapable of self-
knowledge by means of free association: "the patient cannot
remember the whole of what is repressed in him" (*Pleasure Principle*,
12) and so is obliged to repeat it. This same contradiction is inherent
also in the "liberal" subject, insofar as only an infinity of specific
associations – along the model of what Alan Liu ("Local Transcendence") has recently noted as the "detailism" of new historicist
montage – can testify to freedom from special interest. As Freud's
analogy to the train indicates, however, this subject only *appears* free
from particular (class) interests posed in *The Excursion*. Liberal
education frees the subject to travel (in a "liberal" quasi-
geographical space where "every road is open") but subjects him to
debt, so deep a debt that digression is out of the question, since tenure
or security is always already receding, above all for the Poet, whose

tenure must depend on future generations, who therefore must maintain a constant (consistent) "fidelity to the time to come" (Rancière, 248).

We may therefore trace the production of the disconsolate political subject by way of the complex of liberal social institutions epitomized by Cambridge. As we have come to expect from Wordsworth, the transcendental surplus represented by liberal education is both contrasted to and imaged in the beggar. Distancing himself from the "indolent and vague society" of his contemporaries at Cambridge, Wordsworth nostalgically recalls an earlier age:

> when boys and youths,
> The growth of ragged villages and huts,
> Forsook their homes and – errant in the quest
> Of patron, famous school or friendly nook,
> Where, pensioned, they in shelter might sit down –
> From town to town and through wide scattered realms
> Journeyed with their huge folios in hand,
> And often, starting from some covert place,
> Saluted the chance comer on the road,
> Crying, "An obolus, a penny give
> To a poor scholar." (*Prelude* III.477–87)

The scholar–vagrant offers a positive contrast to the liberally educated subject, for by begging he incurs no debt. We are prepared by this figure for the account of the Pedlar in *The Excursion* as an autodidact, purchasing his education piecemeal:

> to the nearest town
> He duly went with what small overplus
> His earnings might supply, and brought away
> The book that most had tempted his desires ...
> The divine Milton. (I.244–7, 250)

For both of these learners, education is an *end*, provides wandering with a purpose; this "objective" status of education is figured in the book as object, the "large folio" or volume of Milton. By contrast, liberal education is conceived as not an end but a means. In 1792 Wordsworth writes to William Matthews in defense of a traditional equation between liberal education and a free, or democratic, society:

Let me entreat you to guard against that melancholy, which appears to be making daily inroads upon your happiness. Educated as you have been, you

ought to be above despair. You have the happiness of being born in a free
country, where every road is open, where talents and industry are more
liberally rewarded than amongst any other nation of the Universe. (Alan
Hill, 10)

Here liberal education appears to produce the disease for which it is
then touted as the cure. Opening "prospects" for the exercise of
talents and industry, liberal education is consonant with hope
(Matthews should be "above" despair) but infinitely extends the
range of expectation, making a road of all the world. Perhaps this is
the best image of the debt incurred by the liberal subject, whether or
not it is accompanied by a monetary debt to relatives (despite
rhetorically distancing himself from Matthews's condition, Wordsworth too was faced with only "prospects"). In both cases, identity
(propriety) and property are attenuated, stretched out between
origin and destination, promise and achievement. Describing what
he aptly calls "the credit economy *and polity*," Pocock claims that
"property had become not only mobile but speculative: what one
owned was promises" (113); such is the status of *intellectual* property.
Even more perhaps than capital itself, cultural capital recedes from
the horizon of the actual.

Diagnosing Matthews's condition as "melancholy," Wordsworth
thereby identifies the liberally educated subject in a way that
corresponds with Coleridge's diagnosis of a postrevolutionary malaise. "Melancholy" appropriately describes the subject's condition
in a "credit" economy and polity, for the difference between
mourning and melancholy, as Freud reminds us, is the difference
between a lost object and "a loss of a more ideal kind" ("Mourning,"
245). The "analogy" between mourning and melancholia conceals a
key difference: in mourning, "the *world* has become poor and
empty"; with melancholia, we witness "the impoverishment of the
ego" (246). Clearly, this impoverishment, the identification of the
ego with the abandoned or lost object, can be seen as a consequence
of owning only one's own "promise."

Freud's essay helps us configure the odd split in *The Excursion* itself,
to which I alluded in noting how funeral processions and funereal
epitaphs are presented as curatives for the Solitary's supposedly
*political* malaise. *The Excursion* begins with a narrative of "simple"
loss, of mourning: "The Ruined Cottage." But the "graveyard"
books of the poem, which might appear to concern mourning, are
meant to respond to the Solitary's more ideal kind of loss, the loss of

"expectation" for the amelioration of mankind. Wordsworth connects the narratives of mourning and melancholia in two ways: first,
Margaret's husband, Robert, suffers from melancholia (a consequence of unemployment); second, the Solitary's loss of *political*
expectation is preceded by loss of *domestic* attachments (his wife and
children die), figured as a loss of "place" or tenure:

> Seven years of occupation undisturbed
> Established seemingly a right to hold
> That happiness; and use and habit gave
> To what an alien spirit had acquired
> A patrimonial sanctity.                    (III.622–6)

By so insisting on their contiguity, Wordsworth implies that
melancholy is a sublime mourning, transcendent to all local
patrimony. What is mourned, I suggest, is the loss of any notion of
positive "right" (notice the equation between right and "occupation," tenancy, is what the Solitary "loses"). The only right
celebrated in *The Excursion* is the inalienable right to die.

For two reasons, then, the Wanderer must serve as the poem's
primary representation of the transcendental surplus. First, his
"wandering" disowns any fixed or permanent sense of self; as I will
demonstrate, Wordsworth's technical aim is to represent the Wanderer in transit. Second, as he metamorphoses from Pedlar to
Wanderer in the course of Wordsworth's several manuscript revisions, we notice that he uses the surplus acquired from "carrying
the pack" to purchase not status or property, but rather *an attitude of
consistency*. Despite retirement, the Wanderer continues his rounds.
The imperceptible difference between the Pedlar who uses his
monetary surplus to buy "the divine Milton" and the Wanderer who
has become Miltonic consists in the latter's entire internalization of
the principle of mobility. Finally, the "surplus" the Wanderer
achieves is formal rather than substantial in nature. When
Wordsworth insists, in perhaps the crucial line of *The Excursion*, that
the Wanderer "could *afford* to suffer," he indicates not acquired
*monetary* wealth (although its form is analogous to money), for what
we chiefly notice is his surplus of sympathy. In his person, the
Wanderer brings together a version of what I have suggested is the
arresting image of liberalism, the juxtaposition of surplus and distress.
In the Wanderer, surplus and distress are incarnated as *moving* and
*being moved*.[6] The Wanderer escapes melancholy because, unlike that

"defaulting citizen," the Solitary who confronts "'a world not
moving to his mind'" (II.314–15), the Wanderer identifies himself
not with the world of objects or the geography of the inhabitant, but
with the money-form (which "wanders through the world") and the
geography of the passerby.[7] The Wanderer in his person and in his
name thus explains the implicit logic of Wordsworth's compositional
progress from "The Ruined Cottage" to *The Excursion*: the cure for
dispossession and unemployment – vagrancy – is walking.

## II: "THE RUINED COTTAGE"

Medicines, in general, accomplish the purpose for which they are admin-
istered, not so much by their actual operation, as by their influence on the
imagination of the patient. But, where the most means are used, and the
greatest pains taken, there will the highest hopes of recovery be naturally
excited. Now, removing from a distance, perhaps, – to the vicinity of a
mineral well, to use its waters, there is so much of pains, of difficulty, such
a change of objects which suggest and regulate the ordinary current of
thought; that, the imagination is unavoidably much more affected, and
more confident hope encouraged, than in the more ordinary application of
medicinal remedies. Besides, almost every disease, under which there can be
any hope of benefit from the uses of mineral waters, yields more or less to the
influence of air and exercise. And, the advantage of these is commonly best
enjoyed in a removal from the scene in which the distemper was contracted.
(Heron, *Journey through Scotland*, 49)

Although "The Ruined Cottage" neither identifies the well adjacent
to Margaret's ruined cottage as a mineral well nor the pains and
difficulty of the Poet's journey there as a curative remedy for a
"distemper" acquired elsewhere (possibly in France), the reasons
vouchsafed for Robert Heron's journey to Scotland offer to explain
how *The Excursion* might seem to Wordsworth an adequate response
to Coleridge's request to write a "philosophical poem" to cure
disenchantment with the speculative *philosophes* of the Enlightenment
and French Revolution – and why Wordsworth might regard the
fragment of "The Ruined Cottage" as its crucial beginning. Heron
writes, in a manner reminiscent of Arthur Young, whose *Travels in
France* are so important a model for *The Prelude*, that his travels and
their written record are attempts "to reconcile the habits of studious,
with those of active life." The habits of studious life, as Heron
describes them, represent a dangerous extreme and have potentially
political implications – "Books turn us to theoretic speculation" –

but the getting and spending of active life cannot entirely counteract the danger, for "the business of the world tends to unfit the imagination, and the Reasoning Faculty for that exercise." The problem: how to *exercise* the imagination without indulging in the "theoretic speculation" associated with the French *philosophes* and their dangerous political disciples? The solution:

[I] lately resolved to try the benefits of a short excursion through some parts of my native country. I pleased myself with the hope that I might, in the way, quicken my powers of observation, by the view of those numberless, unconnected particulars, which in every country, meet the traveller's eye. (*Journey*, 2)

Heron proposes to resist visionary speculation, ironically enough, with the pure sequence which produces the "moving picture" – although, perhaps because of the lag in this case between Heron's idea of the cure and its technical development, cinematography, in his case the written text presents this pure sequence according to the logic of the stereoscope, producing what might be regarded as a false three-dimensionality, or what Dominic LaCapra has called "weak montage" (talk delivered at the University of Pennsylvania, 1983).

The opening lines of "The Ruined Cottage" reveal the Poet temporalizing the difference which a montage successfully reproduces as simultaneity; although shadows "lay in spots / Determined and unmoved," and certainly at some distance from the "bare wide Common" he traverses in the high noon of summer, the Poet interrupts the spatial opposition and distance first by imagining a "dreaming man," and so producing in his mind an immediate "relief" (in the senses both of "the projection of figures from a flat background" and of "easing discomfort"), and then by "fast-forwarding" to the achievement of his goal: "Mine was at that hour / Far other lot, yet with good hope that soon / Under a shade as grateful I should find / Rest..." (1.17–20). Thus in addition to the exercising body, through whose pedestrian intervention what Lukács calls a "teleological positing" or imaginary object might be achieved, Wordsworth shows us the exercising *mind*, or imagination, which, as Heron suggests, works its cure *in medias res*, so that the restoration of health or relief from malaise is half accomplished by the time the Poet reaches the "mineral" well.

Nonetheless, the exercise of the mind seems to emerge as a necessity *out* of the exercising body, the implication being that the "excursive

power" of the mind, whereby I can "see around me here / Things
which you cannot see," is in fact dependent on the excursive body for
its operation, as if the pure sequence of walking is a technique the
experience of which (in the absence of the "moving picture")
suggests to the mind the way in which "here" and "there," those
locations or positions that threaten always to undermine "freedom
from unjustified restraint," represent merely temporal rather than
spatial difference, and how sequence or association may thereby
displace anxiety about freedom – and why, therefore, the Wanderer,
that professional walker, might prove the most able "doctor" for the
incipient malaise of the liberal subject.

It is a critical commonplace that the dreaming man imagined by
the walking Poet proleptically announces the Wanderer, and Paul
Alpers has recently pointed out how this duo – one walking, the other
at rest – recalls Virgil's First Eclogue.[8] But Heron's *Journey through
Scotland* offers a more immediate resource for Wordsworth's representation of the Wanderer; Wordsworth quotes from Heron in the
second edition of *The Excursion* in order to confirm the "real" rather
than purely imaginary possibility of such a learned Pedlar. Heron's
account of the "numberless, unconnected particulars" experienced
during his travels in Scotland includes the following story of an
encounter with a venerable old man:

In a lonely part of the road, at some distance from any habitations, I was
surprised to meet a venerable, old man, who, by his looks, might be about
the age of eighty. He wore a grey cloak, a large, brown wig, and a blue
bonnet on his head. He had a staff in his hand. There was in his countenance
a mingled expression of mildness and dignity. His whole aspect recalled to
my remembrance, those old Scotchmen of whom Taylor, the water-poet, in
the account of his Journey to Scotland, speaks, as men who, notwithstanding
the plainness of their dress, possessed great wealth, and would receive scores
of men in the most liberal, plenteous hospitality. While my imagination was
thus employed, and at every stroke of her pencil, was raising my veneration
for the old man, I came up to him, for he was approaching to meet me on
the road, and was astonished to hear him, with his bonnet in hand, ask my
charity. My respect for his appearance was not diminished by this confession
of his poverty: but I was struck with something like rising horror at the
inconsistency between his appearance and his condition. I answered his
request with kindness and respect, and readily gave the very scanty pittance
which my circumstances could afford. (*Journey*, 155–6)

When we compare Heron's venerable, bonneted old man who begs
relief from distress with the similarly venerable man the sight of

whose hat, "bedewed with water-drops," offers knowledge of proximate relief to the Poet in book 1 of *The Excursion*, we see that Heron's figure appears to challenge the traveller's preconceptions in a way that Wordsworth's does not. The "liberal, plenteous hospitality" that Heron half expects to be offered him – the solicitousness of the host – turns into the solicitation of a vagrant. The "rising horror" that Heron feels in reconciling the actual material conditions and social position of the old man with his speculative preconception is exactly the curative he had in mind when setting forth from his study; whereas the apparently stationary "figures" in books may appear to offer themselves for our pleasure and enjoyment, when mobilized they far more often threaten to disturb our self-absorption by making inconvenient demands upon us. Note that *reading* Heron's account, however, induces a different experience, analogous to "rising horror": we are afflicted by the spectacle of destitution without being able to offer any solution or consolation.

Perhaps this is why, according to Kant, melancholy may itself be a product of reading, that practice of the liberally educated subject:

Since this sort of melancholia (*hypochondria vaga*) has no definite seat in the body and is a creature of the imagination, it could also be called *fictitious* disease, in which the patient finds in himself symptoms of every disease he reads about in books. (*CF*, 187)

Reading, through a process of sympathetic identification, induces brooding over *possible* rather than actual ills; it is, as for Freud, an anxiety without an object. Because it is self-induced, Kant claims, no doctor can cure it, but neither can the subject himself, for the melancholy subject is incapable of "*veto*[*ing*]" anxiety as the normal subject does; the latter "goes on, despite the claim of his inner feeling, to his agenda for the day – in other words, he leaves his oppression (which is then merely local) in its proper place... and turns his attention to the business at hand" (189).

Kant later returns to the subject of *hypochondria vaga* – unlocalized hypochondria, or melancholy – only to recommend the walking reverie as its cure. Like Henry Mayhew, who would later distinguish between the "wandering" and "civilized" tribes we know as the vagrant and the bourgeois by speculating that "in the mere act of wandering, there is a greater determination of blood to the surface of the body, and consequently a less quantity sent to the brain" (2–3), Kant suggests that walking and thinking are antithetical activities.

Undertaken together, walking and thinking produce vertigo, another form of hypochondria, because one has a determinate, the other an indeterminate, location. Thus if the danger of reading and thinking is the production of an imaginary anxiety, walking reverie is its antidote because it teaches how to disengage from the object of distress: "The purpose of walking in the open air is precisely to keep one's attention moving from one object to another and so *to keep it from becoming fixed* on any one object" (*CF*, 199). Like the vertiginous specter of the venerable old man, the determined object cannot be kept in focus.

Paul Hamilton's account of the problem of reading *The Excursion* offers two alternatives, implicitly those of the melancholy and the normative subject:

When readers hear an authentic epitaph in *The Excursion*, such as Margaret's, their position is equivalent to [the Poet's]: they stand still, before remembering that as casual passengers they can move on. The only way to be more committed and to carry sympathy further is to stop reading, to find a character's suffering so awful or important that they cannot bear any more or *cannot accept its incidental status in the poem*. That Wordsworth's success in evoking suffering might stop his readers is a faintly ridiculous notion. Nevertheless, if they keep going, the poem relegates them to the status of casual passenger again, forcing them to acknowledge the practical limitations of their sympathies. Wordsworth's realism here is about as uncomfortable as it could be. (143–4)

These two options – moving on or "becoming fixed," as Kant puts it – are more than mere strategies of reading in *The Excursion*; they are also two ways of figuring vagrancy. In imitation of the vagrant's interruptive function in Heron's and Wordsworth's literary excursions, let me introduce the form of a solicitation offered to me, *on the public road*, by an advocate for the homeless, John Michael Jones:

I. To achieve a better outlook on life, you at once have to achieve a better outlook on your body. If the body is shattered and sapped of vitality, it can easily become a prison of misery and hopelessness, which in turn sets you up for self-destruction. With the body unoperational and the brain beaten by sleeplessness, and far too long battered by extreme changes in wether, you are basically polarized and rendered immobile. Some of us simply lay down when the body begins to show signs of faltering. Some of us are walkers. To the point were the feet swell up and the tendon and muscle to burn and scar tissue to set in. When tensile strength of the muscles begin to go, it is more than a mere indication that the body needs rest – the body better get rest quickly and plenty of it, or it will be rendered beyond repair. So therefore it is only logical that the first phase of this program [a "Human Restoration Center"] be geared to restore the physical aspect of the problem, which for some of us is the root, the very seed from which homelessness has bloomed.

The anatomical specificity of Jones's account, hauntingly evocative of the pain frequently endemic to a "way-wandering life," especially if that life is involuntary, isolates a latent tension in the walking cure as it is delineated in *The Excursion*. If the poem develops its walking cure within and against the extremes of vagrancy and immobility, it fails to indicate the difference between rest that is a matter of choice (the Wanderer's and the Poet's "retirement") and the immobilization that results from bodily or mental incapacity – or, indeed, from death (thus it is that Margaret, and the other inhabitants of the graveyard eulogized by the Pastor in books v–vii, "simply lie down"). But this failure is not an unintentional one; indeed, I would argue that it is Wordsworth's purpose to obscure the difference between the two kinds of "rest," as it is his characteristic tendency elsewhere to obscure the difference between the two kinds of mobility.

Jones's proposal resurrects both these differences. One of the most curious features of his proposal for the Human Restoration Center is an argument for "exercise" as a cure for the faltering steps of homeless "walkers." Having recognized the correlation between the culture of "physical fitness" and social prestige, Jones proposes the following as requirements for his "physical restoration unit":

a. Vitamins
b. Good foods: fresh vegetables fresh fruits lean meats etc.
c. basic medical help.
d. Shiatsu: form of massage that have been proven to be effective in the restoring of damaged and scared muscle tissue.
e. a physical exercise program: Some of us are bent on self-destruction. We need better health. We need stronger bodies. We need vibrant sound minds. We need Restoration.
f. Hygeine: Educate one on the fact that in america with its values (which may be superficial) that cleanliness is a must if one wishes to manuver his/her way into areas of possible employment. We must all try to smell as pleasant as possible. Be [cause?] in america your just short of being labeled sub-human if you don't. If you wish to get your foot in the door of a possible job – wash it.

(This first phase is the most essential to get the body in readiness for the rest of the program. The first step of restoration begins with the body.)

What may strike us as most curious about these proposals is the odd mixture of socially accepted definitions of needs (food, medical attention) with less recognized remedies: the exotic massage technique recommended in (d) and the vision of the homeless set to walking in indoor malls conjured by (e). But this curiosity may be utilized to reveal how the figure of the vagrant – the problem of vagrancy – threatens to undermine the (political) distinction between illness (including mental illness and neuroses) and "social" problems, between private malaise and social disease. Poverty similarly disables the universal efficacy of psychoanalysis, as Timpanaro reminds us; Freud rejected the idea of *pro bono* psychoanalysis not only because the anlaysand's monetary "investment" was a crucial therapy, but also because "neurosis... was beneficial to a poor man because it allowed him to claim 'the pity which the world has refused to his material distress'" (112).

This same disability affects the walking cure; if De Quincey complains that the Wanderer might have offered Margaret a few shillings, relief from her material distress, we might equally complain that he does not offer to take her on one of his "restorative" walks, nor urge her to "quit [her] couch." Just as free association is a technique paralyzed in the face of a wandering mind, so "stepping westward" seems hardly a cure for one who has "wandered much of late." Similarly, although "voting with one's feet" – the freedom to go and to return – is perhaps the most fundamental of freedoms in liberal democracy (without it the principle of tacit consent to citizenship is moot), nonetheless the specifically *political* exercise of freedom – voting – has in most places at least a thirty-day residency requirement. Paul Virilio attributes this restriction to "the wandering body's inability to decide" (87), and we may speculate that precisely this "inability to decide" – evidence of an infinite debt to that future which guarantees value, meaning, or purpose – is the specter that haunts all models of "free association," whether psychological, aesthetic, political, or economic.

As the site of *The Excursion*, the place where the Poet and the Wanderer together form a "community" on the basis of free association, the ruined cottage is itself difficult to read. What kind of "relief" is offered the disconsolate subject by such a space? Since it is no longer inhabited, does it constitute a "place" at all?

One could argue that Wordsworth presents in the Wanderer a figure who still offers the "most liberal, plenteous hospitality" – in a knowledge of the landscape so intimate that he can discern not only the ghostly presence of its former inhabitants but also the location of its nearest well. Such a knowledge replaces the more directly solicitous and ingratiating but not more generous hospitality of Margaret "When she upheld the cool refreshment drawn / From that forsaken spring" (1.504–5). When the Poet, "parched with thirst," seeks "relief" from the burning day, the Wanderer responds merely by pointing out the *source* of relief, as if encouraging those in distress to make their own way in the world – as if relief from distress, in other words, required the use of boots, if not bootstraps: "He, at the word, / Pointing towards a sweet-briar, bade me climb / The fence where that aspiring shrub looked out / Upon the public way" (1.450–3). In effect, the Wanderer's version of hospitality reproduces the travel cure that Heron recommends: to work their cure most effectively, the waters of the mineral spring require the supplement of individual "effort, and expectation, and desire" (*Prelude* vi.541 [1805]). Thus we might say that the Wanderer's "liberal" hospitality, by demanding that the passerby "exercise" his right to relief, opposes the negative condition (itself a malaise) Heron argues has been produced by the introduction of apothecary's shops, which effectively eliminate the necessity of "repairing" to the distant sites of mineral springs.

Of course, the water only relieves physical distress, and has no power to cure the "impotence of grief" later induced by the moving spectacle of Margaret's decline. To understand why *walking* rather than water figures as a psychic and political cure, we again turn to Kant, who so famously adopted Descartes' regimen of walking in his daily life, and here takes the idea of the walking cure to Wordsworthian extreme:

Once, after I had put out the light and gone to bed, I suddenly felt an intense thirst and went, in the dark, to another room to get a drink of water. While I was groping around for the pitcher, I hit upon the idea of *drinking* air through my nose, so to speak, by taking several deep breaths and expanding my chest. Within a few seconds this quenched my thirst completely. The thirst was a pathological stimulus, which was neutralized by a counteracting stimulus. (*CF*, 205)

For Kant, this overcoming of somatic pathologies is proof of mental mastery, of "firm resolution" and the superior power of the will. But it is also, clearly, an effect of imagination; what he calls "the feeling as if one were *drinking* air" (201) is a metaphoric transformation of one element into another. Thus the example nicely corresponds to

*The Excursion*, whose remedies similarly consist of essentially discursive transmutations. And, as "The Ruined Cottage" transfers our attention from well-water to the "water of life," we are perhaps reminded of Marx's trafficker in commodities, who exchanges brandy for a Bible.

The Wanderer himself is the effect of such a discursive transmutation, as manuscript versions of "The Ruined Cottage" demonstrate; he is first identified as a "Pedlar" most familiar with the processes of exchange. His renaming is parallel to his appearance as "host" of that way-station known as "The Ruined Cottage." There, he appears as a figure approximating the condition Coleridge had imagined Wordsworth himself as occupying, of "a man in mental repose, one whose principles were made up, and so prepared to deliver upon authority a system of philosophy";[9] but in early versions his position is far more anomalous. Wordsworth preserves the "history" of the Pedlar's transformation into the Wanderer in the retrospective narration of *The Excursion*. Observed "alone, and stationed in the public way" (38–9), the figure of the Wanderer is first unrecognized, and the Poet, "stricken" by the apparition, approaches "with slackened footsteps" (45–6), reminiscent of the encounter with the discharged soldier. But we are made aware of this initial encounter only after *The Excursion* has introduced us to the reclining Wanderer now reconfigured not as a potential obstacle to progress but as the object of the Poet's strenuous exercise: "I looked round, / And to my wish and to my hope espied / The Friend I sought" (1.31–3).

Thomas De Quincey gives evidence of how difficult it frequently was, in the changing economy and society of the Lake District, to identify the difference between host and vagrant, hospitality and a solicitation for funds. Having eaten nothing since breakfast, Wordsworth and De Quincey find themselves hungry after a long day's ramble, and decide to knock at the door of an isolated house, where they are "showered" with refreshments. However, the ambiguity of the situation strikes home as they prepare to leave:

Could it be, we thought, that, without the formality of a sign, he, in so solitary a region, more that twenty-five miles distant from Kendal... exercised the functions of a landlord, and that we ought to pay him for his most liberal hospitality? (*Recollections*, 228)

One wonders if the Wanderer, stationed first in the public road and then encountered in contemplative repose at the site of the ruined cottage, does not pose a similar epistemological dilemma. As one who can "*afford* to suffer," he might represent with equal accuracy the condition of the beggar, whose "unfortunate" importunity produces a subsistence, and the philosopher, whose sublime detachment from pathological anxiety allows him occasionally to entertain a "moving spectacle."

As the example from Heron's *Journey through Scotland* suggests, the moving spectacle that the title of *The Excursion* announces as its subject is precisely the effect produced by traversing the distance between the vagrant and the Wanderer. The first such moving spectacle, the "Ruined Cottage" narrative, or the "story of Margaret," chronicles the gradual transformation of a solicitous hostess, offering "a daughter's welcome" and "curative" water to the parched traveler, to a vagrant who "has wandered much of late" and who solicits information with a beseeching gaze: "with a face of grief / Unutterably helpless, and a look / That seemed to cling upon me, she enquired / If I had seen her husband" (1.655–8). Margaret is thus a "moving spectacle" in both senses: not only does the dissolution of the domestic economy propel her into motion, but her "face" and "look" register the enforced mobility of dispossession – vagrancy as "being moved" – in an *affective* form; her grief is "moving."

It is so clear to me that Margaret is a type – indeed the archetype – for the abandoned and vagrant women encountered elsewhere in Wordsworth's corpus that it seems almost unnecessary to argue the point, despite numerous excellent readings that suggest she is *too* attached to a place, too immobilized, to free herself from the debilitating grief represented by her circular – and tautological – wandering. It is true that Wordsworth differentiates her from the woman in "The Female Vagrant" who *follows* her husband when he is "swept up" by the war machine, which maintains itself by emptying the streets of the unemployed; Margaret's husband spares her that *form* of vagrancy – "that I should follow with my babes, and sink / Beneath the misery of that wandering life" (1.680–1) – but the effect is the same: "In good truth, I've wandered much of late; / And sometimes – to my shame I speak – have need / Of my best prayers to bring me back again" (754–6). And the fact that Margaret's malaise includes an apparent *lack* of mobility (she is, after all, "fast rooted" to the "wretched spot"), only reinforces her

identity as a vagrant even as it helps to illuminate the threat posed by
vagrancy – *especially* to the Wanderer, who, in his relation to
Margaret, is still and always, until he tells her tale, the Pedlar.

A recent public debate about the relation between mobility and
vagrancy may illuminate the ways in which "moving" and "being
moved" are played out in "The Ruined Cottage" and *The Excursion*.
Edward Koch, then the mayor of New York City, justified actions
taken by the police to remove the homeless from Grand Central
Station, saying, "We thought it would be reasonable for the
authorities to say, 'You can't stay here unless you're here for
transportation.'" But as Rosalyn Deutsche points out, this distinction
misrecognizes the relation of vagrancy to transportation: "Though
we encounter the homeless as figures anchored to a grate or bench or
asleep in the subway as we rush to work, surviving on the streets... is
actually dominated by the constant necessity for movement" (52–3).
While Margaret solicits for information rather than money or food,
her relation to a nearby tollgate (the "Grand Central Station" of the
ruined cottage and its environs) is reminiscent of the position and
function of the old Cumberland beggar:

> and by yon gate,
> That bars the traveller's road, she often stood,
> And when a stranger horseman came, the latch
> Would lift, and in his face look wistfully:
> Most happy, if from aught discovered there
> Of tender feeling, she might dare repeat
> The same sad question.                    (1.894–900)

And as in "The Old Cumberland Beggar," Margaret's proximity to
the tollgate, that impediment to unrestricted movement rendered as
a social "duty," tax, or debt, suggests that the vagrant serves the
same function.

If we needed any further indication of the relation of what has
often been considered Margaret's merely psychological condition to
the social position of that population of the homeless John Michael
Jones describes as "bent on self-destruction" but whom passersby
often regard as soliciting funds for their continued subsistence, the
Wanderer's characterization of Margaret's discourse provides it:

> Most willingly she put her work aside,
> And walked with me along the miry road,
> Heedless how far; and, in such piteous sort

That any heart had ached to hear her, *begged*
That, wheresoe'er I went, I still would ask
For him whom she had lost.        (1.863–8; emphasis added)

In both cases, Margaret's solicitations meet with the response of "tender feeling" rather than "rising horror," as if the social reminder (of debt) that is the tollgate, when humanized, were also domesticated (that is, enclosed, limited). Just as the tollgate allows the traveler to experience that his or her power to move – and hence freedom – is *meta*physical (entry into symbolic exchange is also required) in a way that entirely unrestricted movement would not, the encounter with the vagrant can produce a similar experience, identifying "freedom" not as a condition of independence, but as an entirely *differential* phenomenon. I experience my freedom "positively" when proximate to those under greater constraint; only degrees or increments of freedom, not freedom in an absolute sense, are available to perception. Wordsworth implies as much in "The Old Cumberland Beggar" when he suggests that the poorest villagers feel privileged when they see the figure of the beggar.

What readers see in Margaret is then a "moving spectacle" in more than the sense of a "picture inducing compassion"; in fact, it is the spectacle of pure movement, movement in excess of any use or function (except advertisement, perhaps), that moves to compassion. Margaret's last movements are entirely circular; the "attenuation of affiliative bonds" that defines the vagrant will be ironically represented by the "long-drawn thread" of hemp that girds her waist and connects her to the spinning wheel. As in "Goody Blake and Harry Gill," Wordsworth exploits both the symbolic and the actual historical connection of the textile industry to vagrancy in "The Ruined Cottage"; as mere cloth, the product of weaving, cloth is purely a commodity, but as *clothing*, is represents a kind of essential, almost inalienable property.

The same double trajectory is perhaps visible in the term "cottage industry," since as a form of "domestic" manufacture cottage industry conflates public and private. When Wordsworth tells the tale of Margaret, he also narrates the ruin of this model of manufacture, the breakdown of a successful weaving together of public and private. Though the story centers on Margaret, it also crucially concerns her husband Robert, a weaver by trade. The economic and social changes chronicled in the poem entail their separation, and represent once again Wordsworth's "common" theme: that separation transforms privacy into privation. Most emblematic of this separation, perhaps, is that Margaret's spinning is aided not by her only remaining son, long before apprenticed elsewhere, but by a "neighbour's boy" (861). The domestic economy has been subjected to exchange.

As Liu points out, Wordsworth's representation of domestic manufacture draws on two distinct economies of weaving then current in England: the "independent weaver" of the north, whose participation in the economy of credit and debt, made pervasive by the growth of the fiscal–military state, was mostly limited to small advances from cloth-suppliers, debts that were retired weekly; and the piece-rate system prevalent in the south, where weavers rarely owned their own looms or bought their materials, making them in effect wage-laborers. Robert is situated "in a crux *between* the traditional economies of weaving" (*Wordsworth*, 329), first appearing independent of economic fluctuations, but then occupied only by "casual work" before becoming entirely unemployed, walking to town with "slack steps" and "without an errand" (line 583).

In *The Sinews of Power*, John Brewer gives weighty historical support to Pocock's contention that a "financial revolution" is crucial to the developing concept of the State in late seventeenth and early eighteenth century England, arguing that "the creation of what I call 'the fiscal–military state' was the most important transformation" during this period (xvii). If, as Brewer contends, the image of England as a financial war machine conflicts with the competing vision of an emergent "liberal" state guaranteeing negative liberties and the preservation of private life (the sphere of "domestic affections," as Wordsworth describes the cottage-home of Lake-country "statesmen" in his letter to Fox), it is perhaps no wonder that a similar conflict emerges in the Wanderer's account of the ruined cottage. Robert, whose absence is the efficient cause of the cottage's deterioration, is "seized" both by fever (a "private" malaise) and by "the plague of war."

Once gone, Robert fails to reappear, even in the guise of a discharged soldier whose lapse into vagrancy would serve to indict a tautological structure in which the underemployment created by industrial development creates an embryonic "industrial reserve army" from which the nominal army derives its recruits only to return them to the ranks of that reserve army. This failure to return might be surprising, given *The Excursion*'s emphasis on circulation, were it not for the fact that various *other* discharged soldiers and vagrants do return. Consider in this context the curiously detailed representation of Margaret's "task" when not employed in wandering:

> You see that path,
> Now faint, – the grass has crept o'er its grey line;
> There, to and fro, she paced through many a day
> Of the warm summer, from a bit of hemp
> That girt her waist, spinning the long-drawn thread
> With backward steps. Yet ever as she passed
> A man whose garments showed the soldier's red,
> Or crippled mendicant in sailor's garb,
> The little child who sate to turn the wheel
> Ceased from his task; and she with faltering voice
> Made many a fond enquiry... (1.882–92)

This passage is fascinating not merely because it exhibits in miniature the circularity of Margaret's "path" or walk of life, demonstrating how she is at once "fast rooted" to the spot and nonetheless "restless," but also because it so subtly reflects a pervasive economic structure. Margaret's return to textile manufacture involves not weaving, but rather spinning hemp. Unlike weaving cloth, which suggests the production of an *immediate* use-value, spinning hemp has a far more attenuated relation to improving Margaret's destitute condition, requiring the intervention of a mediated exchange-value, a "pittance" (far less than the "two gold sovereigns" that exchange place with Robert when he enlists in the army). More generally, her return to textile manufacture suggests a cruel irony: Robert's unemployment seems related to an over-production (hence the "ill-requited labour" of artisans [560]) caused by the fiscal–military state and a "national" economy that, like Robert himself, can no longer differentiate "the various tasks / Of summer, autumn, winter, and of spring" (576–7).[10] But it is Robert's departure, after all, that with other similar departures swells the ranks of the military, which in turn resuscitates the textile industry; the military, of course, was the chief consumer of cloths. It is a classic case of uneven development:

surplus-profit can only be achieved at the expense of less productive countries, regions, and branches of production. Hence development takes place only in juxtaposition with underdevelopment; it perpetuates the latter and itself develops thanks to this perpetuation. (Mandel, 102)

And, as Levinson and others have pointed out, the ruined cottage is itself such a case: the surplus-profit or aesthetic value of the cottage depends on a precipitate decline in its "real" value, like the urban space that can only be gentrified once its poorer denizens are evicted.[11]

Margaret's special interest in old soldiers is indicated in a manner that draws attention to the connection between weaving, soldiering, and the "reserve army" of the unemployed: she appears to recognize the connection intuitively, judging the possible knowledge of passers-by of her husband's whereabouts by their garments, garments usually in a state of becoming-thread as the hemp (flax in an earlier draft) which "girds" her waist is in a state of becoming-cloth. War both weaves and unravels. Likewise, the "garb" and "garments" which seem, by the condition of their wearers, to be lapsing into rags, indicate a continually expanding market for Margaret's spinning circle. In this market, the (former) weaver is practically indistinguishable from the discharged soldier: they are equalized by capital.

When we compare this implicit parable of Margaret's spinning to her own description of her alternate occupation – "I have been travelling far; and many days / About the fields I wander, knowing this / Only, that what I seek I cannot find; / And so I waste my time" (1.764–7) – we may note a certain similarity between this "waste" of time and her apparently more productive occupation of spinning hemp: neither model of labor conceives itself or is conceived as capable of fulfilling a given need or desire; its effect, if not its purpose, is to create or renew that need or desire. And, of course, the final irony of the passage in question is the reduction of both weaver and soldier, producer and consumer, to the status of vagrant; just as Margaret's patterns of movement suggest that there is no essential difference between her two occupations, weaving and wandering, so one soldier has been discharged (faded), and the other has become a "crippled mendicant." Not only are they indistinguishable, at least from a distance, from the figure of her long-lost husband, because they are all clad in versions of the same "uniform," but finally, they are hardly distinguishable from Margaret herself; one might say they are merely more tightly clad in the same material, the thread having become woven – and raveled – cloth. Therefore "[their] presence gave no comfort," for they merely extend the narrative of "becoming-vagrant" that is the center of the tale.

I have already suggested how this tale is the obverse of the Pedlar "becoming-Wanderer"; but in fact there is more than a formal equivalence between these transmutations. When Francis Jeffrey comments that the Wanderer's affectation of simplicity consists largely of orations interrupted "with two or three awkward notices of something that the had seen when selling winter raiment about the country," he at least recalls to our attention the economic relation between cottage weavers and pedlars. However perverse it may seem to suggest, perhaps one aspect of the Pedlar's concern for Margaret's lassitude depends on the fact that his visits there cease to contribute to the circulation of goods necessary to his occupation: the more she wanders, the less she has to buy, sell, or trade. Thus there is a dual aspect to, or possible motive for, his extended departure: not only does he rescue himself from the dangers of too great a sympathy for/identification with Margaret-as-vagrant, too close a recognition of the unraveling of production into infinite debt; he also finds more suitable markets that allow him to make the transformation from Pedlar to Wanderer – a transformation whose economic basis receives confirmation from the poem: "This active course / He followed till provision for his wants / Had been obtained" (381–3). The Wanderer's sympathy is a product of surplus.

The conflation of sympathy and surplus visible in Wordsworth's characterization of the Wanderer is linked, as is his "way-wandering life," to the dispossession that enables Margaret to discern the identity between weavers and soldiers, husbands and strangers. Like Margaret in her abandonment, the Pedlar is defined partly by his distance from the bonds of family and community affiliation; his relations with Margaret, as with the youthful poet, are at best adoptive. The cottage is his "home" no more than the nearby village in which he rents a room. For the Wanderer, "daughter" and "home" are entirely metaphorical. But without specific affiliations or local attachments, the Wanderer is able to generate a philosophy that is aptly described as "general welfare," in that the analogical family he constructs is infinitely expandable. The dissolution of the family economy exacerbated by the emergent economy of wage-labor makes kinship an entirely analogical relation, and "grief" is its substitutive patronymic. The "trick" of grief turns even Margaret's biological children into her psychic equivalents; the Wanderer informs us that her baby "Had from its mother caught the trick of grief / And sighed among its playthings" (830–1). We learn from its effect on the Poet that the "trick" of the Wanderer's narrative of the ruined cottage – its intended effect – is to construct a similarly analogical family relation, a symbolic fraternity of grief: "with a brother's love / I blessed her in the impotence of grief" (923–4). Although it appears to reinstall the local attachments disrupted by the operations of a general economy, in fact this affective ethos of "family" sympathy only mirrors the logic of equivalence and infinite expansion.

If the loss of a family member is a proper object of grief, the Poet's loss must be considered a loss of a far more ideal kind, related to melancholia rather than mourning. Like the baby sighing among its playthings, the poet grieving expresses a pathos in the midst of plenty, and therefore suggests that impoverishment is an affective condition of the ego rather than an economic condition of the world. But such grief is not entirely impotent, as Freud's own example of a baby sighing among its playthings will demonstrate.[12]

In *Beyond the Pleasure Principle* Freud describes a game played by his grandson to compensate for the occasional absence of his mother and, later, the disappearance of his father to the war front:

> The child had a wooden reel with a piece of string round it… What he did was to hold the reel by the string and very skillfully throw it over the edge of his curtained cot, so that it disappeared into it, at the same time uttering his expressive "o-o-o-o." He then pulled the reel out of the cot again by the string and hailed its reappearance with a joyful "*da*" ["there"]. This, then, was the complete game – disappearance and return. (9)

Identifying the expressive "o" as a prearticulate version of the German sound for "gone" [*fort*], Freud finds in the game an epistemological dilemma analogous to the "traumatic neurosis" (a "subjective ailment" which "resembles hypochondria or melancholia" [6]) of discharged soldiers who relive their traumas in dreams: given the wish-fulfilling tenor of games and dreams, what explains the compulsion to repeat a distressing experience? Freud offers two explanations, one local, the other general and speculative: both are relevant to the structure of *The Excursion*.

Freud explains the child's sighing among its playthings (I see no reason to *translate* the "o," which adequately marks the pathos of loss) as an expression of and compensation for the loss of his mother; powerless to prevent his mother's occasional absences from home, he controls departure and return in the narrowed circuit of his game. This exchange of a "*passive* situation" for an "*active* part" (10) corresponds to the relation between "being moved" and "moving" that describes the relation between Margaret and the Wanderer. Margaret's last request to the Pedlar – that he bear with him the burden of solicitation, asking of others what she begs of him, information of her husband – appears to precipitate an extended departure from the neighborhood; after that request is made, he never sees Margaret alive again: "We parted then – / Our final parting; from that time forth / Did many seasons pass ere I returned / Into this tract again" (1.868–71). It is as if, in imitation of Robert, he cannot bear to witness her sinking into vagrancy. Also like Robert, he leaves with her some "tokens of regard" meant to memorialize continued affection despite his prolonged absence; these tokens, for her son's use, are presumably the toys among which he later sighs. We learn from this series of connections that both the circuit of exchange embodied in the Pedlar and its abstraction in the money-form imitate Margaret's vagrancy, in the same way that, as Freud reminds us, an organism

is obliged in the course of its development to recapitulate (even if only in a transient and abbreviated fashion) the structures of all the forms from which it is sprung, instead of proceeding quickly by the shortest path to its final shape. (31)

Even as the Pedlar distances himself from Margaret quite literally by moving, the repetition compulsion evident in his way-wandering life suggests the final collapse of any simple distinction between moving and being moved.

In order to represent the Wanderer as a figure of independence and independent means, the liberal face of the vagrant/host, Wordsworth must deemphasize the acquisitive (and therefore solicitous) aspect of peddling. As a consequence, the Pedlar appears less as merchant than as benefactor; others, "*all dependent / Upon the Pedlar's toil*, supplied their wants, / Or pleased their fancies, with the wares he brought" (330–2; emphasis added). Here the Pedlar functions as the "given," the solid, inexhaustible ground of community, and the market as that which provides a common denominator, acts as a harmonizing mechanism, for and of individual desire. Status undergoes a neat reversal: those whom the Pedlar serves grow "dependent," while their own interests and needs gradually *unburden* him. Through this unburdening, whose material form is the transformation of commodities into money, the traveling salesman metamorphoses into a figure of individualism and self-sufficiency. Wordsworth appears to invoke this literal disburdening in figuring the Wanderer as one "for travel unimpaired" (34); unlike early versions of "The Pedlar," in book 1 of *The Excursion* the Wanderer no longer carries a pack, is no longer bent double. He has become a kind of Mr. Moneybags whose sentimental "solicitousness" toward Margaret displaces an economic solicitation, in which "tokens" are those of exchange and debt.

Wordsworth probably derived his idea of the Pedlar as a figure that might "carry the burden" of a discursive shift from the political and the economic to the therapeutic from Heron's *Journey through Scotland* which, in addition to representing the vagrant/host, also offers a history of the traveling salesman–missionary. In the 1820 edition, attempting to verify the authenticity and explain the function of his "philosophical" Pedlar, Wordsworth appended several paragraphs from Heron's account. I quote the appended reference in full:

"We learn from Caesar and other Roman writers, that the travelling merchants who frequented Gaul and other barbarous countries, either newly conquered by Roman arms, or bordering on Roman conquests, were ever the first to make the inhabitants of those countries acquainted with Roman modes of life, and to inspire them with an inclination to follow the Roman fashions, and to enjoy Roman conveniences. In North America, travelling merchants from the Settlements have done and continue to do much more towards civilizing the Indian natives, than all the missionaries, papist or protestant, who have ever been sent among them.

"It is further to be observed, for the credit of this most useful class of men, that they commonly contribute, by their personal manners, no less than by the sale of their wares, to the refinement of the people among whom they travel. Their dealings form them to great quickness of wit and acuteness of judgment. Having constant occasion to recommend themselves and their goods, they acquire habits of the most obliging attention, and the most insinuating address. As in their peregrinations they have opportunity of contemplating the manners of various men and various cities, they become eminently skilled in the knowledge of the world. *As they wander, each alone, through thinly-inhabited districts, they form habits of reflection and of sublime contemplation.* With all these qualifications, no wonder, that they should often be, in remote parts of the country, the best mirrors of fashion, and censors of manners; and should contribute much to polish the roughness, and soften the rusticity, of our peasantry. It is not more than twenty or thirty years since a young man going from any part of Scotland to England, was considered as going to lead the life of a gentleman. When, after twenty years' absence, in that honourable line of employment, he returned with his acquisitions to his native country, he was regarded as a gentleman to all intents and purposes. (Heron, *Journey through Scotland*, I, 89. W. W. [*PW* v.411–12])

Despite Wordsworth's defense of not only the empirical reality but also the economic and cultural value of such rural philosophers, it is important to remember that Heron and Wordsworth argue a much-disputed point. Frequently, English (and Scottish) vagrancy statutes listed itinerant pedlars among other types of the unworthy poor, classifying them as members of the vagabond, hence dangerous, classes. As a Scotsman traveling in England (recall that "The Ruined Cottage" is actually set in the south of England), the Wanderer is a virtual foreigner with little investment in any national concern. By contrast, Heron makes the itinerant merchant not a sower of subversion but an ally of the state, not a barbarian or nomad himself but rather a civilizing influence on the masses. Wordsworth refines this reversal by underlining "*habits of reflection and sublime contemplation*" and thereby drawing attention away from "habits of obliging attention, and the most insinuating address" – those aspects of the pedlar's behavior reminiscent of "beggar's cant."

"Refinement" characterizes both the pedlar's speech *and* his wares, for Heron argues that the difference between the two populations (Mayhew's wandering and civilized tribes) is erased by the "enjoyment of conveniences." The missionaries of convenience – those who bring goods and services to thinly inhabited regions – reduce the vagabondage of the lower classes, who no longer must roam in search of what they cannot find at hand. Mobility is institutionalized and contained in the pedlar, and his "dependents" thus learn the value of centralization and of money.

This quality of refinement is crucial to understanding how the missionary salesman, the Pedlar turned Wanderer, can offer a cure for melancholy. Imagine for a moment that a peasant "wants" the curative of mineral water. Would not the Pedlar who supplies it then curiously represent that bane of individual well-being and the walking cure, the apothecary's shop? A paragraph in Heron's *Journey* elided from Wordsworth's note resolves this apparent contradiction by arguing that the desire for luxuries (which such therapeutic water, like shiatsu massage, must be considered) only arises as a consequence of the pedlar's incursions:

Nothing can be more natural, than that these things should so happen. A rude people will hardly go in search of commodities of which they know not the names, the nature, or the value, and which they have little, if any, money to purchase. Yet, when such commodities are brought among them, exposed to their view, and recommended as fashionable or useful; they seldom fail to take a fancy for them and will often give in exchange anything of however essential utility, that they already possess. They learn to labour, that they may have means with which to purchase those foreign commodities. They learn to disdain the use of those coarse clothes, or rude utensils with which they were before content. And with the new conveniences, they insensibly adopt the improved system of manners to which such conveniences properly correspond. In the stage of the progress of society in which this change is begun, no such alteration could possibly take place, without the intervention of chapmen or pedlars. (*Journey*, 89)

The crucial "progress" of civilization, according to Heron, entails the replacement of one system of value, based on "use," by another, based not only on exchange but also on advertisement (commodities "exposed to their view"). The Pedlar himself functions thus as a kind of "moving spectacle," the trick of which is not to induce compassion but instead cupidity. As the peasant moves from subsistence to a state of "almost epicurean selfishness," buying the mineral water advertised by the Pedlar as a cure for his melancholy, he becomes the therapeutic subject, who needs to learn from Kant how to drink *air* as he strolls along.

The structure of exchange becomes, in Wordsworth, a structure of incompletion, for *his* Pedlar does *not* return after twenty years to become a *property-owner*. In effect, book 1 of *The Excursion* narrates the decline of the eighteenth-century prospect poem, with its stationary perspective of the country-house promontory, and its replacement by a "deterritorialized" control of the landscape, a replacement in turn coincident with the expansion of capital beyond the geographic dimensions at issue in the enclosure movement. Those who obey the old law, that "to be is to inhabit," need not face literal dispossession in order to find themselves entombed in the same cottage garden that formerly provided for their subsistence. Thus Wordsworth does not narrate a tale in which Margaret is forcibly removed from her tenancy by economic conditions, as Robert arguably had been. Rather, she is replaced by a new principle of occupation, or tenancy, that is not in fact tenancy at all, and represents a dichotomy between two models of citizenship, and two models of the subject, readable in Virilio's distinction between "the geography of the inhabitant and that of the passerby," between "the moving-power of invasion and that of the landowner's (or sedentary worker–producer's) relative inability to move, to displace himself, attached as he is to his little parcel of land" (70–1). In contrast to Margaret's, the Wanderer's relation to space is defined by *continual displacement*, and he carries his little "parcel" with him.

The Wanderer exhorts the Poet (and, by extension, the reader) to "no longer read / The forms of things with an unworthy eye" (1.939–40). The *worthy* eye does not belong to the inhabitant nor even to the spectator, but rather to the passerby; hence the recurrence of "pass" and its cognates in the passage in question:

> As once *I passed*, into my heart conveyed
> So still an image of tranquillity...
>
> That what we feel of sorrow and despair
> From ruin and from change, and all the grief
> That *passing* shews of being leave behind,
> Appeared an idle dream, that could maintain,
> Nowhere, dominion o'er the enlightened spirit
> Whose meditative sympathies repose
> Upon the breast of faith. I turned away,
> And walked along my road in happiness.     (1.945–6, 949–56)

The "repose" imagined at the end of "The Ruined Cottage" is at once entirely literal – the moving spectacle that was Margaret has ceased to move – "sleeps in the calm earth" – and entirely metaphysical: "repose" upon the breast of faith takes place while in motion. This latter image makes perfect sense if we consider that faith, like any "token" of regard, requires the future for its redemption. The two gold "sovereigns" that Robert *leaves in place* have no value as long as they remain "fast rooted" to that spot, but require the supplementary *exercise* of the sovereignty they represent, for sovereignty has ceased to *reside* (in kings, in coins, or in land).

Later in *The Excursion*, the Wanderer will represent sovereignty as a vertical rather than horizontal exercise: "*unless above himself he can / Erect himself, how poor a thing is Man!*" (iv.330–1). As a prelude to the "graveyard" books, this reconfigures the movement between "here" and "there" (*fort* and *da*) as the distance between life and death. But the Wanderer's own transmutation, from a Pedlar bent double by his load to one whose "transcendental surplus" marks him as one who "could *afford* to suffer," suggests an alternative reading. First encountered by the Poet in the supine position of the "dreaming man," the Wanderer "erects" himself in order to eulogize Margaret, who lies beneath him: "here she died; / Last human tenant of these ruined walls!" (1.915–16). The figure then conflates surplus and dearth in a way crucial to understanding *The Excursion* as a cure for melancholy that is also its perpetuation. If the melancholiac's impoverished ego signals a "loss of a more ideal kind," death constitutes a "real" loss, and thereby enables a return to mourning. But what "dies" in "The Ruined Cottage" is not merely a species of life and work outmoded by a more mobile society, but space itself, although a nostalgia for space written throughout the poem will consecrate at the same time it announces that death. The game of *fort–da* is truly child's play compared to the model of infinite circulation represented by the Wanderer, which rather corresponds to a "long-drawn-out 'o-o-o-o.'"

### III: THE SPACE OF DEATH

We know that both Margaret and the Wanderer are to be regarded as "moving spectacles" because of the following passage, addressed to the Poet in book II of *The Excursion*:

> "I did not fear
> To tax you with this journey;" – mildly said
> My venerable Friend, as forth we stepped
> Into the presence of the cheerful light –
> "For I have knowledge that you do not shrink
> From moving spectacles; but let us on."          (486–91)

Ironically, book I gives us evidence that the Poet initially "shrinks" from both kinds of "moving spectacles" offered to his contemplation: the spectacle of pure movement represented by the figure poised in the public road whom he approaches with "slackened step," and the "compassionate picture" the Wanderer paints of Margaret. But because the Poet continues onward, in imitation of those moving spectacles, he proves his mettle.

The "moving spectacle" that serves as the ostensible goal of the titular excursion, to which the story of Margaret has been merely a prelude, is the Solitary himself. The destitution of citizen subject represented in the Solitary's history is "moving" partly because, like Margaret, he cannot move on, abandoning anxieties in the manner recommended by Kant. The Solitary, disillusioned by discovering "that all / Which bears the name of action, howsoe'er / Beginning, ends in servitude" (IV.893–5), can be diagnosed as a melancholiac,

unable to attend to business. Like Rousseau, whose sentiments in the
*Rêveries* he here merely echoes, the Solitary abandons all purposes. To
this spectacle of destitution, Wordsworth opposes the "moving
spectacle" of the Poet and Wanderer, who move "on" in a fine
demonstration of purposiveness. For when the Wanderer issues his
command, "let us on," he imagines them deprived of their object:
hearing a funeral dirge, the Wanderer concludes that the Solitary has
died ("He is departed, and finds peace at last!" [384]) even before
they see "a band / Of rustic persons, from behind the hut / Bearing
a coffin in the midst" (386–8). To move on, in this case, is to be a
moving spectacle indeed, for in resisting identification with the
Solitary whose body is "moved" the Wanderer and the Poet seem to
effect a walking cure not only of melancholy but also of death itself.

We quickly discover that the Wanderer is mistaken in his account
of the Solitary's death, however; the coffin they espy holds the body
of another destituted figure, a "homeless Pensioner" and "neglected
veteran" whose history – exposed to a storm, he takes shelter in a
ruined cottage but eventually dies of the exposure – is a naturalized
version of the Solitary's (and the Poet's) exposure to History. The
Wanderer's prevenient burial of the Solitary, however, allows the
Solitary himself to reemerge as the image of transcendental surplus,
erected above this destituted version of himself, so to speak:

> full in view, approaching through a gate
> That opened from the enclosure of green fields
> Into the rough uncultivated ground,
> Behold the Man whom he had fancied dead!     (II.494–7)

Small wonder that the Solitary, thus resurrected, should appear as a
type of the discharged soldier – "A meagre person, tall, and in a garb
/ Not rustic – dull and faded like himself!" (500–1). He is the pure
form of the subject, its hallucinatory double: the vagrant.

In the "Essay upon Epitaphs" appended to *The Excursion*,
Wordsworth describes the pure form of the subject as the epitaph. If
the sepulchral monument is "a tribute to a man as a human being,"
the epitaph "adds something more"; the monument conserves the
particular and historical body, but the epitaph speaks "the general
language of humanity" (*PW* v.451). Representing a man "as
something midway between what he was on earth walking about
with his living frailties, and what he may be presumed to be as a
Spirit," the epitaph is "exposed to all," and "lovingly solicits

regard" (453). Ironically, then, the idealized characterization attempted by the epitaph could well describe the vagrant whose destituted condition and consequent emaciation suggest a premature spiritualization, and its *generalized* address (both to sorrowing survivors and mere "travellers") corresponds to the vagrant's exposure to a "public" that exposure helps to create. The vagrant creates his public by the attenuated affiliative bonds that define his condition; each passerby is "equally" a stranger, and equally a "fellow" man, responding to the spectacle of destitution out of sheer (common) humanity. The epitaph also works by this invocation of a "common" humanity that daily life renders invisible; Wordsworth claims that "to be born and to die are the two points in which all men feel themselves to be in absolute coincidence" (*PW* v, 451).

But this same description of the epitaph could with equal accuracy apply to the Wanderer, also raised above his condition when "walking about with his living frailties," when his body was bent double with a pack. Likewise, since he can "afford to suffer" because of an achieved surplus, the Wanderer exposes himself to moving spectacles, and, even without the commodities by which he might formerly have attracted the attention of strangers, becomes an object of regard. But it is not merely his achieved monetary surplus that enables this transformation; if the destitution of the vagrant brings about a premature spiritualization, the spiritualization of the Wanderer is partly an effect of his advanced years, his proximity to death. In this sense, he shares with the vagrant the condition of having nothing left to lose but life itself.

At first, this representation its universal character may seem to *naturalize* death, and thus to establish a natural basis for human community. The naturalness of death would then establish an ethical principle for the conduct of human life: since death is the natural *end* of humanity, it is also its purpose. The invocation of death corresponds in this sense to the wish expressed by the Wanderer to the Pastor:

> The mine of real life
> Dig for us; and present us, in the shape of
> Virgin ore, that gold which we, by pains
> Fruitless as those of aery alchemists,
> Seek from the torturing crucible...
> Give us, for our abstractions, solid facts;
> For our disputes, plain pictures.          (v.630–4, 637–8)

Whereas in *The Prelude* Wordsworth had sought to displace Enlightenment abstractions of "man" by empirical evidence acquired by encounters with vagrants in the public road, in *The Excursion* the Wanderer seeks his evidence in the churchyard among the mountains. Moreover, although the Pastor responds to his request with stories of death and burial described as "authentic epitaphs," the Wanderer's rhetoric reminds us of Wordsworth's claim in the *Essay on Epitaphs* that the affective power of epitaphs depends partly on their "*close connection with the bodily remains of the deceased*" (*PW* v, 448). For "digging" in the context of the graveyard can only be regarded as a kind of exhumation.

Bodies are most often exhumed when there is some question over the cause of death. Yet the Pastor excludes from consideration anyone whose life is marked by "grievous crimes / And strange disasters" (VI.570–I). There is no mark of violence in any of the deaths recounted; even the would-be soldier, Oswald, dies before he reaches the battlefield. Poems like *The Excursion* thus might be held responsible for Freud's claim, in *Beyond the Pleasure Principle*, that "we are strengthened in our thought" that death is the natural end of life "by the writings of our poets" (38–9). For he points out that the notion of natural death is far from universal; some cultures "attribute every death that occurs among them to the influence of an enemy or of an evil spirit" (39).

Moreover, Wordsworth's intention to naturalize death seems fairly explicit; in the *Essay on Epitaphs* he prefers the "ancient" custom of suburban burial "by the waysides" to the "busy, noisy, unclean, and almost grassless churchyard of a large town" (*PW* v, 449) because "natural" burial effects "analogies" of death: "death as a sleep overcoming the tired wayfarer – of misfortune as a storm that falls suddenly on him" (448). In the context of *The Excursion*, these are not casual analogies, for the homeless Pensioner whose funeral is the moving spectacle of book II dies apparently as a consequence of falling asleep during a storm. But the analogy to nature can hide the efficient cause, and so dehistoricize death, as Sebastiano Timpanaro points out:

For too long the ruling classes have attributed to "nature"... the iniquities and sufferings for which the organization of society is responsible – including certain "natural" calamities (from floods and earthquakes to sicknesses and deaths) which would not have occurred, or would have been much less serious and premature, if the quest for maximum profit and the sub-

ordination of public powers to capitalist interests had not caused ... the most
obvious measures of security and prevention to be neglected. (17)

And indeed, the Solitary offers quite a different account of the
Pensioner's death by exposure to Nature. This exposure itself is a
consequence of "the quest for maximum profits": the housewife who
houses the Pensioner in order to receive part of his pension had
ordered him to collect winter fuel in the midst of the storm.

The idea that death is a "natural" end to life is therefore fraught
with political implications. The Solitary's account of death is almost
Jacobinical in its implicit attribution of death to greed; in the same
spirit that Robespierre declared "Dearth is not the result of lack of
grain...Dearth can only be attributed to the vices of the laws
themselves or their administration," Saint-Just would claim that
"Man is made neither for the hospital nor for the poorhouse"
(Ragon, 301). Medical faculties were abolished by the convention in
the same spirit that would cause Bonaparte to "declare" the end of
mendicancy.

The failure of both the French Convention and Bonaparte to
outlaw either mendicancy or death is the source of the Solitary's
melancholy, as his complaint makes clear:

> Ah! what avails imagination high
> Or question deep? what profits all that earth,
> Or heaven's blue vault, is suffered to put forth
> Of impulse or allurement...
>                if nowhere
> A habitation, for consummate good,
> Or progressive virtue, by the search
> Can be attained – a better sanctuary
> From doubt and sorrow, than the senseless grave?
>
>                       (III.209–12, 220–4)

The anxiety the melancholiac cannot "get beyond" nor leave behind
is the anxiety of death itself, which demonstrates that all earthly
tenure – that of the largest landowner as well as that of the poorest
beggar – is transitory at best. By requesting an exhumation, the
Wanderer seeks to resolve the question of death, now revealed as the
source of melancholy.

In addition to naturalizing death, the epitaphs pronounced by the
Pastor and recommended to the contemplation of the Solitary as a
cure for his despondency may seem to *equalize* death. But this too is an

illusion, as Michel Ragon points out. In *The Space of Death*, he argues that the graveyard

> expresses all the contradictions of our society, which wants to be egalitarian and consoles itself by saying that at least men are equal before death.
> This is not true, however. Everybody, of course, is condemned to death, which is a sort of very relatively consoling equality. But the condemnation to death is accompanied by various tortures, from which some men are exempt, since they die in their sleep. The inequality is flagrant when one considers the time given us to live out our earthly lives and the illness and pain that precede death. (40)

In order to assure equality before the law (of death), then, one would have to establish freedom not only from violent death perpetrated by enemies or spirits, but also from disease, especially from diseases associated with conditions of social inequality – poor housing, nutrition, and sanitation. Then any deviation from the "normal" course of life (what Freud calls its "fixed average duration") would be attributable only to the will of the subject.

Unsurprisingly, none of the rural deaths recounted in *The Excursion* can be attributed directly to such diseases, even though impoverishment often gives rise to pathological behaviors; instead, death is represented as a cure for these pathologies. Take the case of one of the most interesting inhabitants of the graveyard, the "lonely miner" whose tale is recounted in book VI. His is a peculiarly relevant case because he also digs the mine of real life, so to speak, seeking to find its "precious ore." An entire life spent in search of gold might be seen as a cruel parody of *homo economicus*, of getting and spending; the "PATH OF PERSEVERANCE" that links his cottage door to the mine's mouth merely indicates the formal correspondence of his span of life to that of the Cumberland beggar. This would especially be the case had his perseverance gone unrewarded – but indeed he finds the ore. He cannot be said to die, therefore, from the manufacturing of false needs associated with "progress"; instead, he is said to die of "joy." Where the *empty* mine was "the darksome centre of a constant hope" (249), the transmutation of that hope into the (naturalized) form of money collapses the space of desire even as, on a more literal level, the empty mine is filled with ore. His achievement leaves him nowhere to *go* – except that other darksome center, the grave.

Commenting that the story is "true to the letter," Wordsworth expresses surprise at the Miner's fate:

Several times in my life I have heard of sudden influxes of wealth being followed by derangement...But these all happened where there had been little or no previous effort to acquire the riches, and therefore such a consequence might the more naturally be expected than in the case of the solitary Miner. In reviewing his story one cannot help but regret that such perseverance was not sustained by a worthier object. (*PW* v.458)

"Derangement" here indicates primarily a psychic disorder, but given the Miner's history, it may remind us as well of the condition of the female vagrant's father, when his "range of water" is denied by the landlord: both are "unsettled," so to speak. In *Lyrical Ballads*, however, this "derangement," actually an expropriation, had an explicitly historical and economic cause; here, Wordsworth seems to suggest that derangement is the effect of a *mental* deterritorialization ("On the fields he looked / With an unsettled liberty of thought" [238–9]). And, although death is not exactly represented as the "cure" for such derangement, it does *locate* the Miner once again.

The Miner's location in the graveyard must seem "very relatively consoling" to the melancholiac; after all, the Solitary has already dismissed the "security" of housing offered by death (Ragon: "The tomb is a second house" [14]). But the series of authentic epitaphs pronounced by the Pastor gradually suggests Wordsworth's purpose in so representing death as the cure for the anxiety it produces. For the real source of the Solitary's resistance to death – manifested in his solitariness – is its threatened collapse of individuality. And it is true, when individuality is conceived as a set of symptoms, when the ego is defined by its neuroses, that death means the obliteration of individuality. Freud speaks of the melancholiac's tendency to self-denigration as unusually marked by an "insistent communicativeness which finds satisfaction in self-exposure" (247); so, despite his reclusiveness, does Wordsworth's Solitary demonstrate that desire to be *known* that is registered in the epitaph.

By encouraging reflection on this desire to be known, the graveyard is supposed to work its cure. It is not simply a question of the epitaph's success in marking the passage of the individual, memorializing that passage, and so rendering him or her immortal. On the contrary, Wordsworth emphasizes the relative paucity of memorials. As in "The Brothers," the churchyard among the mountains is unmarked by many monuments; the inhabitants of the churchyard are made known through the Pastor's narration, as Margaret had been eulogized by the Wanderer. And if we can see the "path of perseverance" marked by the Miner's passage, to perceive its difference from a stray sheepwalk similarly requires such a narration. We can no longer see any "vestige" of a similar path, of mourning, traced by an unwed mother to the grave of her infant, for example.

What is "knowable" about the inhabitants of the graveyard is their somatic condition, not their psychic disposition. If this seems a severe straitening of the range of knowledge, similar to the "very relatively consoling" equality of death, consider the fact that it is also an extension of knowledge beyond that available to the subject: as Nancy points out, "what community reveals to me, in presenting to me my birth and my death, is my existence outside myself" (*Community* 26). In this context, the Wanderer's exhortation that the subject "above himself... Erect himself" cannot be read merely as a recommendation that the Solitary master his despondency; the mastery or *sovereignty* envisioned here is the impossible concept of the dead man erecting his own sepulchral monument – a moving spectacle indeed. And yet, this impossible sovereignty is precisely what guarantees, not the Solitary's individuality, but his *singularity*, to use Nancy's distinction. Defining the "individual" as "the abstract result of a decomposition" (*ibid.*, 3), Nancy enables us to assimilate two crucial features of the individual, that "unit of account" of liberalism. Individuality as "indivisibility" exposes this concept of the subject as a last effort to protect private property: as the "least common denominator," individuality is an attempt to establish a "proper" name over against the logic of equivalence. Second, we recognize in the individual the "dead" man, for what finally distinguishes the individual from "man in general" is the particular body, tragically subject itself to decomposition. Singularity, by contrast, represents to Nancy a differentiation established not in relation to "man in general," that palimpsest of seriality that is the image of liberal community, but an empty space for sovereignty preserved by the inability of the subject to pronounce its own death. In this sense the space of death, the sepulchral monument and its epitaphic inscription, is the "real" location of what Lefort describes as the empty space of democracy. Both prevent the collapse of representation into immanence.

Associated so profoundly with the logic of infinite circulation, the Wanderer clearly regards death as enabling the "translation" of individuality, its reabsorption or sublation into the pure – *immanent* – idea of community. Death is not the end because "man" is an end, so to speak: the physical decomposition of those features of individuality that preserve difference is what enables the production of the concept "man"; death is a means to the "end" represented by this concept. In this sense, it does not matter whether we conceive of the Wanderer as the purveyor of capitalism or the purveyor of truth; insofar as "man" is discursively configured as producer, even death becomes a "work," something manufactured by human reason. In fact, the Wanderer's notion of death is equally "Jacobinical" in this respect, although death is regarded as the sign of human perfectibility rather than the mark of corruption.

The Wanderer's tendency to regard death as subject to reason, or perseverance in a *prescribed* course of action, is indicated when he curiously interrupts the Pastor's account of a botanist, whose excursive activity mirrors the titular excursion, or Heron's imagined excursion to a mineral spring. To cure his despondency he does not search, as the Solitary first thinks, for "some virtuous herb of power / To cure his malady" (VI.111–12), but rather constructs "A calendar of flowers" (174) clearly meant by Wordsworth to be read as a parody of the French Revolutionary calendar of Nature. By a neat correspondence, the cure for his melancholy (*hypochondria vaga*) becomes the wildflower, that Kantian example of beauty, or *pulchritudo vaga*:

Flowers are free natural beauties. Hardly anyone but a botanist knows what sort of thing a flower ought to be; and even he, though recognizing in the flower the reproductive organ of the plant, pays no regard to this natural purpose if he is passing judgment on the flower by taste. (*CJ* 65)

Reading the Wanderer's interruption –

> "Impute it not to impatience, if," exclaimed
> The Wanderer, "I infer that he was healed
> By perseverance in the course described" (VI.189–91)

– in this context, we are struck by its manifold ironies. First, the Wanderer converts the aesthetic or literary excursion into a regimen, or cure, indistinguishable from the rejected medical model of a search for the virtuous herb. Second, although the Wanderer's prognosis for the botanist transforms means into ends by making "perseverance" or walking itself the source of the cure, his conclusion that the botanist was "healed" is completely ironized by previous information that he had, in fact, already died. If at first we reconcile this contradiction by concluding that the botanist at least did not die of melancholy, we are obstructed in our work of reconciliation by the contention of the Solitary that it is impossible to die "Of pain and grief" alone (VI.117). And indeed, the majority of the graveyard's inhabitants led lives marked by melancholy but died of *natural* causes. The relation of the *therapeutic* subject to the subject of mortality is not a relation of identity.

The relation between the therapeutic subject and the subject of mortality is, as it has been my project to argue, the relation between the transcendental subject and the vagrant. The transcendental subject and the vagrant are finally incarnated in *The Excursion* as the doctor of philosophy and the dead man because the logic of equivalence upon which the concept of "man in general" depends requires the abandonment of *singularity*. If the achievement of surplus in capitalism requires the expropriation of the laborer, the achievement of the philosophical "essence" of Man requires his release from somatic dependencies. Recall that it is the "mine of real life" which finally yields the Wanderer his object; bones are exhumed only to be spiritualized.

Perhaps Wordsworth's graveyard encounter between the doctor of philosophy and the vagrant, "whom he had fancied dead," enables a reconceptualization of Hegel's famous dictum of sublation, "The Spirit is a bone." This reconceptualization would entail a new balancing of those terms, "human" and "nature," the traversing between which has produced both the Romantic poem and the modern subject. When unappeased by the prospect of death, unable to console ourselves that death promises a cessation of *needs*, we register the unsatisfactory logic of liberalism, an idea of community whose moral "purpose" is allied to needs-satisfaction, the principle of production. Like the vagrant who continues to testify to the apparent incapacity of production ever to guarantee needs-satisfaction, the carcass of the dead man exposes the apparent incapacity of philosophy ever to deliver a *concept* of man finally beyond history. But history itself must be reconceived; we cannot content ourselves merely with "historicizing" death, for that had been the project of the French Revolutionaries when they implicitly attributed death to the *ancien régime*. Timpanaro remarks,

The historicist polemic against "man in general," which is completely correct as long as it denies that certain historical and social forms such as private property or class divisions are inherent in humanity in general, overlooks the fact that man as a biological being, endowed with a certain (not unlimited) adaptability to his external environment, and with certain impulses towards activity and the pursuit of happiness, *subject to old age and death*, is not an abstract construction, nor one of our prehistoric ancestors, a species of pithecanthropus now superseded by historical and social man, but still exists in each of us and in all probability will still exist in the future. It is certainly true that the development of society changes men's ways of feeling pain, pleasure, and other elementary psycho-physical reactions, and that there is hardly anything that is "purely natural" left in contemporary man, that has not been enriched and remoulded by the social and cultural environment. But the general aspects of the human condition still remain... to maintain that, since the "biological" is always presented to us as mediated by the "social," the "biological" is nothing and the "social" is everything, would once again be idealist sophistry. (45; emphasis added)

The hypochondria that seems entirely dependent on a certain historical advance – the therapeutic subject *following*, in this sense, the liberal subject even as the paranoid Rousseau follows his invention of citizen subject – will then have to be recognized as a *somatic* condition. Like the *pulchritudo vaga* of the wildflower that derives from our inability to determine its end, its final purpose, so *hypochondria vaga* derives from a somatic resistance to regarding death as the end of desire, or a desirable end.

In an essay whose title, "On the Power of the Mind to Master Its Morbid Feelings by Sheer Resolution," suggests it might have been authored by the Wanderer himself, Kant explains the veneration of old age:

The duty of honoring old age, in other words, is not really based in the consideration that age, because of its frailty, can rightly claim from youth; for weakness is no reason for being entitled to respect. Old age, therefore, claims to be considered something meritorious... not [because] in attaining the age of Nestor one has acquired, by varied and long experience, wisdom for guiding the young; it is only that a man who has survived so long – that is, has succeeded so long in eluding mortality, the most humiliating sentence that can be passed on a rational being ("you are dust and will return to dust") has to this extent won immortality, so to speak. (*CF* 179)

The passage offers us a framework for rereading *The Excursion* against the grain, for rethinking its "humiliating sentence." Kant's version of that sentence, "you are dust and will return to dust," is "the most humiliating sentence that can be passed on a rational being" because it is *tautological*. This tautology is the purest expression of the "natural rights" of man, even as it establishes the basis for universal equality: we are all debts owed to death.

The "humiliation" of the subject, Kant's rational being, takes the form of a tautological sentence because tautology is *irrational*, as Zizek reminds us. It is the irrational, unseemly aspect of rhetoric that one attempts to eliminate from the proposition. And rational being has the form of a proposition – the form of the Wanderer's proposition, "Let us on." In such an economy, death itself is irrational, as Ragon reminds us in *The Space of Death*: because the dead have ceased to *function*, neither producing nor consuming, nor *going* anywhere, they bear a marked resemblance to the vagrant. Symptomatic of this resemblance is the fact that they take up space, demand to be housed.

So it is with old men. Kant remarks on the opposition generated between old age and death:

Why am I not willing to make way for younger people who are struggling upward, and why do I curtail the enjoyment of life I am used to just to stay alive? Why do I prolong a feeble life to an extraordinary age by self-denial, and by my example confuse the obituary list, which is based on the average of those who are more frail by nature and calculated on their life expectancy? (*CF*, 209)

If the humiliation of the rational being by the fatal tautology of "dust" is a consequence of its irrationality, here Kant paradoxically aligns the rational and the irrational: he prolongs his life by a "firm resolution...by which reason exercises a direct healing power," but that very prolongation is irrational. Reason is put in the service of unreason, an unreason generated by the somatic condition of old age. One masters morbidity *not* through sheer resolution, as the title suggests, but through sheer *irresolution*, the incapacity of an old philosopher to decide to die. The spectacle of old age is as "moving" as the spectacle of vagrancy because they both are "remainders" of the logic of equivalence, and therefore suggest a way out of its perfect fatality.

# Notes

## A METHODOLOGICAL PREAMBLE

1 See Lisa Cartwright, "'Experiments' of Destruction," p. 144.
2 Elaine Scarry, *The Body in Pain*, p. 5. Considering the proportional importance (in size and weight) of legs to a given body, it is significant that Scarry's index entry on "Body, Locations within" does not have a subheading for legs; unlike the hands and back, or phallus and womb, those privileged sites for production and reproduction, the legs suggest a transitoriness incongruent with Scarry's idea of the (more or less permanent) artifact. To concretize the relation of walking to the productivist freedom (from pain) Scarry imagines, we may imagine workers as they walk between the workplace and the home.
3 Jameson reproduces a different painting than the one identified by Shapiro as Heidegger's subject in "The Origins of the Work of Art." Since Shapiro's identification tends to go against the grain of Heidegger's own reference to the *series* of shoe paintings, the difference is perhaps unimportant; more telling, however, is Jameson's acceptance of the shoes as those of a peasant, as well as his overlooking of the effect Van Gogh's *serial* portrayal of shoes might have on his distinction between Van Gogh as "high modernist" and the *postmodern*.
4 Quoted from Jacques Derrida, *The Truth in Painting*, p. 367. My discussion of Van Gogh's painting and its criticism is deeply indebted to Derrida's chapter on the subject, "Restitutions."
5 Even historians who dispute the historical reality of "peasant society," arguing that it is largely a *fiction* enabling Marx and others to overemphasize the "massive change" brought about by Acts of Enclosure and the capitalization of land, agree that the important "symbolic" function of "the peasantry" is to invoke "the absence of absolute ownership." See Macfarlane, *The Origins of English Individualism*.
6 Derrida connects Shapiro's idea of the self-portrait, wherein one "renders" oneself, to Van Eyck's self-representational signature in *The Arnolfini Marriage*; see pp. 349–370.

INTRODUCTION

1 An anonymous reviewer is responsible for this wonderful insight.
2 *San Francisco Chronicle*, 23 June 1993, p. A18, col. 2.
3 See Arendt, *On Revolution*, and Lefort, *Democracy and Political Theory*, especially "Human Rights and the Welfare State," pp. 21–40.
4 The phrase is Paul Virilio's: "No one yet suspected that the 'freedom to come and go' so dear to Montaigne would become an obligation to mobility" (p. 30).
5 Liberation is of the *entrepreneurial* subject. See Michael Ryan, "Deconstruction and Social Theory: the Case of Liberalism," p. 156.
6 William Hazlitt records Coleridge's description of Wordsworth's compositional practice in "My First Acquaintance with the Poets," in *Complete Works*, vol. XVII, p. 119.
7 See Lloyd, "Race under Representation," for this apt translation and the argument that the *universal* Kantian subject is a negation.
8 Blake's identification of the God of Judgment, iconographically the equivalent of the Republican *œil de la surveillance*, with "him who walks in the garden at evening time," alerts us to the significance of the evening walk – as practiced, for example, by the speakers of "London" and "My Pretty Rose-Tree." The *evening walk* is the practice of the logic of equivalence, of commodity exchange, and as such the negation of individuation.
9 See Sewell's discussion of "The Abolition of Corporations" in *Work and Revolution in France*, pp. 86–91.
10 The passage appears in Wordsworth's "Letter to the Bishop of Llandaff" (*PrW* I 49). See James Chandler's reading of the passage as a "witty" inference that drunken behavior masks the "sober" shifting of allegiances to advance self-interest, pp. 23–5.

1 ROUSSEAU PLAYS THE BEGGAR: THE LAST WORDS OF CITIZEN SUBJECT

1 Balibar reminds readers of a certain historical "coincidence": "the moment at which Kant produces (and retrospectively projects) the *transcendental* 'subject' is precisely that moment at which politics destroys the 'subject' of the prince, in order to replace him with the republican citizen" (39). Although I find immensely valuable Balibar's careful distinction between the subject politically defined as *subditus*, or one who enters into a relation of obedience, "subjected to" a higher authority, and the *subjectus* as self-authorized, I contend that the regime of liberalism enacts a further split in the definition of the subject: his/her self-authorization occurs not in the political domain but in private, so

that a possible equation between citizen and subject becomes an opposition.

2  Insofar as de Man and Althusser portray the political writings as leading to literature, those texts become so much prefatory material. It is interesting to note in this context de Man's remark that in the preface – that "place in the text where the question of textual mastery and authority is being decided" – "the possibility arises of the entirely gratuitous and irresponsible text... [involving] an intentional denial of paternity for the sake of self-protection" (296). Here he identifies the Preface as the place where the *citizen* belongs – the domain of mastery and authority – but implicitly argues that in Rousseau (hence the reference to a denial of paternity) a usurpation takes place; the *self* replaces the citizen, and "the radical irresponsibility of fiction" the non-fictional *address*. My purpose is not to resist de Man's implication that the Preface is infected by the fiction which follows, but rather to call similar attention to the status of the *post-script* or afterword, which threatens to render the fiction subordinate to the real. To give a "History of the preceding writing" makes the process of composition and distribution more important than the fiction.

3  Rousseau refers strictly to the male body as a sufficient sign of citizenship. Later, in *Emile*, Sophie is encouraged to walk, but her dainty shoes as well as her constitution preclude the kind of rambling, democratizing education developed for Emile.

4  I refer here to historical attempts to render the "literary" as the most universal of categories, subsuming philosophy, politics, and ethics, outlined by Lacoue-Labarthe and Nancy in *The Literary Absolute*. Their identification of a dual tendency in the *Athenaeum* project to recognize the literary "absolute" and literary "exigency" informs my argument in this essay.

5  Although I do not want to engage in a specifically *political* argument here, let me point out that in *The Discourse on Political Economy*, Rousseau's position – "it is therefore one of the most important functions of government to prevent extreme inequality of fortunes; not by taking away wealth from its possessors, but by depriving all men of the means to accumulate it; not by building hospitals for the poor but by securing the citizens from becoming poor" – seems clearly to place him in opposition to the general tendency of poor law reform in the eighteenth century.

6  Rousseau's representation of the conspiracy against him as such a "consolidation of opinion" is an important factor in challenging Althusser's suggestion that the "flight into ideology" represented by the "unprecedented" literary writing occurs as a consequence of Rousseau's collision with the "real" in the form of "social groups" (which negate the opposition particular: general). The contention would be that this collision produces not the flight into but the critique of ideology. If the

existence of social groups produces the political theory – abstract equality as a compensation for real (social) discrepancies – this is exactly what Rousseau suggests when he testifies to the appropriation of that theory *by* such groups. If his writings have an original (or mythical) neutrality, historically the particular and general are categories that come to be inhabited by historical persons or groups, the category of the general usurped by those with real social power, the rest disenfranchised by their relegation to the category of the particular (whose representative is Rousseau).

7 Were it proved that Rousseau actually was responsible for this note, his criticism of the logic of the note might still lend support to my general argument, since the odd phrasing in the note – the poor man "doit un droit a son Roi" – suggests how the conflation of rights and obligations reverts to the model of the social contract Rousseau sought to disrupt.

## 2 MONEY WALKS: WORDSWORTH AND THE RIGHT TO WANDER

1 Subsequently, Marx resorts to two French proverbs to explain the difference between land ("Nulle terre sans seigneur") and the "impersonality" of the money-form ("L'argent n'a pas de maître") (*C* 145 n. 1).

2 In his recently translated *Specters of Marx*, Derrida provides a close reading of the figure of table-turning in *Capital* to which I am deeply indebted. He comments, "Transcendence, the movement of *super-*, the step beyond (*über, epekeina*), is made sensuous in that very excess" (151).

3 In "Female Chatter," Pinch sees Wordsworth's interest in "the power of meter to confer iterability" (840) as an attempt to reinforce gender boundaries, sexuality itself having been rendered as the "heterosexist fantasy" of "similitude in dissimilitude" (the latter phrase is Wordsworth's).

4 It is possible that Wordsworth arranges the line not only to foreground the expanded term of the agricultural "season" (now spread over two years) but also, by ending with "July," to suggest a correspondence between this "denaturing" and the standardization of English. Here, as elsewhere in Wordsworth's poems, "July" fits into the metrical schema as a dactyl; my colleague Stephen Booth alerted me to the *OED*'s claim that, well into the late eighteenth century, rural populations, particularly in the north of England, would have pronounced "July" to rhyme with "truly." But since *Lyrical Ballads* most often adopts dialects or *patois* for an entirely literary purpose, in order to foreground the difference between the "common" (standard English) and the "rustic," it seems likely that Wordsworth wishes the reader to engage both measures in "accounting" for July.

5 Young also embraces engrossment and enclosure in a book called *Farmer's Letters*, where, ironically, he claims that a farm could make

better profits by breeding than by tillage, partly because the former cuts labor costs. It may be that Wordsworth has Young in mind when he tells farmers to "think" in "Goody Blake and Harry Gill"; after all, Young is contributing to the extinction of a class he claims to represent. Other works by Young were less critically received by Wordsworth: Young's *Travels in France*, the record of a journey to revolutionary France predating Wordsworth's by only a year, contains passages which may have suggested elements of Wordsworth's representation of crossing the Simplon Pass and ascending Mount Snowdon.

6  Marx provides a portion of the text of a 1547 statute enacted under Edward VI: "If it happens that a vagabond has been idling about for three days, he is to be taken to his birthplace, branded with a red-hot iron with the letter V on the breast and be set to work, in chains, in the streets or at some other labor" (*C* 687). I refer to a similar measure enacted in France in chapter 1, on Rousseau, above.

7  For a reading of "The Old Cumberland Beggar" which represents the narrator rather than the beggar as a type of profit-seeking and trade, see Robin Jarvis, "Wordsworth and the Use of Charity."

8  "Paper-money [n]ever did, [n]or ever could, CREATE anything of value... though paper-money could CREATE nothing of value, it was able to TRANSFER everything of value... able to take away the wool, that ought to give warmth to the bodies of those who rear the sheep, and put it on the backs of those who carry arms to keep the poor, half-famished shepherds in order" (314). Note how Cobbett's account corresponds closely with the narrative of "Goody Blake and Harry Gill."

9  Hartley Coleridge tells the story. Quoted from Christensen, p. 400.

10  I cite these tautologies – one Hegel's, the other Zizek's – because they will be relevant to my discussion of "Goody Blake and Harry Gill," below, and because they register the *economic* aspect – the transcendental surplus and the empirical deficit – of Wordsworth's tautology that I seek to elucidate.

11  "Usufruct" is a legal term for "the right of temporary possession, use, or enjoyment of the advantages of property belonging to another, so far as may be had without causing damage or prejudice to this" (*OED*). It is distinguished from ownership and consumption.

12  For a similar argument, see Simpson, *Wordsworth's Historical Imagination*.

13  See Ferguson's discussion of depopulation and sublimity in *Solitude and the Sublime*.

14  Cobbett tells of a case which occurred in Wordsworth's "neighbourhood," though I have been unable to find the case in law reports, and therefore cannot date it. The context of his anecdote is significant: it appears subsequent to his attack on "Squire Scott," the erstwhile bricklayer and city-dweller.

However, it is not Squire Scott who has assisted to pass laws to make people pay double toll on a Sunday. 'Squire Scott had nothing to do with passing the New game-laws and Old Ellenborough's Act; 'Squire Scott never invented the New Trespass law, in virtue of which John Cockbain of Whitehaven in the county of Cumberland was, by two clergymen and three other magistrates of that county, sentenced to pay one half-penny for damages and SEVEN SHILLINGS COSTS, for going upon a field, the property of WILLIAM, EARL OF LONSDALE. (150)

This is to imply that the landlords who exercise absolute rights are *strangers*, not "neighbours" in the moral sense.

15 It is odd that Wordsworth should describe *himself* as disinherited, for it seems clear that, in appending his name and preface to the second edition, Wordsworth effectively disenfranchised Coleridge and expropriated his work.

16 See McKendrick, Brewer, and Plumb (eds.), *The Birth of a Consumer Society*, for a revisionist, "demand-side" account of the industrial revolution. See also Campbell, *The Romantic Ethic and the Spirit of Modern Consumerism*, for an interesting if problematic account of the discourse of consumption (modeled on Weber's focus on the discourse of bookkeeping in *The Protestant Ethic and the Spirit of Capitalism*).

17 I am indebted to David Lloyd for the oppression/impression binary to clarify my argument here. The model of reading as "impression" has a long and rich tradition in the Romantic corpus.

18 In addition to redirecting attention in this way, however, we will also have to revise Chandler's salutary criticism of the tendency to regard the poems as offering a "balancing" of epistemologies or "moral philosophies." For while it is true that the rejection of argument in favor of poetic representation is accorded the same preponderance of space afforded to the speaker identified as "William," it is also true that such a spatial, geometrical, or mathematical preponderance does not of itself do away with the possibility of balance.

19 In calling the zero a "non-use-value," I mean to contend for our understanding of its "symbolic" signifying function as a paradigm for the "value" of discourse. The discourses under consideration here – accounting, stenography, law, economics, literature – may be said to rely for their authority on the logic of the zero, insofar as the zero represents a "thing" that does not "count," and therefore does not have to be accounted for. If, according to my more general contention, the modern subject is constructed on the order of analogy, passing from the "man" constructed by the democratic declaration and the discourse of law through to the interiorized subject of psychology, from the public to the private, and never truly "localizable" except by these textual turns and counterturns, the accounting of discourse as a "zero" is necessary for the (imaginary) production of a unified (rather than schizoid) subject. Without wanting to privilege literature as a transcendental

discourse, I do wish to call attention to the way in which the fact (acknowledged by Wordsworth) that literature lacks propriety may serve to undermine this imaginary – in the same way that the "texture" of literary language distracts from the "pure" propositional content.

20  Keats's well-known formulation of a similar "dreaming" condition in "Ode to a Nightingale" ends as if in acknowledgment of Matthew's remonstrance: "Forlorn! the very word is like a bell / To toll me back from thee to my sole self!" The *repetition* (doubling) of the "very word" here produces both the evanishment of the vision (a loss) and a restitution (of selfhood). But this balancing of accounts is another version of the transcendental surplus as empirical deficit, and the self restored by a formalization is a self without neighbors, "sole" and impoverished.

21  See B&G: "Memorandum. If the Printing of the second volume has not commenced, let 'The Brothers' *begin* the Volume" (142 n.). My reading of the poem, which follows, suggests how appropriate such a placement would have been.

22  "Michael" is similar to "The Brothers" in its pairing of the tale with the entail. See Marjorie Levinson's essay, "Spiritual Economics: a Reading of "Michael," in her *Wordsworth's Great Period Poems*.

23  Calenture describes the susceptibility of seamen to an hallucination or delusion whereby the sea becomes a solid ground. In another footnote to the poem, Wordsworth refers readers to Gilbert's *The Hurricane* (B&G, 144).

24  Wordsworth's decision to indicate Leonard's "afterlife" in the conclusion to the poem – "he went on shipboard, and is now / A Seaman, a grey-headed Mariner" (430–1) is significant in this regard, for it suggests the way in which Wordsworth might have come to regard Coleridge's poem as integral to his project as he redefines it in 1800. Not only is the "glittering eye" of the Mariner indicative of his ability to see things that aren't there, thus corresponding with Wordsworth's famous definition of the Poet as possessing "a disposition to be affected more than other men by absent things as if they were present" (*PrW* 1.138). Just as significantly, the mercantile enterprise represented by the ship is the impetus for his emergence as such a visionary.

25  I cannot wholly forbear an etymological speculation upon the name of the family whose history encapsulates the progress of economic transformation, although I offer it more as an instructive emblem of the poem's paradox than as an authorial intention. Walter *Ewbank* is, like Michael, "buffeted with bond, / Interest and mortgages" (211–12); that is, by the texts of *banks*. Upon his death, the Ewbanks must sell their flock (including, one presumes, *ewes*). Thus we may see in the name the jointure of competing economies, although the jointure is confounded by the fact that large flocks of sheep are associated, in the historical

documentation of the period, with the enclosure and engrossment to which the family economy celebrated in "The Brothers" (even the Ennerdale *pastor*'s family is engaged in domestic economy – spinning) is opposed. What in a different economy served as a source of wealth and property now becomes the means of an expropriation and impoverishment.

26 Eilenberg, relegating Marx's "history" of the coin to an endnote, describes his account as a "fancifully mundane explanation" (261). But Marx's "account" is important because it demonstrates the effect of "accounting" on substance. The more a thing is counted, as it were, the less its "substance" *counts*; this is what happens to "another grave" in the course of the poem.

27 As Mantoux points out, criticism of the replacement by pasture of arable land extends at least as far back as More's *Utopia* (152–3 n.). He also usefully distinguishes sixteenth- and seventeenth-century enclosures from the Acts of Enclosure which proliferated in the eighteenth century: "The former had been opposed by the King's administration, the latter on the contrary met with the assistance and encouragement of Parliament" (165).

28 The direction of the missing footway – along the fields to the brooks – suggests that it was an easement; by its pointed absence, therefore, Wordsworth may suggest how such rights of way are aborted by engrossment. Only the public thoroughfare – the habitation of the stranger and the passerby – remains.

29 Note Simmel's oddly Wordsworthian rendering of this capture of advice (congruent with the narrator's accumulation of "hearsay" in "The Thorn," for example). This suggests how *methodology itself*, while seeming to stand outside the economies in dispute, is in fact related to the transformation (by mobility) from a community of neighbors to a community of *strangers*. In contrast to *Hamlet*, where advice similar to that recorded by Simmel is offered in a conversation between father and son, now one has to learn the facts or "language" of real life (money) in the street.

30 Another alteration might also be considered as significant in light of my argument: whereas Darwin clearly identifies the farmer as an inhabitant of Warwickshire, in central England, Wordsworth in the poem claims that Goody Blake "dwelt in Dorsetshire" [line 29]). The obvious explanation for this shift, that Wordsworth wished to set the scene in his "neighbourhood" – Dorset being proximate to Somersetshire – is belied by the fact that other of the *Lyrical Ballads* are set elsewhere – for example, "Simon Lee," set in the "sweet shire of Cardigan." If they have any purpose, that is, the settings for the poems appear to reinforce our sense of a traveling narrator, a passerby and stranger whose "neighbourly" interest is entirely metaphorical.

31  In her essay, Adela Pinch reads the function of the "lusty splinter" differently, arguing for the important resonance established in the poem between the "Stout limbs" of the "lusty" Harry Gill and the "lusty splinters" gathered into Goody Blake's withered arms. I find her reading a valuable enrichment of my own; what she calls "this confusion of body parts, this exchange of sticks and limbs" (842) may be seen as an effect of the logic of the double-entry, a process which entails the transformation of qualities into quantities (Carruthers and Espelande, 58).

32  Although his waistcoats are made of flannel and duffel and seem therefore to correspond to an economy of "use," Wordsworth's modifications – "flannel *fine*" and "*good* duffel grey" – instead suggest a specifically bourgeois form of social prestation whereby "use" becomes an alibi. See Baudrillard's *For a Critique of the Political Economy of the Sign*.

33  Note how Wordsworth encourages an economic understanding of this literal reading: Harry expends all his heat in *acquisition* ("And *fiercely* by the arm he took her, / ... / And *fiercely* by the arm he held her fast" [89–91]). After fire, ice.

34  Although Zizek frequently mentions Marx's analysis of both economic and political forms, he clearly prefers the Hegelian logic of the "double reflection," whereby "symbolic truth emerges via the 'imitation of imitation'" (*KN* 15) (and the Symbolic from the formal dimension – doubling – of the Imaginary). According to Zizek, Marx interpolates a history, relegating the "topsy-turvy world" (the table-turning) of commodity-fetishism to a position *after* "normal," transparent social relations, and fails to consider the way those relations may be an ideal constructed in opposition to (that is, after) commodity-fetishism. Derrida makes a similar point in *Specters of Marx*.

35  I rely here on Antony Easthope's critique of that critical tradition in *Poetry as Discourse*. See especially chapter 5, "The Feudal Ballad," pp. 79–93).

36  In *The Coming Community*, Georgio Agamben points out the etymological connection between "ease" (therefore "easement") and "neighbourhood": "The term 'ease' in fact designates, according to its eytmology, the space adjacent (*ad-jacens, adjacentia*), the empty place where each can move freely" (24).

37  See the "Introduction: General" to chapter XIX, "The Law of Copyright," in *PrW* III.303–6.

38  Although Wordsworth's "harmonies of criticism" are bookkeeping records of the sublime value of poetry, they leave unclear the question of Coleridge's remuneration for his contributions to the 1800 edition. In 1800, Longman offers Wordsworth £80 for two printings of the expanded, two-volume *Lyrical Ballads* (*EY* 244). A letter to Longman after publication of the edition suggests how the complex financial relations between Wordsworth, Coleridge, and their publishers might have benefitted from a more traditional double-entry account:

I consider the £30 which you advanced to Mr Coleridge as advanced on my account; and of course I consider the £80 due to me for the right of printing those two Editions as paid; I must, however, remind you that Mr Coleridge and I conjointly are in your debt for two Copies of Withering's Botany and two botanical microscopes. (*EL* 265)

The payment of £30 seems disproportionately high in light of the £80 Wordsworth was to receive; but when Wordsworth claims that the £30 is advanced to Coleridge "on my account," that is, as a *loan*, the conclusion must be that Coleridge received no remuneration at all from the 1800 edition. It could be contended that Wordsworth thought only of the second volume of the 1800 edition as entirely his own, since (for example) he refers in a letter to Francis Wrangham (January or February 1801) to "*My* 2nd Vol: of L.B." (*EY* 265). But the letter to Richard Wordsworth makes it clear that the £80 is for the printing of *both* volumes: "The first edition is sold off, and another is called for by the Booksellers, for the right of printing two editions, of 750 each of this vol. of poems, and of printing two editions, one of 1000 and another of 750 of another volume of the same size" (243). Moreover, the Preface was appended to the *first* volume; evidence from Coleridge's letters suggests this was a kind of marketing ploy. Urging friends to buy the second volume of Wordsworth's poems, Coleridge almost invariably recommended the second edition of the first volume as well, for its "invaluable preface." A letter to Thomas Poole is characteristic: The Lyrical Ballads will be published by the time this Letter reaches you – for my sake, & Wordsworth's, & your own, you will purchase not only the new Volume, but likewise the second Edition of the First Volume, on account of its invaluable Preface" (*CL* II.665).

39 In "Bodies, Death, and Pauper Funerals," Thomas Laqueur offers a useful framework for understanding Wordsworth's interest in this case – reported in *The Times* in January 1835 – which Wordsworth's editors, Owen and Smyser, tell us was later reported to be a fraud (*PrW* III 278). Having discussed the increased crowding – "Another grave! and then another!" so to speak – of the (urban) parish churchyard, Laqueur cites the relevant law: "In law, anyone dying in a parish had a right to be buried in its churchyard. Though small fees were customary, a clergyman could not refuse burial because of a failure to pay them. *Indeed, parishioners, through the churchwardens in each parish, had a freehold interest in the ground even if surface rights were tediously disputed in courts*" (115; emphasis mine). He later comments, "A respectable funeral was, it appears, the last of the old communal rights to go" (121). It is as if the right to relief has become identical with the right to non-being that Adam asserts in his negated solicitation: the relief one might ask of the parish is a release from mortality – or the "home" James in "The Brothers" is finally afforded by the Priest of Ennerdale: another grave. Since, according to my argument, Wordsworth will be guided in his

argument for copyright by the logic of social security articulated in the "Postscript," it is not surprising that he represents copyright as a life – or, rather, *afterlife* – insurance.

### 3 WALKING AND TALKING AT THE SAME TIME: THE "TWO HISTORIES" OF *THE PRELUDE*

1 Jacques Derrida, "'Like the Sound of the Sea Deep within a Shell': Paul de Man's War," pp 649–50.
2 I use "station" rather than "position" here for two reasons. First, I wish to invoke the vocabulary of the picturesque that must be considered to haunt any poem as locodescriptive as *The Prelude*; that tradition, which frames a given landscape within a perspective established by taking up a "station" or viewpoint, conforms to the model of "local patrimony." Second, I wish to *socialize* this tradition, in a manner already suggested by Alan Liu's analysis (*Wordsworth*) of the pictorial history of Rydal Falls: most verbal and pictorial descriptions depend on the visual advantage of "The Baron's Window" – a view from the summer house of Sir Michael Le Fleming. My argument, that the "perspective" of *The Prelude* methodologically resists such stationing, suggests that Wordsworth attempts to resist the determinations of fixed social "station" or estate.
3 Echolalia, literally the echoing of mumbling, may serve to describe the revolution in poetic language Wordsworth seeks to produce, in *The Prelude* and elsewhere. If the 1800 Preface suggested the aesthetic project of reproducing the "real language of men" as it is determined by the object world, *The Prelude* extends this project by reproducing the "mutterings" of the discharged soldier.
4 Elaine Scarry suggests how central this conflation is to representation within a capitalist regime in reading the logic of Marx's *inversive* tropology: the immateriality of capital gets represented as "Mr. Moneybags" and the objectified body of the worker (labour-power as so many "hands") is rendered statistically – the number of deformed lace-workers, etc. See *The Body in Pain*, especially pp. 268–73.
5 Locke's objection to this typographical innovation, cited by Roger Chartier as a failed resistance to what Henri-Louis Martin terms "the triumph of white over black" or the segmentation of the text and the "visual articulation of the page" (54), has a particularly political resonance that maps onto Easthope's discussion of the ideology of pentameter (see below). The fragmentation of the "continued Discourse" where the "Argument" resides creates "Words" and "Expressions" which Locke calls "*flexible.*" Loosed from their grounding context, these discursive units are then appropriated by sectarian interests, and work not to ensure the toleration that might be imagined to be set in play by the undecidable, but to reinforce "Orthodoxy" and "Opinion."

6 The next paragraph is also relevant, since it is more appropriate for the development of the *English* state:

> Besides the mortgage which capital imposes on it, the small holding is burdened by *taxes*. Taxes are the source of life for the bureaucracy, the army, the priests and the court, in short, for the whole apparatus of executive power... By its very nature, small-holding property forms a suitable basis for an all-powerful and innumerable bureaucracy. It creates a uniform level of relationships and persons over the whole surface of the land. (*EB* 128)

Increases in taxation and the simultaneous growth of the national debt were justified to the English by nationalistic rhetoric that represented the wars of the late eighteenth and early nineteenth centuries as chiefly defenses of *property*.

7 I first became aware of the fact that "term of art" indicates legal terminology during the recent graduate student strike at the University of California (November–December 1992). The major impasse in the negotiations between graduate students and the administration concerning the form future consultation would take was the phrase "in good faith." For the university administration and its lawyers, the inclusion of this phrase was a "term of art" indicating and legitimating a legal obligation to collective bargaining; they refused to include it.

These negotiations were themselves the aftermath of a court decision in the summer of 1992, upholding a university appeal of a lower-court ruling that graduate students were *employees*, and as such entitled to collective bargaining rights.

The difference in status of a student and an employee is not irrelevant to *The Prelude*, since to be an employee is, presumably, to approximate the condition of the "mean pensioner." (Wordsworth is thus a *proper* student of Cambridge when he shows disdain for the *financial* interest represented by a fellowship and goes instead to continue his "education" in France.) Recently this idea of property in liberal education has again become current: the president of the Association of Students of the University of California suggested that the faculty take a 10 percent pay cut rather than the projected 5 percent since "they're not here for the money; they're here for the privilege of being associated with the University of California" (*San Francisco Chronicle*, 20 February 1992). In both cases, the suggestion is that the *proper* form of identity (as student, as faculty) is an internalized, autonomous one that does not rely on a relation to the "outward form" of the institution.

8 Frances Ferguson has also drawn attention to this passage; it is followed by the definition of language as a (deconstructive, in Ferguson's account) "counter-spirit" (*Counter-Spirit*, xvi).

9 Kenneth Johnston identifies the 1798 two-book *Prelude* as a conversation poem, following an argument made earlier by Bishop C. Hunt that an allusion to "Frost at Midnight" is Wordsworth's subtle acknowledgment of Coleridge's formal example (60, 358).

10 See apparatus criticus to the Norton *Prelude* (ed. Wordsworth *et al.*) and the *Fourteen-Book Prelude* (ed. Owen).

11 Many critics have noticed the way in which the walk narrated in the glad preamble appears to anticipate (or retrospectively fulfill) the effects Wordsworth foresaw for that legacy: enabling him " to pause for choice, and walk / At large and unrestrained" (XIII.358–9).

12 Iconicity in poetry is, according to Easthope, the effect of trying "to *contain* the fact of enunciation by holding it in close relation to meaning, attempting – impossibly – to make the signifier a part of the signified" (103). Iconicity is the effect of the failure to produce this absolute coincidence of form and content.

13 The phrase is of course Hartman's, serving as the titular thesis of *Wordsworth's Poetry 1787–1814*. I regard Hartman's brilliant reduction of Wordsworth's poetics to *Siste, viator* as an important "first step" in the kind of critique I attempt here; however, like the critical tendency to read the fifth *promenade* of Rousseau's *Rêveries* as its crux, Hartman's particular interest in "the suspension itself of habitual motion, or an ensuing meditative consciousness" (12) – that is, the moment of "arrest" – has produced a pattern of reading Wordsworth that is itself methodologically *meditative*, preferring the paradigmatic axis (how what is said/written is shaped and disfigured by what is *not* said/ written) even in its historicist and materialist mode.

It is true that reading Wordsworth – reading in general of a "literary" text – encourages or even requires meditation (Wordsworth's neighbors attested to how deviant a practice was Wordsworth's murmuring while in motion). On the other hand, there *is* a temporal and historical dimension to reading – as the mere facts of its general confinement to the sphere of privacy, individuality, and subjectivity, a sphere we now consider to be largely an historical *invention* – would suggest. My own attention to the "physiological" Wordsworth is an attempt to resist the meditative one by focusing on the dimension of experience that is undeniably historical, the syntagmatic.

Hartman's Wordsworthian "Retrospect," offered as a kind of "afterword" to (but placed before) the preface to his book in the 1971 edition, summarizes the irony implicit in the fact that the *halted* traveler should be the hypothetical figure of Wordsworthian imagin-ation: "since the mind is (or is to be) 'lord and master,' should he not write without waiting to be moved by accidents of sense, by peculiar encounters which heighten his consciousness – in other words, should he not turn from occasional and nature poetry to epic?" (xiv). Hartman recognizes that the *Prelude* is riddled with – indeed, is structured by – occasional encounters, but by his own admission, his attention to the *indecisive* in the poetry is limited by his *greater* interest in "the integrity of the mind" (xvii).

14 For a discussion of the conceptualization of (democratic) friendship as

fraternity, the friend as *male*, see Derrida, "The Politics of Friendship." Wordsworth appears to complicate this conceptualization by naming *Dorothy*, both woman and sister, as "Friend" in "Tintern Abbey."

15  Michael Lucey pointed out the Szevo passage to me, and Leslie Kurke explained the relevance of Zeno.

16  Articulating the relation of my argument to Ferguson's is made somewhat difficult by the fact that Ferguson's Wordsworth seems to produce *both* the positions (empiricism and crypto-empiricism) she suggests are mediated by the structure of the poem. In her analysis of "We Are Seven," for example, Ferguson first produces a de Manian argument about the supplementary effect of linguistic materialism on expression, emphasizing the poem's graceless paronomastic jokes on name and number ("the ludicrousness of the accidents of rhyme...and meter" [*Solitude*, 167]), and then counters that reading by supplying an important historical context: arguments against taking an English census. Wordsworth's interrogative mode, in other words, seems to foreshadow the philosophical opposition the poem works to resolve. But the fact that there is such a neat fit between Ferguson's aim and Wordsworth's poetic – in other words, that her subtle readings are so *graceful* – suggests that Ferguson offers less a critical account of Wordsworth than a full articulation of the dual logics he employs.

17  Marx describes Louis Napoleon's *coup* as the act "of a thief in the night" and differentiates him from Cromwell and Napoleon, both of whom faced the Parliaments they were about to dissolve. Louis Napoleon, however, "announces" the *coup* the following day, with "cheap-Jack placards posted early in the morning on all the walls" (*EB* 116).

18  As a vagabond, Louis Napoleon is the historical descendant of Napoleon as *military* persona: discharged from the imperial enterprise, he is a *discharged soldier*.

19  See the entry for "Active citizen" in Scott and Rothaus (eds.), *Historical Dictionary of the French Revolution, 1789–99*, p. 4.

20  In *Marx and the French Revolution* (pp. 17–18), François Furet describes the "two paths" by which liberalism reconstructs the public sphere, both of which are applicable here. The first model, the *petitio principii*, bases the public sphere on the presumption that a harmony of interests will emerge from the conflict of individual interests; this model corresponds to the "charitable gesture" by which the bourgeoisie represents the interests of the disenfranchised. The second corresponds to Constant's classic exposition of the "default" of the public sphere in the regime of liberalism, its reduction to the point of elimination of the power of the state; this model corresponds to what I have called the "negative litany."

21  See Harrison ["Spec(tac)ular Reversals"] for a fuller discussion of "Resolution and Independence" in the context of Poor Law debate.

22  For Wordsworth's relation to and knowledge of Rousseau's corpus, see,

among others, Sabin, *English Romanticism and the French Tradition*, and Chandler, *Wordsworth's Second Nature*. Chandler, arguing that Burke exerts a primary influence upon the argument of *The Prelude*, tends to regard Wordsworth's allusions to Rousseau in the text as largely negative. Evidence of Wordsworth's specific knowledge of Rousseau's "Essay on the Origin of Languages" is more uncertain, although Bewell takes it almost for granted: "In addition to those works that Wordsworth would have known, given his fluency in French and interest in the philosophes – for instance, *Emile*, the *Second Discourse*, the *Social Contract*, the *Confessions*, and the *Nouvelle Héloïse* – it is also likely that he was familiar with the 'Essay on the Origin of Languages,' published in 1781" (p. 82n.). One must acknowledge, however, that the likelihood is somewhat diminished by the fact that the essay was first published in a volume of *Treatises on Music*.

Bewell's book offers important evidence, however, that the aspect of the "essay" I focus on here, the encounter of two strangers, is common to numerous Enlightenment speculations on the origin of languages. One distinctive feature of what I argue is the Wordsworthian version of this "primitive encounter," the meeting with the discharged soldier, does suggest the peculiar relevance of Rousseau's version. Both Mandeville and Condillac imagine an encounter between the two sexes, rather than (as in Rousseau) between a savage and "others" who appear bigger – almost fantastic. For relevant readings of Rousseau, see especially Derrida (*Grammatology*) and de Man.

23 See *The Fourteen-Book Prelude* (ed. Owen), p. 578, for a photographic reprint of the manuscript page in question. Owen follows MS D, but the Norton *Prelude* (ed. Wordsworth), points out that the same lines (and the same query) appeared in MS E, which was the manuscript foundation for the 1850 (first) edition (p. 151).

24 The backward glance of the 1805 edition is subtly rendered – "bidding then / A farewell to the city left behind" (1.97–8) – but the 1850 edition makes the intended echo palpable: "casting then / A backward glance upon the curling cloud / Of city smoke, by distance ruralized" (1.87–9).

25 Here I disagree with Moorman, who claims that the letter refers to two poems; both "The Beggars" and "The Emigrant Mother." Moorman regards the Hutchinsons' objection to the tediousness of the old man's tale as a formal complaint; I regard the emphasis on moral sympathies in the letter, and the distancing of those sympathies from a strictly aesthetic judgment (i.e., whether Sara likes the *poem*) as evidence that Wordsworth here highlights the social content of the poem.

26 In May of 1993, a sudden coalescing of attention to the amount of violence perpetrated by (sometimes discharged) postal workers against other postal workers or supervisors led the Postmaster General to speculate that the intensification of criminal violence might be due in

part to the legislated policy of preferential hiring of veterans, many of whom have mental as well as physical disabilities. His depiction of mentally unstable veterans (implicitly male) trained in violence overlooked the effect of automatism both on mental stability and violence, although many sociologists attributed the increased violence to a dehumanization effected by the "machine-driven" tempo of work rhythms and supervisors' attachment to "rigid" routines. The Postal Service's model of efficiency would be of interest to Wordsworth, as allied both with the systems of education attacked in book v and with the legislation of rates of human movement discussed below.

27 I use the future anterior here both to reinforce the logic of my argument concerning the two temporalities of *The Prelude* (inspired by Marx's *Eighteenth Brumaire*) and to suggest the logical (and political) impetus for Wordsworth's methodological addendum to book iv.

28 Hartman's description of the soldier's "etiolated" condition, which seems a fair characterization of a figure who "Was never seen abroad by night or day," reinforces my contention that the discharged soldier represents at once privation and privacy. At least since Plato, the soldier has frequently figured in the Western political imagination as the epitome of the public man; according to Paul Virilio, the French Revolution brings about the literalization of this figure; beginning by making every man a citizen, it ends by making every citizen a soldier. We may speculate, then, that the condition of the discharged soldier serves as an epitome for the transformation of the "subject" (i.e., Balibar's "citizen subject") that occurs with a shift of his sphere from public to private; in other words, the discharged soldier represents the condition of "defaulted citizenship" I analyze in the next chapter (as Bewell notes, the manuscript of "The Discharged Soldier" belongs to the same period of composition as "The Ruined Cottage").

29 In *The Eighteenth Brumaire* Marx suggestively outlines a way we may consider such vagrancy statutes as the "general rules" of liberalism, the structural equivalent of the "general phrase" of absolute liberty and the marginal note of its abrogation. Laws are "principles" that the bourgeoisie "had itself always interpreted merely as general rules, which one prescribes for others *in order to be able to move all the more freely oneself*" (89).

30 *The San Francisco Chronicle*, Thursday, 13 May 1993, p. B1 col. 1.

31 Mary Moorman identifies the letter-carrier as Fletcher, the local carrier – a likely identification, since elsewhere letters are frequently brought to them by Fletcher. This identification, however, makes it somewhat difficult to explain Dorothy Wordsworth's reference to his travels as beginning and ending a workday – implicitly suggesting that his primary occupation is *not* that of a carrier.

32 Mutinies by sailors were increasingly common in the 1790s as a

consequence of several contributing factors: impressment, the increase in number of Irish seamen, and (suspected) agitation on the part of members of the London Corresponding Society. Royle and Walvin report two strikes in 1797, for example, and note the political tenor of those strikes: "The essence of their case was clearly 'industrial,' but the style of their behaviour and the language they adopted were redolent of the corresponding societies and popular democracy" (82). Evidence of the political bent of the sailors' actions were "the radical device of petitioning" and the use of the term "delegate" (representative).

33 Rousseau's discussion of assembly in *The Social Contract* contributes to our attempt to recover the political aspect of the episode of the discharged soldier from its poetic and critical transformation into an epistemological encounter. The poet, to whom Wordsworth in the 1800 Preface assigns a representative function, encounters in book IV the "chimera" he appears to represent (Rousseau: "The people in assembly, I shall be told, is a mere chimera" [*SC* 261]). As a consequence, the *representative function*, the identity of the poet, becomes the mere chimera: it is the poet, rather than the discharged soldier, who takes on a "ghostly" (political) presence.

34 Translations from the original French are mine.

35 The extent to which the discharged soldier's various aspects of behavior conform to Merleau-Ponty's case study in apraxia is startling. On the "stately" tempo of his speech, for example: "Schneider's general intelligence is intact: his replies are slow, never meaningless, but those of a mature, thinking man who takes an interest in the doctor's experiment" (134). On the "strange half-absence" which characterizes his autobiographical recital, for another:

if a story is told to the patient, it is observed that instead of grasping it as a melodic whole with down and up beats, with its characteristic rhythm or flow, he remembers it only as a succession of facts to be noted one by one...When he tells back the story, he never does so *according to* the account given to him: he finds nothing to emphasize. (132–3)

No wonder he did not stop at the laborer's cottage; it was not in his constricted field of perception: "He never goes out for a walk, but always on an errand, and he never recognizes Professor Goldstein's house as he passes it 'because he did not go out with the intention of going there'" (134–5). As for the formulaic quality of "a soldier's tale": "a conversation with another person does not constitute for him a situation significant in itself, and requiring extempore replies. He can speak only in accordance with a plan drawn up in advance" (135).

36 Robespierre insisted that bread shortages were due entirely to conspiracies of distribution. His belief that mendicancy might be eliminated by legislation was mirrored by findings of the various *Comités de mendicité* formed in the early years of the Republic; like the measure enacted by

Napoleon on 5 July 1808, however (see below), the proposed legislation usually entailed the confinement of beggars, rather than any alteration in the structures that produced such vagabondage.

37 *The Montclarion*, Tuesday, 18 May 1993, p.2, col. 2.

38 "Adventures on Salisbury Plain" is the revised (1795–*c.* 1799) manuscript version of a poem Wordsworth composed in 1793–4 ("Salisbury Plain," or "A Night on Salisbury Plain"), which was further revised and finally published in 1841 as "Guilt and Sorrow." See *The Salisbury Plain Poems* (ed. Gill). All references are to this edition.

39 Since a pun is a play upon the *sound* of a word to alter or ironize its sense, the fact that the sailor's pun is *thought* rather than spoken contributes to its irony. In fact, it is a punning homonym, whose ironization depends entirely upon *tonality* – another aspect of sound that the written text is impotent (intrinsically) to convey.

### 4 THE WALKING CURE

1 As Pocock points out, the "triumph" of this model of liberalism, where the "virtue" of the state is determined in relation to non-interference with "trade," is largely an illusion; the tradition of civic humanism, in which land functions to free its owner from dependence, survives as an "agrarian ideal" (109). However, Pocock's own account of the "Financial Revolution" suggests that the emergence of a specifically capitalist formation made this agrarian model of civic virtue *entirely* ideal.

2 The name given to the French Revolution and its ideological surround by Ernesto Laclau and Chantal Mouffe, following the revisionist accounts developed by Claude Lefort, François Furet, *et al.*

3 The Solitary himself bears traces of this division; his reclusive position parodies that suggested by Coleridge for the eponymous recluse – "the station of a man in mental repose, one whose principles were made up, and so prepared to deliver upon authority a system of philosophy" – and yet his former occupation as traveling minister is undertaken, like the Wanderer's own peddling, "for lack of better hopes" of social advancement (see *PW* v. 47n.).

4 Although Cowper begins his therapeutic epic "I sing the SOFA," in deference to the instruction of his patroness, a "subject supposed to know" the cause of his despondency, singing the sofa leads him by a kind of free association to find his own "walking" cure. To "go for a walk" appears to liberate the subject from a passive position, but the walks undertaken by Rousseau, Cowper, and Wordsworth's poet-figures in fact prove, in the excess of associative contagion organizing their movements, the continuity of apraxia ("a disorder of voluntary movement, consisting in a more or less complete incapacity to execute purposeful movements, notwithstanding the preservation of muscular

power, sensibility, and coordination in general" – M. Merleau-Ponty, *The Phenomenology of Perception*). Liberation cannot guarantee sovereignty (the "cure" for subjection that is citizenship), as an anecdote told by Helen Maria Williams, an early influence on Wordsworth, illustrates:

> When the Bastille was taken, and the old man, of whom you have, no doubt, heard, and who had been confined in a dungeon thirty-five years, was brought into daylight, which had not for so long a space of time visited his eyes, he staggered, shook his white beard, and cried faintly, "Messieurs, vous m'avez rendu un grand service, rendez-m'en autre; tuez-moi! je ne sais pas où aller." (29–30)

5 Review of *The Excursion* appearing in *The Eclectic Magazine* (1816), quoted from Reiman, *The Romantics Reviewed* 31/361.
6 I am indebted to James Chandler for this formulation of my argument.
7 See Paul Virilio, *Speed and Politics*, for a discussion of this geographical shift as part of the legacy of the French Revolution.
8 In "Modern Pastoral Lyricism." I am grateful to its author for allowing me access to his manuscript version.
9 *Table Talk*, 13 July, 1832. Quoted from *PW* v. 364.
10 Duncan Bythell, in an essay on "The Handloom Weavers in the English Cotton Industry during the Industrial Revolution" explains the decline of the handloom weaver as similarly overdetermined, attributable both to "the long war with France (which by raising the rate of interest discouraged investment in plant), and partly to the reluctance of the weavers, many of them women, to leave their homes" (304).
11 See *The Romantic Fragment Poem*'s epilogue on "The Ruined Cottage."
12 I was alerted to the wonderful relevance of the *fort–da* game to "The Ruined Cottage" by an article on the subject by Karen Swann. Swann immediately metaphorizes the child's plaything, seeing the figure of the bobbin in Margaret's body, girt with flax, and thus fails to notice the presence in the poem of an exact replica of Freud's grandson, who may well have been given a bobbin by a pedlar who traffics in staytapes and laces.

# Works cited

Abrams, M. H. "Structure and Style in the Greater Romantic Lyric," in *Romanticism and Consciousness*. New York: Norton, 1970.

Adorno, Theodor. *Negative Dialectics*, trans. E. B. Ashton. New York: Continuum, 1990.

Agamben, Giorgio. *The Coming Community*. Minneapolis: University of Minnesota Press, 1994.

Althusser, Louis. "The Social Contract (*The Discrepancies*)," in *Jean-Jacques Rousseau* ed. Harold Bloom. New York: Chelsea, 1988.

"On the Young Marx," in *For Marx*. Ben Brewster, trans. London: Verso, 1969.

Arendt, Hannah. *On Revolution*. New York: Pelican, 1977.

Baczko, Bronislaw. "Rousseau and Social Marginality," *Daedalus* 107 (Summer 1978), 27–40.

Balibar, Etienne. "Citizen Subject," in *Who Comes After the Subject?* ed. Jean-Luc Nancy. New York: Routledge, 1991.

Barrell, John. *English Literature in History, 1730–1780: An Equal, Wide Survey*. London: Hutchinson, 1983.

Baudrillard, Jean. *For a Critique of the Political Economy of the Sign*, trans. Charles Levin. St. Louis: Telos Press, 1981.

*Simulations*, trans. Paul Foss, Paul Patton, and Philip Beitchman. New York: Semiotext(e), 1983.

Benjamin, Walter. "Paris in the Nineteenth Century," in *Charles Baudelaire: A Lyric Poet in the Era of High Capitalism*, trans. Harry Zohn. London: NLB, 1973.

Bennett, Andrew J. "Devious Feet: Wordsworth and the Scandal of Narrative Form," *ELH* 92 (1992), 142–173.

Bewell, Alan. *Wordsworth and the Enlightenment: Nature, Man and Society in the Experimental Poetry*. New Haven: Yale University Press, 1989.

Blackstone, Sir William. *Commentaries on the Laws of England*. Oxford: Clarendon, 1765–9.

Blanchot, Maurice. "Everyday Speech." *Yale French Studies* 73, 12–20.

*The Step Not Beyond*, trans. Lycette Nelson. Albany: SUNY Press, 1992.

Bourdieu, Pierre. *Distinction: A Social Critique of the Judgment of Taste*, trans. Richard Nice. Cambridge, MA: Harvard University Press, 1984.

Braudel, Fernand. *Capitalism and Material Life: 1400–1800*. Glasgow: Fontana, 1974.

Brewer, John. *The Sinews of Power: War Money and the English State, 1688–1783*. Cambridge, MA: Harvard University Press, 1990.

Burke, Edmund. *Reflections on the Revolution in France*. Garden City, NY: Anchor Books, 1973.

Burrow, J. W. *Whigs and Liberals: Continuity and Change in Eighteenth-Century Political Thought*. Oxford: Clarendon Press, 1988.

Butler, James (ed.), *The Ruined Cottage and the Pedlar*. Ithaca: Cornell University Press, 1979.

Bythell, Duncan. "The Hand-Loom Weavers in the English Cotton Industry during the Industrial Revolution: Some Problems," *Economic History Review*, Second Series, 17 (1964), 339–53.

Campbell, Colin. *The Romantic Ethic and the Spirit of Modern Consumerism*. New York: Basil Blackwell, 1987.

Carlyle, Thomas. *The French Revolution: A History*. New York: A. L. Burt, undated.

Carruthers, Bruce G. and Wendy Nelson Espelande. "Accounting for Rationality: Double-Entry Bookkeeping and the Rhetoric of Economic Rationality," *American Journal of Sociology* 97:1 (July 1991), 31–69.

Cartwright, Lisa. "'Experiments of Destruction': Cinematic Inscriptions of Physiology," *Representations* 40 (Fall 1992), 129–52.

Certeau, Michel de. *The Practice of Everyday Life*, trans. Steven Rendall. Berkeley: University of California Press, 1984.

Chandler, James K. *Wordsworth's Second Nature: A Study of the Poetry and Politics*. University of Chicago Press, 1984.

Chartier, Roger. "Laborers and Voyagers: From the Text to the Reader," *Diacritics* 22:2 (Summer 1992), 49–61.

Christensen, Jerome. *Lord Byron's Strength*. Baltimore: Johns Hopkins University Press, 1993.

Cobbett, William. *Rural Rides*, ed. George Woodcock. Middlesex: Penguin Classics, 1987.

Coleridge, Samuel Taylor. *Biographia Literaria*, ed. George Watson. New York: Dutton, 1975.

*Collected Letters*, ed. Earl Leslie Griggs. Oxford: Clarendon, 1956–71.

Constant, Benjamin. *Political Writings*, ed. Biancamaria Fontana. New York: Cambridge University Press, 1988.

Deleuze, Gilles and Félix Guattari. *Anti-Oedipus: Capitalism and Schizophrenia*, trans. Robert Hurley. Minneapolis: University of Minnesota Press, 1983.

De Quincey, Thomas. *Collected Works*, ed. David Masson. 16 vols. Boston: 1890.

*Recollections of the Lakes and the Lake Poets*, ed. David Wright. New York: Penguin, 1970.

Derrida, Jacques. "'Like the Sound of the Sea Deep Within a Shell': Paul de Man's War," trans. Peggy Kamuf. *Critical Inquiry* 14 (Spring 1988), 590–652.

"The Politics of Friendship," *The Journal of Philosophy* (1988), 632–45.

*Of Grammatology*, trans. Gayatri Spivak. Baltimore: Johns Hopkins University Press, 1976.

*The Truth in Painting*, trans. Geoff Bennington and Ian McLeod. University of Chicago Press, 1987.

*Specters of Marx*, trans. Peggy Kamuf. New York: Routledge, 1994.

Descartes, René. *Discourse on Method*, trans. Donald A. Cress. Indianapolis: Hackett, 1980.

Deutsche, Rosalyn. "Uneven Development: Public Art in New York City," *October* 47 (Winter 1988), 3–52.

Dyer, George. *History of the University and Colleges of Cambridge*. London: Longman, 1814.

Eagleton, Terry. *The Ideology of the Aesthetic*. Oxford: Basil Blackwell, 1990.

Easthope, Antony. *Poetry as Discourse*. New York: Methuen, 1983.

Eilenberg, Susan. *Strange Power of Speech: Wordsworth, Coleridge, and Literary Possession*. New York: Oxford University Press, 1992.

Favret, Mary. *Romantic Correspondence: Women, Politics and the Fiction of Letters*. Cambridge University Press, 1993.

Ferguson, Frances. *Solitude and the Sublime: Romanticism and the Aesthetics of Individuation*. New York: Routledge, 1992.

*Wordsworth: Language as Counter-Spirit*. New Haven: Yale University Press, 1977.

Ferry, David. *The Limits of Mortality: An Essay on Wordsworth's Major Poems*. Middleton, CT: Wesleyan University Press, 1977.

Freud, Sigmund. *Beyond the Pleasure Principle*, trans James Strachey. New York: W. W. Norton, 1961.

"Mourning and Melancholia," in *The Complete Psychological Works of Sigmund Freud*. Vol. 14 (1914–16). London: Hogarth Press, 1957.

*Therapy and Technique*, ed. Philip Rieff. New York: Collier, 1963.

Friedman, Michael H. *The Making of a Tory Humanist: William Wordsworth and the Idea of Community*. New York: Columbia University Press, 1979.

Furet, François. *Marx and the French Revolution*, trans. Deborah Kan Furet. University of Chicago Press, 1988.

Gilbert, Roger. *Walks in the World*. Ithaca: Cornell University Press, 1991.

Godwin, William. *Enquiry Concerning Political Justice and its Influence of Modern Morals and Happiness*, ed. Isaac Kramnick. New York: Penguin, 1976.

Goldsmith, Steven. *Unbuilding Jerusalem: Apocalypse and Romantic Representation*. Ithaca: Cornell University Press, 1993.

Griggs, Earl Leslie (ed.), *Collected Letters of Samuel Taylor Coleridge*. Oxford: Clarendon, 1956–71.

Halpern, Richard. *The Poetics of Primitive Accumulation*. Ithaca: Cornell University Press, 1991.

Hamilton, Paul. *Coleridge's Poetics*. Oxford: Basil Blackwell, 1983.

*Wordsworth*. Atlantic Highlands, NJ: Humanities Press, 1986.

Hammond, J. L. and Barbara Hammond. *The Village Labourer*. London: Longman, 1978.

Harris, Bryan. *An Outline of the Law Relating to Common Land and Public Access to the Countryside*. London: Sweet and Maxwell, 1967.

Harrison, Gary. "Spec(tac)ular Reversals: The Politics of the Sublime and Wordsworth's Transfiguration of the Rustic Poor," *Criticism* 34 (Fall 1992), 563–90.

Hartman, Geoffrey. *Wordsworth's Poetry, 1797–1814*. New Haven: Yale University Press, 1964.

Hazlitt, William. *Complete Works*, ed. P. P. Howe, after A. R. Waller and Arnold Glover. London: Dent, 1930.

Heidegger, Martin. "The Origins of the Work of Art." *Poetry, Language, Thought*. New York: Harper and Row, 1971.

Heron, Robert. *General View of the Natural Circumstance of Those Isles ... of Hebudaie or Hebrides: of the various means which have been employed to cultivate and improve them: and of some other means, which are humbly proposed, as likely to contribute to their farther improvement*. Edinburgh: John Paterson, 1794.

*Observations Made in a Journey through the Western Counties of Scotland, in the Autumn of M,DCC,XCII*. Perth: R. Morrison, Jr., 1793.

Hill, Alan G., ed. *The Letters of William Wordsworth*. New York: Oxford University Press, 1984.

Hill, Howard. *Freedom to Roam*. Ashbourne: Noorland, 1980.

Holdsworth, W. S. *A History of English Law*. London: Methuen, 1930.

Holmes, Oliver Wendell. "The Physiology of Walking," in *Pages from an Old Volume of Life: A Collection of Essays 1857–1881*. Boston: Houghton Mifflin, 1889.

"The Physiology of Verse," in *Pages from an Old Volume of Life: A Collection of Essays 1857–1881*. Boston: Houghton Mifflin, 1889.

Hufton, Olwen. *The Poor of Eighteenth-Century France, 1770–1789*. New York: Oxford University Press, 1974.

Hunt, Lynn. *Politics, Culture and Class in the French Revolution*. Berkeley: University of California Press, 1984.

Hutchinson, Thomas (ed.), *Wordsworth: Poetical Works*, rev. by Ernest de Selincourt. Oxford: 1936.

Jameson, Fredric. *Late Marxism: Adorno, or the Persistence of the Dialectic*. New York: Verso, 1990.

*Postmodernism, or The Cultural Logic of Late Capitalism*. Durham: Duke University Press, 1991.

Jarvis, Robin. "Wordsworth and the Use of Charity," in *Beyond Romanticism: New Approaches to Texts and Context 1780–1832*, ed. Stephen Copley and John Whale. London: Routledge, 1992.

Jeffrey, Francis. Review of *The Excursion* in *Edinburgh Review*, November 1814, p. 30; reprinted in *Romantics Reviewed*, ed. Donald H. Reiman. New York: Garland, 1972. Part *A* (2 vols.) p. 453.

Johnston, Kenneth. *Wordsworth and The Recluse.* New Haven: Yale University Press, 1984.
Kant, Immanuel. *The Conflict of the Faculties,* trans. Mary J. Gregor. Lincoln: University of Nebraska Press, 1979.
*Critique of Judgment,* trans. J. H. Bernard. New York: Hafner Press, 1951.
Lacan, Jacques. "The Agency of the Letter in the Structure of the Unconscious or Reason since Freud," in *Ecrits,* trans. Alan Sheridan. New York: Norton, 1977.
Laclau, Ernesto and Chantal Mouffe. *Hegemony and Socialist Strategy.* London: Verso, 1985.
Lacoue-Labarthe, Philippe and Jean-Luc Nancy. *The Literary Absolute: The Theory of Literature in German Romanticism,* trans. Philip Barnard and Cheryl Lester. Albany: SUNY Press, 1988.
Laqueur, Thomas. "Bodies, Death, and Pauper Funerals," *Representations* 1 (1983), 109–31.
Lefort, Claude. *Democracy and Political Theory,* trans. David Macey. Minneapolis: University of Minnestoa Press, 1988.
Levinson, Marjorie. *The Romantic Fragment Poem: A Critique of a Form.* Chapel Hill: University of North Carolina Press, 1986.
*Wordsworth's Great Period Poems.* New York: Cambridge University Press, 1986.
Littleton, A. C. *Accounting Evolution to 1900.* New York: Russell and Russell, 1966.
Liu, Alan. "Local Transcendence: Cultural Criticism, Postmodernism, and the Romanticism of Detail," *Representations* 32 (Fall 1990), 75–113.
"Wordsworth and Subversion 1739–1804: Trying Cultural Criticism," *Yale Journal of Criticism* 2 (Spring 1989), 55–100.
*Wordsworth: the Sense of History.* Stanford University Press, 1989.
Lloyd, David. "Race under Representation," *Oxford Literary Review* 13 (1992), 62–94.
Lowe, John C. and S. Moryadas. *The Geography of Movement.* Boston: Houghton Mifflin, 1975.
Lukacs, Georg. *The Ontology of Social Being,* vol. III: *Labor.* trans. David Fernbach. London: Merlin Press, 1980.
Macfarlane, Alan. *The Origins of English Individualism.* Oxford: Basil Blackwell, 1978.
Man, Paul de. *Allegories of Reading.* New Haven: Yale University Press, 1979.
Mandel, Ernest. *Late Capitalism.* London: Verso, 1975.
Mantoux, Paul. *The Industrial Revolution in the Eighteenth Century: An Outline of the Beginnings of the Modern Factory System in England,* trans. Marjorie Vernon. University of Chicago Press, 1983.
Marx, Karl. *Capital,* vol 1: *A Critical Analysis of Capitalist Production,* ed. Frederick Engels. New York: International, 1984.
*Das Capital.* Hamburg: Otto Meissner, 1890.
*The Eighteenth Brumaire of Louis Bonaparte.* New York: International, 1987.

Marx, Karl and Frederick Engels. *The German Ideology*, ed. C. J. Arthur. New York: International, 1986.

Mayhew, Henry. *London Labour and the London Poor*, sel. by Victor Neuberg. New York: Viking Penguin, 1985.

McKendrick, Neil, J. Brewer, and J. H. Plumb (eds.). *The Birth of a Consumer Society: the Commercialization of Eighteenth-Century England*. Bloomington: Indiana University Press, 1982.

Merleau-Ponty, Maurice. *The Phenomenology of Perception*, trans. Colin Smith. London: Routledge and Kegan Paul, 1962.

Moorman, Mary. *William Wordsworth: A Biography. The Early Years*. Oxford: Clarendon Press, 1957.

Nancy, Jean-Luc. *The Inoperative Community*, trans. Peter Connor. Minneapolis: University of Minnesota Press, 1991.

(ed.), *Who Comes After the Subject?* New York: Routledge, 1991.

Paine, Thomas. *The Rights of Man*. Garden City, NY: Anchor Books, 1973. *The Age of Reason*. New York: Pantheon, 1984.

Pinch, Adela. "Female Chatter: Meter, Masochism and the *Lyrical Ballads*," *ELH* 55:4 (Winter 1988), 835–52.

Plato. *The Collected Dialogues of Plato*, trans. Bejamin Jowett. New York: Random House, 1937.

Plumb, J. H. "Commercialization and Society," in *The Birth of a Consumer Society: The Commercialization of Eighteenth-Century England*, ed. Neil McKendrick, John Brewer and J. H. Plumb. Bloomington: Indiana University Press, 1982.

Pocock, J. G. A. *Virtue, Commerce, and History: Essays on Political Thought and History, Chiefly in the Eighteenth Century*. New York: Cambridge University Press, 1985.

Porter, Roy. *English Society in the Eighteenth Century*. London: Pelican, 1984.

Ragon, Michael. *The Space of Death: A Study of Funerary Architecture, Decoration and Urbanism*, trans. Alan Sheridan. Charlottesville: University Press of Virginia, 1983.

Rancière, Jacques. *Le Philosophe et les pauvres*. Paris: Fayard, 1983.

Rapaczynski, Andrzej. *Nature and Politics: Liberalism in the Philosophies of Hobbes, Locke, and Rousseau*. Ithaca: Cornell University Press, 1987.

Rieff, Philip (ed.). *Freud: Therapy and Technique*. New York: Collier, 1963.

Reiman, Donald H. (ed.), *The Romantics Reviewed*. New York: Garland, 1972.

Robinson, Jeffrey: *The Walk: Notes on a Romantic Image*. Norman: University of Oklahoma Press, 1989.

Rose, Mark. "The Author as Proprietor: *Donaldson* v. *Becket* and the Genealogy of Modern Authorship," *Representations* 23 (Summer 1988), 51–85.

Rousseau, Jean-Jacques. *Emile*, trans. Barbara Foxley. London: Everyman's Library, 1974. *The First and Second Discourses together with the Replies to Critics and Essay on the Origin of Languages*, ed. and trans. Victor Gourevitch. New York: Harper, 1990.

*Œuvres complètes*, ed. Bernard Gagnembin and Marcel Raymond. Bruges: Bibliothèque de la Pléiade, 1959.

*Rousseau, Judge of Jean-Jâcques: Dialogues. Collected Writings of Rousseau*, vol. 1, ed. and trans. Roger D. Masters and Christopher Kelly. Hanover: University Press of New England, 1990.

*Reveries of the Solitary Walker*, trans. Peter France. New York: Penguin, 1979.

*The Social Contract and Discourses*, trans. and ed. G. D. H. Cole. London: Everyman's Library, 1986.

Royle, Edward and James Walvin. *English Radicals and Reformers, 1760–1848*. Brighton: Harvester Press, 1982.

Ryan, Michael. "Deconstruction and Social Theory: The Case of Liberalism," in *Displacement: Derrida and After*, ed. Mark Krupnick. Bloomington: Indiana University Press, 1983.

Sabin, Margery. *English Romanticism and the French Tradition*. Cambridge, MA: Harvard University Press, 1976.

Scarry, Elaine. *The Body in Pain: The Making and Unmaking of the World*. New York: Oxford University Press, 1985.

(ed.), *Literature and the Body*. Baltimore: Johns Hopkins University Press, 1988.

Schwartz, Robert M. *Policing the Poor in Eighteenth-Century France*. Chapel Hill: University of North Carolina Press, 1988.

Scott, Samuel F. and Barry Rothaus, (eds.), *Historical Dictionary of the French Revolution, 1789–1799*. Westport, CT: Greenwood Press, 1985.

Selincourt, Ernest de, (ed.), *The Letters of William and Dorothy Wordsworth: The Early Years*, vol. 1. Oxford, Clarendon, 1933.

Selwyn, William. *Reports of Cases Argued and Determined in the Court of King's Bench*. 5 vols. London: Butterworth, 1818–22.

Sewell, William H. *Work and Revolution in France: The Language of Labor from the Old Regime to 1848*. Cambridge University Press, 1980.

Simmel, Georg. *The Philosophy of Money*, trans. Tom Bottomore and David Frisby. Boston: Routledge, 1978.

Simpson, David. *Wordsworth and the Figurings of the Real*. Atlantic Highlands, NJ, 1982.

*Wordsworth's Historical Imagination: The Poetry of Displacement*. New York: Methuen, 1987.

Starobinski, Jean. *Rousseau: la transparence et l'obstacle*. Paris: Gallimard, 1971.

Svevo, Italo. *Confessions of Zeno*, trans. Beryl de Zoete. New York: Vintage, 1989.

Swann, Karen. "Suffering and Sensation in *The Ruined Cottage*," *PMLA* 106 (1991), 83–95.

Thompson, E. P. *The Making of the English Working Class*. New York: Penguin, 1982.

Timpanaro, Sebastiano. *On Materialism*, trans. Lawrence Garner. London: Verso, 1980.

*The Freudian Slip*, trans. Kate Soper. London: NLB, 1976.

Tribe, Keith. *Land, Labour and Economic Discourse*. London: Routledge and Kegan Paul, 1978.

Turner, James. *The Politics of Landscape: Rural Scenery and Society in English Poetry 1630–1660*. Oxford: Basil Blackwell, 1979.

Vexliard, Alexandre. *Introduction à la sociologie du vagabondage*. Paris: Libraire Marcel Rivière, 1956.

Vilar, Pierre. *A History of Gold and Money 1450–1920*. London: Verso, 1976.

Virilio, Paul. *Speed and Politics*, trans. Semiotext(e) and Mark Polizzotti. New York: Semiotext(e), 1986.

Volosinov, V. N. *Marxism and the Philosophy of Language*, trans. Ladislav Matejka and I. R. Titunik. Cambridge, MA: Harvard University Press, 1986.

Weber, Max. *The Protestant Ethic and the Spirit of Capitalism*. New York: Charles Scribner's Sons, 1958.

*Economy and Society*. New Brunswick, NJ: Transaction Press, 1956.

Wordsworth, Dorothy. *Journals of Dorothy Wordsworth*, ed. Mary Moorman. New York: Oxford University Press, 1981.

Wordsworth, William. *Descriptive Sketches*, ed. Eric Birdsall. Ithaca: Cornell University Press, 1984.

*An Evening Walk*, ed. James Averill. Ithaca: Cornell University Press, 1984.

*Letters of William Wordsworth: The Early Years*, ed. Ernest de Selincourt. Oxford: Clarendon, 1933.

*Lyrical Ballads and Other Poems, 1797–1800*, ed. James Butler and Karen Green. Ithaca: Cornell University Press, 1992.

*The Prelude 1799, 1805, 1850*, ed. Jonathan Wordsworth, M. H. Abrams, and Stephen Gill. New York: W. W. Norton, 1979.

*The Salisbury Plain Poems of William Wordsworth*, ed. Stephen Gill. Ithaca: Cornell University Press, 1984.

*The Fourteen-Book Prelude*, ed. W. J. B. Owen. Ithaca: Cornell University Press, 1985.

Wordsworth, William and Samuel Coleridge. *Lyrical Ballads, 1798*, ed. W. J. Owen. Oxford University Press, 1987.

Young, Arthur. *Travels, During the Years 1787, 1788, and 1789*. New York: AMS Press, 1794.

Zizek, Slavoj. *For They Know Not What They Do*. London: Verso, 1991.

*The Sublime Object of Ideology*. London: Verso, 1989.

"The King Is a Thing," *New Formations* 13 (Spring 1991).

LAW CASES

*Attorney-General* v. *Antrobus* [1905] 2 Ch 188.
*Blundell* v. *Catterall*(1821) 5 B&Ald 268 [1814–23] All EP Rep 39, 106 ER.
*Ellenborough Park, RE* [1956] Ch 13.
*Entick* v.*Carrington* (1765) 19 State Tr 1030, [1558–1774] All ER Rep 41.

# Index

CAMBRIDGE STUDIES IN ROMANTICISM

TITLES PUBLISHED

DH

821.
7
LAN

Printed in the United Kingdom
by Lightning Source UK Ltd.
129272UK00002B/27/A